FIVE
DISCIPLINES
FOR
ZERO
PATIENT HARM

T0325575

ACHE Management Series

FIVE
DISCIPLINES
FOR
ZERO
PATIENT HARM

HOW
HIGH RELIABILITY
HAPPENS

CHARLES A. MOWLL

ACHE Management Series

Your board, staff, or clients may also benefit from this book's insight. For information on quantity discounts, contact the Health Administration Press marketing manager at (312) 424-9450.

Library of Congress Cataloging-in-Publication Data

Names: Mowll, Charles A., author.
Title: Five disciplines for zero patient harm : how high reliability happens
   / Charles A. Mowll.
Description: Chicago, IL : Health Administration Press, [2019] | Series:
   HAP/ACHE management series | Includes bibliographical references and
   index.
Identifiers: LCCN 2019019324 (print) | LCCN 2019021642 (ebook) | ISBN
   9781640550698 (ebook) | ISBN 9781640550704 (xml) | ISBN 9781640550711
   (epub) | ISBN 9781640550728 (mobi) | ISBN 9781640550681 (print : alk. paper)
Subjects: LCSH: Medical errors—Prevention. | Patients—Safety measures. |
   Medical care—Safety measures.
Classification: LCC R729.8 (ebook) | LCC R729.8 .M69 2019 (print) | DDC
   610.28/9—dc23
LC record available at https://lccn.loc.gov/2019019324

The paper used in this publication meets the minimum requirements of American National Standard for Information Sciences—Permanence of Paper for Printed Library Materials, ANSI Z39.48-1984. ∞™

Acquisitions editor: Janet Davis; Manuscript editor: Deborah Ring; Project manager: Andrew Baumann; Cover designer: Brad Norr; Layout: PerfecType

Found an error or a typo? We want to know! Please e-mail it to hapbooks@ache.org, mentioning the book's title and putting "Book Error" in the subject line.

For photocopying and copyright information, please contact Copyright Clearance Center at www.copyright.com or at (978) 750-8400.

Health Administration Press
A division of the Foundation of the American
   College of Healthcare Executives
300 S. Riverside Plaza, Suite 1900
Chicago, IL 60606-6698
(312) 424-2800

This book is dedicated to

my loving wife, best friend, and partner for nearly 40 years
and a clinical adviser on this book

Darlene (Darby) Mowll, RN

Contents

The Patient Safety Challenge and Setting the Zero Patient Harm Goal

WHY ZERO?

This book brings together for the first time the essential safe care practices learned from highly successful, highly reliable healthcare organizations as a comprehensive strategy to achieve the high-reliability goal of zero preventable patient harm. If you have ever witnessed a loved one or acquaintance suffer from a medical mistake made during their stay in a hospital, you know why zero is the right goal. If you are an executive or senior leader in a hospital who has experienced a serious safety event, you know why zero is the right goal. If you are a physician, nurse, or some other caregiver who has been involved in or witnessed an error that caused harm, you know why zero is the right goal.

Zero preventable patient harm should be the norm, not the stretch goal, in US hospitals. Experts agree that most of the errors that result in pain, injury, or even death during patient care are preventable. For simplicity's sake, in this book zero preventable patient harm is referred to as *zero patient harm*, with the acknowledgment that it always means *preventable* harm.

During my 20-year career as an executive with The Joint Commission, thousands of cases of preventable harm that occurred in US hospitals were reported to The Joint Commission through its Sentinel Event Database. By mid-2017, more than 13,300 serious safety events had been reported to The Joint Commission since it established its mandatory and voluntary event reporting system in 1995. The sentinel event reports and the attendant root cause analyses were very disturbing: patients severely or permanently injured or killed as the result of an error, a series of errors, or latent systems failures. Most of these adverse events were preventable.

As the father of three boys, I remember a sentinel event that occurred in the late 1990s that was particularly upsetting (*Arizona Republic* 1998). An eight-year-old boy weighing 56 pounds (we'll call him Sam) was taken into the operating room (OR) for a procedure to remove a small mass from his neck. The surgeon the family had selected to perform the surgery was still performing brain surgery in another surgical suite, so a substitute surgeon performed Sam's procedure. Another boy, a five-year-old weighing 20 pounds, was also scheduled for an operation that morning to have a cyst removed from his gallbladder. Sam was taken to the OR that was expecting the five-year-old. A half hour into performing the wrong procedure on the wrong site of the wrong patient, the surgeon could not find the cyst on the gallbladder and suggested they check the patient's identity. Now believing that the patients must have been switched, the surgeon sent a nurse to check on the patient in the other OR.

Sam was under anesthesia for more than two hours instead of the expected 30 minutes. After waiting for nearly two hours with no word about how the surgery had gone, Sam's parents were finally informed of the mistake. Although obviously stunned, they agreed to allow the original surgeon, when he became available, to perform the correct operation. It took Sam hours to wake up from the effects of the anesthesia. In addition to the small scar on his neck, he had a five-inch scar on his stomach from the incorrect surgery. When Sam woke up, he wanted to know why his side hurt so bad. He was angry at his parents, refused to talk to them, and demanded to know why they had let this happen to him. Sam's mother wanted to know, "How does this happen?" The surgeon who performed the wrong surgery on the wrong patient said he had done nothing wrong and that surgeons often do not check the patient's identity before incision. The hospital must have agreed, because its action was to simply fire the nurse who had brought Sam to the OR. (A side note: In the 1990s, before the patient safety conscience of US hospitals and healthcare systems was stoked into action, firing the nurse—any nurse—was the typical knee-jerk reaction to fixing flawed patient care processes after a sentinel event. Fire the nurse, problem solved. Of course, red-rule violations and culpable acts also occurred that made dismissing a team member the right decision. However, notwithstanding the violation of safe care practices, the singular action of firing the nurse was and is not an effective way of addressing the underlying weaknesses or correcting the design of healthcare processes and systems. Ignoring these system failures can potentially lead to serious safety events.)

Over the years, Sam's story has served as my constant reminder that the occurrence of preventable harm is unacceptable and the goal of zero patient harm is achievable only in a culture and climate that support *harm-free healthcare*.

THE ANTAGONISTS

Some people just do not believe in setting a goal of zero patient harm, even if it is clarified to mean *preventable* harm. YouTube presentations have been posted that rail against the zero harm concept—and, dare I say, the zero harm movement. The opposition argues that the goal of eliminating all patient harm is unrealistic and unachievable and will leave healthcare staff frustrated with their inability to accomplish the objective. These antagonists suggest that the goal implies the need for perfection, which is difficult or impossible to deliver in a healthcare system that is filled with uncertainty, complex, and in an evolving state of safety science. They also say the goal puts too much pressure on surgeons, other clinicians, and the patient care team, and pressure itself is a known cause of error and its negative consequences.

Moreover, the antagonists argue that an overemphasis on eliminating all patient harm could suppress the provision of treatments or services that could *potentially* be harmful but are otherwise proven or intended to be beneficial to the patient, thus engendering the *do nothing and no harm will occur* mind-set. Last is the concern that encouraging healthcare staff to achieve the zero goal will result in the underreporting of errors and safety events.

The concerns of these opponents are real. However, I don't agree with their rationale. As one high-reliability expert has said, "If you don't pursue perfection and event-free performance, you will never achieve it."

Why must zero patient harm be the goal of every hospital and healthcare system and the objective to which every individual working in these organizations is committed? The answer is that patient injury and death related to hospital-acquired conditions such as medication errors; falls; central line–associated bloodstream infections; ventilator-associated pneumonia; pressure ulcers; inpatient suicide; catheter-associated urinary tract infections; retained surgical items; and wrong-site, wrong-person, or wrong-procedure surgery are largely preventable and grossly unacceptable occurrences.

EXPERT SUPPORT FOR ZERO PATIENT HARM

For decades, one of the many criticisms of the US healthcare system was that it never had an articulated vision and strategic plan for how the system should work and what its quality and cost-control objectives should be. This changed with the 2010 enactment of the Affordable Care Act. The act required the secretary of the US Department of Health and Human Services to establish the nation's first healthcare quality improvement plan—the National Strategy for Quality Improvement in Health Care (the National Quality Strategy, for short). The first National Quality Strategy was issued in March 2011 as one of the three broad national aims to "improve the overall quality, by making health care more patient-centered, reliable, accessible, and safe" (AHRQ 2011). Citing the unacceptably high numbers of healthcare-associated infections (1.7 million), resulting deaths (99,000), and adverse medication-related events (770,000) each year, the National Quality Strategy stated that "health care-related errors harm millions of American patients each year and needlessly add billions of dollars to health care costs." The first strategy was the Making Care Safer initiative, which formally established the national goal of zero patient harm (AHRQ 2011):

> Health care providers should be relentless in their efforts to reduce the risk for injury from care, aiming for zero harm whenever possible and striving to create a system that reliably provides high-quality health care for everyone.

In addition, many healthcare leaders, leading healthcare systems, and national organizations, including the following, are proponents of the zero patient harm goal:

- *National Patient Safety Foundation (NPSF)*. In 2017, the NPSF issued a call to action for healthcare leaders to "initiate a coordinated public health response to improve patient safety and drive the collective work needed to ensure that patients and those who care for them are free from preventable harm." The NPSF's 2015 report *Free from Harm* urged the adoption of a total systems approach to achieve meaningful improvement in patient safety (IHI 2015). The NPSF hoped its report would "prompt substantial movement toward a safer health care system" (NPSF 2017). In May 2017, the NPSF merged with the Institute for Healthcare Improvement (IHI) to "reset and reenergize the patient safety agenda," according to IHI president and CEO Derek Feeley (IHI 2017). Under the banner "Together for Safer Care," IHI/NPSF intend to build on their mutual experience in helping healthcare organizations implement harm-reduction strategies (IHI 2017). Also in 2017, IHI/NPSF and the American College of Healthcare Executives (ACHE) collaborated with some of the most progressive healthcare organizations and globally renowned experts in leadership, safety, and culture to develop *Leading a Culture of Safety: A Blueprint for Success*—an evidence-based, practical resource with tools and proven strategies to help create a culture of safety and achieve zero harm (ACHE 2017).

- *Institute for Healthcare Improvement.* IHI's mission is to improve health and healthcare worldwide. The organization created the *care bundle approach* to preventing harm, and its patient safety initiatives are focused on building safety into every system of care, ensuring that patients receive the safest, most reliable care possible. One of IHI's founding principles was to redesign healthcare into a system without errors or waste. To this end, IHI is involved in developing new measures to move organizations toward harm-free healthcare (IHI 2018).

- *Nationwide Children's Hospital.* This hospital's "Zero Hero" program focuses all staff—from the board and senior leaders to frontline employees—on the fundamental patient expectation of "Do Not Harm Me." Nationwide Children's claims to be the first children's hospital to describe and publicly aspire to a goal of zero patient harm: "Nationwide Children's Hospital is committed to the safety and care of its patients. The idea of zero harm has led to our nationally recognized 'Zero Hero' program. 'Zero' is the only acceptable goal, and one that we all strive for" (Nationwide Children's Hospital 2019).

- *Vidant Health.* With a nine-hospital system serving eastern North Carolina, this system's commitment is "simple. We want zero events of preventable harm and 100 percent exceptional experiences for every person we serve" (Vidant Health 2018).

- *University of Pittsburgh Medical Center (UPMC).* UPMC comprises 30 academic, community, and specialty hospitals serving the greater Pittsburgh, Pennsylvania, area. Patient safety is at the heart of its ability to provide reliable and consistently high-quality patient care. According to UPMC (2018), "The best results occur when everyone is involved in patient safety—from each member of the UPMC health care team to you, our patient. Working together, we are making steady progress toward our goal of zero errors."

- *Memorial Hermann Health System.* This system of 15 hospitals in southeast Texas strives to serve people who "expect hospitals to be high-reliability organizations (HROs) where zero error is the norm. The reality, however, is far different. When we embarked on our journey to become a high reliability organization, we didn't do it to win awards. We did it in the best interest of our patients and their families. We recognize that becoming an HRO is a never-ending quest toward the achievable goal of zero harm to patients under our care" (Memorial Hermann Health System 2013).

- *Solutions for Patient Safety.* This collaborative of more than 100 children's hospitals is driven by the shared goal to "Do No Harm" and to urgently reduce and then eliminate serious harm for all of the children under the care of its facilities. In describing its mission, Solutions for Patient Safety (2018) states, "We are 100+ Children's Hospitals working together to help each individual hospital make progress on a journey to zero harm: so that every child receives safe care every time they enter our hospitals."

- *MedStar Health.* A 10-hospital system serving Maryland and the Washington, DC, area, MedStar Health (2018) puts patient safety as a number-one priority by committing to delivering patient care with zero patient harm.

- *Mark Chassin, MD, president, The Joint Commission.* In an article in the *Milbank Quarterly*, Dr. Chassin posited that "All the constituencies of leadership, both formal and informal, must share the same singular vision of eventually eliminating harms to patients." Citing the exemplary safety improvement record of the US commercial aviation industry for many decades, Dr. Chassin stated that the "lesson for health care is not to be satisfied with modest improvements. Aiming for zero is the first step toward achieving it" (Chassin and Loeb 2013, 468).

- *US Department of Energy (DOE).* The DOE is one of the world's largest high-reliability organizations responsible for the nation's fossil and nuclear power generation, nuclear waste disposal and storage, and maintenance of a safe and secure nuclear weapons deterrent. The DOE's primary objective is the continuous safe, reliable, and efficient production of its operating facilities. DOE training focuses on improving human and facility performance through a dual emphasis on reducing errors and maximizing the controls or defenses that are intended to stop errors from causing a safety event. "Only controls can be effective at reducing the severity of the outcome of error" (DOE 2009, 1-16). Therefore, the DOE's successful strategy for experiencing zero significant events has been to concentrate on reducing errors and managing the controls or defenses.

- *The DuPont Company.* DuPont has been a world leader in safety since its founding along the Brandywine River in Wilmington, Delaware, in

1802. Like most highly reliable organizations, DuPont learned how to be a safe company the hard way. An explosion at its powder mill in 1818 led the way for the creation of a shared owner, leadership, and employee commitment to safe operations every day. In the early 1800s, DuPont implemented safety rules and an expectation for personal accountability for safe operations for every employee. Owner E. I. DuPont "kept safety foremost among his concerns" and, in 1911, created the first safety office and safety officer. For more than 100 years, the company has had an employee recognition and safety incentive program, which rewards employees who have stellar safety records and actively report hazards. Being "Committed to Zero Injuries, Illnesses, and Incidents," DuPont abides by this safety commitment: "We believe that all injuries . . . and environmental incidents, are preventable, and are committed to a goal of zero for all of them" (DuPont 2016).

AND THEN THERE WAS HIPPOCRATES

Evidently, the admonition of and pledge to "first, do no harm" is not specifically in the Hippocratic Oath but was contained in another of Hippocrates' works titled *Epidemics*. But even in this work, the oath is quoted indirectly: "As to diseases, make a habit of two things—to help, or at least to do no harm" (Strauss 1968, 625). No matter; it is a wonderful patient safety mnemonic. Similar to the Hippocratic Oath taken by some medical school graduates, nursing school graduates promise to "abstain from whatever is deleterious and mischievous," which is found in the Florence Nightingale Pledge for nursing graduates (Vanderbilt University 2010).

THE FIVE DISCIPLINES OF PERFORMANCE EXCELLENCE

Organizations that achieve and sustain excellent individual, team, and organizational performance over long periods—from high-risk industries such as commercial airlines to Super Bowl–winning football teams—do the following five things extremely and consistently well:

1. Prepare—through simulation, deliberate practice, and training—for excellent performance.
2. Apply proven offensive strategies that exhibit consistent, excellent individual and team performance.

3. Minimize both individual and team (system) errors through immediate feedback, video playback, and coach interventions.

4. Employ strong defensive strategies that effectively block the potential negative effects of errors, latent hazards, and emerging threats.

5. Coach individuals and teams to achieve consistent, excellent performance in all four areas: preparation, offense, error minimization, and defense.

Examples of safe care practices associated with each of the five disciplines are shown in exhibit A. The fifth discipline, coaching excellence, spans and plays a role in optimizing each of the other four disciplines.

Healthcare professionals—caregivers and executives alike—who implement these five safe practices all the time can accomplish the elusive goal of eliminating adverse events and the preventable injury or death from these events. In other words, these strategies enable the achievement of the desired future state of harm-free healthcare and the safety goal of zero patient harm. I refer to these as the *Five Disciplines of Performance Excellence*.

Exhibit A: The Determinants of a Safe Patient Care Experience: The Five Disciplines of Performance Excellence

Healthcare is disappointingly far behind in consistently adopting and applying these winning strategies, which have been used effectively in sports and in other successful industries. As listed earlier, an expanding cohort of exemplary hospitals and healthcare systems is, however, leading the zero harm movement in creating the patient care culture and practices needed to ensure every inpatient receives safe, harm-free healthcare. In addition, the emergence of simulation centers; evolution of patient care bundles; and adoption of safe practices, error-reduction strategies, and methods to strengthen the controls or defenses learned from high-reliability organizations are encouraging signals of the advances in patient care safety. However, complacency and acceptance of the status quo are prevalent. They are reflected in the slow progress toward accurately identifying, measuring, reporting, and eliminating serious safety events that occur in US hospitals. This tolerance of harm is rampant but is anathema to everything that every healthcare executive, doctor, nurse, allied health professional, and other direct providers of care stand for and are committed to: helping patients get better.

EXCUSES, EXCUSES, EXCUSES

Healthcare leaders, providers, and policymakers have based their tolerance of unacceptable levels of preventable patient harm on a bevy of excuses, such as the following:

- Healthcare is constantly changing, the current healthcare delivery model is complicated, or the healthcare system is too poorly organized for providing standardized, consistent care to patients with chronic conditions.
- Healthcare is highly fragmented and lacks basic clinical information capabilities (IOM 2001).
- Practitioners (doctors and nurses) are frequently interrupted with a continuous flow of information, stressing the limits of human memory and making the system prone to failure (Leonard et al. 2010).
- Harm is an inevitable, small, and acceptable price to pay for the technological and clinical advances of an evolving healthcare system (Leonard et al. 2010).
- Patients are far more complicated and idiosyncratic than airplanes, and the field of medicine is more complex than just about any other field of human endeavor (Gawande 2002).
- Staff are insufficient in number and training. Frontline clinical staff are often fatigued and feel grossly overworked (Dhand 2016).

These excuses somehow give us the peace of mind that, despite the best efforts of healthcare professionals, some unintended patient harm can be expected and is just an unfortunate consequence of a highly stressful, technically complex, and ever-changing environment in hospitals. "The problem of medical errors," says Robert Wachter (2012, xiii), "is not fundamentally one of 'bad apples' . . . but rather one of competent providers working in a chaotic system that has not prioritized safety. Most errors are made by good but fallible people working in dysfunctional systems."

CURRENT STATE OF PATIENT SAFETY

The current state of patient safety in US hospitals is, quite frankly, scary. Just read the headlines within the past decade alone:

- "What Surgeons Leave Behind Cost Some Patients Dearly—Doctors Sew Up Patients with Sponges and Other Supplies Mistakenly Left Inside— Costing Some Victims Their Lives" (Eisler 2013)
- "Pharmacy Error Led to Patient Death, Hospital Confirms" (Associated Press 2014)
- "Diagnostic Errors More Common, Costly and Harmful Than Treatment Mistakes" (Johns Hopkins Medicine 2013)
- "Researchers: Medical Errors Now Third Leading Cause of Death in United States" (Cha 2016)
- "Medical Errors May Cause Over 250,000 Deaths a Year" (Bakalar 2016)
- "Medication Errors Found in 1 out of 2 Surgeries" (McGreevey 2015)
- "Study: Medical Errors Cost U.S. Almost $20 Billion in '08" (Ledue 2010)
- "Hospitals Can Kill You" (Makary 2012)

The current state of delivering harm-free healthcare is unreliable, inconsistent, and porous. This means the negative effects of performance errors often penetrate the gaps in weak defenses. Such errors result in patient harm, and both occur at an alarming rate. But you would have to be a healthcare insider to know the current rate of preventable harm, or know how to find and interpret the academic literature regarding patient safety in hospitals. In most states, hospitals are not required to accurately measure or report their actual patient safety data, whether they are infection rates, medication errors, or any other adverse events. No one—not the state regulators, hospital administration, healthcare providers, patients, or the public—really knows the exact type, frequency, or level of harm that results from the occurrence of serious safety events in hospitals. Therefore, we are left with estimates obtained from published studies or from limited, unaudited reporting systems such as the Hospital-Acquired Conditions (HAC) Initiative. The HAC Initiative was implemented in 2008, mandated by a provision of the Deficit Reduction Act of 2005. With an increased emphasis on value-based purchasing, the HAC Initiative focuses on several *never events* that are reasonably preventable through the application of evidence-based guidelines (Waters et al. 2015).

The 2015 *National Healthcare Quality and Disparities Report* published by the Agency for Healthcare Research and Quality (AHRQ 2017) stated that patient safety in hospitals improved substantially between 2010 and 2014. During this period, hospitals reported a 17 percent reduction in HACs, from 145 per 1,000 discharges to 121 per 1,000 discharges. The leading types of HACs were adverse drug events, pressure ulcers, patient falls, and catheter-associated urinary tract infections. According to the American Hospital Association (2017), there were 33.1 million hospital admissions in 2014, an equivalent measure of the number of hospital discharges. An extrapolation of the 121 HACs per 1,000 discharges for 33.1 million discharges means that an estimated 3.9 million HACs occurred in 2014, for a hospital defect rate of 12.1 percent. In Six Sigma terms, hospitals were operating at a poor safety rate of 2.67 Sigma, with 121,000 defects per million opportunities (DPMO), whereas best-in-class high-reliability industries were operating at better than 6 Sigma, or less than 3.4 DPMO.

"On any given day, about one in 25 hospital patients has at least one healthcare-associated infection." This was the conclusion reached by the US Centers for Disease Control and Prevention (CDC) in its 2016 *National and State Healthcare-Associated Infections Progress Report*. This report was based on the CDC's 2014 Healthcare-Associated Infection (HAI) Prevalence Survey, which estimated that 722,000 HAIs occurred in acute care hospitals and that approximately 75,000 patients with an HAI died during their hospital stay (CDC 2016). Surgical-site infections, bloodstream infections, urinary tract infections, and pneumonia were included in the estimates. As a *Modern Healthcare* article title proclaimed in 2014, "Despite Progress on Patient Safety, Still a Long Way Across the Chasm" (Rice 2014, 8). The chasm referenced here is the *quality chasm* described by the Institute of Medicine (IOM) in its 2001 report *Crossing the Quality Chasm: A New Health System for the 21st Century. Crossing the Quality Chasm* identified the existing, but surmountable, gap between the current state and the desired future state of healthcare quality in the United States. The report stated that "health care today harms too frequently and routinely fails to deliver its potential benefits" (IOM 2001, 1). Moreover, it found that safety flaws were unacceptably common and that safety problems were the result of poorly designed care processes and systems that set the healthcare staff up for failure (IOM 2001). It concluded that the US healthcare system "often lacks the environment, the processes, and the capabilities needed to ensure that services are safe" (IOM 2001, 26).

Collectively, HAC data from AHRQ and the CDC (2018) as well as the 2001 report by the IOM suggest an "epidemic of patient harm in hospitals," which is exactly what John James (2013, 122) concluded in his study of adverse events in US hospitals. James based his conclusion on the review of four studies that used the Global Trigger Tool to identify safety events. He found that a low estimate of preventable harm in hospitals was 210,000 deaths per year, but "the true number of premature deaths associated with preventable harm to patients was estimated at more than 400,000 per year" (James 2013, 122). He observed that the "action and progress on patient safety [were] frustratingly slow" and hoped for an "outcry for overdue changes and increased vigilance in medical care to address the problem of harm to patients who come to a hospital seeking only to be healed" (James 2013, 127). As Dr. Tejal Gandhi (2016), president of the NPSF, has said, "We have a long way to go yet on patient safety."

Desired Future State of Patient Safety

The Five Disciplines for Zero Patient Harm is intended to bring together, as an organized framework, the proven and effective offensive and defensive patient care practices to achieve the National Quality Strategy, Centers for Medicare & Medicaid Services (CMS), and IOM goals of safe care for every patient in every setting every time.

Seeking to improve the health and healthcare of all US residents, the National Quality Strategy involves federal agencies, purchasers, providers, payers, and the public in implementing changes to achieve six priorities. These priorities include promoting effective prevention and treatment practices, better coordination of care, engaging patients and families as partners in their care, and increasing the use of best practices. The number-one priority, however, is "making care safer by reducing harm caused in the delivery of care" (AHRQ 2011, 3). As an example of these "Priorities in Action," the current initiatives that are successful in achieving the priorities are listed and updated monthly on AHRQ's website (see www.ahrq.gov/workingforquality/priorities-in-action/index.html). Following the directive that "no patients should be harmed by the health care they receive," AHRQ's 2014 progress report to Congress, *Working for Quality: Achieving Better Health and Health Care for All Americans* (AHQR 2014, 7), cites the significant progress that Connecticut hospitals have made in reducing the rate of bloodstream infections. Using the Comprehensive Unit-based Safety Program (CUSP), these hospitals were able to reduce central line–associated bloodstream infection rates by nearly 50 percent—from 1.99

infections to 1.05 infections per 1,000 central line days. The CUSP method involves the coordinated use of safety checklists, standardized processes, the identification and mitigation of defects, communication training, and improvements in the safety culture (AHRQ 2011).

CMS designed the CMS Quality Strategy to align with the National Quality Strategy and to encompass and implement several CMS priorities. The Partnership for Patients, Hospital Value-Based Purchasing, and patient-centered medical homes are examples of CMS programs that "reward providers for adopting best practices that can decrease harm" (AHRQ 2011, 19). The strategic vision of the CMS Quality Strategy "is to optimize health outcomes by improving quality and transforming the health care system" (CMS 2017). To accelerate progress toward the number-one priority of Making Care Safer, CMS provides financial incentives to providers that develop and implement best practices designed to reduce patient harm. Moreover, CMS payment incentive programs support the cultivation of cultures of safety, elimination of inappropriate and unnecessary care that may contribute to patient harm, and reduction of HAC rates (CMS 2016). In addition, the Making Care Safer initiative focuses on preventing or minimizing harm in all settings of care delivery by improving medication error rates, decreasing patient falls, and reducing HAIs (CMS 2016).

The IOM created the strategic quality framework and priorities that influenced both the National Quality Strategy and CMS Quality Strategy. The IOM was created in 1970 by the National Academy of Sciences, a private, not-for-profit society focused on scientific and engineering research. Under a congressional mandate, the academy is required to provide advice to various federal agencies. In 2001, the IOM's Committee on Quality of Health Care in America, comprising 19 well-respected national healthcare quality experts, issued its comprehensive assessment of the state of healthcare in the United States, titled *Crossing the Quality Chasm: A New Health System for the 21st Century* (discussed earlier), and detailed solutions for making healthcare better. To improve the twenty-first-century healthcare system, the IOM (2001, 41–42) proposed six specific aims:

1. *Safe*—avoiding injuries from care that is intended to help
2. *Effective*—providing services based on scientific knowledge to patients who can benefit from the service and not to those who are unlikely to benefit
3. *Patient-centered*—ensuring that patient values guide all clinical decisions and that care is respectful and responsive to patient preferences and needs
4. *Timely*—reducing waits and sometimes harmful delays in treatment
5. *Efficient*—avoiding waste, particularly the waste of equipment, supplies, ideas, and energy

6. *Equitable*—providing care that is consistent in quality to patients regardless of their gender, race/ethnicity, geographic location, or socioeconomic status

The IOM's vision for the future state of patient safety is that the "health care environment should be safe for all patients, in all of its processes, all the time" (IOM 2001, 47). In other words, this environment is a culture of harm-free healthcare with the goal of zero patient harm.

The Big Y Formula: $Y = f(X_1, X_2, \ldots X_x)$

This formula means the *Big Y* is a function of, and depends on, the critical input variables X_1, X_2, and X_3. In Six Sigma speak, the Big Y is the most important result that is linked to the critical customer requirements and expectations. Six Sigma is a management methodology developed in 1986 by Motorola as a statistically based process for reducing variation and product defects. The formula $Y = f(X_1, X_2, \ldots X_x)$ provides an analytic structure to define and measure the functional relationships between input and output variables (BusinessBalls 2017).

Applying the formula to the challenge of improving the safety of care provided in hospital settings and achieving the Big Y of zero patient harm yields the following formulaic representation of the essential concepts of the Five Disciplines of Performance Excellence:

> *Big Y* = *ZPH*, or zero patient harm
> X_1—*P*, or prepare to deliver safe care
> X_2—C_s, or apply proven safe care or offensive strategies
> X_3—E_{min}, or minimize errors and mistakes
> X_4—D_{max}, or maximize controls or defenses
> X_5—*CE*, or coach individuals and teams for excellent performance
> $ZPH = f\,CE\,[P + C_s + E_{min} + D_{max}]$

Hospitals and healthcare systems can achieve the desired future state of zero patient harm by implementing the five disciplines, distilled into the formula $ZPH = f\,CE\,[P + C_s + E_{min} + D_{max})$.

We—the leaders, caregivers, and others invested in improving patient safety—know what processes or care practices can reduce surgical-site infections or patient falls, for example. We know that to become as highly reliable as a nuclear power plant, a commercial airline, or a theme park, we need to deliver excellent service consistently over a long period to every patient, every time. We must not allow the

LESSONS FROM HIGH-RELIABILITY ORGANIZATIONS

The US Department of Energy

High-reliability organizations operate safely for many years, not just for days or months, and deal with many of the same challenges that hospitals face. They often make decisions under pressure, operate in high-risk situations, work with inadequate information, and are subject to catastrophic consequences if their system controls or defenses fail to prevent a hazard from occurring.

The US Department of Energy (DOE) is widely regarded as an HRO. It has more than 14,000 employees and is responsible for protecting the safety of the nuclear weapons stockpile, energy security, 24 research laboratories, 2 million acres of nuclear waste, and all nuclear and fossil fuel energy delivery in the United States. It is an expert in human factors and human performance as they relate to maintaining consistently safe operations. Through its Human Performance Center, the DOE has developed extensive training materials to train its staff and contractors; these materials are also available to the public. The DOE's *Human Performance Improvement Handbook* states that "the primary objective of our operating facilities is the continuous safe, reliable, and efficient production of mission-specific products" and that "the strategic approach for improving performance is to reduce human error and manage controls [defenses, safeguards, or barriers] so as to reduce unwanted events and/or mitigate their impact" (DOE 2009, v, 1-1).

The DOE uses the formula $R_e + M_{c/d} = OE_s$ to provide a strategic reminder to all DOE staff and contractors of the critical disciplines necessary to consistently perform with zero significant events (OE_s). Reducing errors (R_e) and effectively managing the controls, barriers, or defenses ($M_{c/d}$) have proven, over decades of experience, to be an effective management and operational model for securing a hazard-free, adverse event–free performance record. The Big Y formula for achieving zero patient harm ($ZPH = f\,CE\,[P + C_s + E_{min} + D_{max}]$) draws heavily from the DOE's $R_e + M_{c/d} = OE_s$ and the *Human Performance Improvement Handbook*.

normalization of deviance to create a culture in which adverse events are accepted as a by-product of a complex, dynamic, and pressure-oriented healthcare environment. We must not allow complacency to diminish our commitment to creating a zero harm environment in which patients never experience an iatrogenic injury or death as a result of failures in the healthcare system itself.

ORGANIZATION AND CONTENTS OF THIS BOOK

The Five Disciplines for Zero Patient Harm is a guide for leaders of hospitals and healthcare systems, but it is also useful for frontline clinical staff who provide patient care at the "sharp end."

The Five Disciplines of Performance Excellence—preparing to deliver safe care, applying proven safe care or offensive strategies, minimizing errors and mistakes, maximizing the controls or defenses, and coaching individuals and teams—are fully developed in parts II through VI of the book. Part I highlights the importance of mastering the skills necessary to effectively bring about the behavioral changes that lead to harm-free healthcare and prepare both individuals and teams to deliver safe care. Part VI focuses on coaching to facilitate safe care. Exemplary hospitals and healthcare systems have implemented peer-to-peer patient safety coaching programs with impressive results. Organizational culture is the result, not the cause. Changes in individual attitudes, beliefs, values, actions, and behaviors result in changes in the culture of the organization and the achievement of a desired safety culture. Therefore, part VII describes leadership's role in guiding the cultural transformation into a safe care culture and climate. Each chapter includes specific, implementable safe care practices, which are recommended action steps to achieve a harm-free healthcare culture and the goal of zero patient harm.

Part I (Mastering Change to Enable Safe Care) is the first section of the book for a good reason. It would be very difficult, if not impossible, for a hospital or healthcare system to install any of the high-reliability safe care practices described in the book and sustain them over time without first mastering the disciplines of change facilitation, change management, or change acceleration. Change occurs through people. Meaningful change will not happen unless the hospital staff *want* that change to happen. Therefore, the healthcare leader must become a master change agent with the ability to engage, enlist, encourage, educate, and empower staff to see and feel the need for change, embrace it, and commit to changing their own behavior in the service of the change initiative.

Part II (Preparing to Deliver Safe Care) explores how HROs, much like winning sports teams and record-holding athletes, prepare for excellent performance through deliberate practice and simulation, which are fundamental contributors to success. These chapters show how successful organizations and emerging leaders in healthcare have worked to enhance the technical and nontechnical skills of their team members and to set behavioral expectations for individual performance that counter complacency and establish an urgency for safe, harm-free healthcare. Training individuals to actively participate on teams and using safety communication tools are fundamental to enhancing team performance and results. Communication among caregivers and care teams is a major factor in the delivery of safe patient care; thus, the safety communication tools and methods used by HROs are presented and discussed. Although physicians, nurses, and other healthcare professionals may have strong clinical or technical skills, they may lack the social and cognitive skills to complement their clinical or technical knowledge and capabilities. Included in part II (chapter 2) is Rhona Flin, Paul O'Connor, and Margaret Crichton's research into enhancing nontechnical skills in healthcare.

Part III (Performing Safe Care Practices: The "Offensive" Strategy) focuses on the proven safe care bundles and other clinical guidelines published and recommended by AHRQ and other authoritative sources. Ten of the top high-risk threats to patient safety and harm-free healthcare are described, and the attendant guidelines or care bundles are presented as safe care practices (e.g., steps to prevent ventilator-associated pneumonia, infections, medication errors, and patient falls). This part also emphasizes the need for resilient adaptability in the field of care delivery, the role of technology in patient safety, and the conduct of after-action reviews to facilitate team learning about what went right and what could be improved in care, treatment, or service delivery.

Part IV (Minimizing Errors and Event Precursors) recognizes that the prevailing construct in healthcare safety science is that errors will always occur in a complex, dynamic system. The current approach to patient safety seems to be to accept as an intractable problem the errors that result from the extensive human-to-human and human-to-machine interfaces in healthcare delivery. HROs do not accept this premise and work hard to reduce the occurrence of error. They work diligently to minimize active and latent errors and to strengthen the controls (defenses, safeguards, and barriers) that protect against and prevent harm. This part describes classification and reporting systems for near misses and serious safety events, management of human factors, system improvements to reduce latent organizational weaknesses, and early intervention and harm prevention strategies. The process of catching and correcting errors before they can cause harm is a central practice of HROs and is described in the chapters in part IV.

Part V (Maximizing Defenses and Barriers: The "Defensive" Strategy) discusses one of the most important disciplines of HROs—understanding the complexities of the system they work in and then anticipating, with great accuracy, where failures will occur in the system. These organizations use causal analysis, failure mode and effects analysis, and barrier effectiveness analysis to trace past failure causes, proactively predict future risks, and critique the effectiveness of existing defenses and barriers. To counter the inevitable errors in the care delivery process, they develop controls and defenses to protect the patient from potential harm. This part demonstrates how HROs have successfully maintained and sustained a safe or winning performance. They routinely conduct various analyses to learn how existing controls or defenses are performing, whether the defensive strategy is effective in blocking potentially harmful errors, whether the defensive strategy was worked around, and whether defenses are in place.

Part VI (Coaching to Facilitate Safe Care) describes the desirable characteristics and performance traits in an individual interested in becoming a patient safety coach. The chapters in this part present the major roles and responsibilities of such a coach and how to effectively coach a care team. Teaching individuals and teams to adopt and consistently apply safe care practices, avoid complacency, and catch and correct errors before they can cause harm is central to this role. The safe care practices in this part include how team members should engage in respectful communications with one another and adhere to the controls, defenses, and safeguards against potential harmful error. The coaching skills useful in this regard are described, and examples are provided to demonstrate how performance data can be used to improve a team's safety performance. Moreover, advice is offered to prospective patient safety coaches on how to deal with staff complacency and resistance as well as what approaches are helpful in changing behaviors to keep patients safe. These recommendations guide coaches in answering the most challenging questions they will encounter and in convincing a disparate group of physicians, nurses, and other providers to listen and change their behaviors. Even talented players need a great coach to elevate their individual and team performance. This is as true in healthcare as it is in competitive sports or in high-reliability industries in which error-causing accidents can have catastrophic consequences.

Part VII (Creating a Safety Culture and Climate) discusses creating the organizational culture and climate that encourage and facilitate safe care. Eight specific behaviors and practices based largely on James Reason's work are presented, and leadership's role in promoting a culture of safety is explored.

The Golden Circle Approach: Start with the Why

The material in each chapter is presented according to Simon Sinek's golden circle principle. By first asking and then answering the why (rather than the what or the how) of safe care practice, readers will want to learn more about it and how it is pursued or implemented. In his book *Start with Why: How Great Leaders Inspire Everyone to Take Action*, Sinek (2011, 1) says that "if we're starting with the wrong questions, if we don't understand the cause, then even the right answers will always steer us wrong." By first communicating the reason for achieving the goal of zero

Exhibit B: The Why, How, and What of Achieving Zero Patient Harm

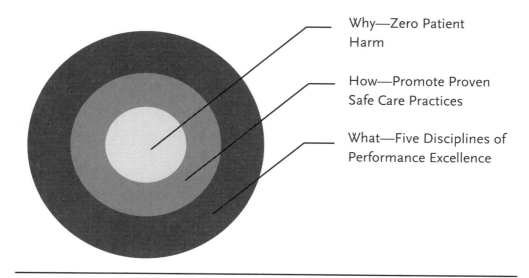

Why—Zero Patient Harm

How—Promote Proven Safe Care Practices

What—Five Disciplines of Performance Excellence

harm—so that healthcare is safe for every patient, every time—I invite (and hopefully inspire) others to learn about it, to believe in it, and to take action by changing their behaviors and practices (exhibit B). The recommended practices and tools throughout the book are well defined, tested, and proven to be effective.

Note About Clinical References

To be clear, *The Five Disciplines for Zero Patient Harm* does not suggest changes in medical practice or procedures. Medical protocols, procedures, and practices are the purview of the medical community. Any clinical practices cited in this book are derived from the existing literature, mostly the patient safety practices described in *Making Health Care Safer II: An Updated Critical Analysis of the Evidence for Patient Safety Practices* (AHRQ 2013). Many other credible clinical guidelines and sources are cited as well.

CONCLUSION

The disciplined actions that enable a football team to win a Super Bowl or a nuclear power plant to operate safely year after year can also be applied to healthcare to protect patients from harmful errors in care delivery. Thousands of preventable adverse events occur in US hospitals each year that permanently injure or kill patients. If hospitals and healthcare systems applied the successful strategies of HROs, patients would be a lot safer during their hospital stay. The Five Disciplines of Performance Excellence presented in this book are modeled after the exemplary practices of successful healthcare organizations, HROs, and sports teams. These "Disciplines" have been proven over decades of use to help high-risk industries and high-performing organizations achieve consistent, highly reliable performance excellence. Hospitals and healthcare organizations can apply these five disciplines with equal success.

REFERENCES

Agency for Healthcare Research and Quality (AHRQ). 2017. "National Healthcare Quality and Disparities Report." Accessed March 18, 2019. www.ahrq.gov/research/findings/nhqrdr/nhqdr17/index.html.

———. 2014. *Working for Quality: Achieving Better Health and Health Care for All Americans*. National Strategy for Quality Improvement in Health Care 2014 Annual Progress Report to Congress. Published September. www.ahrq.gov/sites/default/files/wysiwyg/workingforquality/nqs2015annlrpt.pdf.

———. 2013. *Making Health Care Safer II: An Updated Critical Analysis of the Evidence for Patient Safety Practices*. Rockville, MD: Agency for Healthcare Research and Quality.

———. 2011. "National Strategy for Quality Improvement in Health Care." Accessed March 18, 2019. www.ahrq.gov/workingforquality/reports/2011-annual-report.html.

American College of Healthcare Executives (ACHE). 2017. *Leading a Culture of Safety: A Blueprint for Success*. Accessed February 13, 2019. http://safety.ache.org/blueprint/.

American Hospital Association. 2017. "Trends in Inpatient Utilization in Community Hospitals, 1995–2016." Chartbook Table 3.1. Accessed April 12, 2019. www.aha.org/system/files/2018-05/2018-chartbook-table-3-1.pdf.

Arizona Republic. 1998. "Surgery Answers Sought—Boy's Parents Plan Lawsuit over Mistaken ID." October 2, B-1.

Associated Press. 2014. "Pharmacy Error Led to Patient Death, Hospital Confirms." Fox News. Published December 9. www.foxnews.com/health/pharmacy-error-led-to-patient-death-hospital-confirms.

Bakalar, N. 2016. "Medical Errors May Cause over 250,000 Deaths a Year." *New York Times*. Published May 3. https://well.blogs.nytimes.com/2016/05/03/medical-errors-may-cause-over-250000-deaths-a-year/.

BusinessBalls. 2017. "Six Sigma Definitions, History Overview." Accessed March 18, 2019. www.businessballs.com/performance-management/six-sigma-definitions-history-overview/.

Centers for Disease Control and Prevention (CDC). 2018. "HAI Data." Updated October. www.cdc.gov/hai/surveillance.

———. 2016. *National and State Healthcare Associated Infections Progress Report.* Accessed February 13, 2019. www.cdc.gov/HAI/pdfs/progress-report/hai-progress-report.pdf.

Centers for Medicare & Medicaid Services (CMS). 2017. "Quality Measure and Quality Improvement." Modified August 24. www.cms.gov/Medicare/Quality-Initiatives-Patient-Assessment-Instruments/MMS/Quality-Measure-and-Quality-Improvement-.html.

———. 2016. "CMS Quality Strategy." Accessed January 25, 2019. www.cms.gov/Medicare/Quality-Initiatives-Patient-Assessment-Instruments/QualityInitiativesGenInfo/Downloads/CMS-Quality-Strategy.pdf.

Cha, A. E. 2016. "Researchers: Medical Errors Now Third Leading Cause of Death in United States." *Washington Post.* Published May 3. www.washingtonpost.com/news/to-your-health/wp/2016/05/03/researchers-medical-errors-now-third-leading-cause-of-death-in-united-states/.

Chassin, M. R., and J. M. Loeb. 2013. "High-Reliability Health Care: Getting There from Here." *Milbank Quarterly* 91 (3): 459–90.

Dhand, S. 2016. "The Big Problem with the Airline Versus Healthcare Safety Comparison." Published February 23. http://suneeldhand.com/2016/02/23/the-big-problem-with-the-airline-versus-healthcare-safety-comparison/.

DuPont. 2016. "DuPont Position Statement on Safety, Health, and Environment Commitment." Published April. www.dupont.com/corporate-functions/our-company/insights/articles/position-statements/articles/safety-health-environment-commitment.html.

Eisler, P. 2013. "What Surgeons Leave Behind Cost Some Patients Dearly." *USA Today.* Published March 8. www.usatoday.com/story/news/nation/2013/03/08/surgery.

Gandhi, T. 2016. "Q&A: We Have a Long Way to Go Yet on Patient Safety." *Modern Healthcare.* Published April 16. www.modernhealthcare.com/article/20160416/MAGAZINE/304169899.

Gawande, A. 2002. *Complications: A Surgeon's Note on an Imperfect Science.* New York: Picador.

Institute for Healthcare Improvement (IHI). 2018. "Patient Safety." Accessed January 25, 2019. www.ihi.org/Topics/PatientSafety/Pages/default.aspx.

———. 2017. "IHI and National Patient Safety Foundation Agree to Merger." Press release, March 13. www.ihi.org/about/news/Pages/IHI-NPSF-Announce-Merger.aspx.

———. 2015. *Free from Harm: Accelerating Patient Safety Improvement.* Accessed April 12, 2019. www.ihi.org/resources/Pages/Publications/Free-from-Harm-Accelerating-Patient-Safety-Improvement.aspx.

Institute of Medicine (IOM). 2001. *Crossing the Quality Chasm: A New Health System for the 21st Century*. Washington, DC: National Academies Press.

James, J. T. 2013. "A New Evidence-Based Estimate of Patient Harms Associated with Hospital Care." *Journal of Patient Safety* 9 (3): 122–28.

Johns Hopkins Medicine. 2013. "Diagnostic Errors More Common, Costly and Harmful Than Treatment Mistakes." Published April 23. www.hopkinsmedicine.org/news/media/releases /diagnostic_errors_more_common_costly_and_harmful_than_treatment_mistakes.

Ledue, C. 2010. "Study: Medical Errors Cost U.S. Almost $20 Billion in '08." *Healthcare Finance*. Published August 9. www.healthcarefinancenews.com/news/study-medical -errors-cost-us-economy-almost-20-billion-08.

Leonard, M., A. Frankel, T. Simmonds, and K. Vega. 2010. *Achieving Safe and Reliable Healthcare: Strategies and Solutions*. Chicago: Health Administration Press.

Makary, M. 2012. "Hospitals Can Kill You." *Newsweek*, September 24, 44.

McGreevey, S. 2015. "Medication Errors Found in 1 out of 2 Surgeries." *Harvard Gazette*. Published October 25. https://news.harvard.edu/gazette/story/2015/10/medication -errors-found-in-1-out-of-2-surgeries/.

MedStar Health. 2018. "Quality and Patient Safety." Accessed February 2, 2019. www .medstarhealth.org/qualityandpatientsafety.

Memorial Hermann Health System. 2013. *Leading the Nation in Quality: 2013 Quality Report*. Accessed January 25, 2019. www.memorialhermann.org/about-us/quality-report -high-reliability-healthcare/.

National Patient Safety Foundation (NPSF). 2017. "Preventable Health Care Harm Is a Public Health Crisis." Published March 13. www.npsf.org/page/public_health_crisis.

Nationwide Children's Hospital. 2019. "Do Not Harm Me." Accessed January 25. www .nationwidechildrens.org/impact-quality/patient-safety.

Rice, S. 2014. "Despite Progress on Patient Safety, Still a Long Way Across the Chasm." *Modern Healthcare*. Published December 6. www.modernhealthcare.com/article/20141206 /MAGAZINE/312069987.

Sinek, S. 2011. *Start with Why: How Great Leaders Inspire Everyone to Take Action*. New York: Portfolio.

Solutions for Patient Safety. 2018. "Our Mission." Accessed January 25, 2019. www.solutions forpatientsafety.org/about-us/our-mission/.

Strauss, M. B. 1968. *Familiar Medical Quotations*. Boston: Little, Brown and Company.

University of Pittsburgh Medical Center (UPMC). 2018. "Patient Safety." Accessed January 25, 2019. www.upmc.com/about/why-upmc/quality/patient-safety.

US Department of Energy (DOE). 2009. *Human Performance Improvement Handbook*, vol. 1, *Concepts and Principles*. Published June. www.standards.doe.gov/standards-documents/1000/1028-BHdbk-2009-v1/@@images/file.

Vanderbilt University. 2010. "Florence Nightingale Pledge." *Vanderbilt Nurse*. Published Fall. https://nursing.vanderbilt.edu/news/florence-nightingale-pledge/.

Vidant Health. 2018. "Patient Care." Accessed January 25, 2019. www.vidanthealth.com/Patients-Families/Patient-care.

Wachter, R. 2012. *Understanding Patient Safety*, 2nd ed. New York: McGraw-Hill Medical.

Waters, T., M. J. Daniels, G. J. Bazzoli, E. Perencevich, N. Dunton, V. S. Staggs, C. Potter, N. Fareed, M. Liu, and R. I. Shorr. 2015. "Effect of Medicare's Nonpayment for Hospital-Acquired Conditions: Lessons for Future Policy." *JAMA Internal Medicine* 175 (3): 347–54.

PART I

Mastering Change to Enable Safe Care

Accelerating Change and Changing Behaviors

WHY FOCUS ON CHANGE?

Here is a straightforward reality: A hospital or healthcare system that aspires to transform its patient safety performance from harmful to zero patient harm *must change*. It must stimulate adjustments in behaviors and practices, and this requires individual caregivers who *want* to change the way they do things. It must redesign patient care processes and modify embedded defenses, and this requires the active participation of frontline staff in developing and implementing the changes necessary to minimize error traps and improve safety. It must strengthen existing structures and systems to support the consistent delivery of safe care, and this requires active leadership and adequate resources to sustain the benefits derived from the change. Transforming behaviors, processes, and practices and the resultant difference in attitudes, values, and beliefs require a mastery of change facilitation methods and skills. Healthcare leaders must become master change agents if they want to motivate and lead their organization in pursuing transformational improvements in patient safety that will result in zero patient harm.

Which came first—the chicken or the egg? This timeless riddle and folk paradox describes a causality dilemma or the problem of origin and first cause. It raises the question, "What needs to happen first?" Did the chicken come first, or was it necessary to have an egg for the first chicken to hatch? This riddle is a metaphoric expression used when it is not clear which of two factors is the cause and which is the effect. The causality dilemma for hospitals that aspire to ascend to the high-reliability level, in which zero patient harm is the norm, is whether safe practices or safe thoughts come first. Does a change in thoughts (beliefs and attitudes) cause a change in practices and behaviors? Or does a change in practices and behaviors cause a change in thoughts? Does it matter?

Based on the high-reliability organization research of Karl Weick and Kathleen Sutcliffe (2007) and the study of human factors and safety culture by James Reason (Reason and Hobbs 2003), the following discussion suggests that changing practices and behaviors is a far more direct and effective way to achieve the zero harm goal than first trying to modify attitudes, beliefs, and values throughout the organization. A change in behaviors and practices comes first, resulting in improved attitudes, beliefs, and values that, in turn, cause a transformation in the organizational culture.

Hospitals and healthcare systems that aspire to put in place a consistently safe, highly reliable patient care environment must have a competency in effecting change in practices and behaviors. Facilitating this change and adopting the safe practices of high-reliability organizations is the most effective and direct route to eliminating preventable patient harm. Visioning is important; as Douglas Smith (1996, 230) has said, "Visionless people do not change." But visioning or thinking about and believing in a goal alone is not sufficient for goal realization. Changing practices and behaviors is the critical delta necessary to achieve and sustain zero patient harm (see exhibit 1.1).[1]

This is why chapter 1 is devoted to change. Change facilitates the achievement of zero patient harm, which requires the acquisition of knowledge, skills, and abilities (KSAs) necessary for becoming an excellent agent of change. Job number one for leaders of organizational efforts to eliminate all patient harm is to learn how to create a sense of urgency for change, clearly communicate the vision of a more successful future, gain staff's commitment to and engagement in the change effort, reduce complacency and resistance to change, and provide ongoing support and resources to ensure the successful implementation of the change.

WHY IS CHANGING PRACTICES AND BEHAVIORS CRITICAL TO ACHIEVING A CULTURE OF SAFETY AND CONSISTENTLY SAFE PATIENT CARE?

How often do we think about doing something, create a mental plan for accomplishing it, and dream about the potential results, but then procrastinate and fail to take the action necessary to realize the goal? Getting from A (the current state) to B (the desired future state) requires change. Most people are fearful of change and the uncertainty it represents. But as our experience with making changes in either our personal or professional life grows, we learn that change often provides new opportunities for both personal and professional success. It is an unassailable fact that people need to take action to actualize their thoughts and aspirations. To change the outcomes of something, people need to change their practices and behaviors.

Exhibit 1.1: Effects of Change

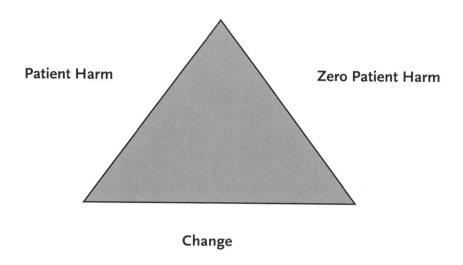

The same is true for an organizational change effort. Actualizing the aspiration of zero patient harm can only occur through action or doing—specifically, following the Five Disciplines of Performance Excellence: (1) preparing (through simulation, practice, and training) to deliver safe care, (2) applying proven safe care or offensive strategies, (3) minimizing errors and mistakes, (4) maximizing the controls or defensive strategies, and (5) routinely receiving guidance and feedback from patient safety coaches.

In the pursuit of a culture of safety, organizations may find it harder to change attitudes and beliefs than practices and behaviors. "Effective practices . . . will eventually bring attitudes and beliefs into line with them" (Reason and Hobbs 2003, 156). Although action is the key determinant of goal achievement,

> Organizations act their way into what they become.
> —Karl Weick and Kathleen Sutcliffe (2007)

action is only possible if the people affected are convinced of its merits and are motivated to take or support it. In other words, action is dependent on effective change facilitation and competent agents of change. "No matter how well a system or solution is conceived, designed, and executed, if people do not like it, it will fail. The goal of the change leader is to . . . create well-designed solutions that will gain wide acceptance" (Bulger and Weber 2005, 372). In addition to being a visionary and charismatic champion for patient safety, today's healthcare leaders must have a mastery of the KSAs of change facilitation to be able to define, reward, and expect the practice of safe behaviors by all staff. According to John Kotter (1996, 151):

Culture changes only after you have successfully altered people's actions, after the new behavior produces some group benefit for a period of time, and after people see the connection between the new actions and the performance improvement. Changing the culture should never be the first step in a major change effort.

According to Jeffrey Hiatt and Timothy Creasey (2012, 1), change management provides the bridge between solutions and results: "The bridge between a quality solution and benefit realization is individuals embracing and adopting change." Organizational transformation occurs because the people in the organization are convinced that, after the change, they will be better off and the organization will be in a better position to meet its objectives. People change the organization, what it does, and what it is able to accomplish. Healthcare leaders must become competent agents of change to facilitate the changes in staff practices and behaviors and the adoption of safe care practices.

> Change is part of organizational life and essential for progress. Those who know how to anticipate it, catalyze it, and manage it will find their careers, and their companies, more satisfying and successful.
> —Richard Luecke (2003)

Change involves patient care teams doing their jobs differently. "A perfectly designed process that no one follows produces no improvement in performance" (Hiatt and Creasey 2012, 1). Therefore, leaders who want to achieve a level of performance excellence must use effective change facilitation tools, including being a champion for change; creating a shared need for change; explaining how the change will benefit both staff and the organization; building a coalition of support for the change; mobilizing the commitment for change; and motivating, monitoring, and rewarding action.

CHANGE TO IMPROVE PERFORMANCE

The four major targets and resulting benefits of organizational change initiatives are as follows:

1. *Structural.* These changes are focused on reorganizing the organization's operating units or parts to improve efficiency and performance. Such change efforts might include acquiring new parts through acquisition or shedding some operating units through divestiture.

2. *Efficiency.* These changes are focused on cost reduction, elimination of nonessential activities, and identification and elimination of waste.

3. *Process.* These changes alter how things get done in the organization. The objective is to make processes more reliable, safer, less costly, more effective, and faster.

4. *Cultural.* These changes focus on modifying the norms, attitudes, beliefs, and behaviors of the organization to support a new vision.

All four of these targets facilitate the organizational changes necessary for a hospital to become highly reliable, to eliminate all preventable patient harm, and to achieve a level of consistent performance excellence. Given that changes in staff behaviors (setting clear behavior-based expectations) and the adoption and consistent application of safe care practices are a top priority in delivering safe care, making *process changes* should be the first order of change in the organization. Along the way, hospitals should make *efficiency changes*, applying Lean Six Sigma tools and techniques to root out waste and inefficiencies in care processes and design, to ensure that only the critical and high-quality characteristics remain.

Effective change management requires leaders to introduce *structural changes* to structures and systems that will support the hospital's evolution to an environment of high reliability and zero patient harm. Visioning, revising or creating policies, providing training, and providing positive reinforcement are examples of the type of structures needed to support the practical changes in patient care practices and behaviors. Leaders must avoid the appearance of change for change's sake and clearly and regularly communicate the desired harm-free healthcare objective. As a result of the changes in priorities, processes, and practices, *cultural changes* occur in the form of new norms, attitudes, and beliefs. As Smith (1996, 98) says, "A performance focus forces everyone to consider the consequences and benefits of changing

> The primary objective of change is performance, not change.
> —Douglas Smith (1996)

or not changing." Managing and facilitating change in the hospital setting is "the ultimate human challenge" in that the leaders, functioning as change agents, transform organizational performance and practices of a large group of people by learning new skills, behaviors, and working relationships.

ASPIRING TO CHANGE

The management of *organizational change*—change that is meaningful and enduring—will be carried out in three stages. Phase 1 establishes the shared aspiration for improvement through change. Phase 2 involves making the change happen through those most affected by the change. Phase 3 entails assimilating the change and related new behaviors and habits throughout the affected parts of the organization.

An aspiration is an ardent desire to accomplish something new. The safety-related aspiration for hospitals is a culture in which every patient receives harm-free healthcare. Leading change, creating a shared need, and shaping the vision for change are the first three pillars of the Change Acceleration Process model (Six Sigma Institute 2019). In this model, the leader's role is to articulate the reason for change as well as explain why the change is important, how it will help them, and how it will benefit the organization. The CEO and senior leadership must be champions for the change initiative and, as such, must demonstrate public commitment to and support for the change. Visioning spotlights the desired outcomes of the intended change and defines the adjustments in behaviors needed to realize the benefits of the change. Creating a shared need for the change happens when the perceived need for change exceeds the resistance to change.

Following are the five determinants of the rate of change adoption that leaders must proactively address to enable the change initiative to succeed (Bulger and Weber 2005):

1. *Relative advantage.* If those affected by the change perceive it as relatively better than the current situation, the change is more rapidly adopted.
2. *Compatibility.* Change adoption is faster when staff perceive the change to be consistent with their values, past experiences, and needs.
3. *Complexity.* The simpler the change, the more likely it is to be adopted.
4. *Trialability.* The perception of risk is lowered if the change can first be implemented on a trial basis before it is adopted.
5. *Observability.* The adoption of the change is enhanced if the affected staff can observe others who are trying the change first.

Facilitating the change initiative will require leaders to create a sense of urgency about the need for change, to overcome the organizational tendency toward homeostasis. *Homeostasis* is the ability to maintain a relatively stable internal state through feedback mechanisms despite the influence of external changes. As Esther Cameron and Mike Green (2012, 140) note, "The forces of homeostasis act to preserve the status quo in any organization." Leaders have to assess the organization's propensity for change before announcing a change initiative. This assessment should include a review of the following (Cameron and Green 2012):

- *Nature of the change.* Five types of change can each provoke a different response from those potentially affected by the change: evolutionary or revolutionary, externally driven or internally motivated, one time or routine, minor or transformative, and contraction or expansion.

- *Consequences of the change.* Those affected by the change will want to know who the potential winners and losers will be; who will benefit; who will be "hurt"; and what the specific consequences will be for employees, customers, and the organization.
- *Past experience with change.* How the organization has handled change initiatives in the past, how it has resourced changes, and what its capacity is to support change should be considered when launching a new change initiative.
- *Individual change factors.* Change is accomplished through the individuals in the organization; therefore, it is important to understand what values motivate them (e.g., money, power, status, inclusion), what personality types may be affected by the change, and what their past experience has been with organizational change initiatives and their *adaptive resilience* to handle change.

"We aspire to be a hospital that consistently provides excellent patient care that is safe and free from harm" is an example of a patient safety vision. Setting such a vision must be based on a clearly defined business problem (eliminating preventable patient harm), must describe an altered and improved future (delivering harm-free healthcare), and must inspire the commitment and energy of all of the staff affected by the change (adopting the safe care practices of high-reliability organizations) (Luecke 2003). Turning the aspirational change objective into action requires change in behavior or practice; leaders need to decide and announce what they specifically want people in the organization to become continually better at doing. Then, they need to provide the support and facilitation that will enable people to learn and adopt the expected and desired change (Smith 1996, 261–67).

In preparing to implement a change initiative, the organization should determine its readiness with the following tasks (Smith 1996, 259):

1. Identify the people who will be affected by the change, and determine how their behaviors and activities will need to shift.
2. Articulate the from/to aspect of the changes in job functions (e.g., ensure peer checking for high-alert medication administration) and individual behaviors (e.g., consistently ensure that all aspects of the fall prevention policy are enforced, including installing bed alarms for at-risk patients and answering the call for ambulation assistance quickly).
3. Assess the sources of readiness.

4. Assess the sources of reluctance.
5. Create the inspirational vision and purpose of the change and effectively communicate them.
6. Describe the "how" of making the change happen.
7. Describe the expected or desired behavior or practice during the change initiative.

ACTUALIZING THE CHANGE

The goal of this book, which should be the principal goal of every hospital or healthcare system, is to facilitate the adoption of best practices, including the Five Disciplines of Performance Excellence (each of which is discussed in its own chapter), that if consistently followed or incorporated into day-to-day performance will lead to excellence and the elimination of preventable patient harm. These practices demand a commitment to changing behaviors and adopting new safe care practices. This commitment, in turn, requires leaders to be smart about initiating and executing change as well as convincing the staff that change is critical to protecting patients from harm. This commitment enables the gains in improved patient safety to be sustained for a long time.

Actualizing the change—to make it a reality—takes a skilled approach. Several effective models for actualizing the change are available, including John Kotter's Eight Accelerators, Edgar Schein's Model of Transformative Change, Cameron and Green's Seven Stages of Change, Smith's Ten Management of Change Principles, the Prosci ADKAR Model of Individual Change, Hiatt and Creasey's Foundational Tenets for Change Management, and Beer's Eight Steps to Create Real Change. Leaders will want to become familiar with the advantages of each model. Kotter's and Schein's change models are discussed here.

Kotter's Eight Accelerators

Kotter's Eight Accelerators model, published in 2012, expands on the Eight-Step Process of Creating Major Change introduced in his 1996 book *Leading Change*. The change accelerators are intended to help organizations "stay competitive amid constant turbulence and disruption" and make significant operational changes that enable the constant adjustment to an ever-changing environment (Kotter 2012). According to Kotter (1996, 30), organizations need to respond to mounting complexity and rapid change with greater agility, speed, and creativity by accelerating strategic change:

Managing change is important. Without competent management, the transformation process can get out of control. But for most organizations, the much bigger challenge is leading change. Only leadership can blast through the many sources of corporate inertia. Only leadership can motivate the actions needed to alter behavior in any significant way. Only leadership can get change to stick by anchoring it in the very culture of an organization.

The accelerators are different from the original eight steps in that the accelerators (1) are concurrent and always at work, (2) involve as many people in the organization as possible as a "volunteer army," and (3) require the flexibility and agility of a network. The accelerators "serve as a continuous and holistic strategic change function" that jump-starts the organization's momentum to improve and become more agile. Recruiting and training many volunteers as change agents who are personally inspired and motivated to participate is a key success factor in bringing about meaningful change. Leaders need to appeal to the individual's emotions and genuine desire to contribute. The leader's role in the change "game is all about vision, opportunity, agility, inspired action, and celebration" (Kotter 2012). The following is a summary of the eight accelerators:

1. *Create a sense of urgency around a single big opportunity.* This urgency to realize a strategically rational and emotionally exciting opportunity is the bedrock on which a change initiative is built.
2. *Build and maintain a guiding coalition.* A broad range of skills, departments, and levels of staff must be represented on the coalition. Coalition members should be knowledgeable about both external influences and internal operations as they are charged with making good enterprisewide decisions about which strategic change initiatives to pursue and how to implement the change.
3. *Formulate a strategic vision and develop change initiatives designed to capitalize on the big opportunity.* The right vision provides a "picture of success" and is feasible, emotionally appealing, and focused on taking advantage of a big opportunity.
4. *Communicate the vision and the strategy to create buy-in and attract a growing volunteer army.* The communication should be memorable and authentic. Its goal is to attract staff to join the volunteer army and support (or not resist) the change initiative.
5. *Accelerate movement toward the vision and the opportunity by ensuring that the network removes barriers.* When barriers to change are identified, a member of the coalition volunteers to be the leader and

recruit others to help. Together, they develop a practical solution to remove the barriers quickly.

6. *Celebrate visible, significant short-term wins.* To silence the skeptics, leaders find evidence that the change benefits the organization or results in short-term success. This proof must be presented immediately, because success breeds success. Celebrating short-term wins helps buoy the volunteer army and prompts more staff to buy in. The description of the win should be unambiguous, obvious, and clearly related to the change vision.

7. *Never let up. Keep learning from experience. Don't declare victory too soon.* The organization must carry the strategic initiatives through to the end. Along the way, it should adapt to shifting environments, enhance its competitive position, and continue to control the rise of cultural or political resistance.

8. *Institutionalize strategic changes in the culture.* Strategic change initiatives will sink or be embedded into the organizational culture when they are incorporated into day-to-day activities. For this to happen, the change initiative must produce visible and positive results and provide a strategically better future for the organization.

In *Leading Change*, Kotter (1996, 4–12) identifies several change management errors that leaders should be aware of and avoid: (1) allowing complacency, (2) failing to create a powerful guiding coalition, (3) lacking a sensible vision, (4) undercommunicating the vision, (5) allowing obstacles to block the new vision, (6) failing to create short-term wins, (7) declaring victory too soon, and (8) neglecting to anchor changes in the corporate culture.

Edgar Schein's Model of Transformative Change

Schein's Model of Transformative Change describes the change process in three steps, as follows (Cameron and Green 2012):

1. *Unfreezing.* Leaders and change agents must engender a feeling of psychological safety for individuals. In this way, people are able to overcome their learning anxiety, and leaders can create the motivation to change.

2. *Learning.* Individuals learn new concepts and new meanings from old concepts through trial and error, scanning for solutions, and role models.

3. *Refreezing.* This step involves internalizing the new concepts and new meanings, incorporating them into self-concept, and employing them in ongoing relationships.

Schein suggests that leaders and change agents must address the learning and survival anxiety of people who are affected by change initiatives. When employees are anxious about learning new behaviors or practices, they fear failing, being temporarily incompetent, and being punished for being incompetent. Employees suffering through survival anxiety are worried they may lose their job, be left behind, or lose their membership in their work group. Sometimes, these characteristics may look like reluctance or resistance to change, but they require interventions to help the affected employee regain confidence and competence.

In preparing for change, leaders should assess staff readiness, acquire project resources, assemble the change management team, and identify the champions and sponsors of the initiative. In managing change, leaders should communicate the plan for change, develop coaching and training plans, and establish strategies to address resistance. In reinforcing change, leaders should implement corrective actions in response to performance feedback, manage the remaining resistance to the change effort, celebrate success, and reward performance (Hiatt and Creasey 2012).

> Today's most urgent performance challenges demand that you learn how to manage people through a period of change. You already know you must have a vision for what the organization will be like after change has been mastered. But such visions are not enough. People facing change need more than an understanding of the end of their journey. They need guidance about how to make the journey itself.
> —Douglas Smith (1996)

ASSIMILATING THE CHANGE

To assimilate a change means to incorporate it into the organizational culture—that is, to conform with the existing customs, norms, attitudes, and values shared by staff. This third phase of change management is important in sustaining the positive outcomes or gains from the change and protecting against recidivism.

Kotter refers to the assimilation stage (the fifth step in the Change Acceleration Process) as either *institutionalizing* or *anchoring* the strategic changes in

> Change management is about engaging the passion and energy of employees around a common and shared vision so that the change becomes an integral part of their work and behavior.
> —Jeffrey Hiatt and Timothy Creasey (2012)

the culture. Leaders can sustain the change by ensuring that the new practices become common or "the way we do things around here." New practices and behaviors "help produce better products and services. . . . But only at the end of the change cycle does most of this become anchored in the culture" (Kotter 1996, 156–57).

To test the level of assimilation, leaders may analyze the "From/To" aspect, or the skill and behavior shifts among the staff affected by the change. Has the knowledge transfer occurred? Have the new KSAs been effectively adopted and ingrained in the way things are done in the organization?

Motivations

Getting more and more people onto the change wagon or to be actively involved requires an understanding of the different approaches to motivating individuals to change or accept change: behavioral, cognitive, psychodynamic, and humanistic (Cameron and Green 2012). These four approaches are described as follows, along with the related interventions to facilitate change:

1. *Behavioral.* This approach uses positive and negative stimuli or rewards and punishment to encourage people to adopt the preferred practices or to discourage them from unwanted behaviors. Interventions needed: performance coaching, rewards, 360-degree feedback, skills training, and values translated into behaviors.

2. *Cognitive.* This approach gets people to realize that their old way of thinking is limiting them from experiencing new things or new ways of being. Interventions needed: results-based coaching, visioning, goal setting, and performance framework (e.g., behavior-based expectations).

3. *Psychodynamic.* This approach helps leaders better understand the reactions of their staff during a change process and develop better ways to deal with them. When individuals go through change, they experience a variety of psychological states, including the Kübler-Ross stages of grief or response to profound change (denial, anger, bargaining, depression, and acceptance). Interventions needed: counseling, surfacing hidden issues, and addressing emotions.

4. *Humanistic.* This approach is based on the understanding that individuals have a choice in how they think, feel, and act and are ultimately responsible for their own situation. Interventions needed: emphasizing healthy development and growth, living the values, addressing emotions, fostering communications, and consultation.

Understanding what motivates the employees affected by the change initiative will help leaders prepare them "to get invested and involved in the design and execution of change processes and to facilitate [change] implementation so that there is sufficient buy-in to make change sustainable" (Porter-O'Grady and Wilson 1995, 20–21). Leaders must provide the training and resources necessary for staff to assimilate the change into daily practice. Such support, along with ensuring the person's capacity for change, can protect against staff burnout, work overload, and frustration.

Resistance and Complacency

The goal of assimilating change is to sustain the resulting improvements into the future. Major threats to sustaining the gains are employee resistance and complacency. "This, too, shall pass" may be heard at the water cooler among the resisters. Assessing whether staff are ready, reluctant, or actively or passively resistant will help determine whether the change will stick. In *Taking Charge of Change*, Smith (1996) says that most people are neither resistant to nor ready for change. Faced with the reality of impending change, individuals become anxious and reluctant about what is to come. The leader's role as master change agent is to convert this reluctance into readiness, not resistance, by getting staff involved in the practical performance of change. Smith proposes seven tactics for leaders to use when responding to a reluctant employee:

1. Explain the need for change and how the new skills and behaviors will benefit both the person and the organization.
2. Clarify the specific skills and behaviors required by the change.
3. Assess if the person has the minimum capabilities required by the change.
4. Make sure the person is emotionally invested in the change and feels the change is essential.
5. Check that the person has a plan of action and personal commitment to specific performance goals.
6. Assess if the person has taken action to achieve her specific goals.
7. Provide support and reinforcement when the person takes action.

Complacency can cancel the positive effects of change. Complacent staff may feel that everything is going just fine and that change is not needed, wanted, or valued. Complacency may be caused by (1) low individual performance standards, (2) lack of external performance feedback, (3) absence of a major and visible crisis,

> If you continue to carry on doing what you are doing, you will continue to get what you are getting.
> —Esther Cameron and Mike Green (2012)

(4) focus on functional goals, and (5) too much "happy talk" by senior leaders who believe that "the company is doing great" (Kotter 1996, 40).

Leaders need to involve complacent and reluctant staff in the design and discussion of change, sharing information about the real challenges the organization faces. Leaders must create opportunities for staff to educate management about their frontline perspectives and experiences. The goal of staff engagement is to develop a mutual understanding of organizational problems, challenges, threats, and opportunities for improvement—that is, the reasons that change is needed.

ROLE OF THE CHANGE AGENT

Change agents are a volunteer corps of staff from various departments. They receive specialized training in change management or change acceleration tools and techniques, and they facilitate change initiatives. Change agents are a critical part of any serious change efforts.

The responsibilities of change agents include providing structured guidance and advice, facilitating meetings of the change implementation team (CIT), resolving conflicts, and educating the CIT on the proper use of change facilitation tools (exhibit 1.2). Although they have no direct-line authority over the members of the CIT, they lead the discussion as they have a thorough understanding of the change process. They provide support to leaders and the sponsors of the change initiative by clarifying the general direction of the change and guiding the implementation of the change, mobilization of key stakeholder groups to work through the transition, and integration of the change (Cameron and Green 2012).

Exhibit 1.2: Change Facilitation Tools (CFTs)

CFT 1: Bounding

When to use: At the beginning of the change initiative
Why: To determine the scope and focus of change
How: Create an "Includes–Excludes" list to help narrow the scope of the change initiative by defining the Fives Ws (What, Why, When, Where, and Who) to be included or excluded from the initiative. Alternatively, draw a picture frame on a flip chart and have the change facilitation team use Post-it notes to identify

---

(continued)

issues to be included in the scope (place the note inside the picture frame) or to be excluded (place the note outside the picture frame).

CFT 2: SIPOC Diagram

When to use: At the beginning of the change initiative
Why: To identify all the relevant elements of the process to be changed or improved
How: The change facilitation team uses flip charts with the headings S-I-P-O-C. Then, the following are defined or identified: four to five high-level steps in the Process (P) to be changed/improved, then the Outputs (O) of the process, then the Customers (C) who will receive the outputs of the process, then the Inputs (I) required for the process to function, and then the Suppliers (S) of the inputs that are required by the process. The resulting SIPOC diagram helps clarify who the suppliers of the inputs are, what specifications are placed on the inputs, who the true customers are of the process, and what the customers' requirements are. Working through the SIPOC discovery helps the team to clearly understand the elements of a process that is the subject of the change initiative and to narrow the scope to be manageable.

CFT 3: Team Charter

When to use: At the beginning of the change initiative
Why: To develop the team charter, probably the most important activity in the change process
How: The team charter defines all of the critical elements of the planned change initiative, including a clear and concise mission statement of the goal (40 words or fewer), the specific issue or problem that will be addressed, and a list of what is included or excluded from the scope of the initiative. The charter also must include SMART (Specific, Measurable, Achievable, Relevant, and Time-oriented) goals, a list of the change facilitation team members, and key milestones and dates. The charter sponsor, champion of the change initiative, the process owner, finance representative, and change agent must all be specifically identified.

CFT 4: ARMI Analysis

When to use: At the beginning of the change initiative
Why: To identify the key staff in the organization that will be Approvers, Resources, Members of the team, or an Interested party

(continued)

Exhibit 1.2: Change Facilitation Tools (CFTs) *(continued)*

How: List the names of all key members of the staff who might have an important and influential role in the change initiative:

> A—Approvers of the scope, resources, and change recommendations
> R—Resource staff who may provide expertise, skills, or influence
> M—Members of the team with working knowledge of the process and related issues or problems
> I—Interested party who should be kept informed about the progress and conclusions of the change initiative

The ARMI assessment should be completed at the start of the change initiative, updated as the initiative unfolds, and reviewed at the conclusion of the initiative.

CFT 5: GRPI Team Effectiveness Assessment

When to use: If/when the change facilitation team is experiencing interpersonal challenges or conflicts
Why: To build team trust, clarity of roles, and collegiality
How: Using a low to high 5-point rating scale (1 to 5), each team member assesses the team's effectiveness in GRPI (Goals, Roles, Processes, and Interpersonal):

> *Goals*—How clear is our agreement on the team's mission and goals for this change initiative?
> *Roles*—How well do we understand, agree on, and fulfill the roles and responsibilities for our team?
> *Processes*—To what extent do we understand and agree on the way in which we approach our change initiative?
> *Interpersonal*—Are the relationships, including the level of openness, trust, and acceptance, on our team working well so far?

CFT 6: More/Less of Project Shaping

When to use: After the original vision and project mission have been chartered
Why: To shape and narrow the focus of the change initiative
How: As a team/group exercise, individual change facilitation team members contribute suggestions about what they expect to see more of and less of when

(continued)

Exhibit 1.2: Change Facilitation Tools (CFTs) *(continued)*

the change initiative has been completed. By identifying both the favorable and unfavorable attributes to be either enhanced or eliminated through changing behaviors, the team paints a picture of the desired future state of the process undergoing change.

CFT 7: The Elevator Speech

When to use: During the introduction of the change initiative to gain acceptance
Why: To convince others of the merits of the change initiative; may include a request for support (the *ask*)
How: The elevator speech is a short and simple statement that has four parts: intent; importance; impact; and an invitation to support, be involved in, or contribute to the initiative. For example: "The zero harm change initiative is about changing behaviors and processes to eliminate all preventable patient harm. It is important because all too often patients are harmed by the very care that was intended to make them better. Your help is needed to encourage your staff to be active and supportive participants in the change effort."

CFT 8: TPC Analysis

When to use: To identify the root cause of resistance to mitigate it
Why: To help encourage staff commitment to the change initiative, identify the sources of resistance, and better understand the reasons certain staff are resisting the potential change
How: The three main sources of resistance to change are technical, political, and cultural. Staff resistance can be categorized into one or more of these sources, which will help change agents and sponsors design interventions targeted at the source(s) of the resistance. Identify what is important to key stakeholders, their reasons for resisting change, the level of resistance, and the strategic action to counter the resistance.

CFT 9: Force Field Analysis

When to use: Early in the design phase of the change initiative
Why: To understand the forces or influences that will either help or hinder the implementation of the change initiative, and to formulate plans to close the gap between where you are and where you want to be

(continued)

How: Hindering forces (restrainers) create barriers and obstacles against the change to a desired future state. Helping forces (enablers) facilitate the change.

Current	Helping Forces	➡	Desired
State	⬅	Hindering Forces	Future
			State

CFT 10: WWW Action Plan

When to use: After every change facilitation team meeting
Why: To make sure that intended actions and assigned responsibilities are completed as planned
How: A team member should be asked to maintain the WWW (Who, What, and When) plan during each team meeting, follow up with the stakeholders who have been assigned responsibilities, and report at subsequent team meetings the progress on implementing the WWW plan.

CFT 11: Plus/Delta Assessment

When to use: At the completion of every change initiative
Why: To assess what went well (plus) and what the team would do differently the next time (delta, which is used in mathematics to signify change)
How: As the change facilitation team debriefs at the conclusion of the change initiative, each team member should write on Post-it notes their assessment of what worked well during the change initiative and their suggestions for changing the process for the next initiative. Next, these notes are posted on one of two flip charts labeled "Plus" and "Delta" and then summarized by the change agent for group discussion.

CFT 12: Changing Systems and Structures

When to use: Any time during the change initiative
Why: To assess the need for changing the supporting systems and structures integral to the successful implementation of change
How: The change facilitation team conducts a review of the current systems and structures and determines if a modification is needed to better facilitate the change. The team considers staffing issues, measures and metrics, rewards, communication, organizational design, information systems, and resource allocation.

Cameron and Green (2012) identify the five stages of the consulting process used by change agents and the specific KSAs needed to effectively manage the organization through a change initiative:

1. *Entry.* This stage requires knowledge of project planning; knowledge of appropriate application of relevant tools and models; effective communication, sincere inquiry, and deep listening skills; strategic and analytical skills; ability to cope with mixed emotions; ability to conduct a change readiness assessment; ability to build relationships, build trust, and gain commitment; and political savvy.

2. *Contracting.* This stage requires knowledge of the charter process; knowledge of establishing accountabilities and measures of success; project management skills; ability to use interventions in the discovery process; ability to generate achievable objectives and metrics; ability to develop effective proposals with specific goals, actions, expectations, and responsibilities; ability to manage resources; and ability to develop mutual contracts that define expectations and the way of working.

3. *Diagnosis.* This stage requires knowledge of the operating environment in which the change initiative is needed; diagnostic and data-interpretation skills, and ability to resist the urge for complete data; ability to coach, discuss, and tutor others in the diagnostic methods of change management; ability to provide meaningful feedback to the CIT, leaders, and sponsor; ability to facilitate stakeholder understanding of data, option generation, and securing agreement for action; ability to gather *sensing data* through interviews and conversations; ability to assess the organization's readiness for change; ability to identify specific interventions and viable options for action; and ability to share feedback and relevant, descriptive, and understandable information for sponsor and team consideration.

4. *Intervening.* This stage requires the ability to discern when engagement rather than a mandate for change is appropriate; design sessions that are participative rather than merely presentations; apply methodological leadership to change management interventions; balance theoretical insights and designed methods; design interventions informed by identified change challenges; develop creative and innovative interventions; encourage difficult public exchanges; and put real choices on the table.

5. *Evaluating.* This stage requires knowledge of designing, implementing, and monitoring evaluation methods and metrics; intervention cost–benefit analysis skills; ability to assess the success of the interventions;

ability to explain to all stakeholders whether the objectives have been achieved; and ability to train the staff and units affected so they can manage the change going forward.

In *Diffusion of Innovations*, Everett Rogers (1983) defines the change agent as one who (1) works through others to translate intent into action, (2) motivates people to change, (3) stabilizes the adoption of innovation, (4) is accepted as trustworthy and competent, and (5) fosters self-renewing behaviors in others to minimize the need for the change agent in the future. Change agents should have the ability to ask *catalytic questions* throughout the stages of the change process and thereby help others through the learning cycle (Cameron and Green 2012). These questions may include the following: What could we have done differently? How did that work out? And what are the implications of not changing?

CONCLUSION

Creating a culture of safety in a hospital or healthcare system in which harm-free healthcare is not just wishful thinking but a daily reality is largely dependent on the organization's ability to change. More precisely, achieving the high-reliability goal of zero patient harm is dependent on leaders' ability to convince their staff of the need for change so they will willingly change their behaviors and specific patient care practices. Changing behaviors and practices will lead to a change in attitudes, values, and beliefs, which in turn will transform the organizational culture into a culture of safety. Healthcare leaders must first be masters of change facilitation so they are able to fully engage staff in this behavioral transformation, the antecedent of consistently safe, highly reliable healthcare.

CHAPTER 1 SAFE CARE PRACTICES

1. Aspire to achieve a healthcare environment in which zero patient harm is the norm. Effect change in practices and behaviors first, and change in organizational beliefs, values, and attitudes will follow. These changes are the foundation of a cultural transformation.

2. Improve performance by making structural, efficiency, process, and cultural changes. These organizational changes are necessary for becoming highly reliable and eliminating all preventable patient harm.

→

---

3. Assess the organization's readiness for change using Douglas Smith's seven-item checklist. Among these seven tasks are identifying the people who will be affected by the change, and determining how their behaviors and activities will need to shift.

4. Make the change a reality with guidance from existing models, including John Kotter's Eight Accelerators and Edgar Schein's Model of Transformative Change. Kotter's accelerators provide a methodology for making significant operational changes to constantly adjust to an ever-changing environment. Schein's model suggests that leaders and change agents must address the learning and survival anxiety among the people affected by the change effort.

5. Assimilate the change into the organizational culture. In other words, reinforce and continually support the change initiative until the existing customs, norms, attitudes, and values reflect the desired change.

6. Convert employee reluctance into readiness by involving them in the practical performance of change. As a master change agent, the leader should apply proven tactics to address reluctance and resistance.

7. Ensure that change agents are part of the change effort. Change agents provide critical support by clarifying the general direction of the change and guiding the implementation of the change, mobilization of key stakeholders, and integration of the change.

8. Sustain the change by ensuring the new practices become common practices and "the way we do things around here."

NOTE

1. The uppercase delta, the fourth letter of the Greek alphabet, is used as a symbol of change in mathematics and science.

REFERENCES

Bulger, J., and V. Weber. 2005. "Implementing Healthcare Quality Improvement: Changing Clinical Behavior." In *The Healthcare Quality Book*, edited by S. Ransom, M. Joshi, and D. Nash, 371–96. Chicago: Health Administration Press.

Cameron, E., and M. Green. 2012. *Making Sense of Change Management*, 3rd ed. London: Kogan Page Limited.

Hiatt, J., and T. Creasey. 2012. *Change Management: The People Side of Change*. Loveland, CO: Prosci Inc.

Kotter, J. 2012. "Accelerate!" *Harvard Business Review*. Published November. https://hbr.org/2012/11/accelerate.

————. 1996. *Leading Change*. Boston: Harvard Business School Press.

Luecke, R. 2003. *Managing Change and Transition*. Boston: Harvard Business School Press.

Porter-O'Grady, T., and C. Wilson. 1995. *The Leadership Revolution in Healthcare*. New York: Aspen Publishing.

Reason, J., and A. Hobbs. 2003. *Managing Maintenance Error: A Practical Guide*. Burlington, VT: Ashgate Publishing.

Rogers, E. 1983. *Diffusion of Innovations*. New York: Free Press.

Six Sigma Institute. 2019. "Change Acceleration Process." Accessed January 29. www.sixsigma-institute.org/Six_Sigma_DMAIC_Process_Define_Phase_Change_Acceleration_Process_CAP.php.

Smith, D. K. 1996. *Taking Charge of Change: 10 Principles for Managing People and Performance.*. Cambridge, MA: Perseus Publishing.

Weick, K. E., and K. M. Sutcliffe. 2007. *Managing the Unexpected: Resilient Performance in an Age of Uncertainty*. San Francisco: Jossey-Bass.

PART II

Preparing to Deliver Safe Care

Enhancing Individual Competence, Behavior, and Performance

WHY FOCUS ON COMPETENCE, BEHAVIOR, AND PERFORMANCE?

In healthcare, the technical competency or proficiency of the entire team at the *sharp end* of patient care—physicians, nurses, allied health professionals, and other caregivers—obviously has a profound effect on the quality and safety of the care being delivered. But being technically competent isn't enough to keep patients safe or result in harm-free healthcare. Individual behaviors (e.g., what a person says, how a person acts and interacts with others) have been proven to be a critical contributing factor to safe patient care and, in other industries, the overall safety performance of the organization. Moreover, a patient care team member can be technically competent and consistently display safe behaviors but may still perform suboptimally and deliver less than desirable results. Individual competence, behavior, and performance are interdependent variables, and each directly affects the quality and safety of patient care.

As exhibit 2.1 shows, overall results can drop dramatically if any one of the three attributes (competence, behavior, and performance) of an individual's work is subpar; if all three attributes are weak, the overall result suffers substantially.

As the US Department of Energy (DOE 2009, 1–12) suggests in its *Human Performance Improvement Handbook*, "Consistent behavior is necessary for consistent results." With an annual budget of more than \$28 billion, the DOE is responsible for a system of high-reliability organizations, including 100 nuclear power plants, security for all nuclear waste and nuclear weapons, and the nation's energy production system. It places great emphasis on minimizing human error to achieve consistent, highly reliable performance. According to the DOE, about 80 percent of

Exhibit 2.1: Interrelationships Among Competence, Behavior, and Performance

Competence (Input)	Behavior (Input)	Performance (Input)	Overall Result (Outcome)
100%	100%	100%	100%
100%	100%	50%	50%
100%	50%	100%	50%
50%	100%	100%	50%
50%	50%	50%	12%

all adverse safety events in the energy industry are attributable to human error, and this proportion may be as high as 90 percent in some industries. "Clearly, focusing efforts on reducing human error will reduce the likelihood of events," according to the *Human Performance Improvement Handbook* (DOE 2009, 1–10). These errors are largely facilitated by latent organizational weaknesses and by individuals interfacing with equipment and organizational systems.

Following an analysis of significant safety events at nuclear power plants over a five-year period, the Nuclear Regulatory Commission concluded that "the risk is in the people—the way they are trained, their level of professionalism and performance, and the way they are managed" (DOE 2009, 1-10). In its role of overseeing high-reliability organizations, the DOE (2009) aims for "event-free performance" and is diligent in the following:

- Helping workers to be and remain competent by providing ongoing training and ensuring that the right people on the job have the knowledge, skills, and abilities (KSAs) that are aligned with the job's task requirements
- Identifying potential job-site safety challenges that might impede error-free performance
- Requiring workers to maintain a sense of uneasiness and a high degree of situational awareness during the execution of tasks (so they can anticipate, prevent, or catch active errors, especially for processes that require error-free performance) and to rigorously use human performance improvement tools
- Reporting feedback to both managers and workers regarding the quality of their work and preparation as well as observations about individual

behaviors and performance on the job. Unsafe attitudes and at-risk behaviors are defined, and workers are observed, trained, and evaluated on the basis of how their demonstrated behaviors and competencies influence their performance and results.

CONFRONTING INCOMPETENCE

Incompetence among healthcare workers was a major concern reported in a 2010 study conducted by the American Association of Critical-Care Nurses (AACN), the Association of periOperative Registered Nurses, and VitalSmarts. A traditional survey was completed by 4,235 nurses, and the responses to a story collector were provided by 2,383 registered nurses (Maxfield et al. 2010). Four out of five respondents were concerned about the negative effects on patient safety of staff shortcuts, incompetence, and disrespect. One in four respondents reported witnessing either shortcuts or incompetence that led to patient harm (Maxfield et al. 2010). Nurse concerns about caregiver incompetence are as follows:

- *Incompetence is common.* Eighty-two percent of nurses revealed working with people who lacked the required skills for the tasks and had outdated knowledge about medications, procedures, and other clinical protocols.
- *Incompetence is dangerous.* The lack of appropriate KSAs led to a near-miss event (according to 31 percent of nurses), affected patients (26 percent), and harmed patients (19 percent).
- *Incompetence is often not discussed.* Only 48 percent of nurses said they spoke to their manager about the person who posed a danger to patients.

Five years earlier, in a similar survey conducted by VitalSmarts and the AACN, more than half of the 1,700 healthcare workers who responded reported witnessing (1) broken rules, (2) mistakes, (3) lack of support, (4) incompetence, (5) poor teamwork, (6) disrespect, and (7) micromanagement. Many of the respondents (which included nurses, physicians, clinical care staff, and administrators) revealed that some of their colleagues cut corners, made mistakes, and demonstrated serious incompetence (Maxfield et al. 2005). Specifically, 81 percent of physicians and 53 percent of nurses and other clinical care providers had concerns about the competency of some nurses or other clinicians they worked with. Moreover, 68 percent of physicians and 34 percent of nurses and other clinical care providers had concerns about the competency of at least one physician on their team (Maxfield et al. 2005). These competency issues ranged from poor clinical judgment, to decision-making beyond one's expertise or proficiency level, to a lack of basic KSAs for the job or task (Maxfield et al. 2005). According to this study, the seven crucial safety concerns identified by respondents were strongly associated with medical errors, patient safety, quality of care, and staff commitment and satisfaction.

This study recommended strategies for having crucial conversations among patient care team members and other workers. Such conversations are necessary to address the deeply rooted competency, behavioral, and performance problems in healthcare delivery. "People see others make mistakes, violate rules, or demonstrate levels of incompetence" repeatedly (Maxfield et al. 2005, 16), over long periods, and in ways that harm patients, but they remain quiet about these failures and inadequacies. Instilling in staff the confidence and ability to speak up is a powerful step toward improving patient safety as well as employee competency, behavior, and performance (Maxfield et al. 2005).

The findings and lessons from both surveys, although conducted many years ago, are still relevant today. And they will be applicable for as long as the US healthcare system grapples with preventable patient harms.

REDUCING THE EFFECTS OF PRESENTEEISM ON INDIVIDUAL COMPETENCE

Competence and performance expectations for healthcare professionals are increasingly being challenged by *presenteeism* and an aging workforce. Presenteeism occurs when workers come to work sick or physically or mentally impaired, which can dramatically affect productivity and safe performance. A growing number of older people (those aged 65 years or older) in the United States continue to work, either convinced they have not saved enough money for retirement or simply keen on retaining the benefits of working and being productive (Kohanna 2014). In light of these trends, organizations should develop a comprehensive program for assessing employees' *fitness for duty*, or competence to perform the assigned tasks effectively and efficiently.

> An employee who is fit for duty has the physical, mental, and emotional capabilities to perform the essential functions of the job.
> —Fred Kohanna (2014)

Concerns about fitness for duty are heightened when the employee (1) takes frequent sick or unpaid leaves, (2) exaggerates medical symptoms, (3) commits a higher than usual number of errors, (4) has reduced levels of productivity, or (5) experiences more work-related injuries. Fitness for duty and individual work performance are negatively affected by presenteeism, which is, in turn, exacerbated by stress, a health condition, medication use, substance abuse, mental illness, or family issues. Presenteeism is observed even among individuals who appear to be physically, mentally, and emotionally capable of performing their job responsibilities. "Presenteeism also takes a toll on safety" (Kohanna 2014, 52), as demonstrated by the following initiative.

In the 1970s, prompted by safety and public health concerns, the Nuclear Regulatory Commission (NRC) and the commercial nuclear power industry in the United States started addressing fitness for duty (FFD) at nuclear power plants. The NRC published its first Fitness-for-Duty Programs rule in 1989 and substantially strengthened the programs in 2008. Since then, the US Department of Transportation and the Federal Aviation Administration have adopted similar comprehensive FFD programs. The NRC's FFD program is "aimed at ensuring that nuclear power plant personnel would perform their tasks in a reliable and trustworthy manner and would not be mentally or physically impaired from any cause" (NRC 2017). Nuclear power plants across the country are required to establish, maintain, and enforce an FFD program that addresses worker hours and fatigue and monitors the potential influence of any substance (legal or illegal) that may impair the workers' ability to perform their duties safely and competently (NRC 2017).

MASTERING NONTECHNICAL SKILLS

Nontechnical skills are cognitive and social abilities that complement technical competencies and contribute to safe and efficient task performance. Nontechnical skills are what high-performing individuals possess that allow them to achieve consistent excellence in high-risk, highly complex work settings (Flin, O'Connor, and Crichton 2008). In the healthcare environment, for example, the safeguards, controls, or defenses built into the care delivery system help protect patients from the potentially harmful effects of error. The healthcare staff, including physicians, nurses, and other caregivers, are the enforcers or enablers of these controls, adhering to these defensive processes and conducting an ongoing assessment of the strength of these defenses. Effective nontechnical skills allow care providers to maximize the effectiveness of these defenses and to catch and correct their own errors and those of their fellow caregivers. In addition, nontechnical skills help caregivers better manage their personal stress and fatigue levels (Flin, O'Connor, and Crichton 2008).

Understanding how nontechnical skills improve team and individual performance and mitigate the effects of errors and adverse safety events is an idea born of necessity by the aviation industry in the 1970s. Following several major airline accidents, NASA hosted an airline industry conference in 1979 to discuss "how to identify and manage the human factors contributing to accidents" (Flin, O'Connor, and Crichton 2008, 4). With the assistance from cockpit voice recordings, the aviation industry concluded that human factors were contributors to the accidents:

> When workers are attentive, make sound decisions, share information and co-operate with fellow workers, then errors and accidents are less likely to occur.
>
> —Rhona Flin, Paul O'Connor, and Margaret Crichton (2008)

failures in leadership, poor team coordination, communication breakdowns, lack of assertiveness, inattention, inadequate decision-making, and personal limitations resulting from stress and fatigue (Flin, O'Connor, and Crichton 2008).

Nontechnical skills underpin safe and efficient competencies, behaviors, and performance. It is true in the aviation industry, and it is true in hospitals and healthcare systems, where the team composition is ever-changing, shift and staff rotations are frequent, and the customer or patient population is dynamic. Because human error is inevitable but nevertheless potentially dangerous, systems must be designed and staff must be trained on these systems to minimize the likelihood of errors and their serious consequences. "An ever expanding evidence base, now beginning to appear in systematic reviews, is establishing the correlation between good team and nontechnical skills and high-level clinical performance" (Sevdalis 2013, 6).

The development of *crew resource management* (CRM) training modules for the aviation industry has motivated anesthetists to create a similar approach, producing the Anesthetists' Non-Technical Skills (ANTS) training program. Other training and assessment tools for enhancing the nontechnical skills of clinicians have been developed and are now in use, including Non-Technical Skills for Surgeons (NOTSS), revised Non-Technical Skills (NOTECHS), and Scrub Practitioners' List of Intraoperative Non-Technical Skills (SPLINTS) (Sevdalis 2013). The cultivation of nontechnical skills among the members of technically oriented patient care teams can substantially reduce preventable errors that may potentially harm patients.

SEVEN ESSENTIAL NONTECHNICAL SKILLS

The seven essential nontechnical skills are situational awareness, decision-making, communication, teamwork, team safety leadership, stress minimization, and fatigue minimization. The following descriptions are drawn from the book *Safety at the Sharp End* (Flin, O'Connor, and Crichton 2008).

Situational Awareness

This skill involves perception and attention to detail and is characterized by knowing what is going on and being able to detect any changes in the work environment.

Both stress and fatigue can retard situational awareness; a person's cognitive capacity and processing of new information can be reduced when the individual is tired or anxious because of stress (Flin, O'Connor, and Crichton 2008). Several safety practices for enhancing situational awareness have been developed by high-reliability organizations in the commercial aviation and nuclear power industries. These practices are applicable in healthcare: (1) Conduct a pre-job briefing with a formal assessment of any anticipated safety risks to prepare workers for or help them better understand the potential safety risks of a particular task *before* starting the work; (2) make sure all team members meet physical and mental FFD requirements, assessing for stress, fatigue, and drug impairment, for example, given that these conditions may diminish situational awareness; (3) minimize distractions and interruptions during critical tasks; and (4) maintain a "sterile cockpit" rule, which prohibits patient care team members from performing nonessential tasks during safety-critical processes or procedures.

> Competence in decision-making is significantly influenced by technical expertise, level of experience, familiarity with the situation and practice in responding to problem situations.
> —Rhona Flin, Paul O'Connor, and Margaret Crichton (2008)

Decision-Making

This nontechnical skill concentrates on operational real-time decision-making by frontline staff as opposed to strategic decisions made at the executive level. Decision-making is a cognitive skill affected by several factors, including distractions, interruptions, noise, stress, and fatigue. Stress-related influences on decision-making include (1) overselective attention or tunnel vision, (2) loss of working memory capacity, (3) restricted retrieval from long-term memory, and (4) favoring simple solutions over complex ones. High-risk work environments, such as hospitals, require practitioners to make "decisions quickly, in distracting conditions and often [while] hampered by inadequate information and changing goals" (Flin, O'Connor, and Crichton 2008, 59). An effective method of assessing an individual's decision-making capabilities in safety-critical work settings is to use simulators. Methods for rating observed nontechnical behaviors include the NOTECHS. Good decision-making behaviors include (1) gathering information and identifying problems, (2) reviewing causal factors with other team members, and (3) considering and sharing information about the risks of alternative courses of action.

Communication

This skill is the exchange of information, feelings, ideas, feedback, and responses and is a major part of good teamwork. Effective communications help build relationships, share knowledge, create predictable patterns of behavior among the team members, and maintain a focus on the task at hand. Four tactics for improving communications are predominant in high-reliability organizations: explicitness, timing, assertiveness, and active listening. *Explicitness* requires that the desired action, and the person responsible for taking the action, be clearly stated. *Timing* of the communication depends on the existence of an immediate threat to patient safety. If an emerging safety concern is observed, communicating the concern immediately using safety communication techniques—such as CUSS (I'm Concerned, I'm Uncomfortable, there's a Safety issue, we need to Stop the process or procedure) or Stop When Unsure—will help protect patients from harm. *Assertiveness* lies between passive and aggressive behaviors and is characterized by speaking up in a way that does not disrespect others while maintaining a focus on the issue and avoiding becoming defensive or emotional. *Active listening* includes being patient, asking questions, being supportive, paraphrasing what was said, making eye contact, and using positive body language. Team leaders should (1) establish a positive work environment by soliciting input from team members, (2) listen without evaluating others, (3) identify bottom-line safety concerns, and (4) establish contingency plans. Team members should (1) verbally indicate their understanding, (2) acknowledge the contingency plans, (3) provide consistent verbal and nonverbal signals, and (4) respond to queries in a timely manner.

Teamwork

This skill is a core competency in CRM training that focuses on making individuals more effective team members. Team members who exemplify effective teamwork are supportive of the other members, maintain an openness to cooperation and coordination, and are accountable for their own performance. Effective team member participation involves constructive conflict, which fosters useful debate and an exchange of information that ensure all team members are able to carry out their responsibilities and meet their performance goals. High-performing teams (1) comprise individuals who are competent at completing their own tasks and have excellent teamwork skills, (2) exhibit clear and concise communications among members, (3) are driven by a common motivation to perform well, and (4) work toward a shared goal and mission. Effective team participation requires knowledge-based, skill-based, and attitude-based competencies.

Team Safety Leadership

This skill refers to a manager's or supervisor's ability to lead, guide, or inspire others in adopting practices and behaviors that result in achieving safety objectives and safe outcomes. Safety leadership involves (1) monitoring and reinforcing safe behaviors, (2) participating in organizational safety activities, (3) being actively supportive of all safety initiatives, and (4) emphasizing safety over productivity. Under stressful circumstances—characterized by high-risk tasks, time pressure, changing conditions, uncertainties, and too much or too little information—the team leader carries a great deal of responsibility for guiding the team through environmental complexities to achieve performance goals. The situational demands on the leader require clear decision-making, communication, teamwork, and situational awareness. The literature has identified 12 team leader skills that reflect effective team leadership in stressful situations: (1) provide immediate feedback to team members, (2) collect performance information from team members, (3) communicate specific and unambiguous role expectations, (4) discuss role strategies in advance of a potential crisis situation, (5) discuss team member interdependencies and role interrelationships, (6) use strategic and concise communication, (7) educate team members on how to recognize unexpected events, (8) educate team members on what actions to take in an emergent situation, (9) provide team members with specific goals for the task being performed and with motivational guidance, (10) communicate information that encourages team member involvement in meeting team goals, (11) remain aware and responsive to team member needs, and (12) be approachable and unintimidating to team members.

> The most significant stressors in acute stress situations are event uncertainty, workload management, time pressure, fatigue, and performance anxiety.
> —Rhona Flin, Paul O'Connor, and Margaret Crichton (2008)

Stress Minimization

This important nontechnical skill helps the care team meet its patient safety goals. Caregivers must learn to manage stress and the stressors in the work environment by identifying the causes of stress, recognizing the symptoms and effects of stress, and implementing coping strategies. Mediating factors—such as personality, coping strategies, previous experiences, and physical fitness—can either reduce or exacerbate the effects of stress that individuals experience. Other stressors include the occurrence of a novel or unexpected event, an unknown event progression, missing critical information, conflicting goals, or the failed implementation of an action plan. Reducing the level of stress or removing the stressors in high-risk work settings like hospitals may be impossible, but staff who have had adequate professional training and experience are less likely to experience acute stress. "The importance of training for stress-proofing personnel cannot be overemphasized. Realistic exercises and simulator sessions, i.e. being prepared through practical exercises, are a major stress-reduction mechanism" (Flin, O'Connor, and Crichton 2008, 181). An organizational process for chronic stress prevention has three steps: (1) Look at workload, work pace, work schedules, and work roles to identify workplace stressors that can be reduced or eliminated; (2) improve the ability to recognize and address stress-related problems as they arise; and (3) help staff cope with and recover from stress-related problems at work.

Fatigue Minimization

This skill is crucial in safety-critical work environments in which staff have to cope with long working hours, difficult conditions, and shift work. Fatigue is the diminished capacity for productivity as a result of deficits in attention, perception, decision-making, and performance. "Fatigue has been shown to have detrimental effects on cognitive performance, motor skills, communication and social skills" (Flin, O'Connor, and Crichton 2008, 194). Fatigue countermeasures help individuals stay alert while performing their assigned tasks; these countermeasures include educating managers on the effects of shift work on performance and alertness, improving sleep hygiene behaviors that promote improved quality of sleep, and taking rest breaks when possible. Ultimately, "the only way of recovering from fatigue is through sleep" (Flin, O'Connor, and Crichton 2008, 196).

SETTING BEHAVIORAL EXPECTATIONS

Which individuals model the most desirable attitudes, values, and behaviors in your organization? Staff who exemplify value-driven, patient-centric, safe behaviors and a commitment to operational excellence are the organization's *positive deviants* (Seidman and Grbavac 2013). Identifying these positive deviants serves as a starting point for changing the cultural expectations regarding individual competence, behaviors, and performance.

HARM-FREE HEALTHCARE: EXEMPLARY PRACTICE

Sharp HealthCare's Attitude Is Everything

At Sharp HealthCare, San Diego's leading healthcare system, "Attitude Is Everything." Sharp's 2,600 affiliated physicians and more than 18,000 employees work to provide their patients with an extraordinarily high level of care the system calls *The Sharp Experience*. The organization's 12 behavior standards are intended to "provide a clear and simple description of exactly what is expected of every Sharp employee—essentially what it should look like, sound like and feel like at Sharp" (Sharp HealthCare 2017).

Starting with "Attitude Is Everything," the behavioral expectations for all staff related to safe care practices are as follows (Sharp HealthCare 2017):

- I thank people for speaking up to reduce harm and prevent defects.

- I communicate with courtesy and clarity.

- I build up my team, sharing in our successes and failures.

- I anticipate and correct problems before they become complaints.

- I ensure my comments and actions produce zero harm and zero defects.

- I speak up when I observe disrespectful behavior.

- I take ownership for safety concerns, whether they are environmental, clinical, or behavioral.

- I always speak up to reduce harm and prevent defects.

- I report potential safety concerns immediately.

- I use proper tools and equipment and do not take shortcuts that compromise safety.

- I follow policies and procedures that are designed to keep everyone safe.

Sharp has made a strong organizational commitment to maintaining a safe environment to achieve "zero harm to employees, our patients and their families" (Sharp HealthCare 2017).

The *four positives*—positive deviance, positive images, positive practice, and positive reflection—change methodology is useful for motivating the widespread adoption of positive deviant behaviors (Seidman and Grbavac 2013). With this approach, positive images of desired attitudes and behaviors must be continuously demonstrated throughout the organization, with the intention that those who observe these images will want to emulate them. Repetition of positive practice, such as *appropriate assertion*, aids in modeling, teaching, and ingraining the safe care practice. Positive reflection allows time for leaders, care teams, and individuals to think about their progress in bringing about change and modifying their expectations to speed adoption.

Leading healthcare organizations define the behaviors vital to keeping patients safe. An example of a safe behavior is *200 percent accountability*: Each patient care team member is 100 percent accountable for following safe care practices and 100 percent accountable for making sure other team members follow safe care practices (Maxfield et al. 2010). Staff who exhibit positive deviance are thankful when a team member reminds them of a positive practice and encourage fellow team members to hold them accountable for practicing safe care. Role-playing among physicians, nurses, and other members of the care team helps them develop empathy for each other and an appreciation for each other's contributions to the team's success. Sharing stories about experiences with patient safety challenges as well as processes that worked and processes that failed embodies positive reflection and promotes positive deviance.

The following *six sources of behavioral influence* explain how staff can be motivated and enabled to adopt positive deviant behaviors (Patterson et al. 2008):

1. *Personal motivation.* Use of personal experiences can appeal to a care provider's own values, stimulating her passion for keeping patients safe.
2. *Personal ability.* Training and skills development must be provided to all care team members to prepare them to be 200 percent accountable for safe care practices.
3. *Social motivation.* Motivation is built and maintained through the support and encouragement from managers and coworkers.
4. *Social ability.* This ability is strengthened by managers and physician champions in each patient care area, who provide the support that staff need to be 200 percent accountable.
5. *Structural motivation.* This type of motivation includes incentives and rewards that are built into the performance review process. Staff should be recognized and rewarded for consistently following safe care practices.
6. *Structural ability.* The process for reviewing, improving, and enforcing safe care practices must be in place. Physicians, nurses, and other

caregivers with structural ability routinely review safe care practices for effectiveness, and the consistency of compliance with these practices is measured and tracked. Cues, reminders, and protocols are developed and used to enable 200 percent accountability.

Behavior reflects an individual's personal values, beliefs, and attitude. Attitude and behavior can be shaped by the organizational commitment to sustaining a safety culture and cultivating safe behaviors. Certain personal beliefs have a significant influence on harm-free performance, such as the beliefs that (1) absolutely safe environments do not exist, (2) human beings are fallible, (3) people want to do a good job, (4) human error is normal, (5) there is no such thing as a routine task or activity, (6) adverse events are organizational failures, and (7) errors present opportunities to learn and improve organizational effectiveness (DOE 2009). What people believe tends to drive their attitudes and behaviors.

> The organization is perfectly tuned to get the performance it receives from the workforce. All human behavior, good and bad, is reinforced, whether by immediate consequences or by past experience. A behavior is reinforced by the consequences that an individual experiences when the behavior occurs. The level of safety and reliability of a facility is directly dependent on the behavior of people.
> —US Department of Energy (2009)

An individual's state of mind or feeling toward work and the working environment is reflected in his attitude; this attitude, in turn, affects his behavior toward safety and error-prevention practices at work (DOE 2009). The following attitudes promote safe behaviors: (1) an uneasiness toward human fallibility, whereby individuals acknowledge their capacity to err; (2) a questioning attitude and vigilant situational awareness to detect potential causes for error, unsafe or hazardous working conditions, and unusual circumstances; (3) a conservative approach to care delivery, whereby actions and decisions err on the side of safety rather than proceed in the face of uncertainty; and (4) avoidance of unsafe attitudes detrimental to reliability and safe performance, including heroics, pride, fatalism, complacency, and invulnerability to error.

ADDRESSING DISRUPTIVE BEHAVIOR

Creating and sustaining a proactive and equitable approach to addressing disruptive behavior in the healthcare organization are important responsibilities

> Accidents are often attributed to employee carelessness or poor safety attitudes [but] most are triggered by deeply ingrained unsafe behaviors.
> —BSMS (2017)

HARM-FREE HEALTHCARE: EXEMPLARY PRACTICE

Sentara Healthcare's Behavior-Based Expectations

Sentara Healthcare launched a systemwide initiative in 2002 to significantly reduce the occurrence of serious safety events that cause harm to patients. Sentara has sustained its leadership as a high-reliability organization for more than 15 years by adopting a culture of safety, maintaining strong board and senior leadership commitment, and embedding behavioral accountability throughout the healthcare system. One of the four core strategies for creating a strong safety culture was to adopt behaviors for error prevention and convert these behaviors to work habits over time. Specific *behavior-based expectations* were created for all Sentara staff, with additional expectations for leaders and physicians (Yates et al. 2005).

Sentara established five behavior-based expectations with associated error-prevention tools for staff (Yates et al. 2005, 688):

1. Pay attention to details and use the STAR (Stop, Think, Act, Review) tool to focus attention and think before acting.

2. Communicate clearly (e.g., use clarifying questions, *read-backs* [a process in which the receiver of a communication reads back the information to confirm its accuracy], and phonetic clarifications).

3. Have a questioning attitude, and validate and verify steps in the process.

4. Perform handoffs effectively (e.g., use the Five Ps for effective handoffs—Patient, Plan, Purpose, Problems, and Precaution).

5. Never leave your wingman, and use peer checking and peer coaching. Leaders are expected to "Make It Happen, Make It Real, and Make It Stick."

Two additional behavior-based expectations were created to clarify communications with physicians when seeking a consultation and the coordination of a patient's overall care. Personal accountability for doing the right thing is a central pillar of Sentara's safety culture. Staff who demonstrate a high degree of personal accountability for following safe care practices are recognized and rewarded (Burke, LeFever, and Sayles 2009). Safety coaches are trained to reinforce safe care, encourage their coworkers,

→

and point out missed opportunities to follow the safe practices. Sentara adopted the *sterile cockpit* concept from aviation, which restricts cockpit conversations to tasks related to takeoff and landing when in flight from 0 to 10,000 feet. Sentara placed red tiles around the Pyxis (medication-dispensing system) station to clearly mark the area as a no-interruption zone, a practice that has proven efficacious in US hospitals and healthcare systems (OR Manager 2013). This process, an application of practical error-prevention techniques, reinforces the Sentara behavior-based expectation of paying attention to details.

As Sentara has done, hospitals and healthcare systems can involve their employees in the process of changing incident-causing behaviors by observing individual and team behaviors, motivating staff to achieve improvement targets, and monitoring behaviors to sustain and recognize those improvements.

for senior executive and medical staff leadership. The medical staff leaders "must not be afraid to suspend or dismiss providers who [are] unable or unwilling to conform to codes of conduct. They are responsible for making sure that the providers adhere to team norms in order to cultivate the best environment for providing quality care to the patients they serve" (Simon 2009). Specifically, Mark Simon (2009) recommends the following five-step process for defining and enforcing the behavioral expectations for physicians: (1) Clearly delineate the expected behaviors, (2) define the consequences of diverging from these expectations, (3) align the penalty or disciplinary action with the severity of the infraction, (4) increase the severity of penalty or disciplinary action for repetitive infractions, and (5) clearly communicate with the disruptive physician at each and every instance of infraction.

The Joint Commission's (2008) *Sentinel Event Alert* on "Behaviors That Undermine a Culture of Safety" advises healthcare organizations on how to address the problem of intimidating and disruptive behaviors that threaten the performance of patient care teams. It states that intimidating and disruptive

> Fundamentally, disruptive behavior by individuals subverts the organization's ability to develop a culture of safety. Two of the central tenets of a safe culture—teamwork across disciplines and a blame-free environment for discussing safety issues—are directly threatened by disruptive behavior.
> —Patient Safety Network (2019)

behaviors can foster medical errors and contribute to preventable adverse outcomes. Although it recognizes "a history of tolerance and indifference to intimidating and disruptive behaviors in health care," it recommends 11 actions for addressing these undesirable behaviors. The suggested actions include educating all staff on appropriate professional behavior, as defined by the hospital's or healthcare system's code of conduct; establishing a policy of zero tolerance for intimidating and disruptive behaviors; and providing skill-based training and coaching for all leaders and managers in relationship building and collaborative practice. Nonretaliation clauses should be included in all policies related to behavioral expectations to protect from retribution those who report intimidating, disruptive, or unprofessional behavior.

To successfully implement and sustain behavior-based and safety-related expectations, organizations should be aware of the pitfalls and threats that can impede their progress. First, staff observations of behaviors are not a reliable primary tool for change. As Jerry Pounds (2000) explains, "performing observations . . . does not necessarily lead to changes in the way people behave at work. In most instances, it only changes the way they behave when they are being observed." Hospitals and healthcare systems should avoid lengthy observations of a long list of behaviors and keep observations no longer than five minutes. Only two or three behaviors should be watched at a time, and findings from the observations should be integrated into work processes (Pounds 2000).

Second, the most effective behavior-based safety processes focus on making safe behaviors a habit and transforming unsafe habits into safe habits.

Third, "delivering regular positive reinforcement for safe behaviors is the key to replacing unsafe habits with safe habits" (Pounds 2000, 4–5). People engage in unsafe behaviors and risk-taking because they think doing so would save them time or energy; the perceived savings in time and energy are natural positive reinforcers.

Fourth, everyone in the organization, including senior management, must be trained in the behavior-based safety processes; in fact, leaders should receive extra training in adopting the supportive behaviors needed to motivate and encourage staff.

Identifying positive deviant behaviors, setting clear behavior-based expectations, and avoiding the potential pitfalls of implementing behavior-based programs will help the organization cultivate a culture of harm-free healthcare.

ENHANCING INDIVIDUAL PERFORMANCE

Performance is different from competence. Competence describes a person's KSAs to perform a task or job, whereas performance (output) is the result of a multitude of factors and influences (input), including competency, behavior, and attitude. To enhance individual performance, the employee and the organization must first reach a common and clear understanding of what goals, behaviors, and actions are expected. The SMART (Specific, Measurable, Attainable, Relevant, Timely) method can be used to establish performance objectives that are reasonable, measurable, and attainable. An employee's behaviors, attitudes, and actions are the means to accomplishing these performance objectives. Safety-related behavioral expectations should include (1) customer service or patient-centeredness, (2) teamwork, (3) effective communication, (4) problem-solving, (5) decision-making, (6) adaptability, and (7) fostering safety and a safe environment.

An individual's performance is shaped by the organization in which she works. Organizational policies, procedures, programs, training, and culture influence a person's behavior (DOE 2009). Individuals tend to be error-prone, but serious safety events are also products of error-prone tasks and work environments, which are both controlled by the employer. Thus, efforts to improve individual performance must also consider the environmental and organizational factors that either facilitate or impede desired behaviors and results.

Healthcare workers are faced on a daily basis with challenging patient care decisions that demand some combination of skill-, rule-, and knowledge-based actions, depending on the situation. Assessing, modifying, and improving the performance of staff in a high-risk, complex work environment like a hospital require a thorough understanding of the differences among skill-based performance, rule-based performance, and knowledge-based performance.

- *Skill-based performance.* This involves highly practiced, physical actions undertaken in familiar situations, usually from memory or without significant thought (DOE 2009)—for example, taking a patient's blood pressure and vital signs. The error mode for skill-based performance is inattention, which is characterized by action slips, lapses in memory or concentration, or unintentional omissions. Skill-based performance requires the right tools to minimize these errors of execution. Workers should not be interrupted or distracted while performing their duties.
- *Rule-based performance.* This performance is a response to a change in the situation, requiring the worker to apply memorized rules or procedures that have been learned through formal training or on-the-job experience with the care team. Rule-based performance relies on an if/then thought process, whereby the individual bases his or her actions and decisions on relevant knowledge and training (DOE 2009). The effectiveness of this performance is dependent on the person's ability to select the most appropriate response or action after assessing and interpreting the situation—for example, prescribing the right type and dose of a blood pressure medication according to certain parameters

of the patient's condition. The error mode for rule-based performance is misinterpretation. When caregivers do not correctly interpret the patient care situation they are addressing, errors can occur as a result of (1) deviating from an approved procedure or protocol, (2) applying the wrong rule or approach to the situation, or (3) applying the correct procedure to the wrong situation. Accurate, complete, and unambiguous written procedures and policies as well as reference guides are critical to rule-driven work. Staff should have access to subject matter experts to confirm the selection of and proper use of the rules.

- *Knowledge-based performance.* This performance, or, more accurately, the "lack of knowledge" mode, is employed in situations in which practiced skills (skill-based performance) or memorized procedures (rule-based performance) do not present an immediate solution. According to the *Human Performance Improvement Handbook*, "Knowledge-based behavior is a response to a totally unfamiliar situation [where] no skill or rule is recognizable to the individual. The person must rely on his or her prior understanding and knowledge, their perceptions of present circumstances, and similarities of the present situation to circumstances encountered before" (DOE 2009, section 2-25). The error mode for knowledge-based performance is an inaccurate mental model. A person's decision-making is erroneous if his real-time problem-solving process is based on incorrect information. Bad information leads to the individual developing an inaccurate picture or mental model of the patient care situation. Under these circumstances, the chance of error is extremely high. Knowledge-based performance may be enhanced through collaboration with the patient care team, other experts, or experienced individuals to help the problem-solving and decision-making process.

Error modes are also important to understand in any kind of performance because they can potentially undermine the work of the individual. Awareness of these error modes and any major threats (see exhibit 2.2) provides the patient care team an opportunity to anticipate, prepare for, and control the negative effects on performance and safety.

Hospitals and healthcare systems need to provide employees with awareness-building training as well as adaptive solutions and controls to counter the potential adverse effects of safety performance threats. For example, the *place-keeping* technique is used to compensate for the mind's limited short-term working memory. These limitations can lead to forgetfulness and omissions during task performance. Place keeping helps staff cross out the steps that have been completed or are not applicable to ensure that critical steps are not omitted or repeated. Another technique

Exhibit 2.2: The 16 Threats to Reliable Performance

1. Unfamiliarity with or lack of awareness of the expectations related to the task or procedure
2. Lack of knowledge or factual information necessary to complete the task successfully
3. Lack of skill in a particular work method or process
4. Lack of experience or proficiency
5. Inability to develop strategies to resolve problem scenarios
6. Unsafe attitude for critical tasks
7. Lack of physical rest leading to fatigue
8. Stress
9. Ingrained habit patterns or actions attributable to the repetitive nature of frequently performed tasks
10. Tendency to make assumptions without verifying facts
11. Complacency and overconfidence
12. Preconceptions and tendency to see only what the mind is tuned to see
13. Inaccurate perception of the risks, hazards, potential dangers, or uncertainties of a given situation
14. Mental shortcuts and biases (e.g., confirmation bias, frequency bias)
15. Limited or short-term memory and forgetfulness
16. Imprecise communication habits that lead to misunderstanding among team members

Source: Information from US Department of Energy (2009, 2-41–2-43).

is *pre-job briefing*, which helps staff identify the error traps to avoid and the steps to accomplish. There is only one recommended solution for fatigue: adequate rest or sleep. Finally, *self-checking* (STAR method) is an effective tool for maintaining attention on performance.

CONCLUSION

This chapter offers proven strategies to enhance individual competence, behavior, and performance. Competence, attitudes, and behaviors significantly affect a person's ability to perform work responsibilities safely and efficiently. Study results and other data explain why improving individual competence, behaviors, and performance is so critical to reducing preventable harm to patients. Technical and nontechnical skills are separately examined as attributes of professional competence. Examples are provided of how exemplary healthcare organizations have adopted safety practices to improve individual competence, behavior, and performance.

CHAPTER 2 SAFE CARE PRACTICES

1. Understand that competence, behavior, and performance are interdependent variables, each of which directly affects the quality and safety of patient care.

2. Reduce the effects of presenteeism. Hospitals and healthcare systems should maintain and enforce a fitness-for-duty program that addresses worker hours and fatigue and monitors the potential influence of any substance (legal or illegal) that may impair the worker's ability to perform her duties safely and competently.

3. Enhance nontechnical skills. Effective nontechnical skills allow care team members to maximize the effectiveness of the organization's defenses and to catch and correct their own errors as well as those of their fellow teammates. These skills include decision-making, team safety leadership, communications, teamwork, and situational awareness. Mastering these and other nontechnical skills will help individual caregivers as well as the hospital or healthcare system minimize and better manage the ill effects of both stress and fatigue.

4. Set behavioral expectations. Leading healthcare organizations define the behaviors that are vital to keeping patients safe by setting individual behavior-based expectations. The staff who exemplify value-driven, patient-centric, safe behaviors and a commitment to operational excellence are the organization's positive deviants. Identifying these models of positive attitudes and behaviors serves as a starting point for changing the organizational cultural expectations related to individual competence, behaviors, and performance.

5. Address disruptive behaviors. Creating and sustaining a proactive and equitable approach to addressing disruptive behaviors is an important role of the senior leaders and medical staff leadership.

6. Enhance individual performance. Assess, modify, and improve the performance of workers in a high-risk, complex environment like a hospital.

→

> This safe care practice requires a thorough understanding of the differences among skill-based, rule-based, and knowledge-based performance.
>
> 7. Eliminate threats to reliable performance. Hospitals and healthcare systems must actively address and mediate the 16 threats to safe and reliable individual performance (exhibit 2.2).

REFERENCES

BSMS. 2017. "Strategic Safety Culture Roadmap." Accessed August 20. www.behavioral-safety.com/free-behavioral-safety-resource-center/level-2.

Burke, G. H., G. B. LeFever, and S. M. Sayles. 2009. "Zero Events of Harm to Patients." *Managing Infection Control.* Published February. https://insidekentuckyonehealth.org/Portals/0/Learning/Documents/4-15%20Culture%20of%20Safety.pdf.

Flin, R., P. O'Connor, and M. Crichton. 2008. *Safety at the Sharp End: A Guide to Non-Technical Skills.* Boca Raton, FL: CRC Press.

Joint Commission. 2008. "Behaviors That Undermine a Culture of Safety." *Sentinel Event Alert* 40. Published July 9. www.jointcommission.org/assets/1/18/SEA_40.PDF.

Kohanna, F. 2014. "Addressing Fitness for Duty, Practical Steps." *Professional Safety* 59 (4): 52–53.

Maxfield, D., J. Grenny, R. Lavandero, and L. Groah. 2010. "The Silent Treatment: Why Safety Tools and Checklists Aren't Enough to Save Lives." Accessed August 10, 2017. https://faculty.medicine.umich.edu/sites/default/files/resources/silent_treatment.pdf.

Maxfield, D., J. Grenny, R. McMillan, K. Patterson, and A. Switzler. 2005. "Silence Kills: The Seven Crucial Conversations for Healthcare." *VitalSmarts.* Accessed August 10, 2017. www.aacn.org/nursing-excellence/healthy-work-environments/~/media/aacn-website/nursing-excellence/healthy-work-environment/silencekills.pdf.

OR Manager. 2013. "Adopting a 'No Interruption Zone' for Patient Safety." Accessed February 6, 2019. www.ormanager.com/adopting-a-no-interruption-zone.

Patient Safety Network. 2019. "Patient Safety Primer: Disruptive and Unprofessional Behavior." Updated January. https://psnet.ahrq.gov/primers/primer/15/disruptive-and-unprofessional-behavior.

Patterson, K., J. Grenny, R. McMillan, D. Maxfield, and A. Switzler. 2008. *Influencer: The Power to Change Anything.* New York: McGraw-Hill.

Pounds, J. 2000. "The Six Biggest Mistakes in Implementing a Behavior-Based Safety Process." *EHS Today.* Published December 31. www.ehstoday.com/news/ehs_imp_33991.

Seidman, W., and R. Grbavac. 2013. "Creating a Culture of Patient Satisfaction: The Four Positives Change Method Can Lead to Better Focus on Patients." *Hospitals & Health Networks Daily*. Published March 7. www.hhnmag.com/articles/5794-creating-a-culture-of-patient-satisfaction.

Sevdalis, N. 2013. "Non-technical Skills and the Future of Teamwork in Healthcare Settings." The Health Foundation. Published June. https://patientsafety.health.org.uk/sites/default/files/resources/non_technical_skills_and_the_future_of_teamwork_in_healthcare_settings.pdf.

Sharp HealthCare. 2017. "The Sharp Experience." Accessed August 20. www.sharp.com/about/sharp-experience/.

Simon, M. N. 2009. "How Hospitals Should Deal with Disruptive Physician Behavior." KevinMD.com. Published September 20. www.kevinmd.com/blog/2009/09/hospitals-deal-disruptive-physician-behavior.html.

US Department of Energy (DOE). 2009. *Human Performance Improvement Handbook*, vol. 1, *Concepts and Principles*. Published June. www.standards.doe.gov/standards-documents/1000/1028-BHdbk-2009-v1.

US Nuclear Regulatory Commission (NRC). 2017. "History of the NRC's Fitness-for-Duty Requirements." Updated May 8. www.nrc.gov/reactors/operating/ops-experience/fitness-for-duty-programs/history.html.

Yates, G., D. Bernd, S. Sayles, C. Stockmeier, G. Burke, and G. Merti. 2005. "Building and Sustaining a System-wide Culture of Safety." *Journal of Quality and Patient Safety* 31 (12): 684–69.

Training Individuals to Effectively Participate on Teams

WHY IS TEAMWORK IMPORTANT TO PROVIDING SAFE PATIENT CARE?

When individuals are able to complement their excellent clinical skills with the ability to work collaboratively with other members of the patient care team, patient care and patient safety are enhanced. An Agency for Healthcare Research and Quality (AHRQ) report on team training in healthcare found that the odds of complications and deaths increase when surgical teams rarely engage in the desired teamwork behaviors, share less information during the intraoperative phase, and exhibit less briefing during the handoff phase (Weaver and Rosen 2013). Moreover, the AHRQ report cited other studies that found that teamwork and communication issues were the root cause of 52 percent to 70 percent of adverse events. The report concluded that teamwork and communication are critical components of safe healthcare delivery and that clinical performance is dependent on situational monitoring, communication, trust, and shared mental models—in other words, effective teamwork.

> Improved teamwork can improve patient safety. The seamless integration of multiple knowledge, skill, and affective components is a mechanism to improve patient safety and avoid errors.
> —Eduardo Salas, Dana Sims, Cameron Klein, and C. Shawn Burke (2003)

The stresses of the hospital patient care environment can threaten the ability to sustain high-level competencies and the commitment to performance excellence of any patient care team member. An absence or excess of information, ambiguity regarding the patient's condition or care plan, time pressures, performance pressures, and the severe consequences of a potential error all add to the complexity of the patient care process (Salas et al. 2003). As discussed in chapter 2, individual competence, behavior, and performance matter. As the skills of individual team members improve, so will the speed and accuracy of the team's performance (Baker et al. 2012). But under stress, the limits of consistent individual performance are challenged.

Teamwork, through collaborative problem-solving, coordination, and improved communication, combines the knowledge, skills, and abilities (KSAs) of each of the team's individual members. This allows the team to be proactive in catching errors before they can harm a patient and to improve patient safety. Breakdowns in teamwork and communication among team members are leading contributing factors to patient care errors (ASRN 2008). Effective teams can avoid or minimize the potential for error by adopting a safe care plan, cultivating effective relationships built on mutual trust, and adapting to changing circumstances quickly and competently.

CHARACTERISTICS OF EFFECTIVE TEAMS

Effective teams are characterized by the following behaviors and actions that lead to safe care practices (ASRN 2008):

- Proactively and reactively adapting to changing circumstances
- Using information from the task environment to adjust the care plan
- Demonstrating clear and concise closed-loop communication—that is, verifying that sent messages are both received and correctly interpreted by the intended party
- Monitoring teammate behavior and providing backup behavior
- Demonstrating strong leadership
- Managing conflicts appropriately
- Making informed decisions
- Promoting coordinated action by synchronizing the team's task requirements
- Having a shared understanding or mental model of how the care plan or procedure should be carried out
- Involving the patient as part of the care team

According to Dr. Jennifer Weller (2015, 2), "While an individual may be competent, what matters to the patient is the collective competence of the team and their ability to perform." Failures in teamwork and communication lead to treatment errors, inefficiency, and workplace tension. The following four attributes of effective teamwork help improve team performance, collective knowledge, and attitude and lead to better patient outcomes:

1. *Situational monitoring.* Team members track each other's work to ensure it is performed as expected and that proper procedures are followed.
2. *Mutual support.* Team members provide feedback and coaching to improve individual and team performance. Members help each other perform tasks, particularly when colleagues are overwhelmed, or offer support when a lapse is detected.
3. *Leadership.* Team members demonstrate leadership by directing and coordinating team member activities, assessing team performance, allocating tasks, motivating the team, planning and organizing team activities, and maintaining a positive team environment.
4. *Communication.* Clear communication among team members requires that the receiver of a message acknowledge receipt and that the sender verify the message was received and understood. This is also known as *closed-loop communication.*

TEAM KNOWLEDGE, SKILLS, AND ABILITIES

Adopting and consistently demonstrating team-based KSAs that are proven to have a positive impact on patient care outcomes is just as important as mastering the KSAs of competent individual performance. Since team membership is constantly changing in patient care settings like hospitals and healthcare systems, team training needs to focus on the development of team-based KSAs.

Teams should strive to develop the following core capabilities (Salas et al. 2008):

- Knowledge of effective team leadership qualities
- Mutual performance monitoring
- Backup behavior
- Team orientation
- Adaptability

These competencies are established by using closed-loop communication techniques, developing a shared mental model for the team, and establishing mutual trust among team members. Backup behavior, for example, requires that team members anticipate and respond to one another's needs by recognizing workload distribution problems and reassigning task duties accordingly. For instance, an Australian health services survey covering a 10-year period ending in 2005 revealed that knowledge of organizational goals and strategies and self-awareness of one's strengths and weaknesses are important factors contributing to effective healthcare team performance (Leggat 2007).

Key team skills and behaviors include (1) managing the team through coordinating, monitoring, and supporting team activities; (2) managing the task by planning, prioritizing, and using resources; and (3) developing a shared mental model among team members (Weller 2015). Leadership, the ability to influence others, and negotiating skills are desired team leader attributes aimed at building a shared mental model and cohesiveness among team members (Leggat 2007). Team attitudes of mutual trust and respect, and a team orientation in which members prioritize team goals above their own individual goals, improve the team's interdependencies and potential for achieving their common goal of a safe care experience for all patients. The development of team-based KSAs can help team members work collaboratively to resolve hierarchical attitude challenges, power differences among members, and the fragmentation of patient care that can result from the siloed approach used in professional training (Weller 2015).

In nursing, for example, teamwork has been shown to result in higher job satisfaction, less staff turnover, better patient satisfaction, and better patient outcomes. Effective nurse KSAs include the use of daily goal sheets, caregiver-to-caregiver reports, and unit huddles that improve team communication (*Nurse Journal* 2017). Additionally, nursing teamwork behaviors such as monitoring one another's performance, backing each other up, and engaging in open communication and conflict resolution have made a positive impact on patient care.

Communication is critically important to managing and resolving conflict among team members. More than 70 percent of medical errors are attributable to dysfunctional team dynamics (AAMC 2016). However, high-functioning healthcare teams facilitate improved patient outcomes.

Patrick Lencioni (2002) identifies five dysfunctions that cause teams to fail: (1) absence of trust, (2) fear of conflict, (3) lack of commitment, (4) avoidance of accountability, and (5) inattention to results. Erosion of trust among team members and the fear of conflict driven by hierarchical power differences undermine team performance.

To build trust and mutual support among patient care team members and address interpersonal conflicts that are detrimental to overall performance,

> The people you work with are the people who can understand you the best and be the best source of support, but they also have the power to make your life miserable; what people refer to as a socially toxic workplace. So the quality of those social relationships and how to make them function as positively as possible is really critical in terms of making things go well.
>
> —Christina Maslach
> (AAMC 2016)

several healthcare organizations have implemented a tool called CREW—Civility, Respect, and Engagement at Work. CREW was developed by the Veterans Health Administration in 2005 to address concerns regarding the impact of civility among healthcare workers on patient safety; CREW was found to improve perceptions of workplace civility (AAMC 2016).

TEAMS, TEAMWORK, TASKWORK, AND TEAM TRAINING

Patient care teams in hospitals are composed of a small group of individuals working together in various patient care units such as intensive care, operating rooms, labor and delivery, and the emergency department. The caregiving team, including physicians, nurses, technicians, and other healthcare professionals, "must coordinate their activities to make safe and efficient patient care a priority" (Baker et al. 2012, 186). Team members have unique and complementary KSAs that contribute to the success of the team goals and common purpose. Effective teams recognize the reliance on and interdependence of each team member and work collaboratively to adapt to changing circumstances.

The following are three dimensions of a great team, and questions that can assess team effectiveness (Aguilar 2016):

1.   *Product.* Has something of high quality, value, and usefulness been accomplished?
2.   *Process.* Has the team managed unproductive conflict well, communicated effectively, and used coordination skills?
3.   *Learning experience.* Have team members improved their KSAs?

Teamwork involves collaborative practice as team members collectively work to improve the quality and safety of patient care. As Salas and colleagues (2003, 5) state, "Safety is improved through interdisciplinary teamwork." While patient care teams often change members, teamwork disciplines and communication methods create a common platform for team member participation. By developing teamwork KSAs, team members adapt quickly to dynamic changes in team assignment or patient care situations, often under stress or time pressures. "Teamwork requires the KSAs that allow interdependent coordinating action toward a shared goal. In the health care field, that goal is patient well-being" (Salas et al. 2003, 6). Teamwork involves a sense of togetherness, cohesion, and mutual trust. High-performing teams synchronize the team's tasks and believe that, by collaborating, they can solve complex problems and adapt to changing circumstances.

Taskwork and *teamwork* are the two components of the team process. Taskwork reflects the individual team member responsibilities in performing the patient care task, understanding the task requirements, interacting with the equipment, and following the proper policies and procedures. It represents the operational or technical skills related to what teams do to provide care, services, or treatment to a patient (Baker et al. 2012).

TRAINING PROGRAMS

Team training in healthcare focuses on improving specific team competencies and behaviors while letting team members practice communication, coordination, and collaboration skills and receive feedback on areas that need improvement. The use of simulation allows healthcare teams to practice procedures and care processes and improve their teamwork skills and interdependencies without risking harm to patients.

Medical team training programs began in the early 1990s with the creation of the Anesthesia Crisis Resource Management (ACRM) program at Stanford University's School of Medicine. ACRM provides training in technical skills and team KSAs and takes place in a simulated operating room. The US Department of Defense implemented its MedTeams training in US Army and US Navy hospitals between 2000 and 2006. AHRQ and the Defense Department collaborated to develop TeamSTEPPS for healthcare, a philosophy launched in 2006. TeamSTEPPS—Team Strategies and Tools to Enhance Performance and Patient Safety—is now widely used in the US healthcare system for training in teamwork (Baker et al. 2012).

Creating an environment centered around effective teamwork and communication offers several benefits for an organization, including the following:

- Contributes to the consistent delivery of patient care
- Is essential for managing the complexity of patient care in a setting that often exceeds the capabilities of an individual clinician
- Ensures staff safety
- Allows staff to learn from mistakes rather than place blame
- Provides a more satisfying and rewarding work environment for staff
- Fosters an environment in which healthcare organizations can attract and retain critically important employees.

—Michael Leonard, Suzanne Graham, and Bill Taggart (2010)

Team training can help alleviate some of the common communication breakdowns that contribute to patient harm, including the following (Leonard, Graham, and Taggart 2010):

- Providing care with incomplete or missing information
- Executing poor patient handoffs because relevant clinical information was not clearly communicated
- Failing to share and communicate known information
- Showing reluctance to speak up about a safety concern
- Assuming the right outcome and the safety of care

ELEMENTS OF EFFECTIVE TEAMWORK

Effective teamwork requires structure and accountability, controlling for team errors, flattened hierarchy, situational awareness, sensitivity to red flags, team debriefings, appropriate assertion, team KSA competencies, a reality-based team orientation, and patient engagement.

Structure and Accountability

An effective, structured patient care team features a framework in which all members know what is expected of them, what their roles and responsibilities are, and who the team leader is. Successful teams also possess an intense sense of accountability. Team members are accountable to each other and to achieving the goal appropriate to the situation. The team works collaboratively and cooperatively to quickly respond and adapt to whatever unexpected situation occurs (Brady, Battles, and Ricciardi 2015).

> Not all teams are created equal. Teamwork is not simply an automatic consequence of placing people together. In fact, we know that well-functioning teams make fewer mistakes than do individuals, especially when responsibilities are clearly delineated, members are empowered to speak up, and everyone feels responsible for and vested in the outcome.
> —P. Jeffrey Brady, James Battles, and Richard Ricciardi (2015)

Controlling for Team Errors

A *team error* is a lapse in performance of one team member that causes another member to err. As teams perform their tasks, members may be inattentive to the task or procedure because of the influence of their coworkers. Just because two or more people are performing a task, that does not ensure it will be done correctly. Performance can be negatively affected by interactions between team members, but communication techniques can be applied to control or minimize team errors—for example, assertively speaking up about a performance concern or applying the team skill of *backup behavior*, whereby team members monitor each other's performance and identify any lapses or mistakes in the other team member's actions (DOE 2009).

Flattened Hierarchy

Hierarchy is a significant barrier to effective team performance and to providing safe care. Team members' perceptions about hierarchy influence their feelings about speaking up when they suspect something is going wrong or questioning the decisions or performance of a teammate. Team leaders are responsible for flattening the hierarchy, minimizing power distances, and creating an open atmosphere of respectful communication and teamwork. Team cohesion is created when all members of the team have input into the care plan, feel valued, and are encouraged to speak up if they have a concern about safety or quality of care (Leonard, Graham, and Taggart 2010).

Situational Awareness

It is essential for team members to know what is going on in the task environment in which the team is performing. Situational assessment is the process of establishing the state of situational awareness where team member perceptions and attention to detail let them detect changes in the environment. Situational awareness is a cognitive skill that can be impeded by stress and fatigue, which reduce an individual's cognitive capacity for processing new information. Maintaining situational awareness among team members in safety-critical tasks is vitally important to safe patient care.

Four strategies contribute to improved team situational awareness: (1) conducting pre-job briefings (sometimes with a formal risk assessment) to allow team members to understand the nature and risks of a particular task *before* starting the work; (2) establishing fitness-for-work expectations for each team member's physical and mental fitness for duty to recognize and control for the diminishing effects that fatigue, stress, drug addiction, or illness can have on situational awareness; (3) minimizing distractions and interruptions during safety-critical tasks; and (4) applying the "sterile cockpit" rule that flight crews use on all commercial airlines, as required by the Federal Aviation Administration. This rule prohibits crew members from performing nonessential duties while the aircraft is in a critical stage of the flight, which helps reduce distractions and maintain situational awareness (Flin, O'Connor, and Crichton 2008).

Sensitivity to Red Flags

Red flags are valuable indicators that the situation has changed and become riskier; team members need to recognize these red flags and initiate discussion to interpret and respond to the safety threat. The most important sign of a potential problem is a sense that "things just don't feel right." If a team member's intuition is signaling that there may be a problem, then the team needs to stop. "Stop when unsure" is a proven high-reliability safety tool used by teams when confronted with a situation that creates a question about the task, procedure, or situation. When the chances for error are high in a safety-critical process or procedure, the best course of action is to take a brief time-out to reassess the situation. Ambiguity, poor communication, confusion, trying something new under pressure, deviation from established norms, verbal violence, fixation on a task, boredom, and being rushed should all be red flags that alert team members that the patient's safety is at risk (Leonard, Graham, and Taggart 2010).

Team Debriefings

Also called *after-action reviews*, team debriefings are positive and constructive team discussions held soon after a patient care process or procedure has ended. Debriefings represent an excellent opportunity for team learning and for the team leader to recognize team members' exemplary efforts. Generally, the debriefing will address these questions: What did we do well? What did we learn? What would we do differently next time? Did any systems or equipment issues present a problem? Who will accept responsibility to make sure any systems issues are corrected?

Appropriate Assertion

Appropriate assertion describes the clear, timely, and professional verbal communication by a team member that she has a performance or safety concern. As Leonard, Graham, and Taggart (2010, 52) state, "It is critically important that healthcare workers be taught to politely assert themselves in the name of safety." Personal assertion should be persistent but not hostile or confrontational and should offer constructive solutions to the emerging risk, if possible. Effective assertion tactics include (1) getting the person's attention by using his name, (2) making eye contact, (3) expressing concern, (4) stating the problem clearly and concisely, (5) proposing an action, (6) making sure all team members understand the proposed action, (7) reaching a decision, (8) making sure all team members understand the decision, and (9) reasserting if necessary (Leonard, Graham, and Taggart 2010). An effective communication tool in unclear situations in which a team member is concerned about a potential safety risk is CUSS: "I'm Concerned, I'm Uncomfortable, there's a Safety issue, and we need to Stop the process."

Team Competencies

Team KSAs reflect the knowledge, skills, and abilities that high-performing teams exhibit:

- *Knowledge.* Effective teams know to monitor the performance of teammates, provide constructive feedback on both good performance and individual errors, and offer advice for performance improvement.
- *Skills.* Team members anticipate and respond to one another's needs through an accurate understanding of teammates' responsibilities. Backup behavior provides the ability to shift workload among team members to achieve balance during busy periods. Teams must demonstrate their adaptability to changes in the environment based on new information and the ability to reallocate intrateam resources. Team leadership is responsible for directing and coordinating the activities of the team, assessing team performance, motivating the team, assigning tasks, and establishing a positive atmosphere.
- *Abilities.* A safety-oriented team shares the belief that team goals take priority over individual team member goals because they have been involved in goal setting and active team communications. These KSAs are enacted on a base of mutual trust, a willingness to admit mistakes and accept feedback, the adoption of a shared mental model among team members, and the consistent use of closed-loop communication (O'Leary et al. 2011).

Reality-Based Team Orientation

In a hospital, healthcare professionals—physicians, nurses, technicians, pharmacists, and other staff members—work with various teams to care for numerous patients 24 hours a day, 7 days a week. The composition of patient care teams is ever-changing. Patient assignments are ever-changing. Therefore, team orientation and teamwork training have to be uniquely designed to recognize these dynamic variables. Simulation-based training provides an opportunity for teams to come together off the "playing field" to practice their team and procedural skills without risking patient harm. Behavior-anchored rating scales (BARS) are useful in assessing individual and team-related performance. Higher BARS survey ratings of collaboration and teamwork have been associated with better patient outcomes (O'Leary et al. 2011).

Kevin O'Leary and colleagues (2011) offer four interventions to improve teamwork in hospitals:

1. Through the localization of physicians, increase the frequency of communications between nurses and physicians.
2. Daily goals of care forms and safety checklists provide structure to interdisciplinary team discussions and ensure input from all team members.
3. Teamwork training emphasizes improved communication behaviors to guide team interactions.
4. Interdisciplinary rounds provide a forum for regular interdisciplinary communication.

Patient Engagement

Involving patients in care planning and delivery benefits both the patient and the care team and improves patient outcomes. AHRQ's (2017b) "Guide to Patient and Family Engagement in Hospital Quality and Patient Safety" recommends that hospitals partner with patients in their healthcare by (1) providing patients with timely and complete information about their care, (2) asking about and listening to the patient's concerns, (3) explaining things in a way the patient can understand, (4) encouraging the patient's involvement in making care decisions, and (5) involving family and friends if the patient wants to do so. AHRQ's engagement strategies include giving patients information on how to ask questions, how to get help when they need it, and how to participate in their care. Moreover, patients can support safe handoffs by being involved in the change-of-shift report for nurses. Patients

A nurse caring for 4 patients may interact with 4 different hospitalists. Similarly, a hospitalist caring for 14 patients may interact with multiple nurses in a given day. Team membership is ever-changing because hospital professionals work in shifts and rotations. Finally, team members are seldom in the same place at the same time because physicians often care for patients on multiple units and floors, while nurses and other team members are often unit-based. Salas and others have noted that team size, instability, and geographic dispersion of membership serve as important barriers to improving teamwork. As a result of these barriers, nurses and physicians do not communicate consistently, and often disagree on the daily plan of care for their patients.

—Kevin O'Leary, Niraj Sehgal, Grace Terrell, and Mark Williams (2011)

and their families should also be involved in the transition from hospital to home. A Commonwealth Fund study of patient-centered medical homes found that nearly all respondents described patients as a member of the care team. Patient involvement includes identifying health goals, carrying out care plans, and making decisions about their care (O'Malley et al. 2014).

THE FIVE Cs OF EFFECTIVE TEAMWORK

According to Agrawal (2014, 21), "Teamwork is . . . not an automatic result of placing people together in one place. Teamwork involves a shared set of teamwork skills and shared goals." In developing an effective strategy to improve teamwork in patient care teams, hospitals must be aware of and create solutions to address the many existing barriers that impede good teamwork: lack of information sharing, dynamic changes in team member composition, hierarchy, complacency, fatigue, doctors and nurses having different communication styles, workload, lack of role clarity for team members, and time pressures. Teamwork change management should begin with a discussion of the Five Cs of Effective Teamwork (Agrawal 2014; Katzenbach and Smith 1992, 22) and continue with an implementation plan focused on improvement of team performance in all five areas:

1. *Common goal.* Team members share and believe in the goal of the team.
2. *Commitment.* Team members are committed to attaining the goals.
3. *Competence.* Team members have the knowledge, skills, and abilities necessary to accomplish their roles in team activities.
4. *Communications.* Team members apply safety communication techniques.
5. *Coordination.* Team members work together with technology, people, and resources to accomplish the goals.

> Often the best teams are not made up of the best individuals. Rather, they are a collection of talented and committed players who are willing to do the little things together that lead to championships. For the Patriots—sure, Tom Brady received a great deal of well-earned credit as the quarterback, but it was the offensive and defensive lines, the secondary, the receivers, the running backs, and the coaches who won the Lombardi Trophy. That's the secret to the truly great teams.
>
> —Nick Saban (2004), Head Football Coach, University of Alabama

TEAM TRAINING IN HEALTHCARE

Sallie Weaver and Michael Rosen (2013, 473) define team training as "a systematic methodology for optimizing the communication, coordination, and collaboration of health care teams that combines specific content with opportunities for practice, formative feedback, and tools to support transfer of training to the daily care environment." In healthcare, team training focuses on strengthening teamwork competencies, such as proactively identifying anomalies in the patient care process that might pose a risk to patient safety. Team training—carried out through information transfer, behavioral modeling, and simulation—aims to enhance the KSAs that are essential for high-performance teamwork.

Members of patient care teams come to work every day concerned about keeping patients safe from harm. Teamwork training provides the knowledge and skills necessary to both minimize the potential for error and the ability to "catch and correct" mistakes before a hazard turns into harm. Effective communication skills facilitated by learning new ways of speaking up and interacting with teammates, as well as non-judgmental assertion techniques, let team members monitor and cross-check each other's performance.

> Providing safe health care depends on highly trained individuals with disparate roles and responsibilities acting together in the best interests of the patient. Communication barriers across hierarchies, failure to acknowledge human fallibility, and lack of situational awareness combine to cause poor teamwork, which can lead to clinical adverse events.
> —Patient Safety Network (2019)

TeamSTEPPS

TeamSTEPPS is now widely used in hospitals to improve teamwork and the performance and safe care practices of healthcare teams. The four core components of TeamSTEPPS are (1) leadership, (2) situation monitoring, (3) mutual support, and (4) communication. These skills complement the teamwork knowledge and attitude that are critical to effectively supporting the task interdependencies and team dynamics that drive excellent performance.

TeamSTEPPS has been shown to contribute to higher quality, safer patient care, increased team awareness, clearer team roles and responsibilities, and better information sharing among team members (AHRQ 2017a). The TeamSTEPPS training program aims to create highly effective patient care teams that optimize the use of information, people, and resources to achieve the best clinical outcomes for patients. Hospitals can either enroll small patient care teams in the training or have lead staff members complete the train-the-trainer course individually and then share their learning. Applicants for the Team-STEPPS training go through a three-step process that includes a pretraining assessment of the hospital's readiness for the changes necessary to make the training effective, the training itself, and then a period of sustaining the positive impact of TeamSTEPPS training. Through the TeamSTEPPS "dosing strategy," hospital patient care teams can choose to learn and implement all the tools and strategies at once, to implement them in only selected units or departments, or to implement only selected tools.

In 2016—10 years after hospitals began implementing the TeamSTEPPS methodology—Baker, Battles, and King (2017, 3) conducted a meta-analysis of 129 studies on team training in healthcare and found "a significant association between programs like TeamSTEPPS and participant learning, training transfer, and organizational outcomes. A decade of research indicates that TeamSTEPPS improves the care delivered to patients. We feel that interprofessional education is foundational for improved care coordination and enhanced patient safety."

> Calling a group of assembled people a team does not make them one. Telling employees they need to collaborate does not translate into collaboration. Teams do not just happen naturally. Teams are, in the very truest sense, volunteer organizations. You cannot force someone to cooperate; you can't mandate teamwork. A high level of cooperation is a product of choices—choices made one person at a time for reasons that are often unique to the team member.
> —David Thiel (2009)

Team Alignment

The first step in team training is to establish a common purpose among the team members—a clear, common, and compelling purpose—that is well defined, inspiring, and spells out what success is supposed to look like. It is the team's purpose that provides the reason for collaboration (Thiel 2009). When patient care team members become emotionally bonded around the mission of improving the patient's condition by providing safe and effective care, they become jointly committed to the team effort. Team training should aim to improve team member alignment with the team's purpose, which will lead to a more cohesive and effective team performance.

Team alignment can be nurtured through the practice of five team-building essentials (Thiel 2009):

1. *Clarity.* "I see it." All team members understand the benefits of team effort.
2. *Relevance.* "I want it." The team's goals and purpose align with the goals and interests of the individual team members.
3. *Significance.* "It's worth it." The team's objectives are of sufficient magnitude and importance to make the work worth the effort.
4. *Achievability.* "I believe it." All members believe the team's purpose and objectives are realistic and attainable.
5. *Urgency.* "It needs to be done now!" There is a sense of urgency and time pressure that motivates team behavior.

Team training programs should be evaluated to determine their effectiveness in changing—ideally, improving—team interrelationships and KSAs. This four-question assessment of the program, conducted routinely over time, will give the organization valuable feedback about the training's efficacy (Salas et al. 2008):

> In short, no team purpose, no team.
> —David Thiel (2009)

1. Did the trainees like the training and find it useful?
2. Did the trainees increase their understanding of the team competencies reviewed in the training?
3. Did trainees change—and, ideally, improve—their behavior to align with desired behaviors?
4. Did the training achieve important results or outcomes?

CONCLUSION

Chapter 3 identifies several safe care practices for training individuals to effectively participate on teams. These practices provide actionable advice on structuring patient care teams to excel, based on team KSAs and the competencies developed by Salas and colleagues (2003). The chapter also presents the safe care practices of high-reliability teams, such as situational awareness, appropriate assertion, and the "red flags" that signal unexpected and unwanted variation. These practices answer the challenge "How to turn a team of experts into an expert team" (Salas et al. 2003, 8).

CHAPTER 3 SAFE CARE PRACTICES

1. Facilitate the development of individual team participation skills to emulate the elements of effective teamwork: structure and accountability, controlling for team errors, flattened hierarchy, situational awareness, sensitivity to red flags, team debriefings, appropriate assertion, team KSA competencies, a reality-based team orientation, and patient engagement.

2. Provide opportunities for patient care team members to participate in ongoing training to strengthen their team KSAs, including the Five Cs of Effective Teamwork: Common goal, Commitment, Competence, Communications, and Coordination.

3. Ensure that individual team members understand how both taskwork and teamwork (and the safe care of patients) depend on their competent performance. Team members must master the four teamwork competencies of situational monitoring, mutual support, leadership, and communication.

4. Encourage patient care team members to employ the safety communication techniques described in exhibit 3.1 to improve team member communications and keep patients safe from harm.

Exhibit 3.1: Safety Communication Techniques

TeamSTEPPS training highlights 13 safe care practices:

Briefing at the start of a patient care process or procedure to discuss the team and team member roles, establish expectations, set the climate, anticipate the desired outcomes, and discuss contingencies if things do not go as planned.

Team huddles can be effective to reestablish situational awareness, reinforce the care plan, problem-solve, and assess the need to adjust the plan.

Debriefing lets the team provide feedback following a patient care process or procedure; it is designed to improve team performance.

Situation monitoring involves continually scanning the environment to assess what is going on around you to maintain situational awareness.

STEP is a tool to aid situational awareness and refers to Status of the patient, Team members, Environment, and Progress toward the goal.

Shared mental models require team members to share information they have about the environment and the task they are involved in to make sure everyone is on the same page.

Cross-monitoring is an error-reduction strategy in which team members monitor the performance of their teammates to make sure any mistakes are caught quickly and corrected before any harm comes to the patient.

SBARQ is a technique for communicating critical information that requires immediate attention and stands for Situation, Background, Assessment, Recommendation and Request, and Questions.

CUSS is a communication tool that can be used by team members to "stop the line." It stands for I am Concerned, I am Uncomfortable, this is a Safety issue, and I don't feel like this is Safe!

(continued)

Exhibit 3.1: Safety Communication Techniques *(continued)*

The two-challenge rule is used when a team member's initial assertion wasn't effective or was ignored. The team member must assertively voice concern at least twice to ensure it has been heard. This lets a team member stop the process if he or she senses or discovers a safety breach.

Callouts are used to communicate important information to all team members simultaneously to improve communications during team patient care events.

Check-backs or read-backs are closed-loop communications in which the receiver restates what was said or written to ensure the information conveyed by the sender was understood as intended by the receiver. Also referred to as *closed-loop communication* or *three-way communication*, these messages are directive or safety-critical in nature and must be communicated using these steps as a safety precaution: (1) The sender gets the attention of the intended receiver using the person's name and then speaks the message; (2) the receiver repeats the message in a paraphrased form, which helps the sender verify that the receiver understands the intended message; and (3) the sender acknowledges that the receiver heard and understood the message.

I'M SAFE checklist lets team members assess their own fitness for duty and safety status through a self-check process by evaluating whether any of these conditions is impeding their ability to perform their assigned duties: illness; medication; stress; alcohol or drugs; fatigue; or eating and elimination.

Other human performance safety tools include the following (TVA 2017):

The *two-minute rule* requires workers to take time before starting a task or procedure to become aware of the immediate work environment and to detect any conditions that were unanticipated in the care planning process. If the team doesn't have two minutes, that time can be reduced to 60 or 45 seconds, but this pre-procedure step is critical to patient safety.

(continued)

The team makes a brief review of the job site to detect any abnormalities, error precursors, or hazards that could result in harm to the patient.

The *phonetic alphabet* should be used when the sender or receiver feels there may be the possibility of misunderstanding verbal messages when communication is undertaken in a high-noise area, when things being discussed sound alike, or when telephone reception is poor.

Place-keeping is used to mark the steps in a process or procedure as they are completed or bypassed to ensure steps are not accidentally omitted or repeated. First, all critical steps are clearly marked on the checklist during the pre-job briefing. Second, all the steps are read before performing the process or procedure. Third, the steps are performed by the team or team members. Finally, each step is marked as it is completed, either by individual sign-off, check mark, or the "circle-slash" method, in which all critical step numbers are circled and then the circles are slashed through when that step is completed.

STAR or self-checking is particularly effective during the completion of skill-based tasks that can often be performed without much conscious thought. STAR stands for the following:

STOP. Pause before performing the procedure, especially at critical steps or decision points.

THINK. Focus attention on the step to be performed. Verify that the action is appropriate, anticipate the expected results of those actions, and consider a contingency plan in case unexpected results occur.

ACT. Perform the care process or procedure.

REVIEW. Verify that the anticipated results were obtained, or implement the contingency care plan if unexpected results occurred.

(continued)

Exhibit 3.1: Safety Communication Techniques *(continued)*

During important steps in a patient care process, self-checking helps team members maintain focus and stay alert to potential safety hazards. This technique is most useful during the completion of safety-critical steps or when the caregiver is under time pressure, stress, or the threat of interruption.

Stop when unsure is employed by individuals when they find themselves in an uncertain or confusing situation. When something "just doesn't feel right," the individual care provider should stop and get help or expert advice.

SAFER is a safe care practice in which the care team Summarizes the critical steps in the care process, Anticipates all error-likely situations, Foresees the consequences of potential errors, Evaluates the defenses, and Reviews any related previous experience that will help inform and improve the safety of this procedure or process.

During patient transfers, or staff handoff of patient information or responsibility, the *5P safety check* can improve the accuracy and continuity of care. Before the handoff or transfer, staff members review the *patient*, the *purpose* or desired outcome, the *plan* for what should happen next, any known *problems* or challenges with the patient, and any potential *precautions* or unusual circumstances related to this patient.

Peer checking provides an important verification of the steps or actions to be taken before performing a safety-critical task. The task performer self-checks all tasks to be performed, the peer confirms that the correct task is about to be performed, the performer and the peer agree on the action to be taken, and then the performer executes the task. If the action is not consistent with the intended action, the peer stops the performer.

Sources: Information from AHRQ (2017a) and TVA (2017).

REFERENCES

Agency for Healthcare Research and Quality (AHRQ). 2017a. "About TeamSTEPPS." Accessed March 20, 2019. www.ahrq.gov/teamstepps/about-teamstepps/index.html.

———. 2017b. "Guide to Patient and Family Engagement in Hospital Quality and Patient Safety." Accessed March 20, 2019. www.ahrq.gov/professionals/systems/hospital/engaging families/index.html.

Agrawal, A. (ed.). 2014. *Patient Safety: A Case-Based Comprehensive Guide*. New York: Springer Science & Business Media.

Aguilar, E. 2016. *The Art of Coaching Teams: Building Resilient Communities That Transform Schools*. San Francisco: Jossey-Bass.

American Society of Registered Nurses (ASRN). 2008. "Facilitating Patient Safety Through Teamwork." *Chronicle of Nursing*. Published June 1. www.asrn.org/journal-chronicle -nursing/364-facilitating-patient-safety-through-teamwork.html.

Association of American Medical Colleges (AAMC). 2016. "Teamwork: The Heart of Health Care." Published September 27. https://news.aamc.org/medical-education /article/teamwork-heart-health-care/.

Baker, D. P., J. B. Battles, and H. B. King. 2017. "New Insights About Team Training from a Decade of TeamSTEPPS." Agency for Healthcare Research and Quality, Perspectives on Safety. Published February. https://psnet.ahrq.gov/perspectives/perspective/218 /New-Insights-About-Team-Training-From-a-Decade-of-TeamSTEPPS.

Baker, D. P., E. Salas, J. B. Battles, and H. B. King. 2012. "The Relation Between Teamwork and Patient Safety." In *Handbook of Human Factors and Ergonomics in Health Care and Patient Safety*, 2nd ed., edited by P. Carayon, 185–97. Boca Raton, FL: CRC Press.

Brady, P. J., J. B. Battles, and R. Ricciardi. 2015. "Teamwork: What Health Care Has Learned from the Military." *Journal of Nursing Care Quality* 30 (1): 1–6.

Flin, R., P. O'Connor, and M. Crichton. 2008. *Safety at the Sharp End: A Guide to Non-Technical Skills*. Boca Raton, FL: CRC Press.

Katzenbach, J. R., and D. K. Smith. 1992. *The Wisdom of Teams: Creating the High-Performance Organization*. Boston: Harvard Business School Press.

Leggat, S. G. 2007. "Effective Healthcare Teams Require Effective Team Members: Defining Teamwork Competencies." *BMC Health Services Research* 7: 17.

Lencioni, P. 2002. *The Five Dysfunctions of a Team: A Leadership Fable*. San Francisco: Jossey-Bass.

Leonard, M., S. Graham, and B. Taggart. 2010. "The Human Factor: Effective Teamwork and Communication in Patient Strategy." In *Achieving Safe and Reliable Healthcare:*

Strategies and Solutions, edited by M. Leonard, A. Frankel, T. Simmonds, and K. Vega, 37–64. Chicago: Health Administration Press.

Nurse Journal. 2017. "When Nursing Teamwork Suffers." Accessed March 20, 2019. https://nursejournal.org/community/when-nursing-teamwork-suffers/.

O'Leary, K. J., N. L. Sehgal, G. Terrell, and M. V. Williams. 2011. "Interdisciplinary Teamwork in Hospitals: A Review and Practical Recommendations for Improvement." *Journal of Hospital Medicine* 7 (1): 1–7.

O'Malley, A., R. Gourevitch, K. Draper, A. Bond, and A. Tirodkar. 2014. "Overcoming Challenges to Teamwork in Patient-Centered Medical Homes: A Qualitative Study." Commonwealth Fund. Published November 18. www.commonwealthfund.org/publications/journal-article/2014/nov/overcoming-challenges-teamwork-patient-centered-medical-homes.

Patient Safety Network. 2019. "Patient Safety Primer: Teamwork Training." Updated January. https://psnet.ahrq.gov/primers/primer/8.

Saban, N. 2004. *How Good Do You Want to Be?* New York: Ballantine.

Salas, E., D. Diaz, S. J. Weaver, and H. King. 2008. "Does Team Training Work? Principles for Health Care." *Academic Emergency Medicine* 15 (11): 1–12.

Salas, E., D. Sims, C. Klein, and C. Burke. 2003. "Can Teamwork Enhance Patient Safety?" *Risk Management Foundation Forum*, July, 5–9.

Tennessee Valley Authority (TVA). 2017. "Human Performance Program." Accessed April 11, 2019. www.nerc.com/pa/rrm/hp/2012%20Human%20Performance%20Conference/TVA%20%20Human%20Performance%20Program.pdf.

Thiel, D. 2009. "A Process to Build High-Performance Teams." *Design Intelligence*. Published July 7. www.di.net/articles/a-process-to-build-high-performance-teams/.

US Department of Energy (DOE). 2009. *Human Performance Improvement Handbook*, vol. 1: *Concepts and Principles*. Published June. www.standards.doe.gov/standards-documents/1000/1028-BHdbk-2009-v1.

Weaver, S. J., and M. A. Rosen. 2013. "Team-Training in Health Care: Brief Update Review." In *Making Health Care Safer II: An Updated Critical Analysis of the Evidence for Patient Safety Practices*, 472–79. Rockville, MD: Agency for Healthcare Research and Quality.

Weller, J. 2015. "Assessing Teamwork and Communication in the Health Professions." Society of Critical Care Medicine. Accessed April 11, 2019. https://ecitydoc.com/download/assessing-teamwork-and-communication_pdf.

Preparing Through Deliberate Practice and Simulation

WHY SHOULD PATIENT CARE TEAMS BE INVOLVED IN DELIBERATE PRACTICE?

Psychologist Anders Ericsson (2016, xxi), an expert on how people improve performance, explains best why deliberate practice is so important: "Desire and hard work are not enough to lead to improved performance—the right sort of practice carried out over a sufficient period of time leads to improvement. Nothing else."

Increasing the right sort of guided practice for patient care teams has been shown to improve both individual and team competencies and to result in less patient harm and better patient outcomes. Several studies support the conclusion that practice—deliberate, purposeful, simulated practice that includes reflection and feedback—contributes to procedural mastery and safer patient care.

The Agency for Healthcare Research and Quality (AHRQ) sponsors systematic reviews of patient safety practices, including the deliberate practice of simulation, and has concluded that "simulation interventions do improve the technical performance of clinicians and health care teams during critical events and can be viewed as an effective patient safety strategy" (AHRQ 2013). In particular, a study of simulation exercises found the following:

- A randomized trial of first-year gastroenterology fellows showed that although fellows trained using simulation exercises outperformed traditionally trained fellows on their first 80 colonoscopy procedures, the difference in performance dissipated after 80 procedures. The study concluded that to achieve the desired level of procedural mastery, performance of at least 200 colonoscopies during practice training was necessary (Schmidt et al. 2013b, 443).

- A meta-analysis of laparoscopic training for surgical residents revealed that residents who were randomized to receive simulation training on laparoscopic cholecystectomy exhibited fewer errors in exposing, clipping, and dissection during their first 10 cholecystectomies than traditionally trained clinicians. These simulation-trained clinicians were found to make "three-fold fewer total errors and an eight-fold decreased variation in error making totals" (Schmidt et al. 2013b, 444).

- Another meta-analysis of simulation-based education in central venous catheter (CVC) techniques demonstrated that simulation-based practice improves learners' performance and outcomes when actual procedures are performed. The study found that CVC simulation training and deliberate practice resulted in fewer needle passes and reduced pneumothoraces. An estimated 48 percent of hospital patients in the intensive care unit have indwelling CVCs, totaling more than 15 million CVC patient days each year. Catheter-related bloodstream infections are among the most common healthcare-associated infections. "Simulation promises to exert protective effects against risks involved with the insertion process, including pneumothorax, arterial puncture, bleeding, and deep vein thrombosis" (Schmidt et al. 2013b, 446).

AHRQ's Patient Safety Primer on simulation training notes that "considerable evidence documents the dangers posed by inexperienced clinicians and poorly functioning clinical teams. Based in part on its success in other industries such as aviation, simulation-based training has therefore emerged as a key component of the patient safety movement and is increasingly being used to improve clinical and teamwork skills" (PSNet 2019).

The goal of simulation-based training is for clinicians to engage in deliberate practice to enhance their skills or learn new skills and to receive focused, real-time feedback about their performance. Deliberate practice through simulation training contributes to the development of individual expertise and the cultivation of effective team skills. Moreover, simulation gives clinicians the opportunity to learn new procedural skills without risking harm to patients. Deliberate practice through simulation allows practitioners to improve their foundational clinical skills as well as the more advanced cognitive and motor skills necessary to carry out their job functions safely and with confidence and mastery. Teamwork training also benefits from simulation by allowing team members to enhance multidisciplinary team communications, especially in preparing for safety-critical situations.

Exhibit 4.1: Procedural Safety Improvements from Simulation-Based Training

Targeted Procedural Skill	Safety Improvement Realized
Colonoscopy	Better initial performance by physicians in actual procedures
Laparoscopic cholecystectomy	Improved clinician performance and fewer errors
Cataract surgery	Lower rate of complications
Central venous catheterization	Improved learner outcomes and performance during actual procedures
Medication administration	Fewer medication administration errors

Source: Information from Schmidt et al. (2013a, 428–29).

Simulation also aids the usability testing of new equipment and new technology in a real-world environment. Safety defenses can be tested for efficacy and latent safety issues can be identified so that process improvements can be designed to protect patients from harm when the equipment or technology is used.

Exhibit 4.1 lists examples of specific procedural safety improvements resulting from simulation-based training.

WHAT IS DELIBERATE PRACTICE?

For more than 30 years, Ericsson has studied the most accomplished performers in the areas of sports, medicine, music, business, education, and sales to understand the factors that contribute to their success. Looking at individuals such as composer Wolfgang Amadeus Mozart, top gun fighter pilots, and grand-master chess players, Ericsson has examined the ingredients of expertise. He concludes that it is not innate talent that differentiates expert performers from the rest of us, but the amount of time they devote to deliberate, purposeful, guided practice. All of us have the cognitive adaptability to learn and master new skills, and we can develop these new abilities through dedicated training and practice that drives changes in the brain and, sometimes, in the body (Ericsson 2016, xvii).

Matthew Syed (2010, 9, 13), a leading expert on the science of high performance, has noted, "We like to think that sport is a meritocracy—where achievement is driven by ability and hard work—but it is nothing of the sort. It is practice, not talent, that ultimately matters." In his study of expert performers, Syed found that top performers transformed their minds and bodies through specialized practice and a lifelong, deliberate effort to improve their skill level and overall performance.

Syed includes a quote in his book *Bounce* from Jack Nicklaus, one of the most accomplished golfers in the history of the game:

Nobody—but nobody—has ever become really proficient at golf without practice, without doing a lot of thinking and then hitting a lot of shots. It isn't so much a lack of talent; it's a lack of being able to repeat good shots consistently that frustrates most players. And the only answer to that is practice.

Extraordinary golfers such as Nicklaus spend just as many hours practicing perfection as they spend on the golf course in a competitive round. Ben Hogan, one of only five players to have won all four major golf tournaments, has said, "Every day that you don't practice is one day longer before you achieve greatness."

Phil Mickelson, the winner of 25 PGA Tour events and four major golf tournaments, has dramatically improved his performance over the years through deliberate practice, including expert coaching, reflection on practice improvement opportunities, and focused feedback. At the beginning of each season, Mickelson spends countless hours at the Callaway Performance Center in California, working with his coaches and practicing every aspect of his game. During a typical practice day, Mickelson hits 1,500 golf balls using his driver, woods, irons, and wedges, working on control and precision. He aims at small targets to practice chipping and makes hundreds of putts from a three-foot circle around the hole.

> We live in a world full of people with extraordinary abilities—abilities that from the vantage point of almost any other time in human history would have been deemed impossible. But while the abilities are extraordinary, there is no mystery at all about how these people developed them. They practiced. A lot.
> —Anders Ericsson (2016)

Before playing in a tournament, Mickelson practices for one to two hours on the driving range, where he works on distance control, and then spends about the same amount of time on the practice putting green, working on longer 15- to 20-foot putts—the typical length a golfer needs for a birdie (one stroke under par). "If I have to hit a shot 132 yards, I do not hit it 137 yards. A slight miscalculation can mean the difference between a birdie and a bogey" (Mickelson 2005, 11).

Mickelson's coaches, Dave Pelz and Rick Smith, have worked with him to refine his game and to identify areas where Mickelson needs to improve, what to practice, and how to practice better. Like all great performers, Mickelson is always striving for improvement in his performance and competitive excellence. Pelz, Phil's short-game coach and a former NASA scientist, used more than 30 years of performance

> Practice is everything. We want to create an environment that will permit each of our players to reach his maximum potential, and one of the ways we do that is by practicing with great focus. A player who is fully prepared on the practice field will feel ready to meet whatever comes his way on game day. If you practice something consistently enough, when the critical moment comes in a game, the players . . . will be comfortable with the situation and make the right decisions. If you compete day in and day out to excel at something in a systematic way, you can't help but improve.
> —Pete Carroll (2010), head coach of the Seattle Seahawks—one of only three coaches ever to have won both a Super Bowl (Seahawks) and an NCAA Collegiate Football Championship (University of Southern California)

data from expert golfers to help Mickelson improve his performance. "Phil has the ability to hit a wedge shot 132 yards rather than 137 yards," Pelz says. "But it took years of training to be able to gain that skill. It's a combination of perfecting swing mechanics without [making] fundamental errors" (Mickelson 2005, 107).

The disciplines of great performers in areas such as competitive sports can be directly applied to the goal of making healthcare safer—deliberate, purposeful practice guided by an expert coach who provides learners with specific feedback, goals for improvement, and time for personal reflection.

Syed (2010, 19) notes that "once the opportunity for practice is in place, the prospects of high achievement take off. If practice is diminished, no amount of talent is going to get you there." Top performers, from pilots and military generals to winning athletes and surgeons, spend countless hours refining, improving, and mastering their professional skills through structured, purposeful practice. Ericsson calls this the "Iceberg Illusion": Outsiders see only the tip of the iceberg—stellar performance—but don't know what lies beneath the surface: countless hours of practice, and dedication to continuous improvement in skill to achieve a superior level of performance. Achieving performance excellence requires purposeful practice, concentration, dedication, the right training, and the right coach (Syed 2010, 92).

Ericsson (2016, 14–17) differentiates deliberate practice from what he refers to as "naive practice." Naive practice entails merely doing a task over and over again and expecting that repetition alone will improve performance. Deliberate or purposeful practice involves well-defined and specific goals and focused feedback. It requires individuals go beyond their comfort zone to achieve mastery.

An important aspect of providing safe patient care is the ability to anticipate and respond effectively to emerging threats to patient safety. One benefit of deliberate practice is the ability to see patterns in task performance that might otherwise seem random. This ability allows the clinician to envision possible outcomes, sort through the options, and make a decision that favors the most promising action (Ericsson 2016, 63–64).

Ericsson (2016, 99–10) has identified 12 attributes of deliberate or purposeful practice:

1. Effective training techniques are established.
2. Practice is overseen by a teacher or coach who is familiar with the abilities of expert performers and knows how to develop those abilities.
3. Individuals practice outside their comfort zone and beyond their capabilities.
4. Performance improvement targets are well defined with specific goals.
5. Coaches develop a training plan that guides individuals through a series of small changes or improvements that eventually lead to a larger change that is necessary to achieve task mastery.
6. Practice requires individuals' full commitment, attention, and actions to achieve progress and improvement.
7. Individuals concentrate on the specific goal for their practice activity.
8. Practice sessions involve feedback and modifying practice in response to that feedback.
9. Coaches monitor individual performance, pointing out problems and offering suggestions to improve performance.
10. Individuals involved in practice monitor their own performance through mental representations, spotting mistakes and adjusting their practice session accordingly.
11. Practice focuses on helping individuals improve their mental representations so that as performance improves, mental representations become more detailed and effective.
12. Individuals modify and improve their skills through practice, which eventually leads to expert performance.

LESSONS FROM HIGH-RELIABILITY ORGANIZATIONS

Simulation Training as an Effective Form of Deliberate Practice in Aviation

Researchers Michael Green, Rayhan Tariq, and Parmis Green (2016, 1) note that "one of the most important reasons cited for the improvement in the safety of [the] aviation industry has been the routine use of aviation

→

---

simulators in the training of pilots." Simulation-based training for airline pilots was introduced in the early 1920s with the Link Trainer, also known as the Blue Box or the Pilot Trainer. Created by Link Aviation Devices, this pilot training simulator was used by air forces around the world as a safe way to train pilots to fly by instruments. This early attempt at simulating, in a risk-free laboratory, the real-time challenges that pilots face in the air spurred the adoption of simulation training more broadly by the US Federal Aviation Administration. Subsequently, this led to its adoption as a method of training in safe procedures in many other industries, including healthcare.

Simulation training in aviation is now required for all pilots, progressing through four levels based on the pilot's responsibilities: (1) cockpit procedures training, including basic training on procedures and the use of checklists; (2) basic aviation training; (3) flight training; and (4) full-flight simulation.

The aviation industry's experience with simulation provides an important lesson: Just because someone has completed simulation training, that does not mean task mastery has been achieved. Rather, organizations, coaches, and trainees need to assess whether the simulation training actually succeeded in transferring skills from the simulated environment to real-world execution of the task. The organization "needs to understand the transfer relationship between performance on the simulator and performance in the game" (Lee, Chamberlin, and Hodges 2001, 133). This, of course, is the goal of simulation—the positive transfer of skills developed during the simulated training to the performance of the task in a real situation.

Deliberate practice through simulation has had a significant positive impact on commercial airline safety over the past 60 years. Approximately 3.3 billion passengers were expected to fly commercially during 2014, up from 106 million passengers in 1960. This period saw a remarkable decrease in the number of fatal airplane accidents and crashes as a result of the industry's collective commitment to improve airline safety. Today, fewer than 2 passenger deaths occur for every 100 million airline passengers, compared with 133 passenger deaths per 100 million passengers in the 1960s and 1970s (Allianz 2014).

A 2014 Global Aviation Study cited several positive trends that have led to impressive improvements in airline safety performance since the 1950s:

→

> (1) advances in aircraft design, including the advent of the jet engine; (2) enormous improvements in the culture of safety; (3) much higher standards of training for crew members; (4) improved air traffic control technology; (5) a focus on identifying problems before they create a significant event; (6) the development of navigation equipment and anti-collision control systems; (7) the implementation of crew resource management (CRM) training; and (8) "recurrent training" for pilots and crew (Allianz 2014, 2). Recurrent training allows pilots and airline crew members to practice their cognitive, motor, and nontechnical skills through simulation training and to prepare for an unexpected, unusual, or emergent situation.

ADVANTAGES OF SIMULATION IN HEALTHCARE

Learning through simulated practice has the advantage of building into the practice session variable patient and environmental conditions, equipment problems, and other anomalies that help prepare the practitioner for unexpected clinical challenges when caring for a real patient. An AHRQ issue brief on healthcare simulation notes that "with respect to safety, simulation enables the training of tomorrow's practitioners without putting today's patients at risk. When practice on the job is not acceptable because of safety concerns, simulation provides the opportunity to reach proficiency on difficult and critical skills that are needed for safe and reliable system performance" (AHRQ 2015, 3).

Simulation training, equipment, and tools may vary according to the training objective. Simulated activities can range from simple role-playing to complex, highly technical procedural training using high-fidelity simulators. Standardized patients can be used to teach basic skills, such as taking a patient's history and physical examination, while high-fidelity mannequins are designed to be lifelike and simulate physiologic changes (Ross 2012). According to Christine Park, president of the

> While technology has helped drive improvements in the aviation industry's safety record, great strides in safety management systems and insights into human factors have also contributed significantly. Flight training has become a more controlled and professional environment with the development of recurrent training. The utilization and technological enhancement of flight simulators has been one of the biggest changes.
>
> —Allianz (2014)

HARM-FREE HEALTHCARE: EXEMPLARY PRACTICE

Deliberate Practice Through Simulation in Healthcare

In 1987, Dr. David Gaba at Stanford University developed the Comprehensive Anesthesia Simulation Environment as a realistic physical simulation for use in the Anesthesia Crisis Resource Management training program—anesthesia's version of CRM (Green, Tariq, and Green 2016, 3). High-fidelity patient simulators, including SimMan, HAL, and METI Human Patient Simulators, are in wide use in anesthesiology training programs around the world. "Simulation training has been objectively shown to increase the skill set of anesthesiologists. It is rational to assume a relationship between simulation training and patient safety" (Green, Tariq, and Green 2016, 1). Simulation-based practice is now used in healthcare to help practitioners improve their procedural skills and acquire new ones, as well as to help the patient care team anticipate responses to emerging or uncommon safety risks and hazards.

The simulation practice session begins with a pre-procedure briefing and ends with a debriefing in which the practitioner/trainee and patient care team discuss (1) how they handled unexpected events, (2) the effectiveness of the team's communication, (3) improvement opportunities, and (4) whether the goal of the care practice was achieved. Gaba envisioned ongoing training of clinical personnel and patient care teams in which they would "undergo continual systematic training, rehearsal, performance assessment, and refinement in their practice" (Gaba 2004, 127). His goal was inspired by the safety accomplishments of high-reliability organizations such as those in commercial aviation. Gaba urged the adoption of simulation training to improve patient safety, facilitate the recruitment and retention of skilled personnel, and enable culture change in healthcare (Gaba 2004, 2).

Simulated practice can be used to (1) assess practitioners' competency in both technical and nontechnical skills, (2) provide a venue for teams to rehearse a complex procedure before performing that procedure on a patient, (3) evaluate the human–machine interfaces between the patient care team and medical equipment in a low-risk setting, (4) practice CRM skills, (5) refresh skills for procedures that are not performed often, (6) improve teamwork, and (7) allow novices to practice extensively before they perform safety-critical processes or procedures on patients (Gaba 2004, 127–30).

→

When medical residents and novice practitioners practice techniques and procedures on real patients, there are always concerns about potential harm to patients. As Dr. Robert Wachter (2012, 310–13) of the University of California, San Francisco Medical Center explains, "With the patient safety movement, most believe that learning on patients is unethical so healthcare is increasingly looking to simulation. It will be important to remember that simulators can help augment trainees' technical competence, but are highly unlikely to fully replace the need for trainees to learn their craft—as safely as possible—with real patients."

Society for Simulation in Healthcare, instead of the traditional physician education model of "see one, do one, teach one," healthcare's "mantra should be 'See one, simulate many, do a few more, and then teach one' because simulation enhances training experiences before we do things in real life" (*Modern Healthcare* 2017).

There are a variety of approaches to simulation training in healthcare, each designed to provide individual practitioners and patient care teams with realistic clinical challenges through the use of part-task trainers, high-fidelity full-body mannequins, team training, virtual reality, standardized patients, and in situ simulation (AHRQ 2015, 5–6):

- *Part-task trainers* are used to develop specific clinical or procedural skills through simulation. For example, an anatomically correct reproduction of the upper torso and head is used to simulate real-world challenges when performing intubation, ventilation, and suction tasks. Other applications include cardiac assessment, vascular access, and lumbar puncture.
- *High-fidelity full-body mannequins* offer the trainee and team an opportunity to practice on a full-body mannequin with anatomical landmarks and physiological features such as vital signs, blood gas exchange, and heart sounds. Mannequins are used to practice physical examinations and rapid response to failing patient conditions.
- *Team training through simulation* focuses on improving the functionality of the patient care team, thereby reducing the potential for patient harm. Simulated practice sessions for teams emphasize clear, concise, and safety-oriented communication; clarification of individual roles and responsibilities; decision-making under pressure; and accountability for safe care practices.

- *Virtual reality* provides a computer-generated environment in which learners are immersed in a highly realistic clinical environment such as an operating room, intensive care unit, or emergency department. Learners interact with the simulated environment, which, in turn, is influenced by their decisions and actions.
- *Standardized patients* are trained actors who are used to simulate real patients for the purpose of teaching basic history and physical examination skills and providing feedback on the practitioner's behaviors during challenging clinical situations. For example, a trainee could practice disclosing an error to a patient or family member.
- *In situ simulation* refers to simulation performed in an actual clinical environment with the providers who normally work with patients in that area. In situ (a Latin phrase meaning "in the situation") simulation provides a more realistic training ground in which to practice new skills and knowledge and is better suited to identifying latent safety threats.

A commitment to eliminating preventable harm to hospitalized patients must include the ongoing engagement of practitioners in deliberate practice and simulated training. Mastering the procedural skills required to place a central line or perform surgery requires excellent perceptual, cognitive, psychomotor, and decision-making skills—skills that can be enhanced through simulation without the risk of patient harm. An individual's cognitive and procedural skills can diminish over time as a result of the infrequent performance of a task or a lack of participation in deliberate practice. Mastery learning—rigorous, competency-based instruction in which learners must demonstrate attainment of a high performance standard—is a form of deliberate practice that can contribute to acquiring and maintaining a superior level of technical performance (AHRQ 2015, 7).

Schmidt and colleagues (2013a, 427) note that "simulation improves patient safety by allowing physicians to become better trained without putting patients at risk and, importantly, by providing protected time for reflection and debriefing—where most

---

There have now been many studies of elite performers—international violinists, chess grand masters, professional ice skaters, mathematicians, and so forth— and the biggest difference researchers find between them and lesser performers is the cumulative amount of deliberate practice they've had. Indeed, the most important talent may be the talent for practice itself.

—Atul Gawande (2002)

of the learning takes place." They summarize the evidence that simulated deliberate practice contributes to safer patient care:

- Heterogeneous evidence (i.e., evidence across multiple topic areas) shows that training with simulation-based exercises increases technical and procedural performance.
- Heterogeneous evidence shows that simulation-based exercises can improve team performance and interpersonal dynamics.
- Limited evidence suggests that improvements in patient outcomes attributable to simulation exercises can occur at the health system level.

PREPARING TO DELIVER SAFE CARE THROUGH DELIBERATE PRACTICE

Clinical and procedural skills improve with the right kind of practice—deliberate practice. Whether the competency-enhancing objective is to improve current clinical, surgical, or procedural motor and cognitive skills or to practice a new process or procedure, deliberate practice provides a rigorous discipline that allows individuals to succeed.

Deliberate practice sessions must be coached. Together, the coach and the practitioners/learners agree on goals and improvement objectives for each practice session. During and at the conclusion of each session, the coach provides "plus-delta" feedback, highlighting the positive aspects of the learners' performance (plus) and giving suggestions for change or improvement (delta). The learners take time for reflection after the session, critiquing their own performance and identifying opportunities for improvement—learning from the practice experience and using that learning to guide future performance.

Physicians, nurses, students, residents, and other healthcare professionals all benefit from focused training, whether it is to acquire new procedural skills, enhance clinical reasoning and decision-making, cultivate communication skills, or achieve mastery of a particular task. Simulation has emerged as an effective form of applied deliberate practice for healthcare professionals.

Simulation-Based Deliberate Practice

Mayo Clinic researcher David Cook describes three forms of simulation-based education for healthcare professionals. These exercises provide opportunities to rehearse individual and team task performance in a risk-free environment, with repeated and structured deliberate practice, and a coach's feedback and assessment of performance (Cook 2013, 2):

1. *Technology-enhanced simulation* requires an educational tool or device that learners physically interact with to mimic an aspect of clinical care for the purpose of enhancing skills. Such tools and devices include virtual reality systems and low- and high-fidelity mannequins and models.
2. *Virtual patients* are interactive, computer-based simulations that help learners effectively obtain a patient's history and physical examination and make diagnostic and therapeutic decisions.
3. *Standardized patients* are real people who are recruited to provide immediate feedback to learners about the proficiency of their approach— for example, explaining the duration and results of an examination.

The use of both virtual patients and technology-enhanced simulation has been shown to have a positive, statistically significant impact on learners' knowledge, skills, and behaviors. The benefits of simulating direct patient effects, such as complications or mortality, are smaller but still significant (Cook 2013, 3). Simulation training is an effective form of deliberate practice and should be part of a healthcare organization's commitment to competency enrichment for the following (Schmidt et al. 2013b, 441):

- Enhancing clinicians' technical skills and performance
- Practicing complex, high-stakes processes or procedures
- Mitigating authority and power differentials between senior and junior clinicians that may hinder effective communication and result in unsafe care
- Learning from errors committed in practice through reflection and debriefing
- Testing new technologies, especially complex ones that require a steep learning curve
- Improving practitioners' cognitive and decision-making skills
- Enhancing team dynamics, teamwork, and interprofessional cohesion
- Managing the emergence of threatening clinical situations

Principles for Designing Simulation-Based Training

Proven principles and practical tactics can provide guidance to organizations that are either implementing simulation-based training for the first time or strengthening an existing program. The ultimate goal of simulation-based deliberate practice is to improve patient safety by reducing errors, testing and maximizing safety defenses, and improving individual and team competencies. The test of effective simulation-based training is whether the practice fosters the transfer of learned knowledge, skills, and abilities (KSAs) to the actual job (Salas et al. 2008, 6). Organizational psychologist Eduardo Salas and colleagues have identified 10 principles to guide the design and implementation of simulation programs, as well as the instructional content, measures of success, and supporting organizational commitment and climate necessary for program success. Simulation-based training programs should do the following:

- *Focus on reinforcing and promoting the needed competencies.* Individual practice sessions should aim to strengthen the KSAs required to perform a task with confidence and mastery. The organization should conduct a training needs assessment and an analysis of the tasks that will be the focus of the training. Training should be directed at improving individuals' competencies, not performing the tasks themselves. Developing desired learning outcomes for the training sessions will aid in the ongoing assessment of the training program's effectiveness.
- *Adopt a systems approach.* The organization must provide a suitable training environment and ensure that learners receive adequate preparation and orientation so that they know what to expect during the training. When the learners successfully transfer their new skills to the actual patient care experience, they should be recognized and rewarded.
- *Prepare the organization for simulation training.* Cultural support for simulation-based training is critical to its success. The organization should conduct an assessment to determine the climate, identify needed resources, and address constraints that might impede the training program's success. "When the organization establishes a climate for learning and sends positive signals to trainees that training matters, it will be more effective" (Salas et al. 2008, 5).
- *Establish appropriate pre-simulation conditions.* Pre-practice conditions prepare trainees for practice by providing them with information about what they will be doing during the training and strategies to improve their learning. The trainees should understand that the training session is about learning—it is not an assessment of their performance. Moreover, the trainees should be given an assurance of confidentiality and be instructed that making errors in simulated practice is part of the learning process.
- *Ensure trainee motivation.* The organization's leaders must continually emphasize the importance of deliberate practice through simulation

and its impact on safe care practices. Through positive messages, the organization will create a perception of value by demonstrating the real benefits of simulation-based training for provider performance, teamwork, and patient care outcomes.

- *Apply sound instructional principles to the design of the training program.* Specify the training objectives, develop the training content, and create a method of assessing individual performance and a process for providing feedback for improvement. The organization should tailor the instructional strategy to the learning objectives, demonstrate the skills to be learned, match the fidelity of the simulation to the task being learned, provide guided hands-on practice, and provide constructive feedback (debriefing and after-action reviews).

- *Develop performance measures.* Observers or coaches can use checklists to measure both the outcomes of the trainee's performance, such as the number of errors committed, and the process components of the training, such as communication and leadership skills. Measurement should occur throughout the training session—because multiple measurements allow the coach to identify changes in behavior over time. "Trigger events" should be embedded in the simulated scenarios that require the learners to demonstrate the expected KSAs.

- *Establish the simulation environment.* For the simulation training session to be most effective, the simulation setting should be prepared with all of the resources the learners will need, including training equipment and instructional material. The instructors must be properly trained, know the content of the simulation session, and be able to answer questions. The instructors must also be skilled at providing constructive feedback regarding individual learners' performance.

- *Prepare the transfer environment.* The test of the effectiveness of simulation-based training is the completeness of the transfer of skills learned in a simulation to the care of actual patients. Organizations can facilitate the transfer process by creating a continuous learning culture and by demonstrating management support for simulation-based training. In addition, leaders must create opportunities for providers to practice their skills or learn new ones, provide incentives to encourage participation in training, and reinforce the desired behaviors in all staff.

- *Determine training effectiveness.* The organization must evaluate whether its simulation training programs are meeting expectations, such as improving individual and team competencies or lowering error rates and subsequent patient harm. Did the trainees like the training? Did they gain the expected skills and knowledge from the training? Did they later apply what they learned in simulation on the job? What impact did the training have on the organization? Was patient safety improved?

CONCLUSION

This chapter discusses how to prepare staff to deliver safe care through deliberate practice and simulation. The evidence is clear: Practitioner participation in deliberate practice and simulation-based training improves both individual and team performance, and the result is safer care for patients. "There must also be a move away from using experience as a proxy for competence and, on a continuous basis, to analyze a practitioner's skills. Simulation, therefore, has an immense capacity to become an integral part of the drive to build a safer healthcare system for patients everywhere" (Aggarwal et al. 2010, 42).

Deliberate practice and training contribute to the development of individual expertise and the cultivation of effective team skills. Moreover, deliberate practice through simulation provides opportunities to learn new procedural skills without risking harm to patients. Deliberate practice allows practitioners to improve their foundational clinical skills as well as the more advanced cognitive and motor skills necessary to performing their job functions safely and with confidence and mastery. Teamwork also benefits from simulation-based training by allowing team members to enhance multidisciplinary team communications, especially in preparation for handling safety-critical situations.

CHAPTER 4 SAFE CARE PRACTICES

1. Prepare to deliver safe care through deliberate practice, following the 10 principles for the design and implementation of simulation-based training programs outlined by Salas and colleagues.

2. Use guidance such as Anders Ericsson's 12 attributes of deliberate or purposeful practice to understand the benefits of deliberate practice.

3. Provide opportunities for simulation-based deliberate practice. David Cook describes three forms of simulation-based education for healthcare professionals: technology-enhanced simulation, virtual patients, and standardized patients. These methods provide opportunities to rehearse individual and team task performance in a risk-free environment.

→

---

4. Focus on mastery learning—rigorous, competency-based instruction in which learners must demonstrate attainment of a high performance standard. This form of deliberate practice can contribute to acquiring and maintaining a superior level of technical performance.

5. Recognize simulation-based training as an effective form of deliberate practice and make it a part of the organization's commitment to competency enrichment.

REFERENCES

Agency for Healthcare Research and Quality (AHRQ). 2015. "Health Care Simulation to Advance Safety: Responding to Ebola and Other Threats." Issue brief. Published February. www.ahrq.gov/sites/default/files/publications/files/simulation-brief.pdf.

———. 2013. "Simulation Exercises Can Improve Patient Safety." *Research Activities*. Published November/December. www.ahrq.gov/sites/default/files/publications/files/Nov_Dec2013_RA.pdf.

Aggarwal, R., O. T. Mytton, M. Derbrew, D. Hananel, M. Heydenburg, B. Issenberg, C. MacAuley, T. Morimoto, N. Soper, A. Ziv, and R. Reznick. 2010. "Training and Simulation for Patient Safety." *Quality & Safety in Health Care* 19 (Suppl. 2): i34–43.

Allianz. 2014. "Global Aviation Study." Accessed February 21, 2019. www.agcs.allianz.com/insights/white-papers-and-case-studies/global-aviation-study-2014/.

Carroll, P. 2010. *Win Forever: Live, Work, and Play Like a Champion.* New York: Penguin.

Cook, D. A. 2013. "The Literature on Health Care Simulation Education: What Does It Show?" Patient Safety Network. Published March. https://psnet.ahrq.gov/perspectives/perspective/138/The-Literature-on-Health-Care-Simulation-Education-What-Does-It-Show.

Ericsson, A. 2016. *Peak: Secrets from the New Science of Expertise.* Boston: Houghton Mifflin Harcourt.

Gaba, D. 2004. "The Future Vision of Simulation in Healthcare." *Quality & Safety in Health Care* 13 (Suppl. 1): i2–10.

Gawande, A. 2002. *Complications: A Surgeon's Notes on an Imperfect Science.* New York: Picador.

Green, M., R. Tariq, and P. Green. 2016. "Improving Patient Safety Through Simulation Training in Anesthesiology: Where Are We?" *Anesthesiology Research and Practice* 2016: 4237523.

Lee, T. D., C. J. Chamberlin, and N. J. Hodges. 2001. "Practice." In *Handbook of Sports Psychology*, 2nd ed., edited by R. N. Singer, H. A. Hausenblas, and C. M. Janelle, 115–43. Hoboken, NJ: John Wiley & Sons.

Mickelson, P. 2005. *One Magical Sunday*. New York: Time Warner Books.

Modern Healthcare. 2017. "The Rise of Simulation in Healthcare—Empowering Clinicians and Preventing Harm." Sponsored content, June 12.

Patient Safety Network (PSNet). 2019. "Patient Safety Primer: Simulation Training." Updated January. https://psnet.ahrq.gov/primers/primer/25.

Ross, K. 2012. "Practice Makes Perfect." *Health Facilities Management* 25 (11): 23–28.

Salas, E., K. A. Wilson, E. Lazzara, H. B. King, and J. S. Augenstein. 2008. "Simulation-Based Training for Patient Safety: 10 Principles That Matter." *Journal of Patient Safety* 4 (1): 3–8.

Schmidt, E., S. Goldhaber-Fiebert, L. Ho, and K. McDonald. 2013a. "Simulation Exercises as a Patient Safety Strategy: A Systematic Review." *Annals of Internal Medicine* 158 (5): 426–32.

———. 2013b. "Use of Simulation Exercises in Patient Safety Efforts." In *Making Health Care Safer II: An Updated Critical Analysis of the Evidence for Patient Safety Practices*, 439–60. Rockville, MD: Agency for Healthcare Research and Quality.

Syed, M. 2010. *Bounce*. New York: HarperCollins.

Wachter, R. 2012. *Understanding Patient Safety*, 2nd ed. New York: McGraw-Hill Medical.

PART III

Performing Safe Care Practices: The "Offensive" Strategy

CHAPTER 5

Preventing Harm Through Safe Care Practices

WHY PURSUE AN "OFFENSIVE" SAFE CARE STRATEGY TO REDUCE PATIENT HARM?

When teams master the ability to respond effectively to unexpected changes in the work environment and execute individual team member duties with precision, they are better prepared to provide safe care to patients and achieve the goal of zero patient harm. Patient care teams that adopt and consistently apply—through extensive team training—an "offensive" patient safety approach have demonstrated great progress toward the goal of eliminating all preventable patient harm. Offensive strategies involve consistently applying safe care practices that have been tested and proven to reduce the risk of harm to patients.

One such offensive strategy, referred to as a patient care *bundle*, targets the major factors that contribute to patient harm in a process or procedure by applying a small set (three to five) of evidence-based interventions to ensure patient safety. The concept of the care bundle was developed at the Institute for Healthcare Improvement (IHI) in 2001. According to Dr. Robert Wachter (2012, 162), chief of medical services at the University of California, San Francisco Medical Center, "the chances of preventing complications seem to improve with complete adherence to a bundle of preventive strategies. Achieving high bundle adherence rates usually requires reengineering the entire clinical process of care." The goal of the care bundle is to "achieve the highest level of reliability in critical care processes and resultant outcomes, while at the same time introducing concepts of enhanced teamwork and communication" (Resar et al. 2012, 2).

Care bundles and other tested clinical guidelines have been proven to be effective at reducing patient harm when they are consistently and uniformly applied. The following are examples of successful applications of the care bundle approach:

- Vanderbilt University Medical Center in Nashville, Tennessee, used the *Fall Prevention Toolkit* and the Universal Fall Precautions developed by the Agency for Healthcare Research and Quality (AHRQ) to reduce patient falls. The number of injuries caused by falls decreased 45 percent over two years (AHRQ 2016).
- More than 600 hospitals representing 926 patient care units participated in an AHRQ-funded national Comprehensive Unit-based Safety Program called On the CUSP: Stop CAUTI, which was based on the successful Bladder Bundle Initiative developed at the Michigan Health and Hospital Association's Keystone Center for Patient Safety. The unadjusted rate of catheter-associated urinary tract infections (CAUTIs) decreased 22.3 percent (Saint et al. 2016).
- Lankenau Medical Center, part of the Main Line Health system in Wynnewood, Pennsylvania, applied IHI's Ventilator Bundle. It experienced a reduction in the rate of ventilator-associated pneumonia (VAP) from 9.47 to 1.9 cases per 1,000 ventilator days and estimated savings of $1.5 million over one year (Sedwick et al. 2012).
- The University of California, Davis Medical Center in Sacramento implemented strict hand hygiene compliance and IHI's Central Line Insertion Bundle and Central Line Maintenance Bundle. The rate of central line–associated bloodstream infections (CLABSIs) decreased from 9.6 to 2.5 per 1,000 central line days over one year (Donley and Reese 2015).
- OSF Saint Francis Medical Center in Peoria, Illinois, used the Six Sigma methodology to prioritize five solutions to halve the incidence of pressure ulcers in its facility. The Save Our Skin program implemented a home-grown care bundle, resulting in a 70 percent reduction in pressure ulcers (Courtney, Ruppman, and Cooper 2006).

These kinds of practical approaches to eliminating patient harm in safety-critical processes have been developed, tested, and shown to be effective offensive strategies. These solutions involve the consistent application of and adherence to patient care bundles and other tested clinical guidelines that eliminate the threats and hazards in a process or procedure that could cause patient harm.

PATIENT SAFETY PRIORITIES

This chapter discusses proven care bundles and other tested clinical guidelines recommended by authoritative sources such as AHRQ, the Centers for Medicare

& Medicaid Services (CMS), and the National Quality Forum (NQF). Ten of the top threats to patient safety and harm-free healthcare are presented, based on nationally identified patient safety priorities. These priorities target preventable causes of patient harm with unacceptably high incidence. Alongside each patient safety threat, offensive strategies or safe care practices are offered that, if applied uniformly and consistently, can help hospitals and health systems achieve the goal of zero patient harm.

These safe care practices are drawn primarily from three sources: (1) the research on evidence of effectiveness conducted by AHRQ on 158 patient safety practices; (2) the *Sentinel Event Alerts* issued and the National Patient Safety Goals established by The Joint Commission; and (3) the Hospital-Acquired Conditions (HAC) Initiative implemented by CMS under the 2005 Deficit Reduction Act. The HACs identified by CMS are safety threats that (1) are high cost, (2) are high volume, (3) result in a higher diagnosis-related group payment, and (4) could reasonably be prevented through the application of evidence-based guidelines.

The NQF introduced the term *never events* in 2001 to refer to particularly harmful medical errors that should never occur. The 29 never events identified by the NQF were also considered in the identification of the top threats and offensive safe care practices presented in this chapter.

Top 10 Safe Care Practices

AHRQ's 2013 report *Making Health Care Safer II: An Updated Critical Analysis of the Evidence for Patient Safety Practices* "strongly encouraged" the adoption of 10 safe care practices, based on the strength of the evidence of effectiveness in preventing patient harm (AHRQ 2013b):

1. Barrier precautions to prevent healthcare-associated infections (HAIs)
2. "Do Not Use" list for hazardous abbreviations
3. Preoperative/anesthesia checklists to prevent operative events
4. Hand hygiene compliance
5. Bundles to prevent CLABSIs
6. Bundles to prevent VAP
7. Bundles to prevent CAUTIs
8. Real-time ultrasound for central line placement
9. Interventions to prevent pressure ulcers
10. Interventions to prevent venous thromboembolism

AHRQ defines a safe care practice (referred to in the report as a *patient safety practice*) as "a type of process or structure whose application reduces the probability of adverse events resulting from exposure to the health care system across a range of diseases and procedures" (AHRQ 2013b, ES-2). AHRQ prioritized its top 10 safe care practices by considering five aspects of each patient safety problem and attendant practices: (1) the scope of the safety problem, including a review of the frequency of the safety problem and the severity of each average event; (2) the strength of the evidence of effectiveness and the relevance of the patient safety practice; (3) the potential for harmful unintended consequences; (4) the estimated costs of complying with the practice; and (5) the degree of difficulty in implementing the safety practice (AHRQ 2013b, ES-7).

The AHRQ report also "encouraged" the adoption of another 12 practices supported by at least moderate evidence of effectiveness (AHRQ 2013b, x). These practices include interventions to reduce patient falls and adverse drug events, implementation of team training, safe adoption of technology such as computerized provider order entry, and the use of simulation training to enhance patient safety efforts.

Hospital-Acquired Conditions

CMS (2018) published a list of 14 categories of HACs that pose a serious threat to patient safety, are usually preventable, and add unnecessary costs to the healthcare system:

1. Unintended retained foreign object (URFO) after surgery
2. Air embolism
3. Blood incompatibility
4. Pressure ulcers
5. Patient falls
6. Poor glycemic control
7. CAUTIs
8. Vascular catheter-associated infection
9. Surgical site infection (SSI) following coronary artery bypass surgery
10. SSI following bariatric surgery
11. SSI following certain orthopedic procedures
12. SSI following procedures to implant cardiac electronic devices
13. Deep vein thrombosis
14. Iatrogenic pneumothorax with venous catheterization

To encourage hospitals and healthcare systems to take steps to reduce HACs—serious threats to patient safety that are not present upon admission—CMS implemented the Hospital-Acquired Condition Reduction Program beginning in fiscal year 2015. The HAC Reduction Program is mandated by Section 3008 of the Affordable Care Act. CMS may revise the list of HACs from time to time, and it has done so in setting the priorities and payment incentives for hospitals through the HAC Reduction Program. The worst-performing 25 percent of hospitals subject to this provision of the law receive a financial penalty in the form of a 1 percent reduction in Medicare and Medicaid funding. For fiscal year 2018, a hospital's total HAC score, which is used to determine its eligibility for a payment penalty or reduction, is based on six quality measures (CMS 2018):

1. Recalibrated Patient Safety Indicator Composite
2. CLABSI rate
3. CAUTI rate
4. SSI rates for colectomy and hysterectomy
5. Methicillin-resistant *Staphylococcus aureus* (MRSA) rate
6. *Clostridium difficile* infection rate

AHRQ issues an annual analysis of the progress made toward reducing HACs. In its December 2016 *National Scorecard on Rates of Hospital-Acquired Conditions*, it reported that the national focus on HACs together with local hospital efforts to reduce HACs had resulted in a 21 percent reduction in HACs between 2010 and 2015. Further, the report indicated that nearly 125,000 fewer patients died as a result of preventable complications in the hospital and that more than 3 million adverse events were avoided. These collective efforts are estimated to have saved more than $28 billion in healthcare costs. "The National Scorecard update demonstrates that coordinated efforts between federal agencies and private stakeholders . . . can lead to major improvements in patient safety" (ODPHP 2017b).

Never Events

The NQF developed its initial list of 27 never events in 2002. This list has been modified over the years and now consists of 29 "serious reportable events" in seven categories: surgical care, product or device safety, patient protection, care management, environmental safety, radiologic procedures, and criminal events (PSNet 2019b). Never events in surgical care include wrong-site, wrong-patient, or wrong-procedure surgery; URFOs after surgery; and immediate postoperative deaths.

Other examples of never events include patient death associated with the misuse of a device (product safety), patient suicide (patient protection), death or injury related to a medication error (care management), death or serious injury related to the use of restraints (environmental safety), death or serious injury resulting from metal objects in the magnetic resonance imaging area (radiologic safety), and patient abduction (criminal event).

Why have the patient safety initiatives described in this chapter received so much attention from state and federal legislative and regulatory bodies and private sector quality improvement organizations? The answer is simple—America's collective conscience has been disturbed and unsettled by the frequent reports of patients being killed or severely harmed by the care they received in a hospital. Patients, the public, and healthcare providers alike have said "enough is enough," and they are demanding changes in the healthcare delivery system to produce a safe patient care experience in every hospital, every time. Janet Corrigan, former president and CEO of the NQF, has noted (NQF 2010):

> Uniformly reliable safety in healthcare has not yet been achieved. Every day, patients are still harmed, or nearly harmed, in healthcare institutions across the country. This harm is not intentional; however, it usually can be avoided. Systematic, universal implementation of these [evidence-based safe] practices can lead to appreciable and sustainable improvements for healthcare safety. Every individual who seeks medical care should be able to expect and receive safe, reliable care, every time.

TOP 10 THREATS TO PATIENT SAFETY AND OFFENSIVE SAFE CARE PRACTICES TO MITIGATE THEM

The Problem of Patient Falls

Between 700,000 and 1 million patients fall in US hospitals each year, and 30 percent to 50 percent of those falls result in injury. Hospitalized patients can be at risk of falling because of physiological changes caused by their medical condition, the medications they are taking, surgery or other procedures, or diagnostic testing that can leave the patient weakened or confused. Patients who are injured by a fall require additional care and treatment and may have to stay in the hospital longer to recover from the fall-related injury. Research has shown that a fall with injury adds 6.3 days to a patient's hospital stay. The average cost of a fall with injury is approximately $14,000.

Falls with injury are consistently among the top 10 events reported by hospitals to The Joint Commission's Sentinel Event Database. Approximately 63 percent of the falls reported to The Joint Commission resulted in the patient's death. Several factors contribute to patient falls in hospitals, including (1) poor communications among care providers; (2) lack of adherence to protocols and safety practices; (3) inadequate staff orientation, supervision, or staffing levels; (4) deficiencies in the physical environment; and (5) inadequate assessment of the patient's risk of falling (Joint Commission 2015).

Preventing Falls and Fall-Related Injuries

An effective organizational approach to fall prevention requires a systems focus in which care, treatment, and services are coordinated among the care team to ensure patient safety, minimize the use of restraints, and provide for the patient's mobility. "Fall prevention involves managing a patient's underlying fall risk factors (e.g., problems with walking and transfers, medication side effects, confusion, frequent toileting needs) and optimizing the hospital's physical design and environment. A number of practices have been shown to reduce the occurrence of falls" (AHRQ 2013a, 1).

AHRQ's *Fall Prevention Toolkit* is designed to help hospitals and healthcare systems implement a comprehensive fall reduction program and sustain positive results. The *Fall Prevention Toolkit* contains 12 Universal Fall Precautions that "are the cornerstone of any hospital fall prevention program, because they apply to all patients at all times" (AHRQ 2013a). To be successful, hospitals should train all hospital care teams on the importance of fall prevention and embed new practice habits into the organization's safety culture. The Universal Fall Precautions apply across all hospital settings and help safeguard staff, visitors, and patients against injury resulting from a fall (AHRQ 2013a):

1. Familiarize the patient with the environment.
2. Have the patient demonstrate call light use.
3. Maintain call lights in reach of the patient.
4. Keep the patient's personal possessions within safe reach of the patient.
5. Have sturdy handrails in patient rooms, bathrooms, and hallways.
6. Place the hospital bed in a low position when a patient is resting in bed; raise the bed to a comfortable height when the patient is transferring out of bed.
7. Keep hospital bed brakes locked.
8. Keep wheelchair wheel locks in the locked position when stationary.
9. Keep nonslip, comfortable, well-fitted footwear on the patient.
10. Use night-lights or supplemental lighting.
11. Keep floor surfaces clean and dry (clean up all spills promptly).
12. Keep patient care areas uncluttered.

Without assistance, patients are more likely to experience a fall during their hospital stay. Using AHRQ's *Fall Prevention Toolkit* as a guide, hospitals should evaluate their current organizational protocols for preventing and responding to patient falls, provide strong leadership support for implementing a fall prevention program, charter a team to steer the implementation of the fall prevention program, and establish improvement goals based on baseline outcome and process measures. Staff should identify risk factors to guide fall prevention care planning—for example, evaluating patients for delirium, educating patients and family, and following safe care practices for mobilizing patients. The hospital should also have a process for assessing and managing patients after a fall. AHRQ provides a tool for post-fall assessment using root cause analysis.

Following implementation of the Universal Fall Precautions, hospital staff should assess the degree to which fall prevention training has been integrated into the hospital's education practices, collect data about falls and fall-related injuries and their causes, and implement improvement strategies that target areas with weak defenses and error-provoking climates.

The Joint Commission (2015) recommends six actions to help healthcare organizations prevent falls and fall-related injuries. It urges strong leadership commitment to preventing falls and a systematic, data-driven approach to achieving a reduction in fall risks and sustaining improvements.

The Problem of Catheter-Associated Urinary Tract Infections

Urinary tract infections (UTIs) are the most common type of HAI, accounting for about 40 percent of all HAIs in the United States (Wachter 2012, 169). Approximately 560,000 patients develop catheter-associated UTIs each year, leading to longer hospital stays, increased costs, and potential injury or harm to the patient (ANA 2017).

UTIs frequently occur after the placement of a urinary catheter, which is often unnecessary and can be easily forgotten by the care team. More than 1 million CAUTIs occur each year, resulting in an additional cost of $676 per admission, or $2,836 if the infection is complicated by bacteremia.

Preventing Catheter-Associated Urinary Tract Infections

Wachter (2012, 171) notes that "in patients with indwelling catheters, maintaining a closed drainage system, providing appropriate catheter care, and removing the catheter as quickly as possible are all beneficial. [Researchers] have demonstrated that nearly one-third of hospital doctors are unaware that their patient has a Foley catheter, and recommend automatic stop orders (after two days) or written or computerized provider reminders to ensure that catheters are removed when they are no longer needed."

Many CAUTI prevention strategies are bundled into a discrete set of interventions known as a *bladder bundle*. The bundle approach to preventing CAUTIs consists of three components: (1) educational interventions to improve the appropriate use of catheters and staff clinical skills in catheter placement; (2) behavioral interventions to ensure the consistent application of catheter restrictions and removal protocols; and (3) the use of specific technologies to improve care, such as bladder ultrasound (Meddings et al. 2013, 73).

In 2007, the Michigan Health and Hospital Association's Keystone Center for Patient Safety launched a statewide effort to prevent CAUTIs. The CAUTI prevention initiative focused hospitals on optimizing the use of urinary catheters, with a specific emphasis on (1) continual assessment of the patient's need for a urinary catheter and (2) removal of the catheter as soon as possible, especially for patients who have no clear need for a urinary catheter. The bladder bundle developed in Michigan was based on the understanding that most hospital-acquired UTIs are caused by an indwelling urinary catheter and on research showing that only about half of all indwelling catheters are appropriate. The bladder bundle emphasizes reducing urinary catheter use in the first place (Saint 2009, 1–5). It comprises the following protocols and associated measures (Saint 2009, 4):

- Nurse-initiated urinary catheter discontinuation protocol (measure: prevalence rate of urinary catheter utilization)
- Urinary catheter reminders and removal prompts (measure: indication for each insertion)
- Alternatives to indwelling urinary catheterization (measure: prevalence rate of unnecessary urinary catheter use)
- Portable bladder ultrasound monitoring (measure: rate of discontinuation of unnecessary urinary catheters)
- Insertion care and maintenance

Avoiding unnecessary placement of indwelling urinary catheters is critical. Patients cannot develop a CAUTI without a catheter. Research shows that between 21 percent and 63 percent of urinary catheters are placed in patients who do not have an appropriate indication and therefore may not need a catheter (Meddings et al. 2013, 75). Therefore, hospitals should develop and implement catheter restriction protocols, which have proven to be effective at decreasing catheter use and CAUTI rates. The Centers for Disease Control and Prevention (CDC) has issued guidelines for appropriate and inappropriate indications for indwelling urinary catheters (CDC

2017). These guidelines can be tailored to include other indications according to the hospital's experience and specialized patient populations.

Safe care practices that prompt the removal of unnecessary catheters may include a reminder system that alerts nurses and doctors that a catheter remains in place. A *catheter reminder intervention* can take the form of a daily checklist, a sticker on the patient's chart, a note on the catheter bag, or electronic reminders for the care team to reassess whether the catheter is still needed. A *stop order* is a more foolproof method of ensuring that catheter placement is appropriately reassessed, as it requires either the nurse or physician to remove the catheter after a certain amount of time or after a condition has occurred unless the catheter is still clinically justified. A systematic review and meta-analysis of 14 studies demonstrated that the CAUTI rate decreased 52 percent with the use of a reminder prompt or a stop order (Meddings et al. 2013, 77).

The Problem of Inpatient Suicide

The rate of suicide is increasing in the United States, and it is now the 10th-leading cause of death. Nearly 40,000 people in the United States die from suicide each year, and between 1,500 and 1,800 inpatient suicides occur in US hospitals annually (Knoll 2012; SAMHSA 2012). More than 1,000 cases of patient suicide occurring in hospitals were reported to The Joint Commission during the five-year period ending in 2014. Inadequacies in the patient care assessment process and poor assessment of the psychiatric state of the patient are common contributors to patient suicide. "At the point of care, providers often do not detect the suicidal thoughts [or suicidal ideation] of individuals (including children and adolescents) who eventually die by suicide" (Joint Commission 2016, 1).

Inpatient suicide rates correlate strongly with admission rates: 78 percent of patients who committed suicide in a hospital had at least one previous admission. Twenty percent to 62 percent of inpatient suicide occurred in hospitals in which the patient was under intermittent observation, while only 2 percent to 9 percent of suicides occurred in hospitals where the patient was under constant observation (i.e., staff could only leave the patient unattended briefly to perform other duties) (Knoll 2012, 2). The deadly combination of poor or inconsistent suicide risk assessment of patients and uncontrolled environmental suicide hazards leads to preventable suicide in hospitals.

Preventing Inpatient Suicide

The 2012 National Strategy for Suicide Prevention was the result of a collaborative effort between the Office of the US Surgeon General and the National Action

Alliance for Suicide Prevention. "The National Strategy is a call to action that is intended to guide suicide prevention actions in the United States over the next decade. It outlines four strategic directions with 13 goals and 60 objectives that are meant to work together in a synergistic way to prevent suicide in the nation" (Office of the US Surgeon General 2012). The National Strategy calls for the adoption of the goal of zero suicides. The rationale is that setting the goal of eliminating suicide will catalyze systemwide changes to enhance service access and quality through continuous improvement.

Effective suicide prevention programs include adequate suicide risk assessment, support services for suicide-inclined patients, appropriate clinical care, and a safe care environment free of suicide hazards. A common risk concern in inpatient psychiatric units is ligature attachment points that pose a hanging risk for patients. A ligature is a rope, sheet, plastic trash bag, or any other item that could be tied or bound tightly as a device for hanging or strangulation. The greatest risk areas are those where patients are provided privacy (such as the bathroom) or are unobservable by the care team. Physical and environmental hazards for suicide include supports or grab bars in showers, plumbing fixtures, sink drains, bed frames, and drop ceilings. Hospitals must ensure that patients who are considered at risk for suicide are cared for in a safe environment that has been checked and inspected to make sure the architecture is suicide-proof and that all means to commit suicide have been removed (Knoll 2012, 2).

The Joint Commission's recommendations on detecting and treating suicide ideation focuses on "detecting and treating suicide ideation in all settings" (Joint Commission 2016, 1). During the five-year period ending in 2014, more than 1,000 suicide events occurring in hospitals (or within 72 hours of discharge) were reported to The Joint Commission. The most common root cause of inpatient suicide was the absence of an adequate patient assessment, especially a psychiatric assessment. The accurate and timely assessment of a patient's suicide risk factors is the foundation of an effective suicide prevention program and an important diagnostic tool, as patients often do not disclose suicide ideation (Joint Commission 2016). The Joint Commission recommends that hospitals develop "clinical environment readiness" by integrating comprehensive behavioral health, primary care, and community resources to ensure continuity of care for individuals at risk for suicide.

The Joint Commission outlines eight suicide prevention strategies to improve the detection of patient suicide ideation and to provide a hazard-free environment of care. These recommendations include screening all patients for suicide ideation; using a brief, standardized, evidence-based screening tool; educating all staff in patient care settings about how to identify and respond to patients with suicide ideation; and using assessment results to inform the level of safety measures needed, which may include keeping the patient in acute suicidal crisis in a safe care environment.

The Problem of Unintended Retained Foreign Objects After Surgery

URFOs, also referred to as retained surgical items, present a significant risk of infection that can be fatal. Other risks include perforations and granulomas. Research conducted by the Mayo Clinic found that over a four-year period, the rate of URFOs was 1 per 5,500 operations. URFOs are more likely to occur as a result of emergency surgery, unexpected changes in surgical procedure, a patient's high body mass index, and the lack of item counts (Treadwell 2013, 158). Potential complications resulting from URFOs include bowel perforation and sepsis, which can occur early in the postoperative period or even months or years later. During the seven-year period ending in 2012, 772 cases of URFOs were reported to The Joint Commission's Sentinel Event Database. The estimated cost of recovering a URFO and caring for the patient is in the range of $166,000 to $200,000 per incident (AHRQ 2017, tool D.4b).

Preventing Unintended Retained Surgical Items

According to the World Health Organization (WHO) in its "Guidelines for Safe Surgery," hospitals should have a written policy and procedure for counting surgical items in the operating room (WHO 2009). The policy should specify (1) when surgical counts are to be performed; (2) who is responsible for conducting the counts; (3) what items are to be counted; and (4) how the counts, including incorrect counts, will be documented. The WHO recommendations for preventing the retention of instruments and sponges comprise 14 steps, including but not limited to performing a full count of all sponges, sharps, and miscellaneous items; performing a count at least at the beginning and at the end of every eligible case; maintaining a tally of all counted items throughout the operation; counting and recording any items added during the procedure upon entry onto the sterile field; and ideally, using preprinted count sheets for sponges, sharps, and instruments and including them in the patient's record.

The WHO guidelines also outline specific recommendations for counting sponges, sharps, and instruments:

- *Sponge count.* The WHO guidelines recommend that an initial sponge count be completed for all nonexempt procedures (1) before the start of the procedure, (2) before closure of the cavity, (3) before wound closure (at first layer of closure), and (4) at skin closure. Gauze, laparotomy sponges, cotton swabs, and dissectors should be included in the count. The WHO also recommends that only X-ray-detectable sponges (when available) be placed in body cavities. Sponges should be completely separated during counting, and attached tapes should not be cut.

- *Sharps count.* The WHO guidelines recommend that sharps be counted (1) before the start of the procedure, (2) before closure of a cavity within a cavity, (3) before wound closure (at first layer of closure), and (4) at skin closure. Suture needles should be counted and reconciled with the marked number of sutures on the package (counters should verify the number of needles in the package when it is opened). Needles should not be left free on a table; they should be contained in a needle counter or container, loaded onto a needle driver, or sealed with their package.

- *Instrument count.* The WHO guidelines recommend that instruments be counted before the start of the procedure and before wound closure (at first layer of closure). Instrument sets should be standardized, for example, with the same type and same number of instruments in each set. Instruments and component parts should be counted singly and all component parts listed separately. All parts of a broken or disassembled instrument should be accounted for. No instruments should be removed from the operating room until the end of the procedure.

The Problem of Surgical Site Infections

According to an analysis of hospital infection rates conducted by the CDC, an estimated 722,000 HAIs occurred in US acute care hospitals in 2011. Approximately 75,000 patients with an HAI died during their hospitalization (CDC 2016). In its annual progress reports, the CDC reports hospitals' progress toward reducing five types of HAIs: (1) CLABSIs, (2) CAUTIs, (3) SSIs, (4) *Clostridium difficile* infections, and (5) MRSA bloodstream infections.

SSIs are the most common and most costly type of HAI. SSIs account for 20 percent of all HAIs in hospitalized patients, numbering 160,000 to 300,000 each year in the United States. Approximately 80 million surgeries are performed in the United States each year, and it is estimated that 1.5 million of those surgeries will be complicated by an SSI. The incidence of SSIs may be greatly underestimated because of post-discharge follow-up challenges (Preas, O'Hara, and Thom 2017). Each SSI adds 7 to 11 postoperative hospital days to the patient's hospital stay, and patients with an SSI have risk of death that is 2 to 11 times higher. SSIs are estimated to add $3.5 billion to $10 billion annually in unnecessary costs to the healthcare system.

Preventing Surgical Site Infections

In 2017, the CDC and its Healthcare Infection Control Practices Advisory Committee issued an update to its 1999 *Guideline for Prevention of Surgical Site Infection*. The revised guidelines provide new and updated evidence-based recommendations for the prevention of SSIs:

- Before surgery, patients should shower or bathe (full body) with soap (antimicrobial or non-antimicrobial) or an antiseptic agent on at least the night before the operative day.
- Antimicrobial prophylaxis should be administered only when indicated, based on published clinical guidelines.
- Skin preparation in the operating room should be performed using an alcohol-based agent unless contraindicated.
- During surgery, glycemic control should be implemented using a blood glucose target level of less than 200 mg/dL.
- Normothermia should be maintained in all patients.
- Increased fraction of inspired oxygen should be administered during surgery and after extubation in the immediate postoperative period for patients with normal pulmonary function undergoing general anesthesia with endotracheal intubation.

The revised guidelines also recommend *not* withholding transfusion of blood products from surgical patients as a means of preventing SSI and *not* applying topical antimicrobial agents to the surgical incision (Berrios-Torres et al. 2017). The 1999 CDC guidelines include four recommendations related to preoperative care, six recommendations related to intraoperative care, and recommendations for postoperative incision care and surveillance.

The Problem of Central Line–Associated Bloodstream Infections

Central venous catheters (CVCs) provide access to the great vessels of the neck or a site proximal to the heart to provide reliable venous access for clinical activities such as blood sampling, infusion of medications, and hemodynamic measurement. CVCs are also the leading cause of healthcare-associated bloodstream infections (BSIs). Approximately 249,000 BSIs occur in US hospitals each year. About one-third of those BSIs (approximately 80,000) occur in the intensive care unit (ICU). With more than 15 million catheter days in ICUs annually, the impact of CLABSIs is substantial. The negative financial impact of central line–associated BSIs is significant; each CLABSI episode can increase the length of a patient's hospitalization from

7 days to 21 days and result in an additional cost of $37,000 per patient. The annual national cost of caring for patients who have experienced a CLABSI is estimated to be as high as $2.68 billion (Chopra et al. 2013, 88–89).

Preventing Central Line–Associated Bloodstream Infections

The CDC's Healthcare Infection Control Practices Advisory Committee has developed extensive evidence-based guidelines for preventing intravascular catheter-related infections. The *Guidelines for the Prevention of Intravascular Catheter-Related Infections* contain more than 100 recommendations in five areas: (1) educating and training healthcare personnel who insert and maintain catheters, (2) using maximal sterile precautions during CVC insertion, (3) using a >0.5 percent chlorhexidine skin preparation with alcohol for antisepsis, (4) avoiding routine replacement of CVCs as a strategy to prevent infection, and (5) using antiseptic/antibiotic-impregnated short-term CVCs and chlorhexidine-impregnated sponge dressings if the rate of infection is not decreasing despite adherence to other strategies. The CDC's guidelines also support the use of "bundled strategies" for performance improvement (CDC 2011, 8).

AHRQ's recommended safe practices for preventing CLABSIs include Five Practices to Prevent CLABSI at the Time of CVC Insertion, Five Practices to Prevent CLABSI After CVC Insertion, and Three Organizational Practices to Prevent CLABSI.

AHRQ's organizational practices include educational interventions, catheter checklists or bundles, and specialized CVC insertion teams. The use of a bundle of evidence-based safe care practices has proven to be a successful preventive strategy to reduce CLABSI. For example, 67 Michigan hospitals participated in a statewide project to apply a CLABSI bundle in ICU settings. Following the implementation of a five-practice bundle, the CLABSI rate dropped from 7.7 per 1,000 catheter days at baseline to 1.4 per 1,000 catheter days at 16 months (Chopra et al. 2013, 88–97).

The Problem of Medication-Related Errors and Adverse Drug Events

Medication errors can occur at any one of the 11 stages of medication management. According to the National Academies of Science, medication-related errors harm 1.5 million people each year. Medication management begins with the ordering and prescribing process and continues with transcribing the order, dispensing and delivering the medication, administering the medication to the patient, and monitoring the patient after the medication is given (Kong 2014). Medication management is fraught with error traps and potential hazards, including look-alike/sound-alike drugs; the use of confusing abbreviations; illegible or unclear orders; or the selection of the wrong patient, wrong drug, wrong time, or wrong frequency for administering the drug, the wrong dosage, the wrong form of the drug, or the wrong route. An adverse drug event (ADE) is defined as an event that causes harm to a patient as a result of exposure to a medication. Not all ADEs are the result of an error or poor care, but all medication errors are ADEs. Some patients will experience an ADE even when they receive the correct medication in the right form, dose, and route. It is estimated that about 50 percent of ADEs are preventable (PSNet 2019a).

ADEs account for about one-third of all adverse events in hospitals and affect about 2 million hospitalized patients each year. Nearly 5 percent of all hospitalized patients experience an ADE (ODPHP 2017c). Patients experiencing an ADE remain in the hospital an additional 1.7 to 4.6 days.

Four types of medications account for more than 50 percent of ADEs seen in hospital emergency room patients: oral anticoagulants (e.g., warfarin), for which the safety concern is bleeding; antidiabetic agents (e.g., insulin), for which the safety concern is hypoglycemia; antiplatelet agents (e.g., aspirin), for which the safety concern is increased risk of bleeding; and opioid pain medications, for which the safety concern is oversedation, respiratory depression, or accidental overdose (ODPHP 2017a; PSNet 2019a). Other medication-related safety concerns include (1) safe use of opioids such as fentanyl, morphine, and methadone; (2) prevention of infection from the misuse of vials; and (3) administration of high-alert drugs such as insulin, potassium chloride, and the intravenous anticoagulant heparin. High-alert medications account for 48 percent of all ADEs (Pfoh, Thompson, and Dy 2013, 23).

Preventing Medication Errors and Adverse Drug Events

The US Food and Drug Administration's Division of Medication Error Prevention and Analysis administers a medication error-prevention program that analyzes error reports sent to MedWatch, determines causality, and provides solutions to the healthcare community to reduce the risk of medication errors. Prospectively, this division reviews proprietary names, labeling, packaging, and product design prior to drug approval to help prevent medication errors.

According to the American Society of Health-System Pharmacists (ASHP) in its "Guidelines on Preventing Medication Errors in Hospitals" (ASHP 2018, 268), "Medication errors can occur at any point of the medication-use system." To examine and improve systems to ensure that medication processes are safe, "the pharmacist should participate in multidisciplinary committees of the organization and take an active role in the evaluation and monitoring of the medication-use process throughout the hospital or healthcare system" (ASHP 2018, 268). Exhibit 5.1 illustrates the ASHP's 11-step medication-use system. This diagram modifies The Joint Commission's medication management system by adding two steps: patient

Exhibit 5.1: ASHP's 11-Step Medication-Use System

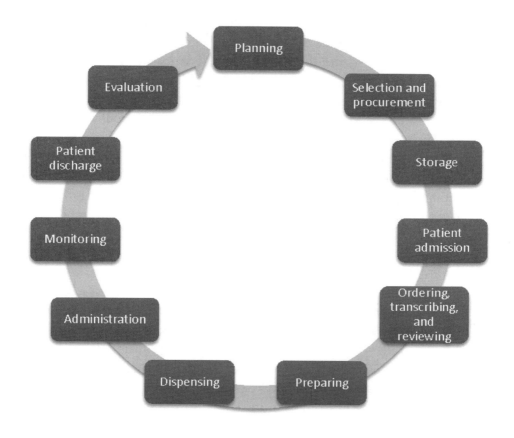

Note: This diagram is a modification of The Joint Commission's medication management system, with the addition of two steps: patient admission and patient discharge. These steps were added to appropriately encompass issues that arise during admission and discharge (e.g., medication history and reconciliation errors, patient education barriers).

Source: Reprinted with permission from ASHP (2018). Copyright © 2018, American Society of Health-System Pharmacists. All rights reserved.

admission and patient discharge. These steps were added to encompass issues that arise during admission and discharge, such as medication history and reconciliation errors and patient education barriers.

The ASHP guidelines are intended to "provide the pharmacists with practical recommendations and best practices for preventing and mitigating patient harm from medication errors in the health-system setting." The following provides a summary of the ASHP's 11-step medication-use system:

1. *Planning for safe medication practices.* Hospitals must have a comprehensive program that includes a medication safety leader, key elements in place to provide a structure for safe medication practices, and a strategic plan. Key supporting elements include a culture of safety built on principles of just culture, an event-reporting system, an interdisciplinary medication safety team, a continuous improvement philosophy regarding the evaluation of errors and harm, and strong designs that assess and reduce the risk of errors (ASHP 2018, 1494–96).

2. *Selection and procurement.* Medication safety includes selecting the appropriate medications that will be stocked in the hospital (the formulary) and safely and effectively obtaining or procuring the medications from manufacturers or wholesalers. Best practices for decreasing the risk of errors during the selection and procurement process fall into five categories: (1) formulary assessment and management, (2) standard concentrations, (3) safety alert monitoring, (4) safe procurement, and (5) medication shortage management (ASHP 2018, 1496).

3. *Storage.* Careful arrangement of medication storage in the pharmacy and throughout the hospital can help reduce the risk of medication errors. Product arrangement can help minimize unintended selection of the wrong product or dosage form. Steps to minimize selection of the wrong product or dosage form in the pharmacy include (1) using bar-code scanning, (2) providing adequate space for each medication and strength, (3) ensuring that labels on bottles face forward, (4) designating separate areas for each dosage form or route of administration, (5) separating frequently confused pairs, (6) segregating high-alert medications and look-alike/sound-alike medications, and (7) using labeling and alerts when appropriate (ASHP 2018, 1498).

4. *Patient admission.* Obtaining a medication history and performing a medication reconciliation at the time of the patient's admission to the hospital is a crucial step in preventing medication errors; the pharmacy should be involved in the process of obtaining an accurate medication history (ASHP 2018, 1499).

5. *Ordering, transcribing, and reviewing.* Common ordering errors include omission, incomplete and unclear orders, wrong drug, wrong time, wrong dose, wrong dosage form, patient allergy, and wrong patient. Providers should consider the following when ordering medications: (1) patient assessment, (2) diagnostic or monitoring tests, (3) diagnoses, (4) patient history, (5) appropriate selection and dose of medication, (6) concomitant therapies, and (7) therapy duration. A single error in any of these steps could result in an ADE. The ASHP guidelines provide

10 recommendations for preventing medication ordering errors (ASHP 2018, 1499–501).

6. *Preparation*. Common preparation errors include wrong concentration, wrong drug, wrong dose, wrong base solution/diluent, wrong volume, preparations made for the wrong patient, or preparations for administration by the wrong route. The ASHP guidelines describe error-prevention strategies for the preparation of medications, including independent double checks, the use of bar coding, safe compounding practices, sterile compounding, and the need for proper education and training of pharmacy personnel (ASHP 2018, 1501–2).

7. *Dispensing*. All medications in nonemergency situations should be reviewed by a pharmacist or an advanced pharmacy technician who is qualified and trained to perform *tech-check-tech*, a process in which one pharmacy technician performs a double check before dispensing the medication. The pharmacist should review the original medication order and ensure that all work performed by supportive personnel or through the use of automated devices is checked by manual or technological means (ASHP 2018, 1503).

8. *Administration*. Common medication administration errors include wrong patient, wrong route, wrong dosage form, wrong time, wrong dose or rate, and wrong drug. Other medication administration errors result from missed doses and errors of omission. Practitioners at the bedside can prevent a significant number of prescribing and dispensing errors from reaching the patient. The ASHP guidelines recommend independent double checks for high-alert medications before administration, when appropriate, by completing independent calculations and checking the patient's allergies. Additionally, the patient's identity must be verified by checking two patient identifiers before administering the medication (ASHP 2018, 1503–4).

9. *Monitoring*. The five primary causes of medication errors in the monitoring process are (1) failure to monitor medication effects, (2) incorrect interpretation of laboratory data used to monitor medication effects, (3) incorrect transcription of laboratory test values, (4) incorrect timing of monitoring, and (5) incorrect timing of serum concentration monitoring. Hospitals should train staff to identify common adverse effects of medications encountered by patients and provide guidance on how to respond to adverse drug reactions (ASHP 2018, 1505–6).

10. *Patient discharge*. Pharmacists can contribute to positive patient outcomes by educating and counseling patients to prepare and motivate them to follow their pharmacotherapeutic regimens and monitoring plans after discharge. The ASHP guidelines describe the benefits of the medication

reconciliation process, particularly at discharge, and the importance of informing the patient of the names of his or her medications, the reasons for their use, the times they should be administered, and the correct dose so that the patient can act as the final safety check in the medication-use system (ASHP 2018, 1506–7).

11. *Evaluation*. Hospitals should continuously evaluate their systems and processes to prevent medication errors. In addition to proactive risk assessment using failure mode and effects analysis, hospitals should use retrospective evaluation methods to determine the root causes of events and develop action plans to improve processes with the goal of minimizing the possibility of event reoccurrence. These methods include root cause analysis, medication-use evaluation, quality improvement, and event detection. Through event detection, clinicians can gain an understanding of the risks that are already present in their hospital in order to reduce preventable medication errors (ASHP 2018, 1507).

The ASHP guidelines describe each of these steps more fully and provide a 92-point Self-Assessment Checklist in Appendix B.

The Problem of Pressure Ulcers

Pressure ulcer rates in hospitals and nursing homes continue to increase as the numbers of obese, diabetic, and elderly patients rise. During the 12-year period ending in 2008, the incidence of pressure ulcers increased approximately 80 percent. It is estimated that 2.5 million patients will develop a pressure ulcer and that 60,000 patients in US hospitals will die from complications related to hospital-acquired pressure ulcers. The costs of treating pressure ulcers are estimated to be more than $11 billion annually. Late-stage pressure ulcers can be life-threatening. Patients with pressure ulcers need more care, more resources, and have longer hospital stays.

Preventing Pressure Ulcers

Pressure ulcers result from damage to the skin or underlying tissue caused by unrelieved pressure. According to IHI, there is strong evidence that when hospitals implement proven best practices, the number of hospital-acquired pressure ulcers can be drastically reduced (IHI 2017). Three preventive strategies for reducing the occurrence of pressure ulcers in hospitalized patients are (1) AHRQ's Pressure Ulcer Bundle; (2) IHI's Six Essential Steps to Preventing Pressure Ulcers; and (3) the *Clinical Practice Guideline for Preventing and Treatment of Pressure Ulcers*, which was developed through a collaborative effort led by the National Pressure Ulcer Advisory Panel.

AHRQ's *Preventing Pressure Ulcers in Hospitals: A Toolkit for Improving Quality of Care* describes the elements and benefits of the Pressure Ulcer Bundle (AHRQ 2012). Implementing the best practices included in the Pressure Ulcer Bundle at the bedside is an extremely complex task, which makes the prevention of pressure ulcers a challenging goal. Pressure ulcer prevention requires an interdisciplinary approach to patient care and a systems focus. Nurses, physicians, dieticians, physical therapists, and patients and their families all need to work together in a multidisciplinary and coordinated way to implement and monitor the pressure ulcer prevention strategies. These strategies should be customized to address the needs of each patient and often must be carried out many times each day to be effective. The Pressure Ulcer Bundle has three components: (1) comprehensive skin assessment, (2) standardized pressure ulcer risk assessment, and (3) care planning and implementation to address areas of risk. The obvious goal is "to implement care practices so that the patient does not develop a pressure ulcer during the hospitalization" (AHRQ 2012, 49).

The National Pressure Ulcer Advisory Panel's *Prevention and Treatment of Pressure Ulcers: Clinical Practice Guidelines* (NPUAP 2014) include 575 specific recommendations for the prevention and treatment of pressure ulcers. The guidelines are based on an extensive literature review and rigorous scientific appraisal process. The guidelines include advice on skin and tissue assessment, risk assessment, preventive skin care, microclimate control, prophylactic dressings, nutrition, repositioning and early mobilization, and wound assessment. (The complete guidelines as well as a Quick Reference Guide can be found at http://npuap.org.)

IHI's recommendations for preventing pressure ulcers identify six essential care practices (IHI 2017):

1. Conduct a pressure ulcer admission assessment for all patients, including an assessment of the patient's risk of skin breakdown.
2. Reassess the risk for all patients on a daily basis.
3. Inspect the skin of at-risk patients daily.
4. Manage moisture, as patients with wet skin are more vulnerable to pressure ulcers.
5. Optimize nutrition and hydration.
6. Minimize pressure by repositioning the patient every two hours and using pressure-reducing surfaces.

The Problem of Ventilator-Associated Pneumonia

Patients on mechanical ventilation are at risk of developing serious complications such as acute respiratory distress syndrome, pneumothorax, pulmonary embolism, lobar atelectasis, and pulmonary edema. VAP is one of these serious complications (Klompas et al. 2014).

VAP is a hospital-acquired pneumonia that typically develops within 48 to 72 hours of endotracheal intubation. Approximately 250,000 VAPs occur in US hospitals each year, and between 8 percent and 28 percent of mechanically ventilated patients will have complications related to it. VAP is the most common infection acquired in hospital ICUs, accounting for 25 percent of all ICU infections.

VAP is the leading cause of death among HAIs: Approximately 15 percent of patients on mechanical ventilation develop VAP, and ventilated patients who develop VAP have a significantly higher mortality rate (46 percent) than those who do not develop VAP (32 percent) (Wachter 2012, 166). The mortality risk of VAP is 10 percent (ranging from 6 percent to 27 percent), resulting in 25,000 VAP-attributable deaths each year. Patients who develop VAP stay an average of four additional days in the hospital ICU with an average additional cost of $23,000. The total additional cost related to the care and treatment of patients with VAP is estimated to be between $2.19 billion and $3.17 billion per year (Winters and Berenholtz 2013, 110).

Preventing Ventilator-Associated Pneumonia

According to Wachter (2012, 166), "Many cases of VAP can be prevented by strict adherence to a variety of preventive strategies. The first is elevation of the head of the bed to semi-recumbent (at least 30°) position, which in one trial resulted in an 18% decrease in VAP cases. A second effective strategy is daily interruption of sedation for ventilated patients. This strategy, when coupled with a program of systematic assessment (usually by trained respiratory therapists) regarding readiness for weaning, results in shorter duration of mechanical ventilation, presumably lowering the risk of VAP." A study of patient safety practices for preventing VAP published in AHRQ's 2013 *Making Health Care Safer II* report estimated that 14,000 to 20,000 lives could be saved each year in the United States if best practices to prevent VAP were universally applied to patients on mechanical ventilation. Four practices are recommended to prevent VAP: (1) elevating the head of the bed to 30 degrees, (2) sedation vacations, (3) oral care with chlorhexidine, and (4) subglottic suctioning endotracheal tubes. The study recognizes that ventilator bundles usually include other interventions that address related complications but are not preventive measures that address VAP prevention directly—for example, deep venous thrombosis or pulmonary embolism prophylaxis and peptic ulcer disease prophylaxis (Winters and Berenholtz 2013, 111).

The Society for Healthcare Epidemiology of America (SHEA) developed its "Strategies to Prevent Ventilator-Associated Pneumonia in Acute Care Hospitals" in collaboration with the Infectious Diseases Society of America, the American Hospital Association, the Association for Professionals in Infection Control and

Epidemiology, and The Joint Commission (Klompas et al. 2014). The SHEA strategies are specific to adult, pediatric, and neonatal populations. The SHEA recommendations for preventing VAP among adult patients include avoiding intubation if possible and using noninvasive positive pressure ventilation whenever feasible; minimizing sedation and managing ventilated patients without sedatives whenever possible; elevating the head of the bed to 30 degrees to 45 degrees; maintaining and improving physical conditioning by providing early exercise and mobilization and minimizing pooling of secretions above the endotracheal tube cuff; and providing endotracheal tubes with subglottic secretion drainage ports for patients likely to require greater than 48 to 72 hours of intubation.

The Problem of Wrong-Site, Wrong-Patient, Wrong-Procedure Surgery

In the three-year period ending in 2016, hospitals reported 297 cases of wrong-site, wrong-patient, or wrong-procedure surgery (WSPS) to The Joint Commission's Sentinel Event Database. A total of 2,524 sentinel events were reported during this same period, making WSPS the second-highest reported event, representing 12 percent of all cases reported. The Joint Commission's Center for Transforming Healthcare, in collaboration with eight of the nation's leading hospitals and healthcare systems, identified 29 main causes of wrong-site surgery that occurred during scheduling, in preoperative care, and in the operating room. These error traps provide opportunities for patient harm if they are not anticipated and controlled. More than 40 million operative procedures are performed in the United States each year. Mortality rates for complex operations in the Medicare population range from 7.5 percent to 17.7 percent for certain procedures (Maggard-Gibbons 2013, 140). Retrospective studies indicate that surgery-related never events (WSWP surgery and URFOs) occur in one out of every 12,248 operations in the United States (Thiels et al. 2015).

Preventing Wrong-Site, Wrong-Patient, and Wrong-Procedure Surgery

Acknowledging The Joint Commission's leadership in developing and mandating the use of a universal protocol in 2003, the WHO offers the Universal Protocol as the solution to its Safe Surgery Saves Lives Objective Number 1: The team will operate on the correct patient at the correct site (WHO 2009, 10–12). The Universal Protocol is a three-step process. Each step is complementary and provides additional safeguards and redundancy in the process of confirming the correct patient, site, and procedure. (A summary of the Universal Protocol follows; the complete WHO Safe Surgery Guidelines and Universal Protocol can be found at http://who.org.)

1. *Verification.* Members of the care team verify the correct patient, site, and procedure at every stage of the process, from the time the decision is made to operate to the time the patient undergoes the operation. Verification occurs when the procedure is scheduled, at the time of admission, upon entry to the operating room, any time that responsibility for care of the patient is transferred to another person, and before the patient leaves the preoperative area or enters the procedure or surgical room.

2. *Marking.* The site or sites to be operated on must be marked. This is particularly important in cases involving laterality, multiple structures (e.g., fingers, toes), or multiple levels (e.g., vertebral column). The mark must be at or next to the operative site, unambiguous, clearly visible, and made with a permanent marker, by the surgeon performing the procedure. (Marking the site may be delegated to another person who will be present during the surgery.) Patient involvement is important, so marking the site should be performed while the patient is alert, when possible.

3. *Time-out.* A brief surgical pause should be taken before the procedure or incision to confirm the patient, procedure, and site of operation. All team members should be actively involved in the process. A checklist is an invaluable tool to ensure that all the steps in the Universal Protocol are completed and performed.

The WHO surgical safety checklist provides guidance on the safe care practices that should be followed before the induction of anesthesia, before skin incision, and before the patient leaves the operating room. While the checklist includes the three main elements of the Universal Protocol, it also serves as a prompt and reminder for several other safe practices: completion of the anesthesia safety check; acknowledgment of patient-specific risks related to known allergies, airway difficulties, and blood loss; anticipation of potential critical events; administration of antibiotic prophylaxis; confirmation of sterility; and instrument, sponge, and needle counts.

CONCLUSION

Chapter 5 describes the top 10 patient safety threats in hospitals and the safe care practices or offensive strategies that have been proven to mitigate those threats and protect patients from harm. These offensive strategies involve the consistent application of and adherence to patient care bundles and other clinical guidelines that focus on eliminating the threats and hazards in a process or procedure that may cause patient harm. Exemplary patient care teams across the country that have adopted and applied—through extensive team training—an offensive approach to patient safety are making great progress toward achieving the goal of eliminating all preventable patient harm. The safe care practices summarized here reflect the current guidelines and proven harm prevention strategies that target the top 10 patient safety priorities.

REFERENCES

Agency for Healthcare Research and Quality (AHRQ). 2017. "Toolkit for Using the AHRQ Quality Indicators." Accessed March 1, 2019. www.ahrq.gov/sites/default/files/wysiwyg /professionals/systems/hospital/qitoolkit/combined/combined_toolkit.pdf.

———. 2016. "AHRQ's Toolkit Helped Vanderbilt University Hospital Substantially Reduce Patient Falls." Published November 21. www.ahrq.gov/news/newsroom/case -studies/201616.html.

———. 2013a. *Fall Prevention Toolkit: Implementation Guide Organized to Direct Hospitals Through the Change Process.* Accessed February 27, 2019. www.ahrq.gov/sites/default /files/publications/files/fallpxtoolkit.pdf.

———. 2013b. *Making Health Care Safer II: An Updated Critical Analysis of the Evidence for Patient Safety Practices.* Rockville, MD: Agency for Healthcare Research and Quality.

———. 2012. *Preventing Pressure Ulcers in Hospitals: A Toolkit for Improving Quality of Care.* Accessed February 27, 2019. www.ahrq.gov/sites/default/files/publications/files /putoolkit.pdf.

American Nurses Association (ANA). 2017. "ANA CAUTI Prevention Tool." Accessed February 27, 2019. www.nursingworld.org/practice-policy/work-environment/health-safety /infection-prevention/ana-cauti-prevention-tool/.

American Society of Health-System Pharmacists (ASHP). 2018. "ASHP Guidelines on Preventing Medication Errors in Hospitals." *American Journal of Health-System Pharmacy* 75 (19): 1493–517. www.ashp.org/-/media/assets/policy-guidelines/docs/guidelines /preventing-medication-errors-hospitals.ashx.

Berrios-Torres, S. I., C. A. Umscheid, D. W. Bratzler, B. Leas, E. C. Stone, R. R. Kelz, C. E. Reinke, S. Morgan, J. S. Solomkin, J. E. Mazuski, E. P. Dellinger, K. M. F. Itani, E. F. Berbari, J. Segreti, J. Parvizi, J. Blanchard, G. Allen, J. A. J. W. Kluytmans, R. Donlan, and W. P. Schecter for the Healthcare Infection Control Practices Advisory Committee. 2017. "Centers for Disease Control and Prevention Guidelines for the Prevention of Surgical Site Infection, 2017." *JAMA Surgery* 152 (8): 784–91.

Centers for Disease Control and Prevention (CDC). 2017. "Guideline for Prevention of Catheter-Associated Urinary Tract Infections 2009." Updated February 15. www.cdc .gov/infectioncontrol/pdf/guidelines/cauti-guidelines.pdf.

———. 2016. "National and State Healthcare-Associated Infections Progress Report." Accessed February 27, 2019. www.cdc.gov/hai/data/portal/progress-report.html.

———. 2011. "Guidelines for the Prevention of Intravascular Catheter-Related Infections." Accessed March 1, 2019. www.cdc.gov/hai/pdfs/bsi-guidelines-2011.pdf.

Centers for Medicare & Medicaid Services (CMS). 2018. "Hospital-Acquired Conditions." Updated August 30. www.cms.gov/medicare/medicare-fee-for-service-payment/hospital acqcond/hospital-acquired_conditions.html.

Chopra, V., S. Krein, R. Olmsted, N. Safdar, and S. Saint. 2013. "Prevention of Central Line–Associated Bloodstream Infections." In *Making Health Care Safer II: An Updated Critical Analysis of the Evidence for Patient Safety Practices*, 88–109. Rockville, MD: Agency for Healthcare Research and Quality.

Courtney, B., J. Ruppman, and H. Cooper. 2006. "Save Our Skin: Initiative Cuts Pressure Ulcer Incidence in Half." *Nursing Management* 37 (4): 36–45.

Donley, V., and S. Reese. 2015. "Reducing Central Line–Associated Bloodstream Infections in Children." *American Nurse Today* 10 (3): 30–32.

Institute for Healthcare Improvement (IHI). 2017. "Relieve the Pressure and Reduce Harm." Accessed February 27, 2019. www.ihi.org/resources/Pages/ImprovementStories/Relieve thePressureandReduceHarm.aspx.

Joint Commission. 2016. "Detecting and Treating Suicide Ideation in All Settings." *Sentinel Event Alert* 56. Published February 24. www.jointcommission.org/assets/1/18/SEA _56_Suicide.pdf.

———. 2015. "Preventing Falls and Fall-Related Injuries in Health Care Facilities." *Sentinel Event Alert* 55. Published September 28. www.jointcommission.org/assets/1/18 /SEA_55.pdf.

Klompas, M., R. Branson, E. C. Eichenwald, L. R. Greene, M. D. Howell, G. Lee, and S. S. Magill. 2014. "Strategies to Prevent Ventilator-Associated Pneumonia in Acute Care Hospitals: 2014 Update." *Infection Control and Hospital Epidemiology* 35 (8): 915–36.

Knoll, J. 2012. "Inpatient Suicide: Identifying Vulnerability in the Hospital Setting." *Psychiatric Times*, May 22.

Kong, M. 2014. "Medication Error." In *Patient Safety: A Case-Based Comprehensive Guide*, edited by A. Agrawal, 103–14. New York: Springer Science & Business Media.

Maggard-Gibbons, M. 2013. "Use of Report Cards and Outcome Measurement to Improve Safety of Surgical Care." In *Making Health Care Safer II: An Updated Critical Analysis of the Evidence for Patient Safety Practices*, 140–57. Rockville, MD: Agency for Healthcare Research and Quality.

Meddings, J., S. L. Krein, M. G. Fakih, R. N. Olmsted, and S. Saint. 2013. "Reducing Unnecessary Urinary Catheter Use and Other Strategies to Prevent Catheter-Associated Urinary Tract Infections." In *Making Health Care Safer II: An Updated Critical Analysis of the Evidence for Patient Safety Practices*, 73–87. Rockville, MD: Agency for Healthcare Research and Quality.

National Pressure Ulcer Advisory Panel (NPUAP). 2014. *2014 Prevention and Treatment of Pressure Ulcers: Clinical Practice Guidelines*. Washington, DC: NPUAP.

National Quality Forum (NQF). 2010. "Safe Practices for Better Healthcare: 2010 Update." Accessed February 27, 2019. www.qualityforum.org/Publications/2010/04/Safe_Practices _for_Better_Healthcare_%E2%80%93_2010_Update.aspx.

Office of Disease Prevention and Health Promotion (ODPHP). 2017a. "New Report Shows Continued Reduction in Hospital-Acquired Conditions." Published January 24. https://health.gov/news/blog/2017/01/new-report-shows-continued-reduction-in -hospital-acquired-conditions/.

———. 2017b. "Overview: Adverse Drug Events." Accessed April 12, 2019. https://health .gov/hcq/ade.asp.

———. 2017c. "The National Action Plan for Adverse Drug Event Prevention: Executive Summary." Accessed February 27, 2019. https://health.gov/hcq/pdfs/ADE-Action-Plan -Executive-Summary.pdf.

Office of the US Surgeon General. 2012. "2012 National Strategy for Suicide Prevention." Published September. www.surgeongeneral.gov/library/reports/national-strategy-suicide -prevention/full-report.pdf.

Patient Safety Network (PSNet). 2019a. "Patient Safety Primer: Medication Errors and Adverse Drug Events." Updated January. https://psnet.ahrq.gov/primers/primer/23 /Medication-Errors-and-Adverse-Drug-Events.

———. 2019b. "Patient Safety Primer: Never Events." Updated January. https://psnet .ahrq.gov/primers/primer/3.

Pfoh, E., D. Thompson, and S. Dy. 2013. "High-Alert Drugs: Patient Safety Practices for Intravenous Anticoagulants." In *Making Health Care Safer II: An Updated Critical Analysis of the Evidence for Patient Safety Practices*, 23–30. Rockville, MD: Agency for Healthcare Research and Quality.

Preas, M. A., L. O'Hara, and K. Thom. 2017. *HICPAC-CDC Guidelines for Prevention of Surgical Site Infection: What the Infection Preventionist Needs to Know*. Association for Professionals in Infection Control and Epidemiology. Accessed February 27, 2019. https://apic.org/Resource_/TinyMceFileManager/Periodical_images/API-Q0414_L _SSI_Guidelines_Final.pdf.

Resar, R., F. A. Griffin, C. Haraden, and T. W. Nolan. 2012. "Using Care Bundles to Improve Health Care Quality." IHI Innovation Series white paper. Accessed February 27, 2019. www.ihi.org/resources/Pages/IHIWhitePapers/UsingCareBundles.aspx.

Saint, S. 2009. "Translating Health Care–Associated Urinary Tract Infection Prevention Research into Practice via the Bladder Bundle." *Joint Commission Journal for Quality and Patient Safety* 35 (9): 1–5.

Saint, S., M. T. Greene, S. L. Krein, M. A. M. Rogers, D. Ratz, K. E. Fowler, B. S. Edson, S. R. Watson, B. Meyer-Lucas, M. Masuga, K. Faulkner, C. V. Gould, J. Battles, and M. G. Fakih. 2016. "A Program to Prevent Catheter-Associated Urinary Tract Infection in Acute Care." *New England Journal of Medicine* 374 (22): 2111–19.

Sedwick, M. B., M. Lance-Smith, S. J. Reeder, and J. Nardi. 2012. "Using Evidence-Based Practice to Prevent Ventilator-Associated Pneumonia." *Critical Care Nurse* 32 (4): 41–51.

Substance Abuse and Mental Health Services Administration (SAMHSA). 2012. "Overview: 2012 National Strategy for Suicide Prevention: Goals and Objectives for Action." Accessed April 12, 2019. https://store.samhsa.gov/system/files/overview.pdf.

Thiels, C. A., T. M. Lal, J. M. Nienow, K. S. Pasupathy, R. C. Blocker, J. M. Aho, and T. I. Morgenthaler. 2015. "Surgical Never Events and Contributing Human Factors." *Surgery* 158 (2): 515–21.

Treadwell, J. R. 2013. "Prevention of Surgical Items Being Left Inside Patient." In *Making Health Care Safer II: An Updated Critical Analysis of the Evidence for Patient Safety Practices*, 123–39. Rockville, MD: Agency for Healthcare Research and Quality.

Wachter, R. 2012. *Understanding Patient Safety*, 2nd ed. New York: McGraw-Hill Medical.

Winters, B. D., and S. M. Berenholtz. 2013. "Ventilator-Associated Pneumonia: Brief Update Review." In *Making Health Care Safer II: An Updated Critical Analysis of the Evidence for Patient Safety Practices*, 110–16. Rockville, MD: Agency for Healthcare Research and Quality.

World Health Organization (WHO). 2009. "WHO Guidelines for Safe Surgery: Safe Surgery Saves Lives." Accessed February 27, 2019. www.who.int/patientsafety/safesurgery/tools_resources/9789241598552/.

Cultivating Resilience and Adaptability

WHY ARE RESILIENCE AND ADAPTABILITY INTEGRAL TO PATIENT SAFETY?

How do hospitals and their staffs cope with the occurrence of a significant safety event that has seriously injured or killed a patient? How do hospitals respond to systemic degradation in patient safety that is causing needless harm? And how do hospitals anticipate, prepare for, respond to, and adapt to sudden and major disruptions to their operations while maintaining safe care practices? Hospitals that effectively respond to and recover from major disruptions or disturbances cultivate *resilience* and *adaptability*—disciplines that allow them to quickly regroup and return to a stable, safe, and desirable level of performance.

Hospital emergency departments (EDs) that get overwhelmed with patients; hospitals that care for the casualties of natural disasters such as floods, fires, and storms; and hospitals that become incapacitated because of a loss of power or other critical service must, as a matter of survival, demonstrate resilience and adaptability. According to Rollin J. Fairbanks and colleagues (2014, 380), hospital EDs provide an excellent example of resilience and adaptability in action: the ED serves as a buffer between the external world and the rest of the hospital; the ED is exposed to an unregulated flow of disturbances that occur at a high rate and with great variety; some disturbances result from catastrophic external events, such as industrial accidents, gun violence, or casualties from natural disasters; and "disturbance management" is an essential element of the training and culture of ED practitioners.

ED management and staff must routinely demonstrate resilience and adaptability as they stretch their capacity in response to increasing demands to avoid gaps in patient care and patient safety—unacceptable failures of the system. ED staff adjust their strategies and recruiting resources to provide adaptive capacity. Christopher Nemeth and colleagues (2008, 7) outline four adaptive strategies that

ED staff use to cope with varying levels of patient load, severity of patient needs, and environmental complexity and to increase the resilience of their operations:

1. *Routine and usual conditions.* Staff anticipate changes to their routine and adapt in apparently seamless ways. (Adaptation: adjust existing resources)
2. *Increasing load and demand.* A key individual recognizes a system degradation and initiates adaptive responses. Practitioners identify and reorganize additional resources to manage the increasing demands and maintain performance at a near-normal level. (Adaptation: identify and reorganize additional resources)
3. *Increasing demand requiring adaptation by the entire department.* An extreme situation challenges the organization's ability to maintain control and sustain operations. Practitioners must anticipate and recognize the change and reorganize activities and resources while they struggle to handle the patient load. (Adaptation: forgo all care except that for life-threatening illness)
4. *Catastrophic event (mass casualty or natural disaster) demand.* Rare but significant demands on the resources of the ED require a complete reorganization of the work and work environment. (Adaptation: completely reorganized work)

The highest level of demand, resulting from a large influx of patients with conditions of varying severity, creates working conditions that are "beyond the range of previous operating experience," and "the resources and coping strategies that would normally provide resilience against variation and the unexpected [soon become] exhausted" (Nemeth et al. 2008, 8). Planning and preparing to maintain control and ensure safe care practices in the face of a catastrophic disturbance can buttress the resilience and adaptive capacity of the organization.

RESILIENCE AND ITS ADVANTAGES

Resilience refers to the ability of an organization or system to respond to an unanticipated disturbance that can lead to failure and then resume normal operations quickly with a minimum decrement in performance (Fairbanks et al. 2014, 376). Resilience allows an organization or system to adjust its functioning before, during, and after disturbances to sustain required operations (Nemeth et al. 2008, 1). Events or changes in the environment that disturb normal hospital functioning, at varying levels of intensity and with a range of impacts, are both expected and unexpected occurrences that hospitals experience as places of care and compassion for their community. Safe patient care and continued safe hospital operations depend on how well the hospital, as a system, and staff at the sharp end of providing care anticipate, monitor, respond to, and learn from disruptive events. A hospital's business continuity and its continuity of providing safe patient care are affected by its organizational resilience and adaptive capacity.

The American National Standard related to organizational resilience (ANSI 2009, 12) sets forth nine benefits derived from an organization's incident prevention, preparedness, and response—in other words, its resilience:

1. Protecting property and the environment affected by the disruptive event
2. Preserving life safety
3. Protecting assets
4. Preventing further escalation of the disruptive event
5. Reducing the length of the disruption to operations
6. Restoring critical operational continuity
7. Recovering normal operations
8. Protecting the organization's image and reputation
9. Mitigating the adverse consequences of a disruptive event

The standard defines resilience as "the adaptive capacity of an organization in a complex and changing environment" (ANSI 2009, 2). The definition is further clarified to include "the ability of an organization to resist being affected by an event or the ability to return to an acceptable level of performance in an acceptable period of time after being affected by an event" (ANSI 2009, 48).

A resilient organization maintains control in the face of environmental and internal disruptions. "Resilience is a form of control" (Weick and Sutcliffe 2007, 70). Resilience allows an organization to withstand the potentially debilitating effects of internal and external disturbances, bounce back from adverse events, learn from them, quickly recover, and regain operational stability. "The fundamental characteristic of a resilient organization is that it does not lose control of what it does but is able to continue and rebound" (Hollnagel and Woods 2006, 348). In their research on high-reliability organizations, Karl Weick and Kathleen Sutcliffe (2007, 71) identify three key abilities that organizations need to operate resiliently:

1. The ability to absorb strain and preserve functioning despite internal or external adversity
2. The ability to recover or "bounce back" from disruptive events and better absorb a surprise rather than collapse
3. The ability to learn from previous episodes of resilient action

Resilience, developed through organizational commitment to preparedness and training individuals on the front line to effectively anticipate, monitor, learn, and respond to disturbances, creates a collective capacity for staff to "cope with a disturbance and learn from their experience" (Weick and Sutcliffe 2007, 73).

The US Department of Energy, one of the world's largest high-reliability organizations, defines three qualities that are necessary for an organization or system to maintain control in the event of an anomaly or disruptive event—that is, to achieve resilience: anticipation, attention, and response. "The organization must constantly be watchful and prepared to respond. Resilience requires a constant sense of unease that prevents complacency [and] a resilient organization must be proactive, flexible, adaptive, and prepared" (DOE 2009, 5-15). These organizational characteristics facilitate stable operations and ongoing provision of safe care while minimizing the disruptive effects of adverse events, external disturbances, and other environmental stressors. Patient safety depends on a hospital's resilience, its resistance to operational hazards, and its adaptive capacity under the constant threat of disruptive events.

> Safety is often expressed in terms of reliability. It is not enough, however, that systems are reliable and that the probability of failure that could cause harm is below a certain value. They must also be resilient and have the ability to recover from irregular variations, disruptions and degradations of expected work conditions. Resilience requires a continuous monitoring of system performance. The fundamental characteristic of a resilient organization is that it does not lose control of what it does, but is able to continue and rebound.
> —US Department of Energy (2009)

James Reason, a world-renowned authority on human error and accident causation, argues that organizational resilience is the product of commitment, competence, and cognizance (Reason and Hobbs 2003, 167–68). First, the leaders of the organization need to formalize their commitment to effective error management and safety management in the face of ever-increasing commercial pressures. Second, the leaders and managers of a safety-critical organization need to understand and recognize the ongoing "safety war" in their organization and the human and organizational factors that contribute to it. Lastly, the organization needs to understand and be competent in the use of safety and error management tools (Reason and Hobbs 2003, 168).

Reason's Human Performance Awareness Checklist defines 30 attributes of resilience in the areas of commitment, cognizance, and competence. This checklist can help hospitals proactively assess their "preparedness for human factors problems" and determine "whether . . . suitable counter-measures have been put in place" (Reason and Hobbs 2003, 170). A low score on the Human Performance Awareness

Checklist indicates that the organization is vulnerable to losses in productivity and capacity and to disruption resulting from errors in performance.

ENHANCING HOSPITALS' CAPACITY FOR RESILIENCE

Jean Pariès (2011, 3), an aviation engineer and human factors expert who has studied resilience in high-reliability organizations, defines resilience as the capacity "to establish now and maintain for the future a readiness to respond at any time to unexpected disruptions or events . . . [and] to have the required resources—people, competence, equipment—available to respond." Pariès distinguishes between *proactive* and *reactive* resilience strategies; real-time organizational resilience requires both. Proactive resilience strategies anticipate potential disruptive situations and develop predefined solutions that are ready to implement. These solutions include emergency response procedures, specific reaction skills for staff, and crisis response plans. Reactive resilience strategies involve training staff to generate, invent, create, or devise ad hoc solutions to emerging threats (Pariès 2011, 3).

Reason's Checklist for Assessing Institutional Resilience is designed to assess how an organization's attitudes and practices match the "ideal" attributes of organizational resilience (Reason and Hobbs 2003). This checklist provides a 20-point assessment tool for hospital leaders to better understand their organization's capacity for resilience. A summary of the assessment tool follows:

1. Managers are always mindful of the human and organizational factors that can endanger their operations.
2. Managers accept occasional setbacks and nasty surprises as inevitable. They anticipate that staff will make errors and train staff to detect and recover from them.
3. Top managers are genuinely committed to maintaining system safety and provide adequate resources to serve this end.
4. Safety-related issues and human performance problems are considered at high-level meetings on a regular basis.
5. Past events are thoroughly reviewed at top-level meetings, and lessons learned are implemented as global reforms rather than local repairs.
6. Top managers seek to identify failed system defenses after adverse events rather than place blame on particular individuals.
7. Top managers adopt a proactive stance toward safety—identifying recurrent error traps and removing them, striving to eliminate workplace factors that are likely to provoke errors, brainstorming new scenarios of possible failure, and conducting regular safety "health checks" on the

organizational processes known to contribute to accidents and serious safety events.

8. Top managers recognize that error-provoking system factors are easier to manage and correct than short-term psychological states such as distraction, inattention, and forgetfulness.

9. The effective management of safety depends on the collection, analysis, and dissemination of relevant information.

10. Managers recognize the necessity of combining reactive outcome data and proactive process information to identify which safety practices are most in need of attention and then carrying out remedial actions.

11. Representatives from all departments and levels attend safety-related meetings.

12. Assignment of staff to monitor safety-related functions or human factors is seen as a fast-track appointment, not a dead end.

13. Policies relating to near misses and incident reporting make clear the organization's stance regarding confidentiality, indemnity against sanctions, and the separation of staff involved in data collection from staff involved in disciplinary proceedings.

14. Disciplinary policies are predicated on agreed-upon distinctions between acceptable and unacceptable behavior. Managers recognize that a small number of unsafe acts are indeed reckless and warrant sanctions, but the majority of such acts should not be punished.

15. Line managers encourage their staff to acquire the mental and technical skills necessary to achieve safe and effective performance. Mental skills include anticipating possible errors and rehearsing appropriate recoveries.

16. The organization has in place rapid, useful, and intelligible feedback channels to communicate the lessons learned from both reactive and proactive safety information systems.

17. The organization acknowledges its errors, apologizes for them, and reassures the victims that the lessons learned from such accidents will help prevent their recurrence.

18. The organization appreciates that commercial goals and safety goals sometimes conflict, and policies and procedures are in place to recognize and resolve such conflicts in a transparent manner.

19. Policies are in place to encourage everyone to raise safety-related concerns.

20. The organization recognizes the critical dependence of effective safety management on the trust of the workforce—particularly in regard to error and incident reporting.

Reason's Checklist for Assessing Institutional Resilience is intended to help organizations examine their policies, overall philosophy, procedures, and practices to determine their level of resilience, as well as their vulnerability to lost productivity and safety interruptions. "High reliability requires intelligent wariness and a continuing respect for the many ways in which things can go wrong. Complacency is the worst enemy" (Reason and Hobbs 2003, 170). Complacency is the antithesis of resilience: Hospitals that lack resilience may first want to look at their organizational culture and safety climate to assess patient safety "mindfulness" and anticipatory capacity.

In their guidebook *Resilience Engineering in Practice*, Erick Hollnagel and colleagues (2011, xxxvi) identify four capabilities necessary for a system to be resilient—what the authors call the Four Cornerstones of Resilience:

1. *Knowing what to do*—the ability to respond to events, disruptions, or disturbances by using prepared responses or adjusting normal functioning. The ability to adjust how the organization functions is a key aspect of resilience.

2. *Knowing what to look for*—the ability to monitor ongoing developments in the organization and in the environment for potential threats.

3. *Knowing what to expect*—the ability to anticipate future developments, threats, and opportunities and potential changes, disruptions, pressures, and their consequences.

4. *Knowing what has happened*—the ability to learn from past experiences, including both failures and successes.

To assess a hospital's capacity for resilience, Hollnagel and colleagues also provide a Resilience Analysis Grid that poses a series of strategic questions for each of the four resilience capabilities. A sample of the assessment questions follows:

1. Questions assessing an organization's *ability to respond* ask whether the organization (1) has a list of events that it has prepared responses for, (2) has clear criteria for activating a response, (3) has adequate resources available to respond, (4) can determine whether a response was adequate, and (5) maintains a readiness to respond.

2. Questions assessing an organization's *ability to monitor* ask (1) what leading, current, and lagging indicators are being used and why; (2) whether there is a regular inspection schedule; (3) whether the validity of leading indicators has been established; and (4) whether the measures are reliable.

3.   Questions assessing an organization's *ability to anticipate* ask (1) how often future threats and opportunities are assessed, (2) how far the organization looks ahead, (3) whether the organization has a model of the future, and (4) whether there is an explicit definition of acceptable and unacceptable risks.

4.   Questions assessing an organization's *ability to learn* ask whether the organization (1) has a process to determine which events are investigated, (2) tries to learn from what is common (successes and things that go right) as well as from what is rare (failures and things that go wrong), (3) provides learning on a continuous basis or as a discrete activity, (4) provides training for data collection, analysis, and learning, and (5) confirms that the intended learning has taken place.

INDIVIDUAL RESILIENCE TRAINING, COMPETENCE, AND AWARENESS

Hospital staff—especially frontline caregivers—are often the first to recognize that a process or system is becoming dysfunctional and spiraling out of control. *Control* here means that the safety precautions—barriers, defenses, safeguards, and controls—designed to protect patients from the unintended harm of error and system hazards are at risk of failing under the pressure of a significant threat.

Hospitals should ensure that all staff are competent to anticipate, monitor, respond to, and learn from significant threats or events. Hospitals should train staff to effectively manage significant hazards, threats, and risks and their effects on their work and work environment. Staff should understand the organization's resilience policies and procedures related to incident prevention, deterrence, mitigation, self-protection, evacuation, response, continuity, and recovery (ANSI 2009, 10). Staff who are involved in performing incident/significant event prevention, preparedness, and response activities should receive training to improve their resilience-related competence. Individuals should be encouraged to take personal responsibility for the prevention, avoidance, deterrence, and detection of a potential disturbance or disruptive event. Situational awareness and decisive and immediate information sharing about emerging events are critical behaviors for staff to possess and employ.

Air Traffic Control, a high-reliability organization collective, defines the competencies for resilient performance among controllers using the T²EAM assessment tool—Taskwork and Teamwork strategies in Emergencies in Air Traffic Management (Malakis and Kontogiannis 2011, 107). This tool defines six competencies:

(1) recognizing and noticing cues, (2) managing uncertainty, (3) anticipating and acknowledging threats and using less busy times to plan, (4) planning for typical events and contingencies, (5) managing workload and prioritizing tasks, and (6) coping with interruptions and distractions. Resilience competencies for teams include (1) coordinating and managing dependencies, (2) communicating and updating situational status, (3) managing errors through error detection and correction, and (4) managing change by detecting and correcting problems in the distributions of tasks.

According to Stathis Malakis and Tom Kontogiannis, the attributes of resilience that individuals should possess include the ability to demonstrate problem-detection skills and the ability to forge new plans in the face of emerging threats. Individuals should be able to gather new information as a threat is unfolding to aid organizational understanding of the nature and severity of the threat. New information helps clarify assumptions and evaluate options. Resilience-prepared individuals must be able to manage uncertainty, recognize problems, anticipate threats, develop contingency plans, and use their cognitive abilities in flexible ways to respond effectively as an event evolves (Malakis and Kontogiannis 2011, 115). In resilient organizations, things go right because people (1) learn to overcome design flaws and functional glitches, (2) adapt their performance to meet demands, (3) interpret and apply procedures to match conditions, and (4) detect and correct when things go wrong (Hollnagel et al. 2011, 258).

SUPPORT FOR STAFF INVOLVED IN ERRORS AND ADVERSE EVENTS

A resilient organization worries about how the organization will return to normal after a significant event and how it will support the emotional and psychological needs of providers and staff involved in the incident. In a study of more than 3,000 physicians, 92 percent reported being previously involved in either a near miss or a serious safety event, and 81 percent reported some degree of stress related to their involvement in an event (PSNet 2019). According to the study, the degree of stress that staff experience depends on the severity of the error, the degree of perceived personal responsibility for the error, and the patient outcome. *Second victims* are healthcare providers who have been involved in a serious safety event or medical error and experience trauma as a result of their involvement in the event. Clinicians who have been involved in a serious safety event often report feelings of responsibility for the patient's outcome, as well as shame, anger, failure, depression, inadequacy, and loss of confidence (PSNet 2019). The intensity of the experience and the level of support provided to the clinician after the event determine how quickly the individual will be able to move on. Second victims go through six stages of recovery (PSNet 2019):

1. *Chaos and accident response.* Clinicians experience turmoil and may be in a state of shock—they are trying to both determine what happened and manage a patient who might be unstable or in crisis.

2. *Intrusive reflections.* Clinicians experience feelings of inadequacy, self-doubt, and loss of confidence—they engage in continuous reevaluation of the situation through "haunted reenactments."

3. *Restoring personal integrity.* Clinicians seek support from trusted people, but they may not know where to turn.

4. *Enduring the inquisition.* Clinicians brace for the institutional investigation and wonder about the impact the event will have on their job and licensure and the potential for litigation.

5. *Obtaining emotional first aid.* Clinicians feel uncertain about confiding in others because of privacy concerns—most clinicians feel unsupported or under-supported.

6. *Moving on.* Clinicians feel internal and external pressure to move on and have three ways of doing so: (1) dropping out by changing roles, moving to a different practice, or leaving the profession; (2) surviving by feeling "OK" after acknowledging the mistake, even though they may have a hard time forgiving themselves and find it hard to "let go"; (3) thriving by making something good come out of the event.

Kaiser Permanente, for example, believes that providing support to its patient care providers following their involvement in an adverse event is "the right thing to do." It seeks to ensure that it takes care of its most valuable resource—its employees—and by doing so increase the quality of care, reduce medical errors, and improve the retention of the affected providers (O'Keefe 2017).

Kaiser Permanente has identified several contributions to improved individual and organizational resilience as a result of its Critical Incident Response program: (1) it allows patient care teams to rebound from the event more quickly; (2) by providing education to staff before and after an event, it supports the emotional needs of staff; (3) by encouraging staff to share their thoughts, feelings, and reactions to adverse outcomes, it facilitates the healing and recovery process and the return to normal; (4) it helps stabilize the workplace more quickly after an event; (5) it mitigates the effects of critical incident stress; and (6) it promotes a return to normal productivity. Organizational efforts to improve its resilience and its adaptive capacity can counteract and diminish the negative potential effects of a critical incident, major disturbance, or serious safety event.

> At the moment of the disturbance, the flexible, adaptive element of the system lies mostly in the sharp-end workers—who call on their knowledge and experience to understand the disruption, anticipate immediate and future demands for performance, and shift work and work processes to meet those demands. To do this well requires a large and diverse fund of knowledge regarding their system's technical and organizational features, the sorts of things that are likely to happen and can happen, what resources are available, and what are the likely consequences of shifting resources in different ways. A hallmark of resilient systems is the presence of multiple interacting goals and the active selection of goals in the face of uncertainty.
>
> —Rollin J. Fairbanks and colleagues (2014)

CONCLUSION

Chapter 6 identifies the safe care practices that cultivate resilience and adaptability in hospitals. Resilience refers to the ability of an organization or system to respond to an unanticipated disturbance that can lead to failure and then resume normal operations quickly with a minimum decrement in performance. Hospitals that effectively respond to and recover from major disruptions or disturbances cultivate resilience and adaptability, which allow them to quickly regroup and return to a stable, safe, and desirable level of performance. The safe care practices described in this chapter include the Four Cornerstones of Resilience described by Erik Hollnagel, James Reason's Checklist for Assessing Institutional Resilience, and the six habits of highly resilient organizations outlined in the Air Traffic Control T²EAM model.

CHAPTER 6 SAFE CARE PRACTICES

1. Assess how organizational attitudes and practices match the "ideal" attributes of organizational resilience using James Reason's 20-point Checklist for Assessing Institutional Resilience.

2. Assess the capacity for resilience and adaptability using Erik Hollnagel and colleagues' Resilience Analysis Grid. This tool poses a series of strategic questions for each of the four capabilities necessary for a system to be resilient—what the authors call the Four Cornerstones of Resilience.

3. Assess, train, and enhance individual competencies in resilience and adaptability using the T²EAM assessment tool developed for use among air traffic controllers. This tool defines competencies for resilient performance.

→

---

4. Consider how the organization will return to normal after a significant event and how it will support the emotional and psychological needs of the providers and staff involved in the incident.

5. Assess the human factors that contribute to organizational resilience using Reason's Human Performance Awareness Checklist. This checklist comprises 30 attributes of resilience in the areas of commitment, cognizance, and competence. A low score indicates that the organization is vulnerable to losses in productivity and capacity and to disruption resulting from errors in performance.

REFERENCES

American National Standards Institute (ANSI). 2009. "Organizational Resilience: Security, Preparedness, and Continuity Management Systems—Requirements with Guidance for Use." Published March 12. www.ndsu.edu/fileadmin/emgt/ASIS_SPC.1-2009_Item _No._1842.pdf.

Fairbanks, R. J., R. L. Wears, D. D. Woods, E. Hollnagel, P. Plsek, and R. I. Cook. 2014. "Resilience and Resilience Engineering in Health Care." *Joint Commission Journal on Quality and Patient Safety* 40 (8): 376–83.

Hollnagel, E., J. Pariès, D. Woods, and J. Wreathall (eds.). 2011. *Resilience Engineering in Practice: A Guidebook*. Burlington, VT: Ashgate Publishing.

Hollnagel, E., and D. Woods. 2006. "Epilogue: Resilience Engineering Precepts." In *Resilience Engineering: Concepts and Precepts*, edited by E. Hollnagel, D. Woods, and N. Leveson, 347–58. Burlington, VT: Ashgate Publishing.

Malakis, S., and T. Kontogiannis. 2011. "Cognitive Strategies in Emergency and Abnormal Situations Training—Implications for Resilience in Air Traffic Control." In *Resilience Engineering in Practice: A Guidebook*, edited by E. Hollnagel, J. Pariès, D. Woods, and J. Wreathall, 101–17. Burlington, VT: Ashgate Publishing.

Nemeth, C., R. Wears, D. Woods, E. Hollnagel, and R. Cook. 2008. "Minding the Gaps: Creating Resilience in Health Care." In *Advances in Patient Safety: New Directions and Alternative Approaches*, vol. 3, *Performance and Tools*, edited by K. Henriksen, J. B. Battles, M. A. Keyes, and M. L. Grady, 1–13. Rockville, MD: Agency for Healthcare Research and Quality.

O'Keefe, J. 2017. "Taking Care of Our Providers and Staff After an Adverse Event." Medically Induced Trauma Support Services. Accessed March 4, 2019. www.mitsstools.org /uploads/3/7/7/6/3776466/kaiser_adverse_outcomes_support_for_staff.pdf.

Pariès, J. 2011. "Resilience and the Ability to Respond." In *Resilience Engineering in Practice: A Guidebook*, edited by E. Hollnagel, J. Pariès, D. Woods, and J. Wreathall, 3–8. Burlington, VT: Ashgate Publishing.

Patient Safety Network (PSNet). 2019. "Patient Safety Primer: Second Victims: Support for Clinicians Involved in Errors and Adverse Events." Updated January. https://psnet.ahrq.gov/primers/primer/30/Second-Victims-Support-for-Clinicians-Involved-in-Errors-and-Adverse-Events.

Reason, J., and A. Hobbs. 2003. *Managing Maintenance Error: A Practical Guide*. Burlington, VT: Ashgate Publishing.

US Department of Energy (DOE). 2009. *Human Performance Improvement Handbook*, vol. 1, *Concepts and Principles*. Published June. www.standards.doe.gov/standards-documents/1000/1028-BHdbk-2009-v1.

Weick, K. E., and K. M. Sutcliffe. 2007. *Managing the Unexpected: Resilient Performance in an Age of Uncertainty*. San Francisco: Jossey-Bass.

CHAPTER 7

Using Technology to Improve Patient Safety

WHY ADOPT TECHNOLOGY TO ENHANCE PATIENT SAFETY?

More than 15 years ago in the *New England Journal of Medicine*, Dr. David Bates and Dr. Atul Gawande (2003, 2526) described the promise and potential of information technology (IT) to improve patient safety:

> Information technology can reduce the rate of errors in three ways: by preventing errors and adverse events, by facilitating a more rapid response after an adverse event has occurred, and by tracking and providing feedback about adverse events. Data now shows that information technology can reduce the frequency of errors of different types and probably the frequency of associated adverse events.
>
> Information technology can substantially improve the safety of medical care by structuring actions, catching errors, and bringing evidence-based, patient-centered decision support to the point of care to allow necessary customization.

Has IT fulfilled the promise and potential that Bates and Gawande described in 2003? Indeed, many examples of the positive role that IT has played in improving patient safety can be cited. However, the benefits of IT must be balanced against concerns about new hazards and risks that IT has introduced into the healthcare system. In his book *The Digital Doctor*, Dr. Robert Wachter (2015a, xi–xiv), chief of medical services at the University of California, San Francisco Medical Center, offers a real-world assessment of the impact of health IT on the practice of medicine:

> While someday the computerization of medicine will surely be that long-awaited "disruptive innovation," today it's often just plain disruptive: of

the doctor-patient relationship, of clinicians' professional interactions and work flow, and of the way we measure and try to improve things. . . . Starting now, and lasting until forever, your health and healthcare will be determined, to a remarkable and somewhat disquieting degree, by how well the technology works.

Technology has played a significant role in advancing the safety and effectiveness of medical care for centuries—since the invention and use of forceps, scalpels (including the double-edged lancet), cautery, surgical needles, and other instruments by the ancient Romans and Greeks around 500 BC. In more recent history, Ignaz Semmelweis, a Hungarian obstetrician, devised a technologic solution in 1847 to reduce the extremely high rate of mortality among birthing mothers at Vienna General Hospital—hand washing! Exhibit 7.1 illustrates the precipitous drop in mortality resulting from puerperal fever after the introduction of hand washing with chlorinated water—a technologic solution (no pun intended) that Dr. Semmelweis referred to as "self-evident" but that had been ignored, rejected, and even ridiculed by the medical community. The mortality rate in the first obstetrical clinic where hand washing was instituted dropped 90 percent, from 18.3 percent to 2.2 percent, and for the first time, the death rate was zero for two consecutive months (Ataman, Vatanoglu-Lutz, and Yildirim 2013, 36)

Exhibit 7.1: Mortality Rates, Vienna Maternity Institution, 1841–1849

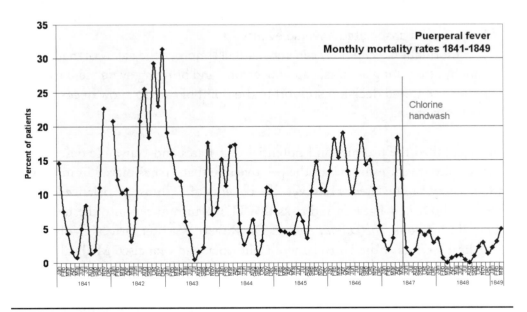

Source: Reprinted from Wikipedia (2019).

Is hand washing considered a "technology"? The World Health Organization (2011, 5) defines a health technology as "the application of organized knowledge and skills in the form of medicines, medical devices, vaccines, procedures, and systems developed to solve a health problem and improve quality of life." So, yes. Unconscionably, many hospitals and their caregiving staffs still struggle to sustain consistent adherence to the lifesaving "technology" of hand washing and hand hygiene.

Over the past 150 years, innovative medical and technologic breakthroughs have contributed to remarkable improvements in the structure, processes, and outcomes of healthcare and patient safety. In the 1850s, the chest-scope or stethoscope became a part of mainstream medicine for auscultation, or listening to the internal sounds of the body. In 1865, Joseph Lister introduced antisepsis to wound treatment. In the 1880s, germ theory was embraced to explain that diseases are caused by microorganisms rather than by air pollution (known as the miasma theory). In 1895, Wilhelm Röntgen discovered X-rays. Ultrasound was discovered in the 1940s and first applied to the human body in 1949. Defibrillators were invented in the 1930s, although the first portable defibrillator was not put to use until 1959. The first commercially viable computerized tomography (CT) scanner was introduced in 1967. The first fully implantable pacemaker was introduced in 1958.

In the 1980s, laser-assisted in situ keratomileusis—LASIK—eye surgery was first performed, and in 1989 it was approved by the US Food and Drug Administration. In the 1970s, medical technology was universally viewed as a core element of good healthcare, attaining almost mystical status and threatening to usurp the physician's role as the central player in modern medicine (Cohen and Hanft 2004, 12). And in 2016, clinicians began using "point-and-shoot" ultrasound with mobile devices to record annotations, complete cardiac scans, monitor heart rate, or measure bladder volume.

A 2008 study of "Patient Care Technology and Safety" published by the Agency for Healthcare Research and Quality (AHRQ) noted that more than 5,000 types of medical devices were then in use around the world by millions of healthcare providers. The study concluded that "device-related problems are inevitable" (Powell-Cope, Nelson, and Patterson 2008, 207). Today, nurses encounter or use more than 50 technologies in direct nursing care delivery; indirect nursing care delivery; patient assessment, monitoring, and surveillance; patient protective devices; nurse protective devices; and communication with others. These devices include patient protective devices such as fall alarms and specialized mattresses, as well as devices that enhance care delivery, such as intravenous (IV) pumps, telemetry, bedside cardiac monitoring, ventilators, and pulse oximetry.

These devices have dramatically changed the delivery of care. For example, before the widespread adoption and use of the pulse oximeter to detect changes in a patient's oxygen saturation level, nurses relied on their observation of subtle changes in the patient's mental status or skin color to detect oxygen depletion and measured arterial blood gases to confirm their suspicion. Pulse oximetry allows the nurse to identify decreased oxygenation before clinical symptoms appear and promptly treat the underlying causes (Powell-Cope, Nelson, and Patterson 2008, 207).

In the book *First, Do Less Harm*, Ross Koppel and colleagues (2012, 63–64) note that IT has been proposed as the solution to a variety of problems in healthcare:

> Medical practice is beset by many woes. The most frequently reported are inefficiency, loss of patient information, fragmented information . . . inadequate patient safety, exorbitant costs, staffing shortages, misallocated staff, and redundant tests and procedures. And that's only a few of the items on a long list of problems. The solution most often proposed for these difficulties is computerized information systems.

The vast array of technologies that have been implemented over the years were designed for a variety of applications: (1) to improve diagnosis of the patient's condition, such as lab tests, X-rays, CT scans, and magnetic resonance imaging; (2) to improve the quality and effectiveness of patient care, such as IV pumps, oxygen and air regulators, and code carts; (3) to improve the safety of care and thereby reduce preventable patient harm, such as bar-code medication administration (BCMA), computerized provider order entry (CPOE), and smart pumps; (4) to improve the safety of practitioners, such as face masks, gloves, gowns, and mechanical lifts; or (5) to enhance communication and decision-making among care providers, such as electronic health records (EHRs) and clinical decision support (CDS).

SAFETY BENEFITS OF TECHNOLOGY

The Office of the National Coordinator for Health Information Technology (ONC) was created in 2009 following the passage of the Health Information Technology for Economic and Clinical Health Act. The primary focus of the ONC is to harness health IT to reduce medical errors and to create platforms and incentives for health IT to facilitate substantial improvements in healthcare quality and safety (ONC 2013, 3). The national Health IT Patient Safety Goal of the US Department of Health and Human Services, of which the ONC is a part, is that "patients and providers have confidence in the safety of the health care system, including its health IT infrastructure, based on evidence of safety" (ONC 2013, 5).

The National Health IT Plan (ONC 2013, 3–4) identifies several positive benefits of health IT and contributions to improved patient safety and care quality:

(1) medication errors can be substantially reduced; (2) EHRs can help eliminate prescription and other errors resulting from illegible handwriting; (3) clinical decisions can more easily be made based on evidence, and (4) patient records can be stored centrally and easily accessed from multiple locations.

The adoption of EHRs provides several opportunities to improve patient safety, by (1) increasing clinicians' awareness of potential medication errors and adverse interactions; (2) improving the availability and timeliness of information to support treatment decisions, care coordination, and care planning; (3) making it easier for clinicians to report safety issues and potential hazards; and (4) giving patients a greater opportunity to more efficiently provide input on data accuracy than the old paper process allowed.

SAFETY THREATS OF TECHNOLOGY

Although health IT offers many benefits, these technologies can also introduce hazards and safety threats that are often unanticipated. These hazards and safety threats may result from the following: (1) the improper or careless use of the technology, (2) the repercussions of introducing a new technology too quickly, (3) the failure to provide training or to consider the organizational culture and clinical settings in which the technology will be applied, (4) poor interface design, (5) inadequate integration into existing systems, (6) the slowdown in clinical work processes, to the point of inefficiency; and (7) the lack of proper servicing and maintenance to maintain safe patient care (Aggarwal et al. 2010).

Four common pitfalls diminish the ability of a technology to enhance care quality and safety: (1) poor technology design that does not account for human factors and ergonomic principles, (2) poor technology interfaces with the patient or the care environment, (3) inadequate planning for the effective implementation of the technology, and (4) inadequate maintenance of the technology (Powell-Cope, Nelson, and Patterson 2008, 207).

Health IT can be cumbersome, unnecessarily error provoking, and insufficiently responsive to the needs

Of course, it was natural for doctors, nurses and pharmacists to expect that, once computers entered our complex, chaotic and often dangerous world, they would make things better. After all, in our off-duty lives we are so thoroughly used to taking out our iPhones, downloading an app, and off we go. But we're learning that the magic of information technology, so familiar to us in the consumer world that it nearly seems "normal," is far more elusive in the world of medicine. Though computers can and do improve patient safety in many ways . . . technology can cause breathtaking errors.
—Dr. Robert Wachter (2015b)

of the clinicians at the sharp end of healthcare delivery (Koppel et al. 2012, 81). "Surprisingly, much of the HIT market is built on a foundation of what economists call 'imperfect information'—an irony for an information technology industry, and an impediment for the health care industry" (Koppel et al. 2012, 84).

SAFE CARE TECHNOLOGIES

Healthcare organizations and device manufacturers collaborate to develop, test, and install technologies that either proactively improve the safety of the patient care process or provide a defense or hazard control to protect the patient from a harmful error. *Proactive* safe care technologies include bedside cardiac monitoring, specialized mattresses to help prevent pressure ulcers, ventilators, and nasogastric, endotracheal, or tracheostomy tubes. *Defense-oriented* technologies include BCMA, CPOE, and radio-frequency identification systems.

Some technologies have been redesigned to build in safety precautions and error reduction features. IV pumps are one example. The design of first-generation IV pumps (traditional pumps) made it difficult for clinicians to access the drug library and easy to override soft alerts or bypass the drug library's decision support feature, and no hard-stop alerts were built in (Rothschild and Keohane 2008). Second-generation IV pumps (smart pumps) introduced drug libraries with standardized concentrations for commonly used drugs, soft alerts with override capability, and hard alerts that could not be overridden. Third-generation IV pumps have now incorporated bar-code technology, adding protections to correctly identify patients and to ensure that the right patient receives the correct drug and dose. Smart pumps now alert caregivers when an inappropriate dosage is selected for a drug through their dose error reduction system; this feature, combined with bar-code-enabled point-of-care technology, provides added protection against delivering a drug to the wrong patient (Reston 2013, 48–49).

The following sections give an overview of some of the most pervasive health technologies that are designed to defend against hazards or harmful errors.

Smart Pumps

Smart IV infusion pumps have been reengineered to mitigate or protect against the harmful effects of errors that occur during the drug administration stage of the medication management process. Errors during drug administration are particularly dangerous because of the risk of overdose, especially for high-risk medications such as insulin, heparin, propofol, and vasoactive drugs (Rothschild and Keohane 2008,

3). Smart pumps provide clinicians with access to the drug library, both soft and hard alerts, and protections that ensure the right drug is administered at the right dosage. *Right patient* protections can be incorporated by linking to a bar-code-enabled point-of-care system.

Bar-Code Technology

Healthcare executive Alicia Torres (2012) notes that "over the past few decades, there have been incredible advances in patient safety, due in part to better technology. One technology that has had a tremendous impact is the bar code. In addition to increased patient safety and identification, this technology offers many other benefits, including improved operational efficiencies." For example, bar-code technology is used in the pharmacy to reduce errors during the dispensing process. Typically, medication- and dose-specific bar codes are affixed to each medication that leaves the pharmacy. Pharmacy staff should ensure that every medication is individually bar-coded and that the bar codes are readable. One pitfall of BCMA systems is that when bar codes are unreadable, the system can be overridden to allow medications to be administered when needed. However, overriding smart pump defenses may negate the benefits of BCMA and create a hazard (Mansur 2008, 6).

BCMA systems help streamline the patient admission process and allow patient care teams to track and identify patients throughout their hospital stay. Patients are provided with a bar-coded wristband upon admission. Medical records, medications, and specimens are all tagged with a corresponding bar-coded label so that clinicians can easily scan and trace critical patient information. For example, each time a medication is administered, a nurse or doctor scans the patient's wristband and the bar code on the medication, and the patient's EHR is automatically updated to reflect the administration of that medication. In this way, bar-code technology provides a safety defense to ensure that the correct treatment or medication is administered to the right patient, "ultimately reducing errors and ensuring patient safety" (Torres 2012, 2).

Researchers Joseph Cummings, Thomas Ratko, and Karl Matuszewski (2005) note, however, that a "BCMA system is only one part of a comprehensive information technology-enabled medication system. The complete system of the future will also incorporate CPOE, eMARs [electronic medication administration records], and smart pumps to ensure patient safety from different aspects of the medication process." An AHRQ-funded study found in a review of more than 14,000 medication administrations and 3,800 order transcriptions in an academic medical center that the use of bar-coded eMARs "substantially reduced the rate of errors in order transcription and in medication administration as well as potential adverse events"

(Poon et al. 2010, 1698). In this study group, patient care units that did not use the bar-coded eMARs had an 11.5 percent error rate, while units that did use the bar-coded eMARs had a 6.8 percent error rate—a 41.4 percent reduction in errors. The rate of potential adverse drug events fell from 3.1 percent without the use of bar-coded eMARs to 1.6 percent with its use, representing a 50.8 percent reduction.

Computerized Provider Order Entry

CPOE allows clinicians to directly enter orders for medications, tests, or procedures into an electronic system, which then transmits the order directly to the individual who is responsible for carrying out the order. Receiving departments might include the pharmacy, clinical laboratory, or radiology department (Ranji, Rennke, and Wachter 2013, 480). In the first decade of the twenty-first century, most clinicians were still handwriting orders for medications, tests, and procedures. The introduction of health IT and "meaningful use" incentives prompted most hospitals to adopt some form of CPOE. Approximately 90 percent of medication errors occur at the ordering or transcribing phrase, because the order either is illegible or uses unclear abbreviations (PSNet 2019). CPOE helps prevent such errors by facilitating standardized, legible, and complete orders. Ranji, Rennke, and Wachter (2013, 480) note that CPOE has the "potential to greatly reduce errors at the prescribing and transcribing stages" of medication and other orders. A 2013 meta-analysis found that the use of CPOE rather than paper-based orders resulted in a 48 percent decrease in prescribing errors, preventing more than 17 million medication errors each year in US hospitals (PSNet 2019).

Coupling CDS systems with CPOE can help prevent both errors of commission, such as ordering a drug in an excessive dose or a drug to which the patient has a known allergy, and errors of omission, such as failing to order prophylaxis against deep vein thrombosis in a patient who has undergone joint replacement surgery (PSNet 2019). Linking CDS and CPOE provides additional defenses against ordering wrong drug doses, wrong route of administration, or wrong frequency of administration and against drug-allergy, drug-drug, and drug-laboratory hazards. CPOE systems offer many other benefits compared with paper-based ordering systems: averting confusion over handwriting; avoiding problems with similar drug names or drug interactions; improving integration with CDS systems; improving integration with adverse drug event reporting systems; allowing faster transmission to the laboratory, pharmacy, or radiology department; and allowing comparison with recommended alternative treatments that might be safer or lower in cost.

Real-Time Ultrasound Guidance During Central Line Insertion

Central venous catheters (CVCs) are a lifesaving technology, but their insertion involves significant risk. CVCs can provide parenteral nutrition, access for vasoactive medications, and hemodynamic monitoring. Percutaneous insertions are often performed blind—that is, the clinician must rely on anatomical landmarks during the insertion process. The use of ultrasound-guided CVC reduces the chance of error and harm by allowing clinicians to detect anatomical variations and the exact vessel location, avoid central veins with preexisting thrombosis that may prevent successful CVC placement, and guide both guidewire and catheter placement after needle insertion (Shekelle and Dallas 2013, 172). The use of ultrasound improves the success rate and reduces the risk of CVC placement, particularly for inexperienced clinicians and for patients in high-risk situations.

Multiple studies have shown that ultrasound guidance in CVC placement is superior to the landmark method. A 2007 study by T. J. Wigmore and colleagues on the effects of the National Institute for Clinical Excellence (NICE) ultrasonography guidelines showed a significant reduction in complications after implementation of the NICE Guidelines, from 10.5 percent to 4.6 percent, with an absolute risk reduction of 5.9 percent (Jacquet and Hong 2014, 21). Compared with the external landmark approach, ultrasound-guided CVC results in fewer complications and is more effective in time and first-attempt success. "Not only has ultrasound guidance in central venous access decreased complication rates, but also it has been shown to decrease total number of attempts, increase first-attempt success, decrease time to insertion, and decrease failure rate" (Jacquet and Hong 2014, 21).

Electronic Health Records

EHRs that are well designed, implemented appropriately, and coupled with strong clinical processes can help improve and monitor healthcare quality and safety. Effective EHRs access important medical history data, provide CDS, and facilitate communication among providers and between providers and patients. Implementation of EHRs has been shown to reduce the number of adverse events—particularly EHR systems with clinical data repository, CDS, CPOE, and provider documentation functionality (Joint Commission 2015).

Several barriers have slowed the adoption of EHRs, however, such as concerns about increased workload for clinicians, system interoperability issues, and security and confidentiality concerns. Managing these concerns and involving end users in the ongoing assessment and operational improvement of EHR systems produce meaningful and sustainable benefits for patients. EHRs have proven to reduce medical errors and inefficiency by making health information more readily available to clinicians and by reducing the number of unnecessary tests. "EHR functionality can be leveraged to improve clinical outcomes and avoid patient harm" (ONC 2013, 8). For example, as a result of the integration of CDS into EHRs, standardized checklists have been developed to prevent central line–associated bloodstream infections, as well as criteria for verifying the proper position of catheters and notifications to discontinue medications or other interventions. CDS/EHR systems can also include risk assessments and prompts to reevaluate the patient's risk level to prevent injury from falls or pressure ulcers (ONC 2013, 8).

Specialized Support Surfaces (Mattresses)

According to an AHRQ-funded study, many specialized beds have been shown to be more effective at reducing the development of pressure ulcers than the standard foam-based beds historically used in hospitals (Agostini, Baker, and Bogardus 2001). Moreover, the study found that placing a dry polymer gel pad on the operating table decreased the incidence of new pressure ulcers by almost half—11 percent for patients placed on the gel pad versus 20 percent for patients placed on a standard operating room table mattress (Agostini, Baker, and Bogardus 2001). Advances in the technology aimed at alleviating bed sores have resulted in more than 100 bed surface options and combinations, including both dynamic systems, which require an energy source to alternate pressure points, and static systems, which rely on redistribution of pressure over a large surface area (Kirman 2018). "The first step in healing a pressure injury is determination of the cause (i.e., pressure, friction, or shear). Turning and repositioning the patient remains the cornerstone of prevention and treatment through pressure relief" (Kirman 2018).

While there is a need for more controlled testing of the effectiveness of various mattresses, clinical trials for prevention and treatment of pressure injuries have been performed on air-fluidized and low-air-loss beds. The evidence from these trials indicates that air-fluidized and low-air-loss beds help prevent or treat pressure ulcers. "Any individual thought to be at risk for developing pressure injuries should be placed on a pressure-reducing device" such as static air, alternating air, gel, or water (Kirman 2018). The National Pressure Ulcer Advisory Panel (NPUAP) has developed uniform terminology, testing methods, and reporting standards for support surfaces. Through its Support Surfaces Standards Initiative, the NPUAP aims to "improve industry understanding of the importance of the support surface body interface, and provide the tools necessary to improve the quality of life and the ultimate outcome for the bed bound individual. Clinicians, patients, and other users would benefit from having product information and test data presented in a consistent manner" (NPUAP 2017).

A 2018 IHI improvement story titled "Relieve the Pressure and Reduce Harm" noted that advanced pressure-reducing surfaces help prevent pressure ulcers, and hospitals are replacing all of their beds with these mattresses. For example, Ascension, a healthcare system of 153 hospitals in 22 states and Washington, DC, has replaced all foam mattresses with surfaces that provide pressure-reducing or pressure-relieving capabilities. Appropriate surfaces include static or air-filled mattresses that do not cycle in time and dynamic surfaces such as air-fluidized mattresses powered by a pump that regularly alternates pressure relief (IHI 2018).

SAFE USE OF TECHNOLOGY

According to Lissane Bainbridge's 1983 precept "ironies of automation," introducing automation into a complex sociotechnical system to improve safety and performance often introduces new problems that degrade safety and performance (Wears and Leveson 2017, 1). When technology is not properly designed, implemented, and applied, it can introduce new safety risks into the healthcare delivery system. For example, if the volume of alerts is too high, clinicians may experience alert fatigue and ignore them. "Many EHRs still are not interoperable, potentially leading to failures in communicating important patient information (such as test results) and delays in treatment" (NQF 2018).

To avoid these risks to patient safety, frontline users should be involved in all stages of applying IT solutions to healthcare problems: planning, design, testing, implementation, operation, and maintenance. The National Quality Forum's 2016 report *Identification and Prioritization of Health IT Patient Safety Measures* concluded that "with proper design, implementation, and use, HIT promises the ability to reduce medical errors and improve quality of care. Yet . . . it can also create new hazards and opportunities for error" (NQF 2016, 2). In its efforts to identify potential measures of health IT safety, the NQF established three goals to guide the work of its Health IT Safety Committee: (1) ensure that clinicians and patients have a foundation of safe health IT, (2) ensure that health IT is properly integrated and used to deliver safe care within healthcare organizations, and (3) ensure that health IT is part of continuous improvement processes to make care safer and more effective.

Sociotechnical systems are the processes and elements of work design related to the interaction between people and technology in the work environment. Koppel and colleagues (2012) provide a 12-point checklist to guide hospital health IT purchasing decisions:

1. Contracts with vendors should specify penalties sufficient to ensure that the vendor is responsive to clinicians' needs and patient safety concerns.
2. Identification and rectification of problems should be clearly spelled out: Who defines a problem? Who is responsible for fixing it? When must it be fixed? Who pays for the fix?
3. Hospitals sharing similar vendor systems should create their own communication channels, in addition to user groups.
4. Efforts to find health IT problems should include investigation of the technology, tasks, organization, patients' issues, and environmental circumstances—in other words, make the technology compatible with the hospital's work processes.
5. All health IT implementation requires meticulous attention to its actual use.
6. Evaluation and implementation teams should work with technology vendors to align hardware, software, user, policy, workflow, and patient safety needs—but hospitals must maintain ultimate control.
7. Health IT system design must incorporate up-to-date standards for user interface.
8. In buying health IT systems, hospitals should focus on basic functionality, flexibility, interoperability, and robust design.
9. Contracts should be negotiated to maximize vendor responsiveness to clinical, workflow, user, and safety needs.
10. Post-implementation assessments to identify user, environment, policy, workflow, and patient issues are critical.
11. Post-implementation assessments should drive hospital education efforts, policy, workflow changes, and requests to vendors.
12. New work-arounds will emerge in response to changes in technology, workflow, and patient types—evaluation of the actual use of technology should be ongoing and assess the impact on communication, workflow, and teamwork.

Ensuring the safe use of technology requires the involvement of frontline caregivers at every stage of technology deployment. AHRQ's *Evidence-Based Handbook for Nurses* (Powell-Cope, Nelson, and Patterson 2008) describes seven tips for nurses to influence technology at the bedside:

1. Organize technology and equipment "fairs" to gain input from key users before technology is purchased.

2. Examine the performance of technology in challenging scenarios in a simulated setting with a small number of untrained representative users.
3. Mentor and oversee temporary (agency) nurses and other personnel during their first use of sophisticated technology.
4. Develop cogent arguments to administration to justify the purchase of new equipment and technologies.
5. Become critical users of technology by identifying problems early on and communicating them to vendors and in-house biomedical engineering staff.
6. Report adverse events associated with medical devices to the US Food and Drug Administration's MAUDE (Manufacturer and User Facility Device Experience) reporting system and/or ECRI Institute's (2018) problem reporting system.
7. Serve as a resource for new technologies on the unit by getting training early, communicating with vendors, training others on the unit, and offering to field questions as new technology is implemented.

USING TECHNOLOGY TO IMPROVE PATIENT SAFETY

The interaction of people and technology in the workplace reflects the organization's sociotechnical system. How well the social aspects of the staff and the technical aspects of the organization's technology perform together is a measure of their *joint optimization*. Joint optimization emphasizes the achievement of both productivity and satisfaction in staff's work lives and technical performance. The introduction of new technologies into complex systems such as hospitals and healthcare systems requires the active commitment of organizational leaders, a supportive culture, and the continuous involvement of frontline staff to achieve joint optimization. The safe adoption of technology depends on leadership, cultural support, and the active engagement of clinical staff at every step of the technology procurement and maintenance process. Hospitals should establish a biomedical and technology team to oversee the integration of technologic solutions into the healthcare environment. This team should conduct routine assessments of the functionality of, staff satisfaction with, and safe performance of all safety-critical technologies.

> Ultimately, it is in society's best interest to see that new technologies are evaluated carefully and that their use in medicine is channeled constructively in ways that temper their highly seductive appeal with clear knowledge of their effectiveness and potential negative consequences.
> —Alan Cohen and Ruth S. Hanft (2004)

SAFETY ASSURANCE FACTORS FOR EHR RESILIENCE (SAFER)

The ONC has published Self-Assessment Guides for High Priority Practices to help healthcare organizations improve the safety and safe use of EHRs. Involving clinicians and staff in completing the self-assessment will help provide an accurate snapshot of the safety of the hospital's EHR system. The self-assessment guides include a checklist, practice worksheets, recommended practices, examples of implementation, and interactive references and support materials (see www.healthit.gov/SAFERGuide). The ONC's goal is "to improve the overall safety of our health care system" (ONC 2016, 1).

The recommended safety practices for High Priority Practices target high-risk safety concerns that pose a threat to the safe use of EHRs. "The potential benefits of EHRs may not be fully maximized unless the people responsible for their implementation, maintenance, and use are prepared for and manage the new challenges and risks they create" (ONC 2016, 2). The risks introduced by EHRs include *social* risks involving people, leadership, workflow, and policies and *technical* risks associated with the EHR hardware, software, system-to-system interfaces, configurations, upgrades, and maintenance. Completing the SAFER Self-Assessment will help hospitals (1) determine a future path to optimize EHR-related safety and quality, (2) set priorities for recommended practices that have not yet been addressed, (3) ensure that a plan is in place to maintain recommended practices that have been implemented, (4) dedicate the required resources to make necessary improvements, and (5) mitigate the highest-priority safety risks introduced by EHRs.

The ONC's High Priority Practices Checklist includes 18 recommended safe practices. The following highlights some of these practices (with their associated checklist numbers):

1.4	Evidence-based order sets and charting templates are available for common clinical conditions, procedures, and services.
1.5	Interactive CDS features and functions (e.g., interruptive warnings, passive suggestions, information buttons) are available and working properly.
1.8	Policies and procedures ensure accurate patient identification at each step of the clinical workflow.
2.2	The human–computer interface is easy to use and designed to ensure that required information is visible, readable, and understandable.
2.4	Clinicians are able to override computer-generated clinical interventions when they deem it necessary.

2.5   The EHR is used for ordering medications, diagnostic tests, and procedures.

2.7   Predefined orders are established for common medications and diagnostic (laboratory or radiology) testing.

3.1   Key EHR safety metrics related to the practice and organization are monitored.

3.2   EHR-related patient safety hazards are reported to all responsible parties, and steps are taken to address them.

3.3   Activities to optimize the safety and safe use of EHRs include clinician engagement.

SAFEWARE: SAFETY-CRITICAL COMPUTING AND HEALTHCARE INFORMATION TECHNOLOGY

Safeware is a comprehensive approach to ensuring the performance of safety-critical computing systems by attending to safety in the design, operation, and maintenance of hardware and software systems (Wears and Leveson 2017). Safeware focuses on hazard analysis and encompasses the entire sociotechnical system over the life cycle of the technology. The following is a summary of the Safeware Guiding Principles developed by Robert Wears and Nancy Leveson and a description of the system safety practices needed to improve the performance of safety-critical computing systems:

- *Safety is a system problem.* Computers are not an inherently dangerous technology, but they can become unsafe when used in an environment in which mishaps and unacceptable losses can occur. Therefore, safety starts at the system level, not at the component or software level.
- *Safety and reliability are sometimes conflicting goals.* Reliable software—that is, software whose performance is invariant—is not necessarily safe, and safe software does not have to be reliable. In some cases, increasing reliability may actually decrease safety—for example, a computer continues to do something even though that behavior is unsafe in the current environment. "Most accidents are caused not by the computer stopping, but by it operating but doing something unsafe."
- *Safety must be built into a system from the beginning.* Once the design of the system has been completed, it is much more difficult to correct a safety flaw.
- *Accident and loss prevention requires a top-down approach.* This approach deals with systems as a whole, not just components of the system.

- *Accidents are not caused by component failures alone.* Accidents are more likely to result from dysfunctional and unsafe interactions among normally operating components.
- *Accidents can be prevented using hazard analysis.* Hazard analysis can be used to eliminate or control hazards. It is a continuous, iterative process applied throughout the development and use of safety-critical processes, computing systems, and other technologies. Identified hazards are eliminated during the design phase or their occurrence is prevented or minimized through safeguards and controls.
- *System safety should be considered at every stage.* System safety needs to be considered during program planning, concept development, system design, system implementation, configuration control, and operations.
- *Safety case analysis is a crucial step.* A formal analysis of all safety-critical systems should be conducted.

> Health care, our most information-intensive industry, is plagued by demonstrably spotty quality, millions of errors, and backbreaking costs. We will never make fundamental improvements in our system without the thoughtful use of technology. Even today, despite the problems, the evidence shows that care is better and safer with computers than without them.
>
> —Dr. Robert Wachter (2015c)

CONCLUSION

The safe care practices described in this chapter can improve patient safety through the effective use of technology. Whether you embrace new technology for its potential to improve the safety and effectiveness of patient care or you eschew technology for more old-fashioned methods, the days of rolling up a sheaf of paper as a chest-scope are—fortunately—in the past. While some clinicians might like to go back to the "good old days" of pen and paper record keeping, wiser heads will prevail and insist that the end users of the next "big thing" in health IT be fully engaged from the design and testing phases to implementation and ongoing monitoring of IT's ability to deliver on its promise.

REFERENCES

Aggarwal, R., O. T. Mytton, F. Greaves, and C. Vincent. 2010. "Technology as Applied to Patient Safety: An Overview." *Quality & Safety in Health Care* 19 (Suppl. 2): 3–8.

Agostini, J. V., D. I. Baker, and S. T. Bogardus. 2001. "Prevention of Pressure Ulcers in Older Patients." In *Making Health Care Safer: A Critical Analysis of Patient Safety Practices*, 281–99. Rockville, MD: Agency for Healthcare Research and Quality.

Ataman, A. D., E. E. Vatanoglu-Lutz, and G. Yildirim. 2013. "Medicine in Stamps—Ignaz Semmelweis and Puerperal Fever." *Journal of the Turkish-German Gynecological Association* 14 (1): 35–39.

Bates, D. W., and A. A. Gawande. 2003. "Improving Safety with Information Technology." *New England Journal of Medicine* 348 (25): 2526–34.

Cohen, A. B., and R. S. Hanft. 2004. *Technology in American Health Care: Policy Directions for Effective Evaluation and Management*. Ann Arbor, MI: University of Michigan Press.

Cummings, J., T. Ratko, and K. Matuszewski. 2005. "Barcoding to Enhance Patient Safety." *Patient Safety & Quality Healthcare.* Published September 1. www.psqh.com/analysis/barcoding-and-rfid-barcoding-to-enhance-patient-safety/.

ECRI Institute. 2018. "Top 10 Health Technology Hazards for 2018." Accessed March 5, 2019. www.ecri.org/Resources/Whitepapers_and_reports/Haz_18.pdf.

Institute for Healthcare Improvement (IHI). 2018. "Relieve the Pressure and Reduce Harm." Accessed March 5, 2019. www.ihi.org/resources/Pages/ImprovementStories/RelievethePressureandReduceHarm.aspx.

Jacquet, J. M., and C. Hong. 2014. "Ultrasound-Guided Central Venous Access." *Critical Decisions in Emergency Medicine* 28 (5): 15–22.

Joint Commission. 2015. "Safe Use of Health Information Technology." *Sentinel Event Alert* 54. Published March 31. www.jointcommission.org/assets/1/18/SEA_54.pdf.

Kirman, C. N. 2018. "Pressure Injuries (Pressure Ulcers) and Wound Care Treatment and Management." Updated June 11. https://emedicine.medscape.com/article/190115-overview.

Koppel, R., S. M. Davidson, R. L. Wears, and C. A. Sinsky. 2012. "Health Care Information Technology to the Rescue." In *First, Do Less Harm: Confronting the Inconvenient Problems of Patient Safety*, edited by R. Koppel and S. Gordon, 62–89. Ithaca, NY: Cornell University Press.

Mansur, J. 2008. "Notes from the Field: When Medication-Related Technology Doesn't Work Correctly." *Joint Commission Perspectives on Patient Safety* 8 (3).

National Pressure Ulcer Advisory Panel (NPUAP). 2017. "Support Surface Standards Initiative." Accessed March 5, 2019. www.npuap.org/resources/educational-and-clinical-resources/support-surface-standards-initiative-s3i/.

National Quality Forum (NQF). 2018. "NQF Provides Guidance on Patient Safety and Health IT." Accessed March 5, 2019. www.qualityforum.org/NQF_Provides_Guidance_on_Patient_Safety_and_Health_IT.aspx.

———. 2016. *Identification and Prioritization of Health IT Patient Safety Measures.* Published February. www.qualityforum.org/Publications/2016/02/Identification_and_Prioritization_of_HIT_Patient_Safety_Measures.aspx.

Office of the National Coordinator for Health Information Technology (ONC). 2016. "Safety Assurance Factors for EHR Resilience—General Instructions for the SAFER Self-Assessment Guides." Published November. www.healthit.gov/sites/default/files/safer/guides/safer_high_priority_practices.pdf.

———. 2013. "Health Information Technology Patient Safety Action and Surveillance Plan." Published July 2. www.healthit.gov/sites/default/files/safety_plan_master.pdf.

Patient Safety Network (PSNet). 2019. "Patient Safety Primer: Computerized Provider Order Entry." Updated January. https://psnet.ahrq.gov/primers/primer/6/Computerized-Provider-Order-Entry.

Poon, E. G., C. A. Keohane, C. S. Yoon, M. Ditmore, A. Bane, O. Levtzion-Korach, T. Moniz, J. M. Rothschild, A. B. Kachalia, J. Hayes, W. W. Churchill, S. Lipsitz, A. D. Whittemore, D. W. Bates, and T. K. Gandhi. 2010. "Effect of Bar-Code Technology on the Safety of Medication Administration." *New England Journal of Medicine* 362 (18): 1698–707.

Powell-Cope, G., A. L. Nelson, and E. S. Patterson. 2008. "Patient Care Technology and Safety." In *Patient Safety and Quality: An Evidence-Based Handbook for Nurses*, edited by R. Hughes, 207–20. Rockville, MD: Agency for Healthcare Research and Quality.

Ranji, S. R., S. Rennke, and R. M. Wachter. 2013. "Computerized Provider Order Entry with Clinical Decision Support Systems: Brief Update Review." In *Making Healthcare Safer II: An Updated Critical Analysis of the Evidence for Patient Safety Practices*, 480–86. Rockville, MD: Agency for Healthcare Research and Quality.

Reston, J. 2013. "Smart Pumps and Other Protocols for Infusion Pumps." In *Making Healthcare Safer II: An Updated Critical Analysis of the Evidence for Patient Safety Practices*, 48–54. Rockville, MD: Agency for Healthcare Research and Quality.

Rothschild, J. M., and C. Keohane. 2008. "The Role of Bar Coding and Smart Pumps in Safety." Patient Safety Network Perspectives on Safety. Published September. https://psnet.ahrq.gov/perspectives/perspective/64/The-Role-of-Bar-Coding-and-Smart-Pumps-in-Safety.

Shekelle, P. G., and P. Dallas. 2013. "Use of Real-Time Ultrasound Guidance During Central Line Insertion: Brief Update Review." In *Making Healthcare Safer II: An Updated Critical Analysis of the Evidence for Patient Safety Practices*, 172–77. Rockville, MD: Agency for Healthcare Research and Quality.

Torres, A. 2012. "The Role of Barcode Technology in Patient Safety and Identification." *Health Management Technology Magazine.* Published September 18. www.hcinnovationgroup.com/home/article/13005150/the-role-of-barcode-technology-in-patient-safety-and-identification.

Wachter, R. 2015a. *The Digital Doctor: Hope, Hype, and Harm at the Dawn of Medicine's Computer Age.* New York: McGraw-Hill.

———. 2015b. "How Technology Led a Hospital to Give a Patient 38 Times His Dosage." *Wired.* Published March 30. www.wired.com/2015/03/how-technology-led-a-hospital-to-give-a-patient-38-times-his-dosage/.

———. 2015c. "Why Health Care Tech Is Still So Bad." *New York Times.* Published March 21. www.nytimes.com/2015/03/22/opinion/sunday/why-health-care-tech-is-still-so-bad.html.

Wears, R. L., and N. G. Leveson. 2017. "'Safeware': Safety-Critical Computing and Health Care Information Technology." In *Advances in Patient Safety: New Directions and Alternative Approaches*, vol. 4, edited by K. Henriksen, J. B. Battles, M. A. Keyes, and M. L. Grady, 1–10. Rockville, MD: Agency for Healthcare Research and Quality.

Wigmore, T. J., J. F. Smythe, M. B. Hacking, R. Raobaikady, and N. S. MacCallum. 2007. "Effect of the Implementation of NICE Guidelines for Ultrasound Guidance on the Complication Rates Associated with Central Venous Placement in Patients Presenting for Routine Surgery in a Tertiary Referral Centre." *British Journal of Anesthesia* 99 (5): 662–65.

Wikipedia. 2019. "Puerperal Fever Monthly Mortality Rates at Vienna Maternity Institution 1841–1849." Accessed May 8. https://en.wikipedia.org/wiki/Historical_mortality _rates_of_puerperal_fever#/media/File:Monthly_mortality_rates_1841-1849.png.

World Health Organization. 2011. *Health Technology Assessment of Medical Devices*. Accessed April 12, 2019. https://apps.who.int/iris/bitstream/handle/10665/44564 /9789241501361_eng.pdf.

PART IV

Minimizing Errors and Event Precursors

Understanding the Specific Causes of Serious Safety Events

WHY MUST HOSPITAL LEADERS UNDERSTAND THE PRECURSORS OF PATIENT HARM?

Achieving zero patient harm—the ultimate goal of a hospital or healthcare system seeking to become a high-reliability organization (HRO)—is contingent on knowing the sources of patient harm (causes, conditions, competencies, capacities, or ineffective controls) and responding effectively to that knowledge. To fix a problem, the cause must be known. The Joint Commission requires that hospital leaders understand and report to the hospital's governing board (1) all system or process failures, (2) the number and type of sentinel events, (3) whether the patients and their families were informed of the events, and (4) all actions taken to improve safety, both proactively and in response to actual safety events (Joint Commission 2017, LD-38). To "improve safety and to reduce the risk of medical errors," The Joint Commission's standards also require that hospital leaders analyze information about system or process failures and the results of proactive risk assessments and then disseminate the lessons learned from these analyses to staff.

Chapter 15 of this book, "Leading the Cultural Transformation to Harm-Free Healthcare," outlines seven critical questions (called the High-Reliability Commitment Index) that healthcare leaders can use to assess whether their organization is on the path to highly reliable, harm-free healthcare. The third of those questions is relevant here: "Do senior leaders know exactly the type and frequency of preventable harm that is occurring in the hospital each day and the specific human and systems-related causes of that harm?" Board members, senior leaders, and hospital staff should be able to cite data on serious patient safety events, close calls, and their precursors. Safety is job number one. Keeping patients safe depends on (1) knowing where the hospital's *error traps* and *error-likely situations* are, (2) knowing what efforts are being undertaken to address *error modes* and to mitigate unsafe acts and behaviors, and (3) knowing what the hospital is doing to strengthen its systems, structures, and controls to reduce *latent organizational weaknesses* that could provoke errors and cause harm.

The three main contributors to patient harm are (1) *unsafe behaviors*, which occur when humans make errors or fail to follow established procedures; (2) *unsafe conditions*, which are often created by latent organizational weaknesses that provoke errors and create error traps; and (3) *unsafe defenses*, which result from the degradation of the safeguards, barriers, and controls that are intended to protect patients from harm. Defining how to identify, modify, and control error precursors and serious safety event precursors is the subject of this chapter; the control of human factors influencing human performance and the control of latent organizational weaknesses will be discussed in chapters 9 and 10.

THE THREE FOUNDATIONS OF ZERO PATIENT HARM

The consistent provision of safe, harm-free healthcare to hospitalized patients is built on three foundational elements:

- Safe acts and safe behaviors (error-free performance)
- Safe care conditions and a safe care environment (free of latent organizational weaknesses)
- Safe care defenses, barriers, and controls (designed to protect patients from harmful event precursors)

Safe acts and safe behaviors depend on the preparation, teamwork, and competent performance expectations described in chapters 2, 3, and 4 of this book. Safe care conditions and a safe care environment depend on the consistent application of safe care practices, organizational resilience and adaptability, and the safe use of technology discussed in chapters 5, 6, and 7. The importance of maximizing an organization's safe care defenses and barriers against harm will be discussed in chapters 11 and 12.

The failure to ensure safe behaviors, safe conditions, and safe defenses can lead to errors, organizational weaknesses, and the degradation of safeguards, often resulting in preventable patient harm. The three main contributors to patient harm are *unsafe behaviors*, *unsafe conditions*, and *unsafe defenses*.

In his book *Managing Maintenance Error*, James Reason describes the importance of acquiring knowledge and ongoing intelligence to create an *informed culture*—a prerequisite for establishing a culture of safety. According to Reason, an informed culture can be achieved only "by creating an atmosphere of trust in which people are willing to confess their errors and near misses. Only in this way can the system identify its error-provoking situations" (Reason and Hobbs 2003, 146). Collecting, analyzing, and disseminating information about close calls and the causes of patient harm can help create a *learning culture* in which both proactive and reactive analyses drive performance improvement and the increased effectiveness of safe care practices.

> We can never guarantee total immunity from bad events, but we can increase the system's intrinsic resistance by strengthening defenses and by identifying and eliminating (as far as possible) the known causal ingredients that are latent in all systems.
> —James Reason and Alan Hobbs (2003)

Hospital leaders can encourage an informed culture by sharing accurate and meaningful data about event causes, error precursors, the integrity of safety defenses (barrier effectiveness analysis), local factor assessments, organizational factor assessments, and proactive failure mode and effects analysis. These analytic tools provide the knowledge necessary to identify, target, and eliminate safety event precursors.

UNSAFE BEHAVIORS

Sometimes patient care staff try to improve the efficiency of their work by taking shortcuts or working around an established policy or procedure. Sometimes staff engage in risky behaviors that violate error-prevention performance expectations. And sometimes staff experience pressure to hurry and "get the job done" despite the risk of patient harm. In these cases, staff are not intentionally trying to injure their patients, but nonetheless, they are exhibiting unsafe behaviors. Although unsafe behaviors often do not contribute to or cause a serious safety event, they represent "a higher probability, or potential, of a bad outcome" (DOE 2009, 2-6).

Examples of unsafe behaviors include following procedures "cookbook style" without thinking about error traps, anomalies, or unique patient factors; having one person perform actions in a safety-critical process without peer checking; failing to follow a procedure when required to do so; attempting to reduce the number of trips necessary to perform tasks; attempting to lift too much weight; signing off on several steps of a procedure before they are actually completed; trying to complete safety-critical tasks while talking on the phone or having a casual conversation; and hurrying through an activity because of workload pressures (DOE 2009, 2-7). "People do not err intentionally. Error is a human action that unintentionally departs from an expected behavior. Error is behavior without malice [and] is provoked by a mismatch between human limitations and environmental conditions at the job site" (DOE 2009, 2-8).

Error Modes

Reason identifies three types of error: (1) an action does not go as planned because of inattention, a procedural *slip* in the completion of a task, or a *lapse of memory*; (2) an action is inadequate because of a *mistake* that occurred when a staff member was faced with a challenging problem; and (3) an action deviates from safe care practices because of a *violation* of the rules (Reason and Hobbs 2003, 40). Procedural slips, lapses of memory, mistakes, and rule violations are characteristics of human performance that threaten the consistent delivery of safe patient care. Understanding the nature and origin of these event precursors should drive an organization's human performance improvement and training efforts.

Minimizing errors, mistakes, and latent organizational weaknesses is one of the Five Disciplines of Performance Excellence that drive high-reliability, high-performing organizations. Slips, lapses of memory, mistakes, and rule violations occur as people are doing their work. People perform their work through one of three approaches: *skill-based performance*, *rule-based performance*, or *knowledge-based performance* (DOE 2009, 2-21–2-27).

Skill-Based Performance

Skill-based performance involves highly practiced, largely physical actions that take place in familiar situations and require little conscious monitoring—in other words, it involves actions that are executed from memory with little conscious thought. In the skill-based mode of performance, individuals perform tasks effectively using preprogrammed behavior sequences.

The error mode for skill-based performance is *inattention*. Skill-based errors usually result from errors in the execution of a task, such as a procedural slip, a lapse of memory, a lapse in concentration, or a lack of attention to the task or the environment. Skill-based errors may also occur when an individual unintentionally omits a step in a process or does not recognize a change in the task requirements, patient conditions, or facility conditions. Slips occur when a physical action fails to achieve its immediate objective. Slips can be caused by changes in the timing or duration of an action or task and may involve performing the wrong action on the correct patient or performing the correct action on the wrong patient. Moreover, a slip may be caused by a change in the sequence of the procedure involving reversal, repetition, or intrusion.

To control skill-based performance errors, "Workers performing skill-based work need adequate tools to minimize action slips, and they need to be free from interruptions and distractions that aggravate concentration, divide their attention, and contribute to lapses in memory that cause error. Workers may benefit from simple job aids and reminders" (DOE 2009, 2-27).

Rule-Based Performance

Prompted by a change in patient conditions or the care environment, individuals may switch from skill-based performance to rule-based performance in their thinking and actions when their preprogrammed behaviors no longer fit the current demands on their knowledge, skills, and abilities. "The work situation has changed such that the previous activity (skill) no longer applies" (DOE 2009, 2-23). Individuals will consider the policies and procedures that apply to the new circumstances and tap into memorized rules or written rules to guide their actions and safe behaviors.

Sometimes individuals may have difficulty fully understanding or detecting the performance requirements of or best response to a particular situation or condition. Rule-based performance requires individuals to interpret the patient care situation using "if/then" logic, which is vulnerable to the error mode of *misinterpretation*. Common rule-based errors involve a clear deviation from an approved procedure, the application of the wrong response to a patient care situation, or the application of the correct procedure to the wrong situation.

To control rule-based performance errors, "Workers need accurate, complete, and unambiguous procedures and guides for reference when doing rule-based work. They may also need access to a subject matter expert when making choices about the rules to select and for correct application of those rules" (DOE 2009, 2-27).

Knowledge-Based Performance

Knowledge-based performance is activated when individuals are uncertain about what action to take in an unfamiliar situation. In these situations, no skill or rule is recognizable, so individuals must rely on their knowledge, perceptions of the present circumstances, and experience with similar situations or circumstances. "Not all hazards, dangers, and possible scenarios can be anticipated in order to develop appropriate procedures. There are some situations in which no procedure guidance exists and no skill applies" (DOE 2009, 2-25).

A mental model is a structured understanding in the mind about how something works. Mental models can help individuals detect skill-based slips and lapses and enhance their ability to distinguish between the desired and undesired state of a system. "Often, decisions are made with limited information and faulty assumptions" (DOE 2009, 2-26). Therefore, the prevalent error mode for knowledge-based performance is having an *inaccurate mental model* of a situation or process.

Causes of knowledge-based performance errors include (1) inadequate understanding or background knowledge of challenging situations, (2) inadequate technical knowledge, (3) poor problem-solving skills, (4) team errors, or (5) ineffective communication among team members that leads to poor decision-making. Simulation training that requires staff to respond to unexpected variations and events during safety-critical processes or procedures can help patient care teams prepare for situations in which knowledge-based performance is required. Knowledge-based errors can be controlled by collaborative team involvement in problem-solving and decision-making in challenging situations.

Violations

"A violation involves the *deliberate* deviation or departure from an expected behavior, policy, or procedure. Such actions may be either acts of omission (not doing something that should be done) or commission (doing something wrong)" (DOE 2009, 2-10). Violations are dangerous and unsafe behaviors on the part of an individual who knowingly deviates from standard procedures, cuts corners, or willfully fails to apply "good rules." Violations are committed intentionally and performed outside the norms of safe behavior (Reason and Hobbs 2003, 49–54). Individuals may be motivated to violate safe care practices because of local error-provoking factors or error-producing conditions in the immediate care environment. Local factors include (1) time pressure, (2) fatigue, (3) inexperience, (4) low points in circadian rhythm, (5) poor communication, (6) unworkable procedures, (7) documentation requirements, (8) inadequate equipment, (9) shift handoffs, (10) task frequency and volume, (11) design deficiencies, and (12) team culture and beliefs (Reason and Hobbs 2003, 63).

Understanding the motivations and intentions behind violations of safe care practices can help shape the best organization response—for example, culpable acts require disciplinary action; violations of flawed rules or procedures require lean Six Sigma process redesign; violations committed by otherwise good employees who lack the requisite knowledge or skills require education, skill development, and training; and violations resulting from local error-provoking factors require human factors reengineering of the work environment.

Understanding Unsafe Behaviors

An *active error* is an action that unintentionally departs from an expected behavior and has an immediate, observable, and undesirable impact on patient care. A *violation*, on the other hand, is a deliberate and intentional act that is committed to evade an established policy or procedure. The majority of actions leading to a safety event are active errors, whose cause must be a focus of the hospital's analytic and event-prevention efforts.

TWIN analysis provides hospitals with a framework to identify the human performance error precursors that are known to cause unsafe behaviors and active errors. The analysis should be performed in daily pre-job briefings, safety huddles, and preparations for high-risk procedures to minimize the impact of error before work begins. TWIN analysis focuses on Task demands, Work environment, Individual capabilities, and the Natural tendencies of humans (B&W Pantex 2008, 102–4):

- *Task demands*—interpretation requirements, high workload, taxing memory requirements, simultaneous multiple tasks, unexpected conditions, time pressure, repetitive actions, monotony, unclear goals, unclear roles and responsibilities, lack of standards, unclear standards, confusing procedures, vague guidance, delays, idle time
- *Work environment*—confusing controls, overconfidence, distractions, interruptions, unexpected equipment conditions, emphasis on production rather than safety, unavailability of equipment or tools, changes or departures from routine processes or procedures, personality conflicts, work-arounds, hidden systems responses, adverse environmental conditions (e.g., heat or cold), poor access to equipment, shift work schedule
- *Individual capabilities*—scheduling pressure to get the work done, first time doing a task, intentional rule breaking, incorrect problem-solving, fatigue, illness, lack of experience with a task, inaccurate mental model of a task, misunderstood communication, no communication, personal issues (e.g., medical, financial, emotional)
- *Natural tendencies of humans*—bad assumptions, inaccurate mind-set, complacency, disorientation or confusion during a task, boring task, dislike of or unfamiliarity with coworkers, on-the-job stress, habits caused by wrong actions left unchecked for long time, inaccurate perceptions of risk or hazard, focus on task rather than the big picture, limited short-term memory, uncertainty about job requirements

UNSAFE CONDITIONS

Darlene, a registered nurse, arrives for her 12-hour shift on 3 North at Safe Care Hospital on a typical morning at 6:30 a.m. She is immediately thrust into the chaos of a busy medical-surgical unit, which requires every ounce of her knowledge, skills, and abilities to lovingly and competently care for the wide variety of patients in her care. Often performing her duties without the benefit of a patient care team to support her, Darlene interacts with physicians, patients, families, other caregivers, nutritionists, technologists, and various biomedical equipment, and she is required to document everything she does in the patient's electronic health record.

Nurses complete patient assessments, conduct patient rounds, and prepare patient reports at shift change. Administering high-risk medications; inserting and monitoring intravenous solutions; monitoring wound care and changing dressings; attending to skin care, special orders, and patient requests for ambulation; and responding to hundreds of monitor alerts, alarms, and patient call light requests are just some of the responsibilities of a hospital-based nurse.

Often, workplace and environmental conditions make the job even tougher: equipment malfunctions; delays in critical test results; poor communications between physicians and nurses; excessive noise, distractions, and interruptions during safety-critical processes. Nurses are often expected to communicate with physicians, pharmacy staff, and other members of the care team by phone or electronically while simultaneously performing other patient care duties. All the while, they contend with antiquated policies and procedures; inadequate staffing, inadequate training, and unsafe practices, policies, and procedures. The conditions under which hospital-based nurses and other members of the patient care team must function every day create a multitude of error traps and error-provoking situations that constantly threaten the delivery of safe care.

Latent Errors

Latent errors are actions or decisions that create organizational weaknesses that go unnoticed until they are detected as a result of a safety event or a proactive hazard assessment. "Latent conditions include actions, directives, and decisions that either create the preconditions for error or fail to prevent, catch, or mitigate the effects of error" (DOE 2009, 2-9). These latent conditions include poorly designed care processes or procedures, automation that is difficult to use or creates safety risks, inadequate staff training, and poorly maintained tools and equipment. System defenses and barriers are designed to prevent a serious safety event by blocking the negative effects of an active human error. Latent conditions can create gaps or weaknesses in these defenses that may allow a threat—an active error—to create a hazard that has the potential to harm a patient.

B&W Pantex is an HRO that contracts with the US Department of Energy "to maintain the safety and security of the nation's nuclear weapons stockpile"

(DNFSB 2019). B&W Pantex's *High Reliability Operations Handbook* describes the organization's systems and structures "as . . . the most important aspect of an HRO. The system used by an HRO must be designed, deployed, and used in a manner that supports high reliability operations" (B&W Pantex 2008, 63). System design influences the work environment and working conditions through operating procedures, communication methods, engineering, process design, maintenance, document control, and safety procedures and culture. Latent conditions arise from system or organizational weaknesses. They are "hidden deficiencies in management control processes or values that create workplace conditions that can provoke errors and degrade the integrity of defenses" (B&W Pantex 2008, 91).

Senior leaders, managers, and supervisors must be diligent in their ongoing assessment of error-prone work environments to identify and mitigate latent organizational weaknesses. Identifying error-likely situations or error traps, error precursors, and unsafe conditions before a patient is harmed is an essential component of a hospital's commitment to the goal of zero patient harm. The Department of Energy's (2009, 1-11) *Human Performance Improvement Handbook* notes the following:

> A traditional belief is that human performance is a worker-focused phenomenon. This belief promotes the notion that failures are introduced to the system only through the inherent unreliability of people. . . . However, experience indicates that weaknesses in organizational processes and cultural values are involved in the majority of facility events. Accidents result from a combination of factors, many of which are beyond the control of the worker.

Understanding Unsafe Conditions

Improving working conditions and making the care environment safe requires the accurate and timely identification and mitigation of latent organizational weaknesses and error-provoking factors. Hospitals can use three assessment tools to proactively identify and prioritize the factors in the workplace and in the care environment that may contribute to active errors and serious safety events. These assessments are performed to head off potential harm from system or organizational weaknesses and to assess the organization's resistance to operational hazards and event-producing factors (Reason and Hobbs 2003, 138).

A *local factors assessment* is a subjective assessment that is routinely completed by frontline staff members who are chosen randomly. Findings are submitted anonymously. Using a 10-point scale, assessors rate the safety of the workplace based on local factors such as morale; staff knowledge, skills, and abilities; equipment functioning and support; fatigue; time and productivity pressures; shift differences; paperwork and documentation demands; and constancy of interruptions.

An *organizational factors assessment* is a broader assessment that is standardized and completed by management or safety improvement staff. This type of assessment is consistent across departments, thereby providing a uniform analysis of latent organizational weaknesses that might be causing active errors to penetrate hospital defenses. An organizational factors assessment looks at systems and structures, people management, availability of needed tools and equipment, staff training, selection and placement of staff, productivity pressures, operational pressures, shift differences, staff scheduling, policies and procedures, and maintenance issues (Reason and Hobbs 2003, 139–41). Improvements in engineered systems and supporting structures, equipment functionality, and workplace conditions all help enhance human performance and reduce human error. "Human error is more likely when tools and equipment, procedures, work processes, or technical support are inadequate" (DOE 2009, 2-34).

Error precursor analysis is designed to identify error precursors at the time of or before the occurrence of a serious safety event. Error precursors are unfavorable factors or conditions present in the patient care environment that increase the chances of error during specific care processes or procedures. An error precursor creates an error-likely situation that often arises when the demands of a task exceed the capabilities of an individual or care team. Accident or safety event precursors are defined by the National Academy of Sciences as the conditions, events, and sequences that precede and lead to accidents. Precursors are the "building blocks" of accidents or safety events, and they can include both internal and external factors. "Recognizing signals before an accident clearly offers the potential of improving safety, and many organizations have attempted to develop programs to identify and benefit from accident precursors. Precursor reporting systems are typically used for technologies in which unforeseen problems can have serious consequences" (National Academy of Engineering 2004, 6–8). Precursor programs help improve organizational awareness of safety threats and provide information to staff that mitigates complacency and improves understanding of latent organizational weaknesses that could create a hazard for patients. Error precursor analysis relies on staff reports of near misses, close calls, and good catches to understand both error precursors and event precursors.

UNSAFE DEFENSES

Safe care defenses, barriers, and controls make up the protective shell that surrounds patients, protecting them from harm caused by human error or latent organizational

LESSONS FROM HIGH-RELIABILITY ORGANIZATIONS

Eliminating Hazards by Recognizing Common Accident Precursors

Hoar Construction, a national construction company that builds commercial office buildings, retail stores, and hospitals around the country, is committed to protecting the safety of its workforce and the communities it builds in. Hoar focuses on working smarter and eliminating hazards in the workplace.

The company provides lessons learned and safety advisories to workers through its "Safety Moment" smartphone app. Workers are instructed to stop their work if they observe one of five red flags—that is, the five most common precursors of an accident. Through daily safety meetings and ongoing communications with workers, the company "eliminate[s] hazards by planning ahead and avoiding these common precursors that cause accidents" (Hoar Construction 2019).

1. *Time pressures.* Being in a hurry is the most common precursor of a safety incident. Workers hurry when things do not go according to plan or when resources are lacking. A shortage of time or trained personnel can also cause staff to hurry.

2. *Personnel changes.* A reduction in the number of personnel, shift changes, new personnel, or changes in management can be event precursors. Anticipating and managing personnel changes will help avoid the negative effects of personnel changes on the people doing the work.

3. *Breakdown in communications.* A hazard may be caused by a change in the work environment or the job site when critical information is not passed on or communicated effectively.

4. *Deviation from the plan.* Planning is an important process to find ways to work faster, smarter, and safer. The plan needs to be communicated to and understood by the entire team. When team members deviate from the plan, they put everyone at risk of an accident.

5. *Improper use or lack of equipment.* Performing a task without the proper tools and equipment is a red flag. New or inexperienced workers must be properly trained on the use of the equipment to avoid creating a work hazard.

weaknesses. John S. Carroll (2004, 127), a professor of organization studies at the Massachusetts Institute of Technology, states the following about high-hazard industries:

> High-hazard industries, such as nuclear power and aviation, that would put many people at risk in the event of a single accident are particularly sensitive to precursors and consider them opportunities to avoid accidents. Accidents happen when precursors occur in combination and/ or when system defenses fail to mitigate a situation. Every precursor event is, therefore, both a test of the adequacy of system defenses and an opportunity to develop and apply knowledge to avoid accidents.

When a member of the patient care team makes a mistake, has a lapse of memory, or experiences a slip in performance because of inattention, a hospital's defenses and barriers help protect the patient from harm. Those same defenses and barriers also protect the patient against latent organizational weaknesses such as unsafe policies, poor training, or poorly maintained equipment. (Defenses and barriers are discussed in more detail in part V of this book, "Maximizing Defenses and Barriers: The 'Defensive Strategy.'")

Defenses and barriers serve two important functions: prevention and mitigation. Prevention barriers serve to prevent a human error, equipment failure, or other latent weakness from creating a hazard and causing harm to the patient. Dose error controls on smart pumps are an example of a prevention barrier in healthcare. Ultrasound-guided central-line insertion is another example. Mitigation barriers are used to reduce, contain, or neutralize a hazard once it has occurred, thereby eliminating or minimizing the negative consequences for the patient. Radio-frequency identification and count controls to avoid the unintended retention of surgical items after surgery are examples of mitigating barriers. Administering a counteracting drug in response to a dramatic and life-threatening drop in a patient's blood pressure and sending a rapid response team to address a sudden deterioration in the patient's condition are other examples of mitigation barriers.

Defenses-in-Depth

Three types of defenses or barriers, when applied in layers, provide the desired *defenses-in-depth* found among HROs that experience few catastrophic events despite operating in a high-risk environment (B&W Pantex 2008, 92–94; DOE 2009, 3-5–3-10):

1.   *Engineered defenses* or design controls are embedded in hardware, software, and equipment in the physical environment to affect people's

behavior, choices, and attitudes. Engineered defenses can be active or passive defenses. An example of an active engineered control or defense is a smart pump that performs specific safety-related functions such as "air-in-line" detection, free-flow protection, and battery backup and includes a dose error reduction system.

2. *Administrative defenses* are written policies, procedures, programs, and plans that instruct people what to do, when to do it, where it is to be done, and how well to do it. Administrative defenses provide training, work plans, and procedural guidance to help staff avoid hazards in the work environment. An example of an administrative defense is the Universal Protocol for Preventing Wrong Site, Wrong Person, and Wrong Procedure Surgery. Marking the surgical site, conducting a pre-procedure confirmation of the patient's identity and the surgical procedure to be performed, and taking a "time out" before starting the procedure are administrative defenses designed to protect patients from injury or death during surgery.

3. *Human defenses* are the values, beliefs, and attitudes that drive individuals' behavior in the workplace and affect the choices they make regarding safety and error prevention. Safe defensive attitudes include (1) uneasiness toward human fallibility, (2) self-awareness of the capacity for error, (3) wariness of conditions that are conducive to error, (4) rigorous application of human performance improvement tools, (5) questioning attitude, (6) vigilant situational awareness of working conditions to detect error-likely situations and unsafe or hazardous working conditions, (7) refusal to proceed in the face of uncertainty, (8) fact-based decision-making, (9) conservative approach to patient care and safety, (10) decision-making that favors safety over production, and (11) avoidance of unsafe attitudes and practices that are detrimental to high reliability.

Understanding Unsafe Defenses

Serious safety events occur in hospitals because defenses, barriers, or controls fail. Patient-protective defenses and barriers must be developed and installed for every process or procedure that poses a significant risk to the patient. Hospitals should routinely test the effectiveness of their defenses by conducting a barrier effectiveness analysis.

Defenses fail to protect patients from harm for one of four reasons: (1) the barrier was in place but was only partially effective (penetrated by the untoward effects of an error), (2) the barrier was in place but was not used, (3) the barrier was circumvented, or (4) no barrier was in place (even though it was required). Barrier effectiveness analysis can help hospitals determine what caused defenses or barriers to fail. This type of analysis also assesses the four characteristics of defenses and barriers:

- *Effectiveness*—Assess whether the defense or barrier met its intended purpose.
- *Availability*—Assess whether the defense or barrier will function when needed.
- *Assessment*—Assess the ease of determining the effectiveness of the defense or barrier.
- *Interpretation*—Assess the extent of human interpretation needed for the defense or barrier to function properly.

Managing defenses and barriers and the use of barrier effectiveness analysis are discussed more fully in chapter 11, "Strengthening Defenses to Prevent Harm."

CONCLUSION

Patient harm is caused by unsafe behaviors, unsafe conditions, and unsafe defenses, barriers, and controls. This chapter describes assessment tools for each of these safety threats. Proactively analyzing the risks that are inherent in patient care processes—especially high-risk processes and procedures—is facilitated by tools such as TWIN analysis, barrier effectiveness analysis, and failure mode and effects analysis.

The first step in prioritizing the high-risk processes to improve is to use a Pareto prioritization process. The safety risks that are identified and prioritized through the Pareto process are then assigned a risk priority number through failure mode and effects analysis, which assesses the severity of impact, frequency of occurrence, and probability of detecting the failure mode of each high-risk process.

CHAPTER 8 SAFE CARE PRACTICES

1. Understand the nature and origin of event precursors and use that knowledge to drive the organization's human performance improvement and training efforts. Procedural slips, lapses of memory, mistakes, and rule violations are characteristics of human performance that threaten the consistent delivery of safe patient care.

2. Identify the human performance error precursors that are known to cause unsafe behaviors and active errors using TWIN analysis. TWIN analysis focuses on Task demands, Work environment, Individual capabilities, and the Natural tendencies of humans.

3. Ensure that senior leaders, managers, and supervisors are diligent in their ongoing assessment of error-prone work environments to identify and mitigate latent organizational weaknesses.

4. Identify and prioritize the factors in the workplace and in the care environment that may contribute to active errors and serious safety events using three assessment tools: local factors assessment, organizational factors assessment, and error precursor analysis.

5. Test the effectiveness of process and procedural defenses by conducting a barrier effectiveness analysis.

REFERENCES

B&W Pantex. 2008. *High Reliability Operations: A Practical Guide to Avoid the System Accident.* Amarillo, TX: Babcock and Wilcox Technical Services.

Carroll, J. 2004. "Knowledge Management in High-Hazard Industries." In *Accident Precursor Analysis and Management: Reducing Technological Risk Through Diligence*, edited by J. Phimister, V. Bier, and H. Kunreuther, 127–34. Washington, DC: National Academies Press.

Defense Nuclear Facilities Safety Board (DNFSB). 2019. "About Pantex." Accessed April 12. www.dnfsb.gov/doe-sites/pantex.

Hoar Construction. 2019. "Five Common Precursors to an Accident." Accessed March 8. www.hoar.com/five-common-precursors-to-an-accident/.

Joint Commission. 2017. *2017 Hospital Accreditation Standards*. Oakbrook Terrace, IL: Joint Commission Resources.

National Academy of Engineering. 2004. *Accident Precursor Analysis and Management: Reducing Technological Risk Through Diligence*. Washington, DC: National Academies Press.

Reason, J., and A. Hobbs. 2003. *Managing Maintenance Error: A Practical Guide*. Burlington, VT: Ashgate Publishing.

US Department of Energy (DOE). 2009. *Human Performance Improvement Handbook*, vol. 1, *Concepts and Principles*. Published June. www.standards.doe.gov/standards -documents/1000/1028-BHdbk-2009-v1.

Influencing Human Performance
and System Performance

WHY WILL INFLUENCING HUMAN PERFORMANCE AND SYSTEM PERFORMANCE PREVENT PATIENT HARM?

Hospitals and healthcare systems must first fully understand the causes of patient harm to positively influence the outcome of patient care. By minimizing, eliminating, or controlling the causes of harm, hospitals and healthcare systems can achieve the goal of zero preventable patient harm. As described in chapter 8, the three main contributors to patient harm are unsafe behaviors, unsafe conditions, and unsafe defenses.

The concept of the "Harm-Free Threes" (exhibit 9.1) provides a framework for thinking about how to minimize errors and error-provoking situations, strengthen defenses and barriers, and eliminate the hazards that lead to patient harm. The first triad outlines the three predictors of harm-free healthcare. These are the main factors that create opportunities for unsafe behaviors, unsafe conditions, and unsafe defenses.

The first predictor is *human performance*, which includes individual and team competence, behavior, attitudes, and beliefs, and individuals' fitness for duty.

The second predictor is *system performance*, which includes information technology support for the care process and caregivers, organizational policies and procedures, resource availability, staffing levels, and organizational culture, all of which influence the local conditions in which care is provided. To optimize both human performance and system performance, hospital leaders should employ human factors engineering methods, which examine the interactions and relationships between humans and systems. Influencing human factors is discussed in chapter 10.

The third predictor is *defense and controls performance*. This involves analysis and strengthening of the defenses, barriers, and controls that are designed to protect patients from the inevitable errors and latent organizational weaknesses that result from human performance or system performance safety failures. Strengthening defenses is discussed in chapter 11.

The Harm-Free Threes framework further defines the elements of unsafe behaviors, unsafe conditions, and unsafe defenses that should be analyzed, managed, and controlled to eliminate all preventable patient harm. Finally, system performance and its contributions to patient harm can be assessed at three levels: the microsystem, or the "sharp" end of the patient care experience; the mesosystem, which comprises the relationships among the systems supporting the patient care experience; and the macrosystem, or the "blunt" end of the patient care experience, which encompasses organizational support, resources, policy, and leadership guidance, and the external

---

Exhibit 9.1: The Harm-Free Threes

Three Predictors of Harm-Free Healthcare

- Human performance (individual and team competence)
- System performance (at the sharp end, among systems, or at the blunt end)
- Defense and controls performance

Three Causes of Patient Harm

- Unsafe behaviors
- Unsafe conditions
- Unsafe defenses

Three Causes of Unsafe Behaviors

- Skill-based errors (procedural slips, lapses of attention or memory, mistakes)
- Rule-based errors (deviating from the proper procedure, applying the wrong response)
- Knowledge-based errors (poor information, unfamiliar situation, wrong mental model)

Three Causes of Unsafe Conditions

- Physical ergonomics (lighting, noise, space limitations, distractions)
- Cognitive ergonomics (people and their interactions with system components, memory, perception, workload, attention)
- Organizational ergonomics (procedural directives, communication and information, job design, teamwork, sociotechnical systems issues)

(continued)

healthcare system that provides regulatory rules and requirements, measurement mandates, and payment parameters.

THREE ANALYTIC APPROACHES TO HARM PREVENTION

Hospitals and healthcare systems should use all three analytic approaches to preventing patient harm: retrospective, prospective, and concurrent analysis.

Retrospective analysis involves looking back to determine the proximate and root causes of serious safety events. This can be done through root cause analysis but also should include barrier effectiveness analysis to assess deficiencies in defenses and barriers.

Prospective analysis involves looking forward to assess the severity and frequency of high-risk processes of care. Prospective analysis helps hospitals and healthcare systems determine their failure modes and the hazards that might result from uncontrolled high-risk processes. This type of analysis is usually performed through the routine conduct of failure mode and effects analysis.

Concurrent analysis occurs during the actual provision of care. Patient safety coaches and patient care team members apply high-reliability safe care practices to "catch and correct" human errors and latent organizational weaknesses before patient harm can occur.

INFLUENCING HUMAN PERFORMANCE

Chapters 2, 3, and 4 of this book described the first of the Five Disciplines of Performance Excellence: preparing to deliver safe care. This first discipline focuses on enhancing individual competence and performance, training individuals to effectively participate on teams, and preparing to deliver safe care through deliberate practice and simulation. Chapter 8 focused on understanding the specific causes of serious safety events and provided a detailed discussion of unsafe behaviors and their causes: skill-based performance errors, rule-based performance errors, and knowledge-based performance errors. Chapter 8 also presented TWIN analysis, which provides a framework for assessing error precursors and unfavorable conditions that can interfere with human performance (DOE 2009, 2-31):

- *Task demands*—the specific mental, physical, and team requirements to perform a task, which may exceed individual capabilities or challenge human limitations, such as excessive workload, time pressures, unclear roles and responsibilities, repetitive actions, concurrent task requirements, and unclear performance or task standards.
- *Work environment*—the influences of the workplace on the care process, including organizational and cultural conditions, such as distractions, interruptions, unexpected equipment problems, changes or departure from routine procedure, team attitudes or disregard for hazards, and personality conflicts.
- *Individual capabilities*—the unique mental, physical, and emotional characteristics of the individual that fail to meet the demands of a specific task, such as unfamiliarity with the task, unsafe attitude, lack of knowledge, unpracticed skills, inexperience, illness and presenteeism, fatigue, imprecise communication habits, and poor problem-solving skills.
- *Natural human tendencies*—the generic human traits, dispositions, and limitations that may incline an individual to make an error or commit an unsafe act, such as the limits of short-term memory, stress, habit patterns, complacency, overconfidence, inaccurate risk perception, and assumptions that are not fact based.

Understanding these human performance characteristics and providing the training, opportunity for practice and development, resources, and environmental conditions necessary for patient care team members to do their best work is vital. We must learn to avoid mistakes—as Dr. Robert Wachter (2012, 305) has said, "We now recognize that learning from mistakes is fundamentally unethical." Wachter points to a growing concern that practicing skills—particularly surgical skills—on patients is unethical. For that reason, healthcare is increasingly using simulation to develop practitioners' skills and reduce the incidence of error and harm.

Wachter (2012, 273) also describes the problem of permissiveness and its contribution to enabling human error: "It can be argued that our permissiveness toward healthcare rule violators is responsible for the high rate of violations of some very important rules, such as hand hygiene." A hospital's governing board, senior leaders, medical staff, and other care providers must share a conviction that safe care practices and safe behaviors must be consistently applied and that at-risk behaviors must be respectfully challenged.

Patient safety coaches can serve as "mindfulness monitors," constantly reinforcing safe behaviors and providing guidance and feedback in response to unsafe behaviors. Safe practices to prevent routine slips and lapses of memory include building in redundancies and cross-checks using checklists, read-back protocols, and other safety steps such as signing the surgery site before an operation and asking patients to affirm their names before administering medication. Decreasing or eliminating distractions and interruptions can also improve the safety of medication administration.

The adoption of safety practices that have been successful in other industries is now saving lives in healthcare. For example, crew resource management, a practice used in the aviation industry, is being employed to improve teamwork and communications among patient care teams; simulation training, another aviation innovation, is helping improve clinicians' motor and cognitive skills; management by walking around is now applied as leadership "walk rounds," in which senior leaders visit daily with frontline clinical staff to assess and respond to safety concerns; bar coding, which is required by the US Food and Drug Administration, is now helping reduce errors in medication administration; and work hour limitations, long used for pilots, now help decrease fatigue among healthcare providers (Wachter 2012, xv, 27).

James Reason states that "put very simply, there are two ways people can go wrong. They can either do something they should not have done, or fail to do something they should have done. The former are errors of commission, the latter are errors of omission" (Reason and Hobbs 2003, 6). According to Reason, human errors are both the cause of safety events and

> Most errors are made by good but fallible people working in dysfunctional systems. . . . The fact that we are now routinely seeking insights from aviation, manufacturing, education, and other industries and embracing paradigms from engineering, sociology, psychology, and management, may prove to be the most enduring benefit of the patient safety movement.
> —Dr. Robert Wachter (2012)

the consequence of local circumstances and conditions, the task being performed, the tools and equipment used, and the workplace. "Human error is often treated as a uniform collection of unwanted acts. In reality, errors fall into quite distinct types that require different kinds of remedial measures" (Reason and Hobbs 2003, 19). System safety and human factors expert Jens Rasmussen outlines three levels of human performance—skill-based performance, rule-based performance, and knowledge-based performance—and their associated errors.

Skill-based performance involves highly practiced actions that are performed in familiar situations, usually from memory. In this performance mode, staff can experience a lapse of memory, omit a step in a process or procedure, or lose concentration, which may lead to an error. Solutions to skill-based errors include creating work zones for safety-critical processes to minimize distractions and interruptions, implementing simple job aids and reminders to counter slips, and applying safe care practices such as STAR (Stop, Think, Act, and Review), place keeping, pre-job briefings, and checklists to avoid both errors of commission and errors of omission.

Rule-based performance is stimulated by a change in the patient's condition or the patient care environment. In this situation, preprogrammed behaviors no longer fit the situation. Errors in this performance mode usually result from misinterpretation of the patient care situation. Staff may deviate from approved procedures, apply the wrong response to the patient care situation, or apply the correct response to the wrong situation.

To address rule-based performance errors, procedures and guidelines need to be current, accurate, unambiguous, and clear. Staff should be knowledgeable about the current procedure for many different situations and trained to effectively respond to changing and unexpected circumstances. An expert should always be available for consultation if the demands of the situation exceed the knowledge, skills, and abilities of the individual patient care team member. Apply safe care practices such as SAFER (Summarize the critical steps in a care process, Anticipate possible error-likely situations, Foresee the consequences of potential errors, Evaluate the defenses, and Review all previous experience that will help improve the safety of the process or procedure to be performed), red flags, or check-backs or read-backs.

Knowledge-based performance is activated when caregivers realize that they are uncertain about what action to take in an unfamiliar patient care situation. Errors are made when staff have limited information and act under faulty assumptions. Staff may develop an inaccurate mental model of the situation that leads to an error. Simulation training that requires staff to respond to unexpected variations and known challenges that might occur during the performance of safety-critical processes or procedures can help prepare them for situations when knowledge-based performance is required. Preparation, practice, and simulation of challenging situations will help develop staff's problem-solving skills, technical knowledge, and communication with team members.

INFLUENCING SYSTEM PERFORMANCE

Historically, analysis of the causes of serious safety events in healthcare has focused on active errors resulting from human performance. A more sophisticated and comprehensive approach to understanding the causes of accidents or serious safety events in high-reliability organizations involves the analysis of the three factors that contribute to safety events: human performance, system performance, and defense and controls performance. "System failures are rooted in the complex interactions between system components and human failures, as the complexity of such interactions increases, accidents caused by dysfunctional component interactions are more likely" (B&W Pantex 2008, 28).

Systems perform a variety of functions: Some are organizational or administrative, while others are operational or sociotechnical (reflecting the interplay between people and technology). As described earlier, the provision of healthcare in a hospital setting involves multiple nested systems: the microsystem of patient care at the sharp end is part of a mesosystem of supporting systems that are all nested in the organization's macrosystem. And, of course, each hospital or healthcare organization is part of an even larger healthcare system (which is not a focus of this discussion). Understanding the complex interdependencies of the various systems that support the patient care experience, as portrayed in exhibit 9.2, will allow hospital leaders to identify hazards and strengthen the defenses that protect patients from materialized threats to patient safety.

In his analysis of the partial nuclear core meltdown at Three Mile Island in 1979, sociologist Charles Perrow concluded that "systems with high degrees of interactive complexity are likely to experience unexpected and often baffling interactions among components, interactions that designers may not have anticipated and operators cannot recognize within the required reaction time. Consequently, they are highly vulnerable to common-mode failures" (B&W Pantex 2008, 28). Understanding and positively influencing the components of the complex systems—micro, meso, and macro—that create hazards, error traps, and error-provoking situations is the job of the organization's management and senior leaders. Hospitals are "dynamically complex." Hospitals are health systems comprising many interconnected and interdependent parts. Harvard University professor Rifat Atun (2012, 6) notes,

Their contexts create extensive networks of feedback loops with variable time lags between the cause and effect of an action and non-linear

Exhibit 9.2: Minimizing Errors Through Systems Improvement

Mesosystem of multiple services supporting the patient care microsystem within the hospital macrosystem influenced by the external health care megasystem

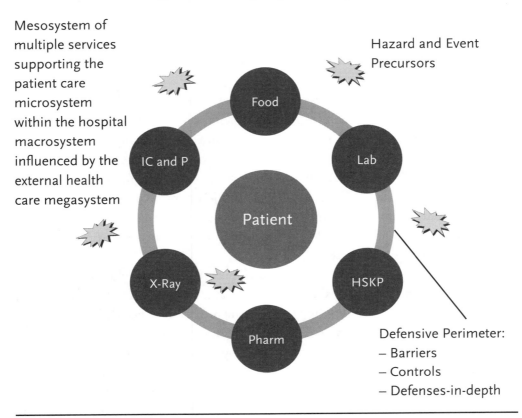

Hazard and Event Precursors

Defensive Perimeter:
– Barriers
– Controls
– Defenses-in-depth

Note: HSKP = housekeeping; IC and P = infection control and prevention.

relationships between system elements, collectively creating a "dynamic complexity." Understanding the interconnectedness and complexity is the essence of systems thinking that views the system as a whole rather than its individual component parts, taking into account behavior of systems over time rather than static snapshots.

System tendencies can have a positive or a negative effect on the conditions of care delivery or the care environment. These tendencies include boundaries, homeostasis, adaptation, reciprocal transactions, feedback loops, and energy throughput. Systems tend to create barriers and boundaries that define their operating space and distinguish the system from other systems in the functioning environment. Systems are homeostatic organizations that want to maintain their unique identity by resisting and being resilient against external influences. Systems are self-adapting organizations that make the internal changes needed to protect themselves and to continue fulfilling their mission and purpose. Systems influence other mesosystems through reciprocal transactions that are mutually beneficial. Systems self-correct based on the input and reactions they receive through feedback loops. Finally, systems have differing rates of throughput energy that is transferred between the systems in the mesosystem and the macrosystem in which they operate. Understanding these common tendencies of "systemness" is a necessary underpinning for creating a systems analysis and improvement plan, or Systems Improvement Plan for short.

Systems Improvement Plan

Hospital leaders who want to adopt the high-reliability practice of analyzing and improving their systems of care, in addition to improving human performance, should engage an interdisciplinary team to create and deploy a Systems Improvement Plan unique to their hospital. Every hospital has different patient populations, resource constraints, physical facilities, staff competencies, and organizational capabilities, which requires a customized Systems Improvement Plan.

System contributions to error can be studied from a variety of perspectives with the goal of learning the following (Amalberti and Hourlier 2012, 389):

- Where are errors occurring in the system?
- What types of errors are occurring?
- How many errors are occurring, and what is the rate of error?
- When are errors occurring (shift, week, weekend)?
- What were the consequences of each error for the patient (short-term effect, permanent injury, death)?
- Were the errors active errors or latent errors?
- For an active error, was it a slip, lapse, or mistake?
- For a latent error, was the organizational weakness that led to the error identified?
- Was a violation of rules involved?
- What was the cause of the error?
- Were defenses and barriers activated and penetrated or circumvented?
- What were the specific systems issues that allowed the error to cause a serious safety event?

When analyzing the "blunt end" of the system for error and event precursors, the assessment should consider staffing policies and practices, process and procedural design, technology support and the safe adoption of technology, leadership commitment to patient safety and the goal of zero patient harm, the adequacy of resources needed to perform safe patient care, provision of training and simulation required for competent performance, and the timeliness of information and lessons learned to support an informed safety culture and safe care practices.

A systems approach to improving performance and keeping patients safe from harm focuses on tracing causal factors. "Remedial efforts are directed at situations, defenses, and organizations. There are schematically two major sources of error-shaping factors: bad system design implying undue work constraints (general architecture, procurement, and personnel management) and bad organizational design (governance, managerial policies, commitment, safety culture)" (Amalberti and Hourlier 2012, 393). Systems analysis and improvement must seriously consider that system factors may be the cause of errors made by caregivers at the sharp end of the patient care process.

Analyzing System Performance Can Be Challenging

Researchers Pascale Carayon and Kenneth E. Wood (2010, 24) note that "medical errors and preventable patient harm can be avoided by a renewed focus on the design of work systems and processes. Redesigning a system can be challenging, especially in healthcare organizations that have limited technical infrastructure and technical expertise in human factors and systems engineering." Improving systems performance in complex adaptive systems such as hospitals and healthcare systems will complement the hospital's efforts to improve human performance by preventing the adverse consequences of faulty system interactions, inconsistent systems performance across the mesosystem, and error-provoking policies and workplace conditions. "Health care is a dynamic complex system where people and system elements continuously change, therefore requiring constant vigilance and monitoring of the various system interactions and transitions" (Carayon and Wood 2010, 26).

Systems thinking does not come naturally—especially to health care professionals. We have been educated and acculturated to recognize our personal responsibility to master the knowledge and skills, and to acquire the wisdom, that enables us to assist sick—and often vulnerable and dependent—individuals. We can be sure that Hippocrates and, centuries later, Florence Nightingale, addressed their dictum to "do no harm" to physicians and nurses as individuals—not to the systems within which they worked.

—Dr. Paul M. Schyve (2005)

According to the World Health Organization (WHO) in its report *Systems Thinking for Health Systems Strengthening*, many hospitals and healthcare systems lack the capacity to measure or understand their own weaknesses and constraints. Interventions to improve the safety and quality of patient care in any part of the system will have an effect on the overall system, and the overall system will have an effect on every intervention (WHO 2009, 1). One of the challenges confronting healthcare leaders as they attempt to improve system performance is that hospitals are complex, nonlinear systems in which the care environment is often unpredictable and resistant to change. "Seemingly obvious solutions sometimes [worsen] a problem" (WHO 2009, 1). The WHO has identified six "building blocks" of a healthcare system that can serve as a framework for system analysis and improvement efforts (WHO 2009):

1. *Service delivery*—patient care services that are provided through personal interventions that are effective, safe, and efficient (with a minimal waste of resources) and the infrastructure for providing the services
2. *Healthcare workforce*—doctors, nurses, and other staff who are responsive, fair, and efficient and available in sufficient numbers
3. *Health information*—reliable information produced and disseminated in a timely manner on health determinants, health system performance, and health status
4. *Medical technologies*—the scientifically sound and cost-effective use of medical products, vaccines, and other technologies ensuring their quality, safety, efficacy, and cost-effectiveness
5. *Health financing*—having adequate funds for health to ensure that people can access and use needed services
6. *Leadership and governance*—leaders ensure strategic policy frameworks that are combined with effective oversight, coalition building, accountability, incentives, and attention to system design

The WHO report identifies five types of skills that are needed for systems thinking: (1) dynamic thinking that looks at patterns of behavior over time, (2) system-as-cause thinking that places responsibility for a behavior on those who manage the policies and system elements, (3) forest thinking rather than tree-by-tree thinking to gain an understanding of the context in which harm occurred, (4) operational thinking that concentrates on causality and understanding how a behavior is generated, and (5) loop thinking that views causality as an ongoing process, not a one-time event. This type of thinking represents a paradigm shift from the historical approach of "blaming and shaming" the individuals who make errors.

Nurses Focus on Systems Thinking

The Quality and Safety Education for Nurses (QSEN) program integrates quality and safety competency development into nursing education curricula. The mission of the QSEN program is to ensure that nurses have the knowledge, skills, and abilities to contribute to the continuous improvement of the quality and safety of the healthcare systems in which they work. "The full effect of the QSEN competencies to improve the quality and safety of care can only be realized when nurses apply them at both the individual and system levels of care" (Dolansky and Moore 2013). Systems thinking can enhance nurses' day-to-day work and their ability to engage in better problem-solving, priority setting, delegation, interactions, collaboration, decision-making, and action taking. These functions are greatly influenced by nurses' understanding of how the components of the system in which they work relate to other components in the mesosystem and the macrosystem as a whole. "Systems thinking links a person's environment to his/her behavior. In the delivery of nursing care, this involves the nurse's understanding and valuing how components of a complex healthcare system influence care of an individual patient" (Dolansky and Moore 2013). QSEN emphasizes that optimal patient care requires nurses to apply both the traditional approach of vigilant individual care and the contemporary approach of vigilant *systems* of care.

Physicians Focus on Systems Thinking

Systems-based practice (SBP) is one of the six core competencies required of residents and physicians to deliver high-quality medical care. The six competencies are patient care, medical knowledge, practice-based learning and improvement, interpersonal and communication skills, professionalism, and systems-based practice. A collaborative effort between the Accreditation Council for Graduate Medical Education and the American Board of Medical Specialties, these core competencies define the proficiencies that physicians must have to deliver safe, high-quality patient care (Johnson, Miller, and Horowitz 2008, 1). "Competency in SBP requires that physicians understand how patient care relates to the health care system as a whole and how to use the system to improve the quality and safety of patient care. Systems thinking is the cornerstone of SBP" (Johnson, Miller, and Horowitz 2008, 1).

Residents are expected to demonstrate the ability to (1) recognize and respond to the larger context and system that they are a part of, (2) call on resources within the system to provide optimal care, (3) work effectively in a variety of healthcare delivery settings and systems, (4) coordinate patient care within the healthcare system, (5) incorporate cost awareness and risk-benefit analysis into patient care, (6) advocate for quality patient care and optimal care systems, (7) work in interprofessional teams to enhance patient safety, and (8) identify system errors and implement potential systems solutions. "An understanding of systems is essential to improve the quality and safety of patient care" (Johnson, Miller, and Horowitz 2008, 2). Physicians in hospital microsystems work collaboratively with other clinicians and staff with a shared purpose to provide safe and effective care to a defined group of patients. This system of care at the sharp end depends on the decisions made at the macrosystem level about staffing, resource availability, information and technology, cultural expectations for safe behaviors, and productivity.

Systems thinking, applied through an organized Systems Improvement Plan, can heighten organizational awareness of the importance of adopting a comprehensive approach to discovering the causes of safety events: improvement in human performance, system performance, and defense and controls performance. "While systems thinking enables new and productive approaches to improving patient safety, it brings with it its own conceptual challenges—challenges that, if not recognized and addressed, will both slow our progress and introduce new harm" (Schyve 2005, 2).

CONCLUSION

Chapter 9 discusses the safe care practices that positively influence both human performance and systems performance. Leaders must commit to analyzing and improving the three factors that create the opportunity for unsafe behaviors, unsafe conditions, and unsafe defenses: (1) human performance, (2) the performance of the supportive systems of care, and (3) defense and controls performance. Hospitals are health systems comprising many interconnected and interdependent parts. Understanding and positively influencing the components of those complex systems—micro, meso, and macro—that create hazards, error traps, and error-provoking situations is the job of an organization's management and senior leaders.

CHAPTER 9 SAFE CARE PRACTICES

1. Prevent patient harm by using three analytic approaches: retrospective analysis, prospective analysis, and concurrent analysis.

2. Engage an interdisciplinary team to create and deploy a Systems Improvement Plan to analyze and improve systems of care. The Systems

→

> Improvement Plan is unique to each hospital or healthcare system, taking into account patient populations, resource constraints, physical facilities, staff competencies, and organizational capabilities.
>
> 3. Use the World Health Organization's six "building blocks" as a framework for system analysis and improvement efforts.

REFERENCES

Amalberti, R., and S. Hourlier. 2012. "Human Error Reduction Strategies in Health Care." In *Handbook of Human Factors and Ergonomics in Health Care and Patient Safety*, 2nd ed., edited by P. Carayon, 385–99. Boca Raton, FL: CRC Press.

Atun, R. 2012. "Health Systems, Systems Thinking and Innovation." *Health Policy and Planning* 27 (Suppl. 4): iv4–iv8.

B&W Pantex. 2008. *High Reliability Operations: A Practical Guide to Avoid the System Accident*. Amarillo, TX: Babcock and Wilcox Technical Services.

Carayon, P., and K. E. Wood. 2010. "Patient Safety: The Role of Human Factors and Systems Engineering." *Studies in Health Technology and Informatics* 153: 23–46.

Dolansky, M. A., and S. M. Moore. 2013. "Quality and Safety Education for Nurses (QSEN): The Key Is Systems Thinking." *Online Journal of Issues in Nursing* 18 (3): 1.

Johnson, J. K., S. H. Miller, and S. D. Horowitz. 2008. "Systems-Based Practice: Improving the Safety and Quality of Patient Care by Recognizing and Improving the Systems in Which We Work." In *Advances in Patient Safety: New Directions and Alternative Approaches*, vol. 2, *Culture and Redesign*, edited by K. Henriksen, J. B. Battles, M. A. Keyes, and M. L. Grady. Rockville, MD: Agency for Healthcare Research and Quality.

Reason, J., and A. Hobbs. 2003. *Managing Maintenance Error: A Practical Guide*. Burlington, VT: Ashgate Publishing.

Schyve, P. M. 2005. "Prologue: Systems Thinking and Patient Safety." In *Advances in Patient Safety: From Research to Implementation*, vol. 2, *Concepts and Methodology*, edited by K. Henriksen, J. B. Battles, E. S. Marks, and D. I. Lewin. Rockville, MD: Agency for Healthcare Research and Quality.

US Department of Energy (DOE). 2009. *Human Performance Improvement Handbook*, vol. 1, *Concepts and Principles*. Published June. www.standards.doe.gov/standards -documents/1000/1028-BHdbk-2009-v1.

Wachter, R. 2012. *Understanding Patient Safety*, 2nd. ed. New York: McGraw-Hill Medical.

World Health Organization (WHO). 2009. *Systems Thinking for Health Systems Strengthening*. Accessed March 12, 2019. www.who.int/alliance-hpsr/resources/9789241563895/en/.

CHAPTER 10

Influencing the Human Factors That Impact Human Performance and System Performance

WHY SHOULD HOSPITALS USE HUMAN FACTORS ANALYSIS AND DESIGN TO IMPROVE HUMAN AND SYSTEM PERFORMANCE?

As described in chapter 9, the "Harm-Free Threes" outline the three predictors of harm-free healthcare: human performance, system performance (the supportive systems of care), and defense and controls performance. Human factors influence the interactions between humans (the caregiving staff) and other parts of the system of care and the effectiveness of barriers, defenses, and controls. These are the main factors that create opportunities for unsafe behaviors, unsafe conditions, and unsafe defenses.

This chapter will describe the human–system interfaces that exist in healthcare; how human factors research and design focus on the physical, cognitive, and organizational characteristics of systems; and how hospitals can influence the human factors that affect safe care delivery to improve both human performance and system performance.

INFLUENCING HUMAN FACTORS

According to the World Health Organization (WHO 2011), "Human factors examine the relationship between human beings and the systems with which they interact by focusing on improving efficiency, creativity, productivity, and job satisfaction, with the goal of minimizing errors." Less formally, the WHO describes human factors as "the study of all the factors that make it easier to do the work in the right way." Human factors analysis in healthcare can help improve high-risk processes that span multiple systems, such as medication management, patient care team communications, and patient handoff or transfer across systems of care.

Human factors engineering involves design solutions for software (e.g., computerized provider order entry), hardware (e.g., smart pumps), tools (e.g., patient beds, scalpels, syringes), and the physical layout of the workplace (e.g., lighting, space, distance). Human factors engineers consider human strengths and limitations in the design and improvement of interdependent systems in which people interact with other people, tools and technologies, and the work environment. A human factors assessment analyzes the physical demands, skill demands, mental workload, team dynamics, aspects of the work environment, and device design that are required to complete a task competently and effectively. The goal of human factors engineering is to "design systems that optimize safety and minimize the risk of error in complex environments" (PSNet 2019). A key directive in high-reliability organizations is learning—and therefore knowing—what the gap is between *work as imagined* and *work as performed*.

HUMAN FACTORS TOOLS AND TECHNIQUES

Human factors engineers use a variety of techniques to assess and improve system safety. *Usability testing* of new systems and equipment in real-world conditions allows human factors engineers to identify potential problems and unintended consequences of the new technology. Usability testing can also identify work-arounds that frontline staff may use to circumvent policies or safety procedures (PSNet 2019). Another aspect of human factors design is the incorporation of *forcing functions*—system design elements that prevent unintended or undesirable actions from being performed or allow actions to be performed only if a prerequisite action is performed first.

Standardization and standardized practices are increasingly being implemented in healthcare to increase reliability, improve information flow, and minimize the need for cross-training (PSNet 2019). The Comprehensive Unit-based Safety Program (CUSP) implemented by the Michigan Health and Hospital Association to dramatically reduce central line–associated bloodstream infections used a checklist as a *cognitive artifact* to ensure that the procedures and expected staff behaviors for central line insertion were clear. Well-designed cognitive artifacts can improve safety performance by improving situational awareness and communication and coordination among patient care team members (Gurses, Ozok, and Pronovost 2011, 349).

Human factors methods and techniques can be classified into six approaches (Carayon and Wood 2010, 29):

1. *General methods*—usually involves the direct observation of work
2. *Data collection*—collecting information about people and the physical measurement of anthropometric dimensions

3. *Analysis and design*—involves time studies and task analysis
4. *Evaluation of human–machine system performance*—involves usability testing, performance measures, error analysis, and accident reporting
5. *Evaluation of demands on people*—for example, looking at mental workload
6. *Management and implementation of ergonomics*—using participative methods

THE THREE FOCUSES OF HUMAN FACTORS

Human factors research and design focuses on the physical, cognitive, and organizational characteristics of a system. Human factors analysis traditionally focuses on the interaction between humans and the systems in which they work, including the work environment, work space, technology and equipment, and processes and procedures. Human factors engineers consider human capabilities and limitations in the design of human–system interfaces to improve system efficiency and safety. Ergonomics is a similar process of workplace improvement that focuses on the relationship between workers and their work environment. Human factors and ergonomics are considered to be synonymous, as both focus on improving the interactions and relationships between people and the systems in which they work.

Human factors or ergonomic analyses consider five types of human–system interactions, assessing operational optimization (efficiency, resiliency, safety, human well-being, overall system performance) across the physical, cognitive, and organizational domains of performance (Carayon 2012, 4–5):

1. *Human–machine interface*—involves the design of controls (e.g., controls in a telemetry monitoring unit), displays (e.g., anesthesia machine displays), work space (e.g., nursing station, distance to patient rooms), and facilities (e.g., hospital ergonomic design)
2. *Human–environment interface*—involves environmental ergonomics and issues of noise, lighting, temperature, airflow, and vibration
3. *Human–software interface*—involves the usability of medical devices and information technology (IT) and considers safety issues such as information overload
4. *Human–job interface*—involves work design ergonomics, workload, work schedules, and work content
5. *Human–organization interface*—examines organizational culture, teamwork, learning processes, work system, and sociotechnical system issues

Across all of these human–system interfaces, latent conditions can contribute to human error when stimulated by an active error. Latent conditions exist at the blunt end of operations, whereas active errors are committed at the sharp end of care. Human factors analysis examines the interactions between human performance (where active errors occur) and system performance (where latent errors originate). The objective of human factors analysis is to design the workplace to optimize system performance and prevent patient harm. Researchers Ayse P. Gurses, A. Ant Ozok, and Peter J. Pronovost (2011, 347) describe the goal of human factors analysis as the "joint optimization of social and technical elements of a system. . . . HFE [human factors and ergonomics] specialists focus on designing user-friendly interfaces that can improve the user's performance and reduce human error." Human factors specialists analyze the interactions between people and the systems in which they work, considering the physical environment, organizational conditions, and cognitive ergonomics and mental processes of the staff (Carayon 2012, 4; Gurses, Ozok, and Pronovost 2011, 348).

Physical Characteristics of the System

The usability of tools and equipment, the physical layout of the workplace, the physical workload of staff members, and the physical characteristics of the users of equipment and technology are examples of human factors that span the human and system aspects of performance. Physical human factors problems include tools whose physical dimensions do not fit the physical characteristics of the users (e.g., too small font size on computer screens), inappropriately designed physical environments (e.g., noisy and distracting environment), and physical layouts that do not support clinician work (e.g., monitoring patients from a central nursing station) (Carayon, Xie, and Kianfar 2013, 326).

Physical environmental conditions include lighting, noise, temperature, workplace layout, distractions, and ventilation. Human factors design principles for the physical environment focus on (1) minimizing perception time and decision time, (2) reducing or mitigating the need for excessive physical exertion, and (3) optimizing opportunities for physical movement (Carayon, Xie, and Kianfar 2013, 332). "It is important not only that each component of the system be designed appropriately, but also that system components be aligned and that system interactions be optimized" (Carayon, Xie, and Kianfar 2013, 332).

Examples of improvements to the physical environment resulting from human factors analysis include designing patient rooms to reduce falls, adding and strategically placing hand-washing stations to increase compliance with hand-washing requirements, and making sure that adequate lighting is available in medication dispensing areas (Gurses, Ozok, and Pronovost 2011, 348). As Kerm Henriksen and colleagues aptly describe, the location and availability of supplies and equipment in the physical work space and the lack of standardization of tools and equipment reflect system weaknesses and latent factors that, when matched with an initiating action, pose hazards to patients. Providers frequently spend a great deal of time "looking for appropriate cables, lines, connectors, and other accessories. In many ORs and ICUs, there is an eclectic mix of monitoring systems from different vendors that interface with various devices that increase the cognitive workload placed on provider personnel. Another microsystem interface problem . . . are medical gas mix-ups, where nitrogen and carbon dioxide have been mistakenly connected to the oxygen supply system. Gas system safeguards . . . have been overridden with adapters" (Henriksen et al. 2008, 9).

Purposefully designing the physical work environment for the nature of the work and those who work in it is a long-standing performance design principle of high-risk, high-reliability organizations. Healthcare organizations have "begun to appreciate the relationship between the physical environment (e.g., design of jobs, equipment, and physical layout) and employee performance (e.g., efficiency, reduction of error, and job satisfaction)" (Henriksen et al. 2008, 9). Henriksen and colleagues identify the following safety improvements resulting from human factors engineering and the design of the physical environment of hospitals:

- Better use of space for improved patient monitoring and reduced steps to the point of patient care
- Mistake-proofing and forcing functions that preclude the initiation of potentially harmful actions
- Standardization of facility systems, equipment, and patient rooms
- In-room placement of sinks for hand hygiene
- Single-bed rooms for reducing infections
- Better ventilation systems for pathogen control
- Improved patient handling, transport, and prevention of falls
- Use of health IT for quick and reliable access to patient information
- Use of health IT for improved medication safety
- Appropriate and adjustable lighting
- Noise reduction for lowering stress
- Simulation suites with sophisticated mannequins that enable mastery of critical skills
- Improved signage

Human factors engineers may study, for example, the design for sound control or the influence of excessive sound and noise on both caregivers and patients by analyzing the impact of sound on human behavior and performance. "Nurses as an occupational group are especially sensitive to building and workplace layout features . . . [these features] have a direct bearing on the quality and safety of care provided" (Henriksen et al. 2008, 10). Human factors considerations for nursing include (1) the distance traveled to care for patients, (2) work surfaces, (3) the lifting of patients, (4) visual requirements for patient monitoring, and (5) space for provider communications and care coordination activities.

Cognitive Characteristics of the System

The design and improvement of systems that support the safe delivery of patient care must also consider human factors related to the cognitive capacity of the people working in the system. Human factors engineer Pascale Carayon (2012, 7) notes that

> Often people in health care are overwhelmed by the number of tasks to perform (e.g., high patient flow in an emergency department, limited time allocated for a primary care physician to visit with a patient), need to work under high time pressure (e.g., quick decision making during a code), or have a hard time coping with information load (e.g., need to keep up with medical knowledge, information overload related to poor design of electronic health record technology). These various aspects of workload can be addressed by understanding the cognitive limitations and abilities of individuals.

Human factors design elements that address the cognitive characteristics of the system and the humans working in it focus on (1) matching technology with individuals' mental models, (2) minimizing the cognitive load on workers, (3) ensuring the consistency of interface designs for workers, (4) allowing for error detection and recovery, and (5) providing feedback to workers (Carayon, Xie, and Kianfar 2013, 332). The potential hazards created by uncontrolled cognitive ergonomic issues—such as decision-making under time pressure, stress on mental capacity or excess workload, and the ability to perform under stress—can be reduced through human factors interventions such as decision support tools to reduce diagnostic errors and usability testing of devices and equipment.

Organizational Characteristics of the System

Henriksen and colleagues (2008, 11) note that "the organizational/social environment represents another set of latent conditions that can lie dormant for some time; yet when combined with other pathogens, can thwart the system's defenses and lead to error." Organizational characteristics of the micro-, meso-, and macrosystems of healthcare range from safety culture and climate to normative values, beliefs, and attitudes toward teamwork, communication, and the design of jobs.

In their contribution to the Agency for Healthcare Research and Quality report *Making Healthcare Safer II*, Pascale Carayon, Anping Xie, and Sarah Kianfar illustrate how human factors assessment and improvement designs have addressed the organizational characteristics related to patient safety in the surgical suite and in the intensive care unit (ICU). "These issues interact as part of the larger work system and produce the vulnerabilities that can lead to patient safety incidents" (Carayon, Xie, and Kianfar 2013, 338). In the surgical suite, they identify the following organizational characteristics in their human factors assessment:

- Teamwork, miscommunication, lack of coordination, and lack of team familiarity and team stability, all of which contributed to errors during surgery
- Poor design and implementation of technology—integration of information across displays, unreliable audible alarms, shape of input controls, and lack of proper training for surgeons
- Design and implementation of surgery checklists
- Poor safety culture and lack of a culture to take responsibility for patient safety, report errors, learn from mistakes, and adapt individual and organizational behavior based on lessons learned from mistakes

In the ICU, they identify these organizational characteristics:

- Design and implementation of guidelines and best practices (e.g., for infection control)
- Workload, stress, and burnout of ICU physicians and nurses
- Information flow and decision-making in handoffs of patients across units, across services, patients discharged, and shift changes
- Design and implementation of technology for remote monitoring of ICU patients

The best approach to improving the organizational characteristics of systems through human factors research and improvement initiatives is to ensure that frontline clinical staff are involved in system design and redesign efforts. While responsibility for organizational human factors rests in the hands of management, a systems approach to understanding the threats to patient safety requires that management and frontline workers communicate openly about the contribution of blunt-end policies and practices to unsafe working conditions. These organizational policies and practices include staffing, communications, workload, patient volume fluctuations, patient production schedules, accessibility of personnel, design and implementation of technology, and poorly designed equipment interfaces.

According to James Reason, "Most of the enduring solutions to human factors problems involve technical, procedural, and organizational measures rather than purely psychological ones" (Reason and Hobbs 2003, 98). Hospitals should identify and prioritize for improvement the situational, organizational, and workplace factors that are detrimental to human performance and contribute to safety events.

Reason identifies nine error-provoking human factors that organizations should prioritize for assessment and improvement: (1) excessive reliance on memory, as lapses of memory are a common error; (2) interruptions, which can cause errors of omission; (3) time pressures, which can lead to risk-taking and cutting corners; (4) fatigue and tiredness, which can cause poor decision-making and judgment; (5) poor communication and coordination among team members, which can result in a lack of clarity about the situation; (6) unfamiliar jobs and tasks that are not part of a staff member's normal duties, which can result in the degradation of practical skills; (7) ambiguity, which creates uncertainty among the patient care team members about what is going on; (8) diffusion of team member responsibilities, which may cause team members to make assumptions about others' knowledge; and (9) highly routine procedures, which are a danger zone for slips and lapses because the tasks are so familiar to the worker, causing attention to wander (Reason and Hobbs 2003, 104).

Organizational factors assessments are routinely completed by management, but they are done less frequently than other systems assessments (e.g., barrier effectiveness analysis, failure mode and effects analysis, root cause analysis, hazard analysis). An organizational factors assessment examines the error-provoking potential of systems and structures, resource availability, staffing and people management, technology and equipment, training, simulation, skills development, production pressures, policies, organizational culture, planning, communication, and facility and equipment maintenance (Reason and Hobbs 2003, 140–41).

FOUR HUMAN FACTORS DESIGN PRINCIPLES FOCUSED ON PATIENT SAFETY

Integral to strengthening the human–system interactions that affect patient safety is knowledge of the human factors—physical, cognitive, and organizational—that threaten the consistent delivery of harm-free healthcare. Human factors engineering involves removing hazards and performance obstacles, enhancing the resilience and adaptability of the system, and paying attention to the interrelationships between systems of care—that is, systems thinking. Carayon, Xie, and Kianfer (2013, 331) outline four human factors design principles focused on patient safety:

1. *Remove system hazards.* An objective of human factors system design is to identify and remove system hazards, starting with the design and continuing through the implementation of a new system feature or improving an existing one. A work system that is not designed according to human factors design principles creates opportunities for errors and hazards.

2. *Remove performance obstacles.* An objective of human factors system redesign is to identify and remove performance obstacles. Performance obstacles in the work system can hinder clinicians' ability to perform their work and deliver safe care. If some obstacles cannot be removed because they are intrinsic to the job, strategies should be designed to mitigate the impact of the performance obstacles by enhancing other system elements.

3. *Support resilience.* Work systems should be designed to enhance resilience and support adaptability and flexibility in human work. A work system that does not support resilience can produce circumstances under which system operators may not be able to detect, adapt to, or recover from errors, hazards, disruptions, and disturbances.

4. *Systems thinking.* Whenever there is a change in the work system, the organization needs to consider how the change will affect the entire work system and how the system can be optimized. Human factors design does not focus on one element of work in isolation because system components interact to influence care processes and patient safety.

APPLYING HUMAN FACTORS THINKING TO THE CARE ENVIRONMENT

Individuals and patient care teams should be trained to understand human factors and to routinely assess their working conditions to determine the "safety health" of the workplace. The WHO offers several suggestions for limiting errors caused by humans (WHO 2011). Although the suggestions are intended for medical students, they apply to all members of the patient care team:

-   *Avoid reliance on memory.* Relying on memory is dangerous when it comes to patient care. Checking actions against a diagram can reduce the load on clinicians' working memory. This is one reason that protocols are so important in healthcare—they reduce reliance on memory.

- *Make things visible.* Using pictures and notices that outline the steps in a process—for example, switching a machine on and off or using a smart pump and properly reading the displays—will help individuals master a skill. Pictorial reminders of the importance of hand washing have also proven effective.
- *Review and simplify processes.* Simple is better. Some healthcare tasks have become so complicated that they are a recipe for error, such as handoff communications and discharge processes. Making the patient handoff process simpler by implementing fewer but clearer communication strategies can reduce errors. Limiting the range of drugs available for prescribing is another example of a process that could be simplified.
- *Standardize common processes and procedures.* Often, units and departments in hospitals do common things differently, forcing staff to relearn procedures when they move from one area to another. Hospitals that standardize the way they do things help staff reduce reliance on memory, thereby improving efficiency and saving time. Examples include standardizing drug order forms and processes, discharge forms, and types of equipment.
- *Routinely use checklists.* Checklists should be used particularly when there is an evidence-based way of implementing a process or treatment.
- *Be vigilant.* Individuals should be alert to possible errors when they are completing lengthy, repetitive tasks. Becoming tired, distracted, or bored during routine activities may lead to error—individuals must avoid becoming complacent and remain vigilant of the potential for hazards and errors.

The Joint Commission's position paper on "Human Factors Analysis in Patient Safety Systems" argues that human factors analysis "is an essential step to designing equipment, procedures, tasks, and work environments because research shows that human failures cause 80% to 90% of errors. The most common root causes of sentinel events are human factors, leadership, and communication" (Joint Commission 2015, 7). The Joint Commission identifies forcing functions, computerized automation, and human–machine redundancies as the most reliable human factors engineering strategies. Other human factors strategies listed as "somewhat reliable" include checklists for high-risk procedures, forced pauses in processes, reminders, standardization of equipment, and planned error-recovery opportunities. The Joint Commission states that human factors should be among the factors considered in both retrospective causal analyses such as root cause analysis and in prospective risk assessments such as failure mode and effects analysis. The Joint Commission (2015, 8) offers a six-question guide for using human factors to analyze the system.

Pamela Cipriano (2008), editor in chief of *American Nurse Today*, notes that "systems thinking can be transformational. It transcends the quality-improvement cycle, producing better and safer patient care. To improve our complex system, we need a new mindset to expand our understanding of work, patients, and co-workers. The new mindset is systems thinking." Healthcare systems such as Johns Hopkins Medicine and the National Center for Human Factors in Healthcare at MedStar Health have successfully applied human factors analysis to improve the design of patient care processes, devices, and the systems that support the safe delivery of patient care.

The MedStar Health National Center for Human Factors in Healthcare (2019) identifies the following benefits of applying human factors and system safety engineering: efficient care processes in medical care, effective communication between medical care providers, better understanding of patients' medical conditions, implementation of effective and sustainable root cause analysis solutions, reduced risk of medical device use error, easier to use or more intuitive devices, reduced risk of health IT-related use error, easier to use or more intuitive health IT, reduced need for training, easier repair and maintenance, cost savings through prevention and mitigation of adverse events, safer working conditions in medicine, and improved patient outcomes.

Johns Hopkins Medicine describes human factors analysis as "a scientific discipline that aims to help people do their best work, improve resilience and overall system performance, and minimize errors. Human factors solutions make it 'easy to do things right and hard to do things wrong.' When errors do occur, they are less likely to lead to patient harm" (Johns Hopkins Medicine 2019). Johns Hopkins lists the benefits of human factors system design as improved clinician performance, increased delivery of evidence-based medicine, enhanced patient and family centeredness of care, improved patient–provider communication, reduced inefficiencies and non-value-added tasks, and reduced burnout and improved job satisfaction. Johns Hopkins Medicine (2019) cites the following example of the positive benefits of human factors analysis and systems improvement:

Human factors engineers, clinicians, outcomes researchers, psychologists, and sociologists sought to proactively identify safety risks in cardiac surgery using a multi-method approach, including observations of 22 surgeries at five well-respected hospitals. Their holistic review uncovered 58 different types of hazards—anything in the work system that has the potential to cause an error—related to flawed devices, suboptimal physical layout design, processes and organizational structures. Hazards included disorganized medication carts that might lead a clinician to select the wrong drug, a surgeon who was introduced to a new cautery gun in the middle of a procedure, and purchasing practices that did not consider the downstream safety impacts of their decisions. Many of the team's recommendations were adopted by the five hospitals, resulting in improvements in areas such as infection prevention and safety of care transitions.

The Clinical Human Factors Group (CHFG) is a broad coalition of healthcare professionals, managers, and service users who have partnered with experts in human factors from healthcare and other high-risk industries to advocate for a healthcare system that places an understanding of human factors at the heart of improving clinical, managerial, and organizational practice. According to the CHFG (2013, 5), "integrating human factors science into the design of healthcare systems, processes and tasks can play a significant role in reducing patient harm." The CHFG lists the following benefits and positive impacts on safety from developing healthcare systems founded on human factors principles:

- Reduction of patient harm through better design of healthcare systems and equipment
- Better understanding of why healthcare staff make errors
- Better understanding of how system factors threaten patient safety
- Improved safety culture of teams and organizations
- Enhanced teamwork and communication among healthcare staff
- Improved approaches to incident investigation
- Better prediction of what could go wrong in the design of new hospitals and healthcare processes

The CHFG's guide *Implementing Human Factors in Healthcare—Taking Further Steps* includes a comprehensive list of human factors methods and applications organized by hospital functional area: reorganizing patient care services; teamwork support; healthcare facilities design; staffing selection, allocation, and training; technology and device design; board and governance support; and safe protocols, processes, and procedures. For example, in reorganizing patient care services, human factors specialists use task analysis and system modeling, prospective risk assessment, hazard identification methods, human reliability assessment, environmental assessment, workload assessment, and safety cases. For technology and device design, human factors analysis and improvement efforts focus on usability testing, interface design and analysis, anthropometrics, mental workload assessment, task analysis and system modeling, safety cases, mock-ups, prototyping, and simulation. (The full set of human factors methods and applications can be found at http://chfg.org.)

LESSONS FROM HIGH-RELIABILITY ORGANIZATIONS

Using Human Factors Analysis to Improve Airline Safety

The US Federal Aviation Administration (FAA) created Human Factors Policy Order 9550.8 to "establish policy, procedures, and responsibilities for incorporating and coordinating human factors considerations in Federal Aviation Administration . . . programs and activities to enhance aviation safety, capability, efficiency, and productivity" (FAA 2014). The goal of incorporating human factors system design into the FAA's acquisition, certification, regulation, and standard setting is to "promote the safety and productivity of the national airspace system." The FAA's application of human factors engineering methods is intended "to generate and compile information about human capabilities and limitations and apply that information to equipment, systems, facilities, procedures, jobs, environments, training, staffing, and personnel management for safe, comfortable, and effective human performance."

In line with the human factors design models described in this chapter, FAA researchers seek to understand the physical, cognitive, behavioral, and organizational characteristics of aviation professionals and the systems in which they work. Professionals working in FAA systems include pilots, air traffic controllers, technical operations specialists, and aircraft maintenance technicians. With a focus on maximizing human–system performance, the FAA's overall goal is to use human factors to support high levels of human–system performance across all aviation domains. Taking a "system of systems" approach that considers the complex interactions among people, technology, procedures, and organizations, the FAA closely coordinates its efforts with the airline industry. Since human factors have been identified as a contributing factor in two-thirds to three-fourths of recent aviation accidents or incidents, the FAA strives to improve aviation safety by reducing the impact of human error (FAA 2014).

While human errors and human factors contribute to airplane accidents, human factors are also a major concern in maintenance practices and air traffic management. For example, human factors analysts at Boeing "work with engineers, pilots, and mechanics to apply the latest knowledge about the interface between human performance and commercial airplanes to help operators improve safety and efficiency in their daily operations" (Graeber

→

1999, 23). Boeing began employing human factors specialists in the 1960s, and the company continues to help its airline operators apply the latest human factors knowledge to increase flight safety. "A sound scientific basis is necessary for assessing human performance implications in design, training, and procedures, just as developing a new wing requires sound aerodynamic engineering" (Graeber 1999, 24).

Boeing's human factors research and improvement efforts focus on the flight crew and maintenance technicians because improving human performance in these roles can help reduce the commercial aviation accident rate. Boeing's human factors work helps airline company operators better manage human error.

Two of the human factors assessment tools used by Boeing are the Procedural Event Analysis Tool (PEAT) and the Maintenance Error Decision Aid (MEDA). When airline personnel make errors, the contributing factors in the work environment are part of the causal chain. The PEAT and MEDA tools help identify the contributing factors and, if possible, eliminate or mitigate them.

PEAT, first used in 1999, is an analytic tool that helps the airline industry effectively manage the risks associated with flight crew procedural deviations. The intention is to develop effective remedies that will eliminate these deviations in the future. A trained investigator interviews the flight crew to collect information about procedural deviations and contributing factors associated with them. MEDA is a tool used to collect more information about maintenance errors and to provide a standardized process for analyzing the contributing factors to error and for developing possible corrective actions.

CONCLUSION

Chapter 10 identifies the safe care practices that influence the human factors related to improving both human performance and system performance. Hospitals that seek to achieve the high-reliability goal of zero patient harm must master the Five Disciplines of Performance Excellence. This chapter describes the discipline of minimizing errors and event precursors by influencing the human factors that impact the interactions between human performance and system performance. The safe care practices for human factors include harm-prevention analytic approaches and human factors design principles related to the physical, cognitive, and organizational characteristics of systems.

REFERENCES

Carayon, P. 2012. "Human Factors and Ergonomics in Health Care and Patent Safety." In *Handbook of Human Factors and Ergonomics in Health Care and Patient Safety*, 2nd ed., edited by P. Carayon, 3–15. Boca Raton, FL: CRC Press.

Carayon, P., and K. E. Wood. 2010. "Patient Safety: The Role of Human Factors and Systems Engineering." *Studies in Health Technology and Informatics* 153: 23–46.

Carayon, P., A. Xie, and S. Kianfar. 2013. "Human Factors and Ergonomics." In *Making Healthcare Safer II: An Updated Critical Analysis of the Evidence for Patient Safety Practices*, 325–50. Rockville, MD: Agency for Healthcare Research and Quality.

Cipriano, P. F. 2008. "Improving Health Care with Systems Thinking." *American Nurse Today* 3 (9): 6.

Clinical Human Factors Group (CHFG). 2013. *Implementing Human Factors in Healthcare—Taking Further Steps*. Accessed April 13, 2019. https://chfg.org/how-to -guide-to-human-factors-volume-2/.

Graeber, C. 1999. "The Role of Human Factors in Improving Aviation Safety." *Aero* 8: 23–31. www.boeing.com/commercial/aeromagazine/aero_08/human.pdf.

Gurses, A. P., A. A. Ozok, and P. J. Pronovost. 2011. "Time to Accelerate Integration of Human Factors and Ergonomics in Patient Safety." *BMJ Quality & Safety* 21 (4): 347–51.

Henriksen, K., E. Dayton, M. A. Keyes, P. Carayon, and R. G. Hughes. 2008. "Understanding Adverse Events: A Human Factors Framework." In *Patient Safety and Quality: An Evidence-Based Handbook for Nurses*, edited by R. G. Hughes, chapter 5. Rockville, MD: Agency for Healthcare Research and Quality.

Johns Hopkins Medicine. 2019. "Human Factors in Health Care." Armstrong Institute for Patient Safety and Quality. Accessed March 15. www.hopkinsmedicine.org/armstrong _institute/centers/human_factors_engineering/human_factors_in_health_care.html.

Joint Commission. 2015. "Human Factors Analysis in Patient Safety Systems." *The Source*. Accessed April 15, 2019. www.jointcommission.org/assets/1/6/HumanFactorsThe_Source .pdf.

MedStar Health National Center for Human Factors in Healthcare. 2019. "What Is Human Factors in Healthcare?" Accessed April 13. www.medicalhumanfactors.net/ what-is-human-factors/.

Patient Safety Network (PSNet). 2019. "Patient Safety Primer: Human Factors Engineering." Updated January. https://psnet.ahrq.gov/primers/primer/20/Human-Factors -Engineering.

Reason, J., and A. Hobbs. 2003. *Managing Maintenance Error: A Practical Guide*. Burlington, VT: Ashgate Publishing.

US Federal Aviation Administration (FAA). 2014. "Role of Human Factors in the FAA." Published December. www.hf.faa.gov/media/RoleOfHF-FAA.pdf.

World Health Organization (WHO). 2011. "What Is Human Factors and Why Is It Important to Patient Safety?" In *Patient Safety Curriculum Guide: Multi-professional Edition*, 111–20. Accessed April 15, 2019. https://apps.who.int/iris/bitstream/handle /10665/44641/9789241501958_eng.pdf.

PART V

Maximizing Defenses and Barriers: The "Defensive" Strategy

Strengthening Defenses to Prevent Harm

WHY SHOULD HOSPITAL LEADERS BE AS CONCERNED ABOUT THE STRENGTH OF THEIR "DEFENSIVE" COMPETENCIES AS THEY ARE ABOUT THEIR "OFFENSIVE" COMPETENCIES?

Defenses, barriers, and controls save lives. When errors occur and hazards are activated, defenses, barriers, and controls provide the protective safeguards that keep patients safe from harm. "Not all of the errors result in patient harm. This is due to the fact that in health care, as in other industries, defenses are in place. Defenses are protective measures put in place to reduce the likelihood of negative outcomes resulting from an unsafe act" (Drews 2012, 332).

Defenses and barriers can be designed for either prevention or protection. "Barriers that are intended to work *before* a specific initiating event takes place, serve as a means of *prevention*. Such barriers are supposed to ensure that the accident does not happen. . . . Barriers that are intended to work *after* a specific initiating event has taken place serve as means of *protection*. These barriers are supposed to shield the environment and the people in it, as well as the system itself, from the consequences of the accident" (Hollnagel 2004, 76). Hospital leaders must understand the adequacy and effectiveness of the organization's defenses and controls and their contribution to keeping patients safe.

Even high-performing organizations can suffer catastrophic failure when they do not maintain effective defenses and controls against harm. The following are a few examples:

- A nuclear power plant that failed to maintain effective defenses against human and system performance failures experienced a partial core meltdown that caused the release of radioactive gases into the atmosphere (Three Mile Island, 1979).

- A commercial airline that failed to maintain its defenses against human error and maintenance error went out of business shortly after one of its planes caught fire in midair and crashed, killing all 110 people on board (ValuJet, 1996).
- A wildland firefighting unit that failed to follow established safety defenses (8 out of 10 Standard Firefighting Orders were compromised) were trapped by a wildfire and died after they were overtaken by the fast-spreading blaze (South Canyon Fire, 1994).
- A major accounting firm that depended on the public's trust in its integrity and strict adherence to accounting standards failed to maintain its defenses and controls, resulting in a conviction for obstruction of justice and criminal complicity that ultimately forced the company to surrender its licenses and right to practice before the US Securities and Exchange Commission (Arthur Andersen, 2002).
- The engineer of a commuter train in New York was found to have been the direct cause of the train's derailment by going three times the mandated speed around a bend in the track, resulting in four passenger deaths and 61 injuries. The engineer had been suffering from sleep apnea, but the National Transportation Safety Board found that if a required safety defense mechanism had been installed (Positive Train Control), the accident could have been prevented (Spuyten Duyvil, 2013).
- A 10-year-old boy died on one of the world's tallest waterslides at a theme park in Kansas City, Kansas, that was later found to have violated international design standards for safe operation and failed to repair and maintain necessary safety defenses such as the brake system (Schlitterbahn Waterpark, 2016).

An adage in professional football is that "defense wins championships." The top-ranked defensive team during the regular season has won 17 Super Bowl championships, whereas the top-ranked offensive team has won only eight times. Forty-three (or 81 percent) of the 53 Super Bowls have been won by a top 10 defensive team. The winner of the 2019 Super Bowl, the New England Patriots, had the seventh-best defense out of 32 teams, while the losing Los Angeles Rams, who were held to just three points, had the twentieth-worst defense in the National Football League (ESPN 2019). Of course, great offensive teams have also had championship seasons. "We found that when it comes to winning a title, or winning in sports in general for that matter, offense and defense carry nearly identical weight. In virtually every sport, you need either a stellar offense or a stellar defense, and having both is even better" (Moskowitz and Wertheim 2012, 1). Excellence on both offensive and defensive provides an even greater chance of success.

What's the point? Healthcare organizations—just like high-risk, high-reliability organizations, high-performing businesses, or championship-winning athletic teams—need to demonstrate defensive competence as well as offensive competence to excel. Offering the best clinical excellence in the world does not much matter if a healthcare system's defenses and controls do not consistently and continuously protect patients from the inevitability of human error. In short, defense saves lives.

THE PURPOSE OF DEFENSES

Broadly, the term *defenses* comprises protections against hazards such as safeguards, barriers, and controls. The difference is semantic: When we design safeguards and barriers, we do so to guard *against* some action occurring—for example, a safeguard against patient falls or a barrier against the spread of infection. When we design controls, we do so to *limit* an action—for example, a control for a smart intravenous (IV) pump limits the free flow of medication or dosing level.

Three types of defenses will be discussed in this chapter: *physical defenses, administrative defenses*, and *human defenses*. Understanding how these types of defenses and controls function and how to effectively develop, deploy, monitor, and improve them is critical to a hospital's efforts to keep patients safe from the potentially harmful effects of human error or system weaknesses. Every member of the patient care team, as well as the leadership team that supports their delivery of safe care, should build the following steps into their patient care practices (DOE 2012, 1-19):

1. *Clarify the scope of work.* Make sure that work expectations are clear and understood by the entire patient care team and that the necessary resources (e.g., supplies, equipment, competent staff) are readily available.
2. *Analyze the hazards.* Identify, analyze, and categorize the hazards associated with the task or process being undertaken.
3. *Develop and implement defenses and controls.* Identify, activate, and implement the defenses and controls that are appropriate for a situation, either to prevent a hazard from causing harm or to mitigate, contain, or divert the harmful effects of a hazard.
4. *Perform work with activated defenses.* Perform work safely with defenses and controls activated and working as designed.
5. *Offer feedback for improvement.* Assess the adequacy of the defenses and controls applied in a particular process or procedure, openly consider whether the defenses were circumvented, or identify the need for new or revised defenses.

Organizational drift from the desired safe care practices of high-reliability health-care organizations is determined by monitoring the gap between *work as planned* and *work as performed*. Achieving harm-free healthcare is contingent on making sure that work as performed reflects the work as planned defined in steps 1–3.

Defenses serve two main purposes—to prevent harm or to mitigate harm. Serious safety events that result in an injury to, or death of, a patient unfold in a five-step dynamic. First, an initiating error or action activates an existing hazard that may lead to patient harm. Second, flawed defenses and controls fail to protect the patient against hazards. *Prevention barriers* or *defenses* are designed to block potentially harmful actions from activating a hazard.

Third, error precursors—unfavorable conditions in the patient care environment—create error-likely situations or error traps. *Mitigation barriers* or *defenses* are designed to contain or reduce the impact of a hazard once it has been activated. For example, suppose that a surgeon and surgical team failed to follow the four-count standard protocol to prevent retained foreign objects and left a retained sponge—*Gossypiboma*—inside the patient. The application of a final preventive defense—scanning the patient using a radio frequency identification wand—was successful, and the retained sponge was removed before final suture. Another example of a mitigating defense is the sprinkler systems in hospitals that are designed to contain the hazard of fire.

Fourth, latent organizational weaknesses create conditions in the patient care environment that provoke errors or contribute to the deterioration of defenses and controls. Deficiencies in management policies, staff training programs, and norms, attitudes, and beliefs that do not reflect a culture of safety are examples of latent organizational weaknesses.

Lastly, when an initiating action by an individual is in error or a rule violation, and flawed defenses, error precursors, and latent organizational weaknesses align, patient harm is a probable outcome of the care process. James Reason defines defenses as follows (Reason and Hobbs 2003, 91):

> Defences, barriers, and safeguards are features of the system that have been put there to help the system cope with unplanned and untoward events that have happened in the past, or have been imagined by the system designers. Unfortunately, gaps in defences may only become apparent after an accident has occurred. These gaps may involve defences that have failed to perform as intended or defences that were inadequate or entirely absent.

Defenses are designed to minimize the potential negative effects of errors—errors that may provoke a hazard and cause harm.

Many preventive defenses in healthcare employ technological barriers to block the effects of errors and avoid triggering a hazard. For example, the use of computerized provider order entry (CPOE) has improved communications among patient care teams, expanded the availability of information, and increased the speed of order processing. CPOE defensive controls help prevent the use of inappropriate medications, administration of the wrong dose of a drug, or administration of a drug at the wrong frequency. CPOE defensive controls also aid with monitoring the medication management process, eliminating confusing and illegible handwriting, and reducing the risk of look-alike/sound-alike drug errors (Wachter 2012, 211).

Bar-code medication administration (BCMA) is another excellent example of a physical and technological barrier designed to protect patients from receiving the wrong medication or the wrong dose or frequency of a medication. The BCMA defense requires nurses to swipe the bar code on the medication, the patient's wristband, and their own badge, thereby establishing a three-way cross-check before the medication can be administered. "Effective use of BCMA technology can substantially reduce medication dispensing errors" (Wachter 2012, 214, 217).

Dr. Robert Wachter, chief of medical services at the University of California, San Francisco Medical Center, cites research by Eric Poon and colleagues (Poon et al. 2010) showing that multiple defenses provide layers of protection. In one case, a closed-loop system that combined CPOE, BCMA, and an electronic medication administration record led to a 50 percent decrease in drug administration errors and potential adverse drug events. High-reliability organizations refer to this strategy as *defenses-in-depth*.

DEFENSES-IN-DEPTH

Defenses and controls are designed, implemented, and strengthened over time to provide a protective barrier between human or system errors and patients. "High-hazard operations attempt to minimize vulnerability from human fallibility by using redundant systems, processes, and employees. Redundancy helps achieve reliability through duplication and overlap of effort" (B&W Pantex 2008, 20). Because any one defense may not be adequate to protect patients from harm, safe systems should build in multiple layers of defenses—defenses-in-depth—to create redundant, overlapping, and complementary defensive functions to block errors from causing patient harm.

Again, an analogy to football works here. Think about the functions of a football team's defensive squad: The collective goal of the defense is to stop the forward progress of the opposing force (in healthcare, the potential harm-producing effects of error). Members of the defense have individual roles to play, but they also complement the defensive efforts of their teammates, and their efforts are often redundant—for example, multiple defensive players might tackle an opposing offensive player. The defense comprises three layers: (1) the front line of defense—that is, the defensive line; (2) the linebackers, who defend against anything that gets past the front line; and (3) the defensive backs in the "secondary" defensive area of the field of play. On each team, two defensive players in the secondary have the responsibility of safeties, meaning that they are the last line of defense against the opposing force.

Who are your safeties? Football teams with excellent defenses-in-depth usually excel at winning games. Hospitals with strong defenses-in-depth win by keeping patients safe from the harmful effects of error and organizational weaknesses. "The presence of sophisticated system or component redundancy, also called defenses-in-depth redundancy, has changed the character of industrial accidents more than any other factor, making modern technological systems largely immune to isolated failures" (B&W Pantex 2008, 21).

LESSONS FROM HIGH-RELIABILITY ORGANIZATIONS

Defenses-in-Depth: Nuclear Power Plants

US nuclear power plants use a defenses-in-depth approach to minimize the possibility of releasing hazardous amounts of radioactive material into the environment. Nuclear power plants use three barriers to prevent the release of fission products into the environment: fuel rods, a reactor vessel and primary cooling system, and containment. While the chances of a single barrier or defense failing is unlikely, the chances of all three defenses failing simultaneously is extremely remote (FEMA 2019).

The US Nuclear Regulatory Commission (NRC) oversees the safety of the nation's nuclear power industry. A defenses-in-depth approach has been a central tenet of the NRC's safety regulations and requirements for nuclear power plants for many years. The defense-in-depth concept for protecting the public from the consequences of a nuclear reactor accident was first applied in the 1950s. "Defense-in-depth recognizes that our knowledge is imperfect. Although we plan for all conceivable accidents, the unexpected may still occur. Our design and operation of nuclear plants needs to be robust enough to compensate for this lack of knowledge" (Drouin 2016). Nuclear power plants implement multiple layers of defenses—defenses-in-depth—to

→

control the hazards associated with nuclear power generation, so that if one layer fails, the other layers of defense will compensate.

Hospitals should consider the three principles of defense-in-depth used by nuclear power plants when designing their hazard-specific defensive protections:

1. *Redundancy.* More than one component or element of the process should perform the same function—for example, having two or more sources of information to verify a patient's identification or performing multiple checks before administering a high-risk medication.

2. *Independence.* The multiple components of a process rely on separate and distinct attributes to function—for example, the prescribing physician, pharmacist, nurse, and peer cross-checking nurse and the technological defenses of CPOE and BCMA all provide multiple independent verifications to minimize the possibility of a medication administration error.

3. *Diversity.* The multiple components of a process that perform the same function rely on different design features to operate—for example, backup power generation and batteries ensure that lifesaving support services such as ventilation and infusion pumps will continue to operate as required.

In the safe design of nuclear power plants and nuclear reactors, defenses-in-depth help (1) maintain reactor stability by limiting the ability of events to disrupt operation, such as seismically designed buildings; (2) protect the reactor if plant operations are disrupted with safety features such as emergency reactor core cooling with redundant pumps; (3) strengthen barrier integrity to guard against the release of radioactive material into the environment with, for example, leak-tight containment structures; and (4) protect the public if a release does occur through emergency preparedness plans (Drouin 2016).

ADMINISTRATIVE DEFENSES

Hazards can be identified and controlled by activating defenses. We know what the most prevalent, significant, and harm-producing hazards are in acute hospital settings. Despite this, hospitals collectively have not developed and implemented the defenses and controls necessary to neutralize these hazards and protect patients from potential harm. Chapter 5 summarized the top 10 threats to patient safety, which include patient falls, inpatient suicide, central line–associated bloodstream infections, and wrong-site, wrong-patient, or wrong-procedure surgery. Exemplar hospitals and healthcare systems in the United States have made great progress in designing defenses and controls to address these known hazards and to provide patient protections in error-likely situations.

For example, the Universal Fall Precautions implemented by hospitals include administrative defenses such as policies that require staff to familiarize patients with their environment and require patients to demonstrate their ability to use the call light. Physical or technical barriers and defenses against patient falls include having sturdy hand rails in patients' rooms, bathrooms, and hallways and keeping hospital bed brakes in the locked position. Human defenses and controls include hourly rounding by staff to continuously check on patients and the physical environment to ensure the elements of the fall prevention precautions are in effect. An important human defense is making sure staff respond quickly to patients activating their call lights.

Administrative defenses and controls are not as reliable as physical or engineered controls because they rely on human training, judgment, and initiative to ensure that administrative policies and procedures are followed completely and correctly (DOE 2009, 3-6). Administrative defenses and controls that "significantly impact human performance" include the following (DOE 2009, 3-7):

- Strategic business planning, including goal setting, budgeting, priority setting, and resource allocation
- Organizational structure, including lines of authority and defined staff roles and responsibilities
- Processes and policies that define how work is to be conducted, including operations guidance, preventive maintenance, and work procedures
- Communications, including routine communications, meetings, and alarms
- Technical and administrative procedures, including human performance, safety, troubleshooting, records, self-assessment, and corrective action
- Training programs
- Personnel qualification standards that establish the physical, psychological, educational, and proficiency standards for each position
- Work management processes, including work initiation, prioritization, planning, and scheduling
- Human resource policies and practices, particularly related to staffing levels

- Human performance expectations and standards
- Information technology and information handling

Checklists are an effective administrative defense against the inherent hazards of complex, multistep processes and procedures, and they have been particularly effective in preventing errors of omission. In his book *The Checklist Manifesto*, surgeon and public health expert Atul Gawande (2009, 13) notes,

> Avoidable failures are common and persistent. And the reason is increasingly evident: the volume and complexity of what we know has exceeded our individual ability to deliver its benefits correctly, safely, or reliably. The checklist is a different strategy to overcome our failures, builds on our experience, and takes advantage of our knowledge.

According to Gawande, checklists remind staff to follow the minimum necessary steps in a process and make the steps explicit. "You want people to make sure to get the stupid stuff right" (Gawande 2009, 51).

The application of checklists as a defense against active errors and latent conditions has been adopted as the Safe Surgery Checklist by the World Health Organization and has proven effective in reducing the rate of central line–associated bloodstream infections in US hospitals. Johns Hopkins developed a checklist of the necessary steps to avoid infections when inserting a central line: (1) wash hands with soap; (2) clean the patient's skin with chlorhexidine antiseptic; (3) put sterile drapes over the entire patient; (4) wear a mask, hat, sterile gown, and gloves; and (5) put a sterile dressing over the insertion site once the line is in (Gawande 2009, 38). Gawande recommends that checklists must be quick and simple tools that are user friendly and modest in length and scope to be functionally useful in complex systems such as healthcare (Gawande 2009, 128).

PHYSICAL AND TECHNICAL DEFENSES

Physical and technical defenses are engineered controls such as hardware, software, and equipment that operate in the physical environment of care delivery. These defenses are designed to affect people's behaviors, choices, and attitudes to avoid error traps, control hazards, and prevent harm (DOE 2009, 3–5). *Active controls* perform specific safety-related functions, such as universal barrier precautions to prevent infections, IV pumps to prevent medication errors, and round-tip surgical blades (scalpels) to prevent sharp injuries. *Passive controls* do not have to be operated or maintained, which makes them more reliable since they do not require human involvement. Physical defenses and engineered controls provide the following advantages:

- Elimination of unnecessary human–machine interactions
- Error-tolerant designs that are used to mistake-proof human–machine interactions
- Interlocks to prevent improper operator actions
- Initiation of automatic protective actions when necessary
- Manager-initiated modifications to eliminate or minimize errors associated with work-arounds
- Resolution of deficiencies in the environment or working conditions to minimize their impact on performance

Physical defenses and barriers must be designed to counter and control the conditions that can contribute to safety events (DOE 2009, 3-6), such as inoperable equipment; poorly functioning controls, alarms, or indicators; work-arounds; temporary repairs; long-term modifications or alterations to the work space; nuisance alarms; excessive noise; missing labels; poor lighting; unusual work space or equipment conditions; cramped conditions; and awkward layout of equipment. In the handbook *High Reliability Operations: A Practical Guide to Avoid the System Accident*, B&W Pantex (2008, 137), the firm that contracts with the US Department of Energy (DOE) to oversee the safe storage of the country's nuclear weapons stockpile, recommends:

> Don't hide those barriers! Safety barriers that employees don't know about or understand are often violated and seldom effective. Don't hide barriers from your employees [and] continually prompt employees to verify the effectiveness of barriers. Your employees need to understand which barriers are meant to defend against which hazards. After all, they have the most to lose if an ineffective or missing barrier leads to systemic failure.

Physical and engineered defenses can provide detection capability as well. Warning and alarm system defenses provide the patient care team with important health assessment and patient monitoring information, while electronic health records are designed with software lockouts that allow only one patient record to be opened at a time to avoid wrong-patient errors. Moreover, forcing function defenses provide hard-stop limits on the programming of smart IV pumps (Wetterneck 2012, 453).

Smart IV pumps provide an excellent example of engineered physical defenses and controls that suppress the hazards of wrong-dose, wrong-rate medication errors. The first programmable IV infusion pumps would accept any infusion rate and programming entry errors—for example, entering the volume as the rate could result in a fatal dose. "Compared to medications delivered via other routes, IV medication errors are twice as likely to cause patient harm" (Vanderveen 2014). Beginning around 2004, smart IV pumps introduced a major defense against intravenous medication errors, the dose error reduction system. Wireless connectivity facilitated the integration of smart pumps with other systems and devices. These technological enhancements and safety defenses represented a major improvement in infusion safety that enhanced nursing productivity, aided clinical decision-making, improved patient monitoring, and reduced the variation in medication infusion processes (Vanderveen 2014).

According to Dr. Tim Vanderveen, smart IV pumps have significantly improved IV medication safety by (1) fostering the development of drug dose limits, (2) promoting the standardization of concentration and dosing units, (3) providing a treasure trove of infusion data, (4) documenting many "good catches" of prevented programming errors, (5) uncovering a high degree of variation in infusion pump practices, (6) identifying human factors–related issues that provide opportunities for better design, and (7) promoting wireless connectivity with server applications.

HUMAN DEFENSES

Nurses or other caregiving staff may sometimes be the cause of human error that threatens a patient's safe care experience. At the same time, however, they are often the last line of defense against a hazard becoming a harm. The knowledge, skills, and abilities of the patient care team members are influenced by their past experiences, decision-making abilities, education, and training—all of which serve as a potent defense against human error and latent organizational weaknesses.

Human defenses are also driven by the cultural norms, values, beliefs, and attitudes of the organization and staff. "Culture is defined by people's behavior, and safe behavior is value-driven. The true values of an organization are reflected in the observed acts of its people" (DOE 2009, 3-8). Thinking about their important role as "safeties"—the last line of defense—nurses and other caregivers at the sharp end of patient care must constantly consider the errors that could occur at each step in critical care processes and the hazards that create error-likely situations.

Performing this defensive function requires situational awareness and the application of readily available reminders of the human performance improvement tools that provide an additional defense against preventable harm. Human defensive actions include (1) pre-job briefings, (2) questioning attitude, (3) self-checking, (4) peer checking, (5) eliminating error precursors at the job site, (6) stopping when unsure, (7) adherence to procedures, (8) second-person verifications, and (9) attention and alertness. These safe care practices and communication techniques were discussed in chapter 3.

FACTORS THAT DEFEAT DEFENSES AND CONTROLS

The Institute of Nuclear Power Operations (INPO) maintains safety standards for the nation's 102 nuclear power plants and conducts routine safety inspections of nuclear facilities. During its many years of oversight of this high-reliability industry, the INPO identified several warning signs reflecting common weaknesses that contribute to the degradation of defenses and controls (DOE 2009, 3-25). Hospital leaders and performance improvement staff should consider these factors and use them to assess the effectiveness of the hospital's defenses:

- *Overconfidence.* Staff are living on past successes and therefore do not recognize low-level problems and remain unaware of hazards.
- *Isolationism.* Benchmarking is seldom done, and best practices are not implemented; therefore, the organization lags others in the industry in many areas of performance and may be unaware of it.
- *Adversarial relationships.* Within the organization, employees are not involved and are not listened to, and they are not encouraged to raise concerns about safety. Adversarial relationships hinder open communications.
- *Informal operations.* Operational standards, formality, and discipline are lacking. Special projects and initiatives overshadow a focus on operations.
- *Weak engineering.* A loss of talent and lack of alignment with operational priorities causes weak engineering and design.
- *Production priorities.* Important equipment problems linger and repairs are postponed—safety is assumed and not explicitly emphasized in staff interactions and communications.
- *Inadequate change management.* Organizational changes are implemented before their impacts are fully considered—processes and procedures do not support strong performance following management changes.
- *Serious safety events.* Event significance is unrecognized or underplayed and reactions to events and unsafe conditions are not aggressive—organizational causes of events are not explored in depth.
- *Ineffective leaders.* Managers are defensive, lack team skills, and communicate poorly. Managers lack knowledge about the organization and lack operational experience. And senior leaders are not involved in operations, do not exercise accountability, and do not follow up.

- *Lack of self-criticism.* Self-assessment processes, such as management observation programs, do not find problems or do not address them—if a problem is identified, the results are not acted on in time to make a difference.

In conducting a thorough analysis of the causes of wrong-site, wrong-patient, and wrong-procedure surgeries, The Joint Commission's Center for Transforming Healthcare identified 29 main causes that stemmed from the organization's culture or occurred during the scheduling process, during the time the patient was in the preoperative holding area, or during surgery. For the wrong-site surgery cases reviewed in the project, controls and defenses were either absent, circumvented, or inconsistently applied. For example, during the scheduling process, unapproved abbreviations, cross-outs of information, and illegible handwriting were identified as event precursors. The inconsistent use of surgical site marking, time-out processes that were inconsistently used or not used at all, and inadequate patient verification by the team because of time pressures or distractions were causal factors in the preoperative holding area. Cultural contributions to surgical mistakes reflect an organization that has an inconsistent focus on patient safety and does not empower staff to voice their safety concerns (Joint Commission Center for Transforming Healthcare 2011).

> We need to ensure that our systems are as error-tolerant as possible. We can do this by ensuring that we have appropriate defenses in place.
> —James Reason and Alan Hobbs (2003)

ANALYZING THE STRENGTH OF DEFENSES THROUGH BARRIER EFFECTIVENESS ANALYSIS

Defenses and barriers should be routinely analyzed to determine their status (present or absent, activated or ignored) and their effectiveness at preventing patient harm. Each barrier or defense should be analyzed to (1) clarify the hazard that the defense is designed to control, (2) determine the threat that the defense is meant to protect against, (3) determine the effectiveness of the defense against the intended threat, and (4) assess the significance of identified weaknesses in the defense and their possible contribution to system safety events (B&W Pantex 2008, 139). High-reliability organizations reduce variability and improve the safety of performance by minimizing hazards, reducing the negative influences of complex interactivity, minimizing human error, and employing redundant independent barriers as backup measures (B&W Pantex 2008, 29).

A thorough barrier effectiveness analysis will reveal five defensive states—six if the hospital is still routinely harming patients—that indicate the effectiveness of the organization's safety defenses:

1. Defense was in place, was activated, and was effective at controlling the hazard and preventing patient harm.
2. Defense was in place, was activated, but was penetrated (ineffective), allowing the hazard to cause harm.
3. Defense was in place but was not activated (possible act of omission).
4. Defense was circumvented (possible act of commission).
5. Defense was not in place and was not required.
6. "What is a defense?" (ignorance of the effective use of defenses, barriers, and controls leads to patient harm).

Barriers and defenses can be assessed retrospectively as part of a root cause analysis to determine how the designed defenses and controls worked, how they might have failed, and how they could be strengthened to provide greater protection from harm in the future. "Investigators use barrier analysis to identify hazards associated with an accident and the barriers that should/could have prevented it" (DOE 2012, 1-21). The effectiveness of defenses can also be assessed prospectively through scenario testing and concurrently by the patient care team and the patient safety coach. Being mindful of the emerging situation as patient care team members or caregivers work through a safety-critical process or procedure should include an awareness of the safety defenses that are supposed to control process-specific hazards and an assessment of their activation and effectiveness. A sample barrier effectiveness analysis for fall-related defenses is outlined in exhibit 11.1.

Barrier effectiveness analysis considers five elements (DOE 2012, 2-64):

1. *Hazard identification*—identify the targeted hazard that the defense is supposed to control.
2. *Barrier identification*—identify each barrier that is supposed to target and control the identified hazard.
3. *Barrier performance*—assess how the barrier or defense actually performed, whether the barrier was in place or not, and whether the barrier failed to perform as designed.
4. *Causes of barrier failure*—identify the probable causes of the barrier's failure.
5. *Consequences*—evaluate the consequences of the barrier's failure and contributions to a safety event.

Exhibit 11.1: Sample Barrier Effectiveness Analysis—Patient Falls

Hazard: Falls
Target: Patients
Event: Patient fell while trying to ambulate alone to access the bathroom; suffered a bruised hip and shoulder, which extended the patient's hospitalization two days.

Defense/Barrier

(Analysis is performed for each defense that is designed to control each hazard.)
Have sturdy handrails in patient rooms, bathrooms, and hallways (the fifth defense of the 12 Universal Fall Precautions).

Defense Purpose

(prevention or mitigation)
Prevention defense

Defense Type

(physical, administrative, or human)
Physical

How did the defense/barrier perform?

This defense was not activated because other defenses failed first; therefore, handrails were never used. Staff failed to respond to repeated call light requests for assistance to go to the bathroom, and the defense of hourly nurse rounding was not performed.

Why did the defense/barrier fail?

This defense did not fail; it was never activated because other layers of defense failed first.

What effect did the defense/barrier have on the serious safety event?

None.

Should the defense/barrier be strengthened in any way?

Not at this time.

In support of the barrier effectiveness analysis, hospitals should also develop a *safety case* for every major error-provoking and harm-producing hazard. The safety case (1) identifies a claim or concern about a safety-critical process or procedure; (2) makes a structured argument to support the claim; and (3) provides evidence that demonstrates the validity of the argument (e.g., facts, research, test data, expert opinion).

For example, a safety case for IV infusion pumps should include a hazard analysis to identify related hazards and provide "an argument that hazards caused by the device have been adequately addressed. This is accomplished through a thorough analysis of hazards and implementation of adequate controls to address the hazards" (FDA 2014, 10–11). The safety case for infusion pumps should make a claim about the safety of the pump, clarify the patients and conditions for which the pump is intended, and establish that effective defenses and controls have been implemented to prevent or mitigate the potential harmful effects of the hazard.

Industrial safety expert Erik Hollnagel (2004, 97–98) has defined a set of "pragmatic criteria" that can be useful for assessing the adequacy and effectiveness of a hospital's patient safety defenses, barriers, and controls:

- *Efficiency or adequacy*—how efficient the barrier is expected to be in achieving its purpose
- *Resources required*—the resources needed to design, develop, implement, and maintain the barrier
- *Robustness (reliability)*—how reliable and resistant the barrier is—for example, how well it can withstand the variability of the environment, including working practices, degraded information or noise, unexpected events, and wear and tear
- *Delay in implementation*—the time from conception to implementation of a barrier
- *Applicability to safety-critical tasks*—safety-critical tasks play a special role in sociotechnical systems
- *Availability*—whether the barrier can fulfill its purpose when needed
- *Evaluation*—whether a barrier works as expected and is available when needed
- *Dependence on humans*—the extent to which a barrier depends on humans to achieve its purpose

LESSONS FROM HIGH-RELIABILITY ORGANIZATIONS

Safety Management in Air Traffic Control

Each day, the Air Traffic Organization (ATO), the operational arm of the US Federal Aviation Administration, guides more than 50,000 flights through 30.2 million square miles of domestic and international airspace. The ATO's mission is to ensure that every flight departs and arrives safely. During the 12-year period ending in 2015, 50 fatal accidents related to air traffic management occurred in the US National Airspace System; only one involved a commercial air carrier. In three of the last five years ending in 2015, no fatal accidents related to air traffic management occurred.

In 2015, air traffic operations totaled 132.1 million flights. Air traffic operations experienced only 19 high-risk events in that year, reflecting a safe performance rate of 99.99451 percent. The US air traffic control system is an exemplary high-reliability organization, operating in an extremely high-risk environment while experiencing very few events. The ATO maintains a comprehensive Safety Management System, which received more than 15,000 reports in 2015 through its Voluntary Safety Reporting Programs—the largest of its kind in the world. The reporting system "allows those on the frontlines of safety—such as controllers, technicians, and flight crews—to document incidents, concerns, and potential solutions without the fear of reprisal" (FAA 2015, 4).

The ATO's primary measure of safety-related performance is the system risk event rate, a 12-month rolling rate that reflects the frequency of serious airborne losses of separation per 1,000 reported events. In September 2015, the rate was 2.62 serious losses for every 1,000 reported losses, well below the ATO's target of 20.

The ATO assesses safety incidents through a rigorous Risk Analysis Process, regardless of whether the event occurred in the air, on an airport surface, or in one of the ATO's technical systems. Assessments are performed by a panel of experts that includes pilots, controllers, and human factors specialists. Significant hazards include runway incursions, degradation of equipment that could affect the safety of air traffic or flight information services, and loss of separation in the air. The most persistent safety problems reported through the ATO's voluntary reporting systems are

→

(1) safety culture, (2) procedural deficiency, (3) equipment design or function, (4) interface with other facilities, (5) compliance with directives, (6) organizational policy, and (7) delegation of work.

A significant safety concern is the growing complexity and congestion of the National Airspace System, which is particularly apparent in the airfield environment. The ATO has enhanced its defenses and controls through the Runway Safety Program, which involves integrating multiple layers of surface surveillance and alerting technology, redesigning problematic runway and taxiway layouts, and improving safety aids such as runway lighting and signage.

Over the 10-year period ending in 2015, improvement in runway-related safety defenses and in the Runway Safety Program overall resulted in a 44 percent decrease in serious runway incursions (incorrect presence of an aircraft, vehicle, or person in a protected area for takeoffs and landings) and prevented damage and injuries from runway excursions (when an aircraft veers off the runway or overruns the runway).

The ATO's Risk Analysis Process involves assessment of the severity and likelihood of recurrence of safety events and assessment of the National Airspace System's defensive layers and barriers. These defenses and barriers represent the "controllability" of the situation. The analysis reviews the systemic factors and human errors that contributed to a safety event and the likelihood that those factors will align again in the future.

The ATO's barriers "fall into three categories: air traffic control, pilot, and [National Airspace System] technology infrastructure. Each category is composed of many discrete barriers designed to prevent a loss of required separation from occurring (termed resolution barriers) or prevent a loss of separation from becoming a collision (recovery barriers)" (FAA 2016, 9). Examples of ATO technology defenses include alerts, advisories, and surveillance systems. Examples of organizational defenses include planning, communications, and supervisory interventions. Examples of human (pilot) defenses include situational awareness, execution, and "See and Avoid." Each defense and barrier is scored for effectiveness. Those scores allow safety analysts "to inspect the effectiveness of barriers and the factors that influence their performance at different locations and at different levels of specificity. We can identify trends in individual or composite barrier performance, which, in turn, help us understand the conditions that contribute to vulnerabilities or successes" (FAA 2016, 10).

PATIENTS DEFENDING THEIR OWN SAFETY

Clearly, no one is more invested in patient safety than the patient. Patients must be encouraged, empowered, and fully engaged as active members of the patient care team in the hospital setting. "Research shows that when patients are engaged in their health care, it can lead to measurable improvements in safety and quality" (AHRQ 2013). According to the Agency for Healthcare Research and Quality's "Guide to Patient and Family Engagement in Hospital Quality and Safety," hospitals should promote better communication among patients, family members, and healthcare professionals beginning at admission and throughout the patient's stay. "When patients speak up—and when health care professionals engage and empower them to do so and then understand and act on what we hear—we strengthen the health care team. We know that successful organizations that are serious about shared decision making and focused on safety encourage patients to" (Brady and Gandhi 2018):

- Ask questions to make sure they understand their diagnosis, treatment options, and care plans
- Speak up about the risks and problems they see or may encounter
- Express their values

Indeed, "patients themselves can help to safeguard their own wellbeing and promote change" (Health Foundation 2013, 3). When patients actively participate in their care, they are involved in decisions about their care plan and kept informed about what is happening to them or about to happen to them. When patients participate, the quality and safety of care improves. Research indicates that greater levels of patient participation are associated with fewer adverse events (Health Foundation 2013, 15).

Patients can engage in three broad behaviors to contribute to their own safety: (1) making sure that their treatment is appropriate for them, (2) making sure that treatment is given as planned and according to appropriate protocols, and (3) helping to identify and reduce problems and risks within healthcare systems (Health Foundation 2013).

AN INTERESTING THOUGHT—MAYBE NOTHING MORE

Our current metrics and measures for evaluating individual job performance are mostly offensive performance measures; however, performance evaluations should also include individuals' defensive contributions to patient care. Leading hospitals assess staff performance against behavior-based expectations, encouraging staff to take personal responsibility for safe care practices and actively report safety concerns. By doing so, they reinforce the hospital's culture of safety and commitment to zero patient harm.

In professional basketball, the key statistical metric for players is their "efficiency" rating—a measure of both the player's offensive production and defensive performance. This rating reflects the player's overall performance. This measure is critically important, since the same five players on the court must excel on both offensive and defensive—just like the frontline "players" who provide care to patients in a hospital.

In professional hockey, players perform in either offensive or defensive positions, but they all have defensive responsibilities while on the ice. All players receive a "plus/minus" rating for their performance during each game. Players receive +1 for every goal the team scores while they are on the ice and −1 for every goal the team gives up while they are on the ice. A player's plus/minus statistic correlates with excellent overall performance and contribution to winning games, both offensively and defensively.

Here's an interesting idea: Every day a member of the patient care team is involved in an event-free day, they get a +1, and every day that the team experiences a safety event, all the team members receive a −1. Hospitals and patient care teams often recognize and celebrate when they have not experienced a central line–associated bloodstream infection, ventilator-associated pneumonia, catheter-associated urinary tract infection, patient fall, or other serious safety event over a long period of time. Providing teams and team members with a "Patient Safety Plus/Minus Score" could provide recognition and reinforcement of new safety behaviors and their impact on saving lives!

THE PARITY ZONE

Psychologist James Reason, in his book *Managing the Risks of Organizational Accidents*, describes the dynamic, often competing tensions and motivations in a high-hazard industry—or almost any organization—between production and protection. An organization's resources are generated through the *production* of goods and services, which makes the funds available for the organization's *protections*. "Since production creates the resources that make protection possible, its needs will generally have priority. . . . This is partly because those who manage the organization possess productive rather than protective skills" (Reason 1997, 4).

Reason explains that the prioritization of production over protection (the organization's defenses against patient harm) is partly attributable to the fact that production information is clear, direct, and readily understood, whereas protection-related information is indirect, discontinuous, and "indicated by the absence of negative outcomes." Reason's assessment of the organizational leader's bent toward production over protection is concerning if it holds true for healthcare executives. If an organization fails to invest in adequate protections (i.e., adequate defenses and barriers against serious safety events), its production will suffer as a result of waste, rework, low patient satisfaction, low morale, and loss of community trust. "In an ideal world, the level of protection should match the hazards of the productive operations—the parity zone. The more extensive the productive operations, the greater is the hazard exposure and so also is the need for corresponding protection" (Reason 1997, 3). Hospital leaders should assess their organization's *parity zone* to establish the right balance between production and protection and to ensure that the entire organization understands that balance. As a hospital or healthcare system leader, what are your protection skills, and how can they be strengthened?

CONCLUSION

Chapter 11 describes the safe care practices that will strengthen a hospital's defenses to protect patients from harm. Even high-performing organizations can suffer catastrophic failure when they do not maintain effective controls and defenses against harm. Three types of defenses are discussed in this chapter: physical defenses, administrative defenses, and human defenses. Understanding how these defenses and controls function and how to effectively develop, deploy, monitor, and improve them is critical to a hospital's efforts to keep patients safe from the potentially harmful effects of human error and system weaknesses.

CHAPTER 11 SAFE CARE PRACTICES

1. Understand the adequacy and effectiveness of the organization's defenses and controls and their contribution to keeping patients safe.

2. Encourage every member of the patient care team, as well as the leadership team that supports their delivery of safe care, to build the following steps into their patient care practices: clarify the scope of work, analyze the hazards, develop and implement defenses and controls, perform work with activated defenses, and offer feedback for improvement.

$\rightarrow$

---

3. Build safe systems that include multiple layers of defenses—defenses-in-depth—to create redundant, overlapping, and complementary defensive functions to block errors from harming patients.

4. Consider the factors that defeat defenses and controls and use them to assess the effectiveness of the hospital's defenses.

5. Assess the organization's "parity zone" to establish the right balance between production and protection and to ensure that the entire organization understands that balance.

REFERENCES

Agency for Healthcare Research and Quality (AHRQ). 2013. "Guide to Patient and Family Engagement in Hospital Quality and Safety." Accessed March 20, 2019. www.ahrq.gov/professionals/systems/hospital/engagingfamilies/index.html.

B&W Pantex. 2008. *High Reliability Operations: A Practical Guide to Avoid the System Accident*. Amarillo, TX: Babcock and Wilcox Technical Services.

Brady, J., and T. K. Gandhi. 2018. "Patient Safety: Distinct Roles, One Goal." *AHRQ Views*. Published March 12. www.ahrq.gov/news/blog/ahrqviews/patient-safety-distinct-roles-one-goal.html.

Drews, F. A. 2012. "Human Error in Health Care." In *Handbook of Human Factors and Ergonomics in Health Care and Patient Safety*, 2nd ed., edited by P. Carayon, 323–40. Boca Raton, FL: CRC Press.

Drouin, M. 2016. "How the NRC Uses a Defense-in-Depth Approach Today to Protect the Public." *US NRC Blog*. Published July 13. https://public-blog.nrc-gateway.gov/2016/07/13/part-ii-how-the-nrc-uses-a-defense-in-depth-approach-today-to-protect-the-public/.

ESPN. 2019. "NFL Team Total Defense Statistics—2018." Accessed April 13. www.espn.com/nfl/statistics/team/_/stat/total/position/defense.

Gawande, A. 2009. *The Checklist Manifesto*. New York: Metropolitan Books.

Health Foundation. 2013. *Involving Patients in Improving Safety*. Published January. www.health.org.uk/sites/default/files/InvolvingPatientsInImprovingSafety.pdf.

Hollnagel, E. 2004. *Barriers and Accident Prevention*. New York: Ashgate Publishing.

Joint Commission Center for Transforming Healthcare. 2011. "Targeted Solutions Tool for Safe Surgery." Accessed March 20, 2019. www.centerfortransforminghealthcare.org/what-we-offer/targeted-solutions-tool/safe-surgery-tst.

Moskowitz, T., and J. Wertheim. 2012. "Does Defense Really Win Championships?" Published January 20. *Freakonomics Blog.* www.freakonomics.com/2012/01/20/does-defense-really-win-championships.

Poon, E. G., C. A. Keohane, C. S. Yoon, M. Ditmore, A. Bane, O. Levtzion-Korach, T. Moniz, J. M. Rothschild, A. B. Kachalia, J. Hayes, W. W. Churchill, S. Lipsitz, A. D. Whittemore, D. W. Bates, and T. K. Gandhi. 2010. "Effect of Bar-Code Technology on the Safety of Medication Administration." *New England Journal of Medicine* 362 (18): 1698–1707.

Reason, J. 1997. *Managing the Risks of Organizational Accidents.* Burlington, VT: Ashgate Publishing.

Reason, J., and A. Hobbs. 2003. *Managing Maintenance Error: A Practical Guide.* Burlington, VT: Ashgate Publishing.

US Department of Energy (DOE). 2012. *DOE Handbook: Accident and Operational Safety Analysis.* Published July. www.standards.doe.gov/standards-documents/1200/1208-bhdbk-2012-v2/@@images/file.

———. 2009. "Managing Defenses." In *Human Performance Improvement Handbook,* vol. 1, *Concepts and Principles,* chapter 3. Accessed March 21, 2019. www.standards.doe.gov/standards-documents/1000/1028-BHdbk-2009-v1.

US Federal Aviation Administration (FAA). 2016. *Transforming Risk Management: Understanding the Challenges of Safety Risk Measurement.* Accessed March 20, 2019. www.faa.gov/about/office_org/headquarters_offices/ato/service_units/safety/media/transforming-risk-mgmt.pdf.

———. 2015. *Air Traffic Organization: 2015 Safety Report.* Accessed March 20, 2019. www.faa.gov/about/office_org/headquarters_offices/ato/service_units/safety/media/2015_safety_report.pdf.

US Federal Emergency Management Authority (FEMA). 2019. "Defense-in-Depth." Accessed April 13. https://emilms.fema.gov/IS3/FEMA_IS/is03/REM0404040.htm.

US Food and Drug Administration (FDA). 2014. "Infusion Pumps Total Product Life Cycle: Guidance for Industry and FDA Staff." Published December 2. www.fda.gov/downloads/medicaldevices/deviceregulationandguidance/guidancedocuments/ucm209337.pdf.

Vanderveen, R. 2014. "From Smart Pumps to Intelligent Infusion Systems—the Promise of Interoperability." *Patient Safety & Quality Healthcare.* Published May 27. www.psqh.com/analysis/from-smart-pumps-to-intelligent-infusion-systems-the-promise-of-interoperability/.

Wachter, R. 2012. *Understanding Patient Safety,* 2nd ed. New York: McGraw-Hill Medical.

Wetterneck, T. B. 2012. "Error Recovery in Health Care." In *Handbook of Human Factors and Ergonomics in Health Care and Patient Safety,* 2nd ed., edited by P. Carayon, 449–61. Boca Raton, FL: CRC Press.

Designing Safer Systems

WHY DOES SYSTEM DESIGN MATTER TO THE DELIVERY OF SAFE PATIENT CARE?

When we think of *systems*, we tend to think *big*. Big systems like the mega US healthcare system or large macrosystems such as Ascension Health, Hospital Corporation of America, Kaiser Permanente, Sutter Health, or Community Health System. But the hospital's intensive care unit (ICU), emergency department, and medical/surgical unit are all systems too! They are the microsystems at the sharp end of healthcare that hospitalized patients are most familiar with, but often they will come in contact with many of the other supporting microsystems as well. Patients will receive care, treatment, or services from systems such as nutrition and dietetics, radiology, clinical laboratory services, housekeeping, and pharmacy services during their hospital stay. And the clinical departments within the hospital, such as pathology, cardiology, surgery, oncology, radiology, anesthesiology, emergency services, and medicine, are also microsystems that are responsible for organizing and delivering care that is safe, effective, high quality, and clinically excellent.

To improve the mesosystems of clinical departments, patient care units, and supporting patient care services, hospital leaders must first understand how each of these individual systems of care contribute to the patient care experience and, second, understand how the systems are interconnected and interdependent. Achieving safety at the sharp end of patient care requires, as organizational theorist Karl Weick has said, a "reluctance to simplify." By paying closer attention to the details, contexts, and complexities of the many systems of patient care, hospitals can counteract the tendency toward oversimplification. By becoming more mindful of the risks of failing to understand the complexities of the systems of care, hospital leaders will gain "a richer and more varied picture of potential consequences, which in turn suggests a richer and more varied set of precautions and early warning signs. HROs [high-reliability organizations] are just as preoccupied with complicating their simplifications as they are with probing their failures" (Weick and Sutcliffe 2007, 53).

THREE STEPS OF SAFER SYSTEM DESIGN

The process of designing safe systems comprises three steps. The first step is knowing the systems—that is, gaining a thorough knowledge of the safety-related impact that each of the microsystems of patient care and supporting services has on patient care. The second step involves assessing the safety and reliability of each safety-critical function and process within each system. The third step requires the application of selected Lean Six Sigma improvement tools to engage frontline staff in the practical design of safer systems of care. Tools such as Lean, value stream mapping, SIPOC (Supplier, Input, Process, Output, Customer), and Design for Six Sigma are useful for (1) simplifying processes and systems to remove wasteful steps and inefficiency, (2) identifying and moderating existing hazards and risks, and (3) strengthening system defenses and barriers to protect patients from harm.

An analogy is useful here: If you want to drive a safe car, you'll take it to a competent service center that will run a comprehensive electronic diagnostic assessment and tell you what needs to be fixed. The service center will fix the parts that do not work well any longer and make sure that all of the car's defensive features—brakes, brake lights, horn, dashboard warning indicators, backup camera—are functioning properly. This process requires an understanding of all of the car's operating systems; the application of a comprehensive diagnostic assessment to determine system weaknesses, hazards, and safety-related problems; and the competent use of the right tools to improve the car's safety and overall functioning. The analogy is not perfect, but it makes the point: knowledge, assessment, and improvement—the three steps of safer system design. There are, of course, two important prerequisites for beginning a safer system design project: input from the customer and mastery of change management (the subject of chapter 1).

SAFETY DIAGNOSTICS AND ASSESSMENT TECHNIQUES

After completing a thorough assessment of the systems that work together to provide patient care, treatment, and services, hospitals should run *diagnostics* on each system to determine (1) opportunities for improvement; (2) error-provoking features of the system; (3) known hazards; (4) the effectiveness of existing defenses or the need for new defenses or barriers; and (5) the history of failure—that is, the incidence of human, system, or human factors–related event precursors. High-reliability organizations use diagnostic tools that are familiar to healthcare, such as root cause analysis and failure mode and effects analysis, as well as less familiar tools such as functional hazard analysis, the safety assessment report, and the development of the safety case. The analysis of system defenses and barriers, or barrier effectiveness analysis, was described in chapter 11.

Functional Hazard Analysis

The US military has employed functional hazard analysis for many years to "identify and classify the system functions and safety hazards" and to assess the consequences associated with functional failure—that is, hazards (System Safety Society 2014, 2). Functional hazard analysis examines the relationship between identified safety-significant functions that are performed within a system and all related hazards. An interdisciplinary team conducts the assessment, considering what mitigation solutions (defenses, barriers, controls) might be applied to neutralize the hazard and protect against any adverse effects that hazard might have on patient care. Estimating the probability of a serious safety event as a result of a functional hazard should be a part of the functional hazard analysis. "Design constraints are recommended for inclusion in the system specifications in order to eliminate or reduce the risk of the identified hazards" (System Safety Society 2014, 2).

The functions or discrete actions that take place within the system define the system's capability. The analysis of system functions is, not surprisingly, completed through a functional analysis. Importantly, the functional hazard analysis will assess both what is required of the system and its functions and how the system should achieve its goals. Functions and hazards should be assessed from several different viewpoints: overall, operational, systems, services, data and information, standards, and capability.

A functional hazard analysis encompasses seven steps (System Safety Society 2014, 5–9):

1. *Gather and interpret system architecture data.* Identify and describe the functions that are performed by the system.
2. *Evaluate functional failures for hazards.* Evaluate each function for the potential impact of functional failure, considering all of the life cycles, activities, and modes that apply to the system.
3. *Identify safety-significant subsystems and interfaces.* Evaluate the correlation between the system's safety-significant functions and all subsystems and interfaces.

4. *Identify existing and recommended mitigations.* For each identified hazard, identify existing and new design constraints that will reduce or eliminate the risk of the hazard contributing to a future safety event.

5. *Decompose safety-significant functions into components.* Decompose system functions to the component level, a more granular level of operational detail that looks at component functionality involving hardware, software, and human performance.

6. *Identify risk levels, software criticality indices, and follow-on actions.* Based on an understanding of existing hazards and causal factors at the component, function, and system levels, assess the safety impact of those hazards and causal factors on the severity and probability of serious safety events.

7. *Document the analysis.* Treat the functional hazard analysis as a critical diagnostic for determining the safety health of a system.

Safety Assessment Report

The safety assessment report (SAR) is a comprehensive evaluation of the safety risks of a system. The SAR is used to identify all safety-related features and functions of a system and the procedural hazards that may be present in the system (Trumble 2014). The SAR must also specify the procedural defenses and controls that should be followed within and specific to the system to prevent an event.

For example, in a hospital setting, an SAR might be performed for the ICU, starting with a general introduction describing the size and scope of the unit's services, followed by a detailed description of the system and its components and functions as well as the identification of all related hazards. Next, the SAR describes all system-specific safety engineering, which provides guidance on safe care practices and protective defenses and barriers. Finally, the assessment offers conclusions and recommendations for safety enhancements, including the identification of residual risks, or the risks that have not been removed from the system and may not be controlled with a barrier or defense. Every senior leader in the hospital should understand the residual risks for every safety-critical process and system in the hospital. The safety engineering portion of the report will be informed by the results of the functional hazard analysis and provides the following (Trumble 2014):

- A description of the hazardous conditions inherent in the system
- A list of all hazards by subsystem or major component
- A description of the actions taken to eliminate or control hazards

- A discussion of the effects of defenses and controls on the probability of occurrence and severity level of serious safety events
- A discussion of the residual risks that remain after defenses and controls are applied or for which no controls can be applied

In the United Kingdom, the Health and Safety Executive (HSE) is responsible for setting standards for workplace safety for more than 20 industries, similar to the Occupational Safety and Health Administration's role in the United States. The HSE's guidance on the use of SARs provides a useful tool for hospitals and healthcare systems (HSE 2017, 135–41). Although the HSE's application of the SAR targets worker and workplace safety, its process safety guidance can also be applied to the assessment of the safety of patient care processes. The HSE's process safety assessment (abridged and modified for use in healthcare) focuses on the following:

- Identifying hazards and major safety event scenarios
- Describing defenses and controls and their link to safety event scenarios
- Outlining decision criteria for selection of defenses and controls to ensure that risks are tolerable
- Demonstrating adequate diversity and redundancy in defenses and controls
- Ensuring that process risks are as low as reasonably possible
- Demonstrating how defensive measures that have been taken will prevent foreseeable failures that could lead to safety events
- Describing how the safety design of a system or process reflects the associated hazard analysis
- Introducing inherent safety designs when reasonably practicable
- Describing additional defenses and controls that are required to reduce risk in high-hazard situations
- Applying the hierarchical approach of inherently safer design (eliminate, prevent, control, mitigate) to select defenses and controls to reduce risks
- Implementing process designs that eliminate or prevent unsafe conditions from occurring
- Demonstrating that the principles of redundancy, diversity, separation, and segregation have been applied to the selection of defenses and controls
- Showing how passive rather than active risk reduction measures are prioritized
- Ensuring safety in the design of the layout of the work space and work environment

- Designing safety-related controls and alarms to prevent or warn of excursions beyond safe operating limits
- Implementing emergency prevention and protection measures

According to the HSE (2017, 141) report, "failure to manage change is a common cause of accidents." The management of change criteria should stipulate when a process change is significant enough to go through the organization's formal change management process and whether a formal hazard analysis is needed.

Safety Case

As a senior leader (a member of the medical staff, a unit manager, or a nurse in the ICU, for example), how do you know if the patient care environment—and the actual care and services being provided in that environment—is safe? A common rule of thumb is that "nothing bad has happened today, so it must be safe."

A more informed, credible, and valid approach is to do what high-reliability organizations do—develop a safety case that makes the argument, supported by credible evidence, that the system is acceptably safe. A safety case should be created for the hospital and for each of the patient care microsystems operating within it.

A safety case is a comprehensive and dynamic document that clearly lays out the circumstances under which a system can operate safely and demonstrates "that the associated risk and hazards have been assessed, appropriate limits and conditions have been defined and adequate safety measures have been identified and put in place" (ONR 2016, 5). The Office of Nuclear Regulation (ONR) in the United Kingdom defines eight qualities that are fundamental to a good safety case, which are modified here for use in healthcare (ONR 2016, 6–9):

1. *Intelligible.* The safety case should be structured to meet the needs of everyone who will use it, from managers to frontline staff.
2. *Valid.* The safety case should accurately represent the current status of the system.
3. *Complete.* The safety case should analyze all of the activities associated with normal operations, identify and analyze safety concerns, and demonstrate that risks are as low as reasonably possible. The safety case should show that the system is adequately safe and discuss what is needed for it to remain safe.
4. *Evidential.* The arguments presented in the safety case should be supported with relevant, verifiable evidence.

5. *Robust.* The safety case should demonstrate that the system conforms (or will conform) to sound safety practices, including defenses-in-depth and adequate safety margins.

6. *Integrated.* The safety case should identify hazards from and dependences on other systems.

7. *Balanced.* The safety case should present a balanced account, identifying areas of uncertainty as well as strengths and describing weaknesses and areas for improvement.

8. *Forward looking.* The safety case should demonstrate that the system will remain safe throughout a defined period, demonstrate adequate defenses and controls against hazards, identify important aspects of operation and management that are necessary to maintain safety, and detail any constraints on maintaining system safety.

The ONR's Nuclear Safety Technical Assessment Guide on "The Purpose, Scope, and Content of Safety Cases" describes a framework for developing a safety case that provides useful guidance to hospital leaders who desire to analyze the safety health of their safety-critical processes (ONR 2016, 5): (1) identifying the facility's (or system's) hazards using a thorough and systematic process; (2) identifying the system's failure modes; (3) demonstrating that the system conforms to sound safety principles; (4) using the concept of defenses-in-depth and adequate safety margins; (5) demonstrating that all structures, systems, and components have been designed, constructed, commissioned, operated, and maintained in such a way as to enable them to fulfill their safety functions; (6) providing a basis for the safe management of people, plant, and processes; and (7) analyzing all identified faults and severe accidents using contemporary fault analysis methods to demonstrate that risks are as low as reasonably possible (ALARP).

By developing a safety case for every safety-critical microsystem within the hospital, leaders, managers, and frontline staff will have a common and current understanding of the safety health of the patient care experience. Knowing is a critical attribute of patient safety: Knowing where the hazards are, knowing where the error traps are, knowing how the defenses and controls are functioning, and knowing the failure modes of the system. This knowledge will lead to safer systems design and safer care. The safety case is an organizing tool for understanding the difference between work as imagined and work as performed. The safety case facilitates a better understanding of how the work is actually performed at the sharp end of the patient care process and the risks, hazards, and controls inherent in it.

USE THE RIGHT TOOLS TO BUILD A SAFE HOME

Across the United States, exemplar hospitals, big and small, have shown that by learning how to use and apply the right improvement tools, they can build a safer, more reliable "home" for their patients. Visitors to the hospital home expect that they will be better off for coming and certainly not harmed by the experience. Creating a caring, compassionate, and safe environment for patients requires the right tools: human performance improvement tools, technology solutions, reliability engineering tools, process improvement tools, simulation and training aids, and tools to eliminate waste and inefficiency in processes and systems.

Lean, Design for Six Sigma, and reliability engineering are rigorous system and process improvement techniques that complement the more familiar Plan-Do-Check-Act iterative process of continuous improvement. Developed by Walter Shewhart at Western Electric Company (AT&T Bell Labs) in the 1920s, the Plan-Do-Check-Act process improvement cycle was later popularized by engineer W. Edwards Deming and has become a basic platform for quality improvement around the world. Sometimes, however, high-hazard and highly complex systems require more powerful tools to design quality and safety into system performance.

Deciding which tool is the right one to tackle a particular quality or patient safety challenge should be driven by an experiential decision matrix. From simple projects to complex systemic improvement undertakings, short-term to long-term, unit based or organizationwide, the improvement tools will vary based on the nature of the problem. For an improvement that is small in scope but for which staff resistance is anticipated, effective change management may be enough to effect the change in performance. For a project that requires a team effort, a Kaizen short-term project might be the best approach. Larger projects aimed at removing waste and inefficiency from a process and eliminating opportunities for error or defects require the application of Lean methods.

Sustainable process improvement may require the rigor of a Six Sigma DMAIC (Design, Measure, Analyze, Improve, and Control) effort that comprehensively engages frontline staff in designing and testing process improvements that meet customer expectations of value. When a patient care process is so dysfunctional that incremental improvements are not enough to create an acceptable level of safety, then Design for Six Sigma is the tool to employ to completely redesign the process from top to bottom.

During my 20 years at The Joint Commission, staff applied a variety of Lean Six Sigma tools to dramatically improve the quality of the accreditation process, deliver better value to both paying customers and the public, and remove waste and inefficiency from a complex service delivery model. The DMAIC model was used for most improvement projects and typically included the following steps: (1)

determination of candidate improvement projects through a Pareto prioritization process with input from all staff; (2) selection of a manageable number of projects each year; (3) assignment of project champions and sponsors, and identification of process owners; (4) creation of a project charter with an inclusion/exclusion list, needed resources, team members, project goal and problem statement, and time-table; (5) team meetings facilitated by a change agent and a green or black belt; (6) "report-outs" from the improvement team for every step of the DMAIC process; and (7) the application of a variety of tools appropriate for the project, including value stream mapping, gathering "voice of the customer" information to guide the improvement effort, and analytic tools such as analysis of variance, stakeholder analysis, SIPOC, and statistical process control. (To read more about The Joint Commission's use of Lean Six Sigma to improve its processes and customer service, see ASQ 2009.)

LEAN IMPROVEMENT

According to James Womack and Daniel Jones (1996, 15), "lean thinking is *lean* because it provides a way to do more and more with less and less—less human effort, less equipment, less time, and less space—while coming closer and closer to providing customers with exactly what they want." Lean techniques drive process improvement based on customer needs by eliminating the non-value-added steps in a process and enhancing the value-added steps to create greater value for the customer. According to the Institute for Healthcare Improvement (2005, 2), "the core idea of lean involves determining the value of any given process by distin-guishing value-added steps from non-value-added steps, and eliminating waste . . . so that ultimately every step adds value to the process." The improvement team works through a "brown wallpaper" value stream analysis of the process under review, identifying and labeling all steps in the process. The value stream leads to "eliminating non-value-added steps; and making value flow from beginning to end based on the pull—the expressed needs—of the customer/patient" (IHI 2005, 2). The focus of the Lean improvement methodology is the elimination of waste in a process or system—anything that does not add value for the customer. Healthcare organizations target eight types of waste to improve the patient care experience (Millard 2016):

1. *Defects and mistakes.* Defects in healthcare can be deadly. Defects include misdiagnosis, administration of the wrong medication, and hospital-acquired conditions. Waste includes the time spent creating a defect, reworking defects, and inspecting defects.

2. *Waiting.* Wasted time is a problem for both patients and providers—patients in waiting rooms, staff with uneven workloads waiting for their next task, emergency room patients and physicians waiting for test results, emergency room patients waiting to be admitted, and patients waiting to be discharged.

3. *Transportation.* Waste occurs as patients are moved from department to department or room to room, medication is moved from the pharmacy to its destination, and supplies are moved from storage to the floor.

4. *Overproduction.* Waste includes unnecessary diagnostic tests, uneaten meals, ordering medications that the patient does not need, and peak staffing during nonpeak hours.

5. *Overprocessing.* Waste occurs when complex diagnostic imagery, for example, magnetic resonance imaging, is ordered when a simpler method would suffice (X-ray). Other forms of waste include unnecessary paperwork, surgical intervention instead of an equally effective medical alternative, and treatment by a specialist that could be done by a primary care provider.

6. *Inventory.* Waste includes medications that may expire, preprinted forms, and excess bedside equipment.

7. *Motion.* Waste includes supplies that are not stored where they are needed, work space layouts that are not consistent with workflow, and equipment that is not conveniently located.

8. *Human potential.* Waste occurs when organizations do not listen to employees, when employees are pressured to cover up problems, and when employees habitually work below their level of licensure.

The basic principles of the Lean methodology are (1) specifying value, (2) identifying the value stream, (3) flow, (4) pull, and (5) perfection (Womack and Jones 1996, 16–26):

1. *Specify value.* Value is defined by the customer and reflects the customer's needs. There must be "a conscious attempt to precisely define value in terms of specific products with specific capabilities offered at specific prices through a dialogue with specific customers."

2. *Identify the value stream.* The value stream is "the set of all the specific actions required to bring a specific product" to the customer. Identifying the value stream for a product or service "almost always exposes enormous, indeed staggering, amounts of *muda* [waste]." While many steps will be found to create value, many other steps will be found to create no value and are "immediately avoidable."

3. *Flow.* All the activities needed to design, order, and provide a product occur in a continuous flow rather than as disconnected and aggregated processes.

4. *Pull.* Customers pull the product that they need from the organization rather than the organization pushing products, often unwanted, onto the customer.

5. *Perfection.* As the first four principles interact with each other, value is more accurately specified, the value stream is identified, the value-creating steps flow continuously, and customers pull value from the organization. "Dreaming about perfection is fun [and] also useful, because it shows what is possible and helps us to achieve more than we would otherwise."

HARM-FREE HEALTHCARE: EXEMPLARY PRACTICE

"Zero Defects with Lean": Virginia Mason Health System

Virginia Mason Health System, based in Seattle, Washington, prioritizes patient safety and is a leader in applying Lean principles to help "optimize the patient's experience" (Virginia Mason Institute 2017). As a regional healthcare system with more than 14,000 hospital admissions annually, Virginia Mason strives to make every patient visit a perfect patient experience. Based on Lean principles, the Virginia Mason Production System is used to identify and eliminate waste and inefficiency in the healthcare experience. Lean is about promoting a culture of continuous improvement at Virginia Mason, and the Lean management system is the "cornerstone to a culture that puts the patient first" (Virginia Mason Institute 2017).

Virginia Mason's system is based on the principles of the Toyota Production System. Virginia Mason's experience with applying Lean improvement principles has shown the following (Lin 2016):

- Lean methods engage people, from maintenance workers to physicians and executives, who participate in and understand how Lean applies to their work.

- A set of wide-ranging tools can work for all parts of the healthcare system.

- Collecting and measuring data is an essential part of the Lean process.

→

- When staff are engaged in Lean work, they sustain that work and keep improving.

- While healthcare is highly variable, Lean is adaptable and flexible enough to be a good fit.

According to Melissa Lin (2016) of the Virginia Mason Institute, "The goal is always to achieve zero defects in all their improvement work. In health care, we should all be engaging our staff every day to find the best ways to reach that vital goal for every patient."

Virginia Mason uses value stream maps for all improvement projects "to improve safety and build reliability into our processes throughout the medical center" (King 2016). According to Rosemary King, a registered nurse, value stream maps have "helped us make significant improvements in early sepsis identification and intervention, patient falls, medication errors, and so many other areas." According to King, the value stream map (1) helps identify waste and direct improvement efforts, (2) helps engage team members and connect them to the work, (3) helps leaders connect processes to organizational goals, (4) helps organizational leaders work together to identify flow issues, (5) helps improve the performance of processes, (6) helps increase capacity by identifying waste so that more patients can move efficiently through the system, and (7) helps the organization become a facile, adaptive system. King says that "when we use a value stream map, people are no longer working in isolation. They're working together like musicians in a symphony."

DESIGN FOR SIX SIGMA

Complexity means more opportunities for failure. Healthcare systems and microsystems are complex composites of human, organizational, and environmental elements that interact in sometimes unpredictable ways. In the never-ending pursuit of perfect systems of care in which patients always receive the safest and most effective care possible, sometimes systems cannot be incrementally fixed and require a complete redesign. "When the current product or process cannot be improved to meet customer requirements, it is time for replacement. Design for Six Sigma is intended for use when you must replace a product instead of redesigning [it]" (Quality One 2019).

Design for Six Sigma includes many of the same characteristics of the Six Sigma DMAIC methodology, but it is tailored for the design of new processes rather than making incremental improvements to a process. One of the most common Design for Six Sigma approaches is the DMADV method—Define, Measure, Analyze, Design, Verify. The five stages of DMADV include the following (Quality One 2019):

1. *Define*. Develop the project charter, communication plan, and a risk assessment plan.
2. *Measure*. Gain an understanding of the customer's needs and then translate those needs into measurable design requirements.
3. *Analyze*. Convert the performance requirements into system, subsystem, and component-level design requirements. Quality function deployment is a useful tool for this purpose. The team develops multiple design options and uses decision-making tools to select the final design.
4. *Design*. Evaluate the design using tools such as failure mode and effects analysis. The team develops a design and validation plan for the new process.
5. *Verify*. Introduce the new process or product and perform validation testing to verify that it meets customer and performance requirements. Often a process failure mode and effects analysis is performed to evaluate the risk inherent in the new process and to resolve any concerns.

A benefit of applying the Design for Six Sigma improvement methodology is gaining a clearer understanding of the gap between customer expectations and the current capabilities of a process (Graves 2014). Customer expectations can be clarified by listening to the voice of the customer, prioritizing customer responses, and identifying a measurable target for the customer requirements.

"CHANGE FOR THE BETTER": KAIZEN

To develop effective and sustainable solutions to persistent problems, it is crucial to engage employees who are closest to the problem in creating the solution. *Kaizen* is a method of continuous improvement that "stresses that the real experts in any organization are the people that actually do the work each day, and these employees should be intimately involved in improving their own workflows" (Congdon 2012). *Kai* and *zen* mean "change for the better," and the Kaizen approach "refers to any activities that continually improve all business functions or processes and involves every employee" (Kanbanchi 2018). A small-step work improvement method, Kaizen emerged in the 1950s as a result of Deming's consulting efforts in Japan to help industry improve the quality of its products. Kaizen emphasizes involving frontline workers in improving their own work processes and empowering them to implement incremental changes that will make the organization as a whole better off. The Kaizen approach to process improvement is based on 10 principles that should guide staff efforts (Kanbanchi 2018):

1. Improve everything continuously.
2. Abolish old, traditional concepts.
3. Accept no excuses and make things happen.
4. Say no to the status quo of implementing new methods and assuming they will work.
5. If something is wrong, correct it.
6. Empower everyone to take part in problem-solving.
7. Get information and opinions from multiple people.
8. Before making decisions, ask *why* five times to get to the root cause.
9. Be economical. Save money through small improvements and spend the saved money on further improvements.
10. Remember that improvement has no limits. Never stop trying to improve.

Ronda Bowen (2011) recommends implementing the 3G approach for decision-making in Kaizen projects: "The 3G approach involves *Gemba* (place or location), *Genbutsu* (the product), and *Genjitsu* (the problem being specifically looked at). By viewing the problem, in a given space, related to the product, it helps you to be specific about the changes you wish to implement."

A Kaizen "blitz" or Kaizen event is designed to address a particular problem or improvement opportunity over a short period. "A Kaizen event is a focused development project that can accomplish breakthrough improvements in a short amount of time [and] have a clear and concise objective along with immediately available resources and rapid results" (Kanbanchi 2018). The continuous cycle of Kaizen activity has seven phases (Choudhury 2017): (1) identify an opportunity, (2) analyze the process, (3) develop an optimal solution, (4) implement the solution, (5) study the results, (6) standardize the solution, and (7) plan for the future. The idea of *gemba* "is that the problems are visible and the best improvement ideas will come from going to the gemba" where the work is actually performed (Kanbanchi 2018). The improvement team working through a Kaizen event will take a gemba walk to observe and gain insight about how the process they are attempting to improve is performed and to discover information helpful to their effort.

CONCLUSION

Chapter 12 discusses safe care practices that facilitate safer system design. Repairing or replacing ineffective, unsafe, and inefficient patient care systems that harbor uncontrolled hazards requires the application of sophisticated diagnostic tools and improvement methods. The design of safer systems for the delivery of patient care can benefit from lessons learned from other high-risk, high-hazard, yet highly reliable industries. Hospitals need to use better tools to achieve better results—safer care, all the time. The process of designing safer

> Safety starts with system design.
> —Federal Aviation Administration (2015)

systems of care comprises three steps: gaining a thorough knowledge of the safety-related impact that each of the microsystems of patient care and supporting services has on patient care; assessing the safety and reliability of each safety-critical function and process within each system; and applying Lean Six Sigma improvement tools to engage frontline staff in the practical design of safer systems of care.

CHAPTER 12 SAFE CARE PRACTICES

1. Understand the three-step process of designing safe systems: (1) gaining a thorough knowledge of the safety-related impact that each of the microsystems of patient care and supporting services has on patient care; (2) assessing the safety and reliability of each safety-critical function and process within each system; and (3) applying selected Lean Six Sigma improvement tools to engage frontline staff in the practical design of safer systems of care.

2. Run diagnostics on each system to determine (1) opportunities for improvement; (2) error-provoking features of the system; (3) known hazards; (4) the effectiveness of existing defenses or the need for new defenses or barriers; and (5) the history of failure—that is, the incidence of human, system, or human factors–related event precursors.

3. Develop a safety case for every safety-critical microsystem within the hospital. By doing so, leaders, managers, and frontline staff will have a common and current understanding of the safety health of the patient care experience.

→

---

4. Choose the right tool to tackle a particular quality or patient safety challenge using an experiential decision matrix. The right improvement tool depends on the nature of the problem: simple project or complex systemic improvement undertaking, short-term or long-term, unit based or organizationwide.

5. Design a sustainable process improvement. Doing so may require the rigor of a Six Sigma DMAIC (Design, Measure, Analyze, Improve, and Control) effort that comprehensively engages frontline staff in designing and testing process improvements that meet customer expectations of value.

REFERENCES

American Society for Quality (ASQ). 2009. "Don't Just Talk the Talk: The Joint Commission Tackles Its Own Processes with Lean and Six Sigma." *Quality Progress*. Published July. www.jointcommission.org/assets/1/18/ASQ7-09Article.pdf.

Bowen, R. 2011. "A Look at the Kaizen Process: Instilling Continuous Improvement." Bright Hub Project Management. Accessed March 22, 2019. www.brighthubpm.com/methods-strategies/71639-understanding-the-kaizen-process-steps-and-goals/.

Choudhury, A. 2017. "Kaizen with Six Sigma Ensures Continuous Improvement." WBIS Consulting & Training. Published September 30. https://wbisct.net/2017/09/30/kaizen-six-sigma-ensures-continuous-improvement-afsar-choudhury/.

Congdon, K. 2012. "Kaizen: The Key to Lean Healthcare?" *Health IT Outcomes*. Published May 2. www.healthitoutcomes.com/doc/kaizen-the-key-to-lean-healthcare-0001.

Graves, A. 2014. "Design for Six Sigma." *Six Sigma Daily*. Published October 27. www.sixsigmadaily.com/tag/design-for-six-sigma/.

Health and Safety Executive (HSE). 2017. "Process Safety Aspects of Safety Report Assessment." Accessed April 13, 2019. www.hse.gov.uk/comah/sram/docs/s12c.pdf.

Institute for Healthcare Improvement (IHI). 2005. "Going Lean in Health Care." White paper. Accessed March 22, 2019. www.ihi.org/resources/Pages/IHIWhitePapers/GoingLeaninHealthCare.aspx.

Kanbanchi. 2018. "What Is Kaizen?" Accessed March 22, 2019. www.kanbanchi.com/what-is-kaizen.

King, R. 2016. "Why Is a Value Stream Map Important for Transforming Patient Care and Decreasing Costs?" *Virginia Mason Institute Blog*. Published May 17. www.virginiamasoninstitute.org/2016/05/value-stream-map-patient-care-decreasing-costs/.

Lin, M. 2016. "Which Is Better for Engaging Health Care Staff: Lean or Six Sigma?" *Virginia Mason Institute Blog*. Published February 10. www.virginiamasoninstitute.org/2016/02 /better-engaging-health-care-staff-lean-six-sigma.

Millard, M. 2016. "The 7 Wastes of Lean in Healthcare." *KaiNexis Blog*. Published May 10. https://blog.kainexus.com/improvement-disciplines/lean/7-wastes-of-lean-in-healthcare.

Office for Nuclear Regulation (ONR). 2016. "The Purpose, Scope, and Content of Safety Cases." Published July. www.onr.org.uk/operational/tech_asst_guides/ns-tast-gd-051.pdf.

Quality One. 2019. "Design for Six Sigma (DFSS)." Accessed March 22. https://quality -one.com/dfss/.

System Safety Society. 2014. "Functional Hazard Analysis (FHA) Methodology Tutorial." Accessed March 22, 2019. https://system-safety.org/issc2014/83_Functional_Hazard _Analysis_Common%20Process.pdf.

Trumble, C. 2014. "Safety Assessment Report Workshop." International System Safety Society, Tennessee Valley Chapter. Accessed March 22, 2019. www.isss-tvc.org/Trumble _SAR_Workshop.pdf.

US Federal Aviation Administration (FAA). 2015. *Air Traffic Organization: 2015 Safety Report*. Accessed April 13, 2019. www.faa.gov/about/office_org/headquarters_offices /ato/service_units/safety/media/2015_safety_report.pdf.

Virginia Mason Institute. 2017. "What Is Lean Health Care?" *Virginia Mason Institute Blog*. Published August 11. www.virginiamasoninstitute.org/2017/08/lean-health-care/.

Weick, K. E., and K. M. Sutcliffe. 2007. *Managing the Unexpected: Resilient Performance in an Age of Uncertainty*. San Francisco: Jossey-Bass.

Womack, J., and D. Jones. 1996. *Lean Thinking: Banish Waste and Create Wealth in Your Corporation*. New York: Simon & Schuster.

PART VI

Coaching to Facilitate Safe Care

Developing Effective Patient Safety Coaching Skills

WHY SHOULD HOSPITALS CULTIVATE PATIENT SAFETY COACHES?

Patient safety coaches are peer healthcare professionals who are embedded in patient care teams and advocate for the consistent, competent, and continuous use of safe care practices to improve patient safety. Patient safety coaches work to ingrain the use of error-prevention tools and tactics into the performance of patient care teams, strengthen safeguards and defenses to protect patients from errors when they do occur, and cultivate a culture of mindfulness to counter the threat of complacency. Coaching is primarily about changing behaviors. According to the Institute for Safe Medication Practices, peer-to-peer coaches have three main roles: They help healthcare staff (1) see the risks associated with their behavioral choices, (2) learn what factors enable at-risk behaviors, and (3) make safer behavioral choices in the future (ISMP 2011).

Factors that contribute to the erosion of safe care practices in hospitals include communication failures among patient care team members; a lack of adherence to protocols and safe care practices; the failure to comply with existing policies and procedures; the absence of policies and procedures; human factors such as lapses and cognitive biases; and errors resulting from time pressures, distractions, and intimidation (Joint Commission 2019). Doctors, nurses, and other caregivers work in an environment that is often chaotic and filled with new and ever-changing information, stresses, distractions, dynamic tensions, challenging workloads, and changes in patients and their conditions. Not surprisingly, without the necessary safeguards and defenses in place, constant attention to patient safety, and consistent adherence to safe care practices, errors will occur, systems will fail, and patients will be harmed.

In hospitals, patient safety coaches are trained and deployed to build awareness of patient safety among their peers and to observe and provide feedback to patient care teams about their safety performance. Patient safety coaches can help improve patient safety in hospitals and reduce the incidence of preventable harm. "Safety coaching is about keeping patients, families, employees, and visitors safe. Safety coaches at Cincinnati Children's include staff from all areas of the medical center. A robust safety coach program is believed to be key in reinforcing error-prevention behaviors throughout the medical center" (Cincinnati Children's Hospital 2019). Cincinnati Children's Hospital Medical Center in Ohio launched its Safety Coaching Program in 2007. It was one of the first of a growing number of hospitals to empower patient safety coaches to "spread the reliable use of expected safety behaviors to reduce harm to patients" (Cincinnati Children's Hospital 2019).

Complacency can lead to a lack of attention to details, poor performance, diminished situational awareness, and failure to recognize emerging safety threats. Complacency can cause patient harm. *Inconsistency* of patient care team member performance and failure to follow safe care practices can lead to undesirable variation in the delivery of care appropriate for each patient's condition. Inconsistency can cause patient harm. *Incompetence* is reflected in diminished knowledge, skills, and abilities (KSAs) to perform the tasks required of patient care team members. Incompetence can cause patient harm. Complacent, inconsistent, and incompetent staff can cause patient harm. *Coaching excellence*—a double entendre referring both to excellent coaches and to their ability to foster excellent performance—can act as a check on the harmful effects of complacency, inconsistency, and incompetence.

CONTROLLING COMPLACENCY

According to Stephen Covey, real change does not come from telling, advising, fixing, or teaching—it comes from the inside-out and from changing a person's thoughts and views (Simpson 2014, 30). Healthcare professionals are not motivated by an authoritarian, command-and-control style of "teaching and telling." Rather, they are driven by a desire for self-awareness, self-reliance, and self-belief and an internal motivation to excel. "The awareness-raising function of the expert coach is indispensable" (Whitmore 2009, 35).

Awareness counteracts complacency. Awareness means knowing what is going on around you, and self-awareness is knowing exactly what your role is and how well you are performing it. Raising awareness helps sharpen the ability to receive new information and perceive changes in the environment. Complacency lowers awareness; it is doing just enough to get by. Patient safety coaches can help individuals and teams strengthen their awareness through daily practice and the acquisition of new skills. "High awareness is vital for high performance" (Whitmore 2009, 36).

Situational awareness of the changing dynamics of the patient care environment and patient conditions is critical to protecting patients from harm. It is a discipline that forces patient care team members to "stay in the moment." Thinking about what could go wrong, about the hazards that could cause harm to a patient, and about the effectiveness of the defenses and controls designed to protect patients from harm are examples of situational awareness. To avoid complacency, team members must constantly reaffirm their commitment to being aware of the complex environment in which patient care is provided.

A sports analogy is useful here: "In basketball, it all comes down to 40 minutes on the court. The players have to make split-second decisions and reactions, with the responsibility of winning or losing on their shoulders." The coach helps train and develop the players, "but only the players on the floor create the results" (Cook and Poole 2011, 94).

> Success narrows perceptions . . . the problem is that if people assume that success demonstrates competence, they are more likely to drift into complacency, inattention, and predictable routines. What they don't realize is that complacency also increases the likelihood that unexpected events will go undetected longer and accumulate into bigger problems. Complacency destroys. Don't let it get a foothold.
> —Karl Weick and Kathleen Sutcliffe (2007)

In the same way, patient care teams provide life-saving care, treatment, and services to patients on a typical day. Winning or losing—that is, saving lives or harming patients—largely falls on the shoulders of patient care teams. No one on the team should become complacent about the behaviors that underly the "winning" provision of safe patient care.

According to Phil Jackson, one of the most successful coaches in the history of professional basketball, situational awareness in basketball means that players must keep their eye on the ball at all times and remain acutely aware of everything that is happening on the court. "We developed a highly integrated style of defense that relied on the collective awareness of all five players rather than one man's brilliant moves" (Jackson 2013, 30). As the coach of 11 championship teams, Jackson emphasized the importance of self-awareness and made sure his players were mentally and physically in the game 100 percent of the time:

> As a coach, I want to prepare them for the inevitable chaos that occurs the minute they step onto a basketball court. I was interested in getting them to take a more mindful approach to the game and to their relationships with one another. At its heart, mindfulness is about being present in the moment as much as possible. . . . When you immerse yourself fully in

the moment, you start developing a much deeper awareness of what's going on, right here, right now. And that awareness ultimately leads to a greater sense of oneness—the essence of teamwork.

Vidant Medical Center in Greenville, North Carolina, implemented a patient safety coaching program in 2006 with the purpose of changing "the culture of the organization through coaching for continuous improvement" (Harton and Ingram 2013, 41). At Vidant, safety coaches are department-based champions who keep team members focused on patient safety by supporting and fostering personal accountability for the safe performance of responsibilities. "Safety coaches have an important role in patient safety. They bring focused awareness to staff members who may have become complacent or drifted away from safe patient practices. They provide coaching in best practices . . . [and] support a proactive focus on patient safety and engage best practices as a preventive tool before a serious safety event occurs" (Harton and Ingram 2013, 45).

CONTROLLING CONSISTENCY

During a typical four- to five-day hospital stay, a patient will encounter many care-givers from a variety of patient care teams, all of them working around the clock: doctors, nurses, nutritionists, laboratory technicians, radiology technicians, pharmacy personnel, and many others depending on the patient's treatment requirements. The nature of the work makes it difficult for patient care teams to maintain consistency because of the continuously changing dynamics of patients, patient conditions, team members, assigned rooms and floors, and the distractions of work, thought, and the constant flow of information. Patient safety coaches who are embedded in patient care teams provide a constancy of commitment to patient safety principles and safe care practices.

Sentara Healthcare, an integrated healthcare system of 12 hospitals and more than 300 sites of care located in Virginia, has been on the road to high reliability since 2002, with the ultimate goal of zero patient harm. At Sentara, patient safety coaches are frontline staff who work as members of patient care teams in each hospital and serve as the patient safety leader on each unit. Sentara's patient safety coaches "play a vital role in observing practices of team members, giving a word of praise when they see a coworker practicing a safe behavior, and offering constructive correction when they observe a missed opportunity" (Burke, LeFever, and Sayles 2009, 46–47). To support consistency throughout the healthcare system, patient safety coaches meet monthly to (1) receive continuing education on safe care practices and safe behaviors, (2) provide input about ways to improve safety processes, and (3) identify systems problems that could compromise patient safety and work together to develop solutions that can be widely disseminated and applied.

The consistent adherence of both individual caregivers and patient care teams to safe care practices and safe behaviors in every patient encounter makes a significant contribution to achieving the goal of harm-free healthcare. Consistency results from sustaining a culture of safety in which all staff follow all safe practices all the time. Sentara Healthcare has identified five key characteristics (Burke, LeFever, and Sayles 2009, 50) that are critical to improving consistency of safety performance and sustaining a culture of safety:

1. Continuous leadership focused on the need for change and improvement
2. Provision of safety tools and techniques that become part of staff's daily activities
3. Leadership commitment and support that is visible and constant
4. Constant vigilance and a relentless commitment to improvement
5. Continuous reinforcement of desired behaviors to ensure that error-prevention behaviors are followed 100 percent of the time

Patient safety coaches are the "consistency coaches" who work within patient care teams to make sure that safe practices and safe behaviors are followed unconditionally.

CONTROLLING COMPETENCE

In his book *Coaching—Evoking Excellence in Others*, professional business coach James Flaherty (2010, 1) notes that the principal intention of a coach is "to leave the person being coached . . . more competent in an activity." According to Flaherty, the purpose of coaching is to achieve (1) long-term performance excellence, (2) individual awareness to self-correct performance, and (3) individual self-improvement through learning, practice, and emulating stellar performers.

The role of the patient safety coach is to be a constant voice for safe practice and a guide for staff efforts in the competent use of safe care practices. Interacting with patient care teams and individual team members, patient safety coaches help caregivers learn the methods, tools, and techniques of patient safety *before* attempting to apply them in the delivery of patient care. Coaches help the caregiving staff practice these approaches to improving patient safety and team communications in simulated and actual patient care settings. Moreover, patient safety coaches praise, spotlight, and encourage the emulation of "stellar performers" who consistently demonstrate the desired safety behaviors.

Positive feedback can be a powerful motivator to help individuals improve their performance. Patient safety coaches provide timely feedback on an individual's performance of patient care tasks so that they can adjust their behavior to achieve the desired results. Positive feedback is intended to help individuals and teams improve their performance, achieve better results in their work, and develop a strong sense of ownership and personal commitment to achieving positive outcomes (Canfield and Chee 2013, 100, 123). Coaching helps patient care team members become great performers by executing their tasks well and reducing inconsistency and bad behaviors (Simpson 2014, 113–14). After observing individual and team performance and behaviors, the patient safety coach will provide candid feedback to the team, seek their perspectives, reach agreement with the team on performance problems and their causes, and identify skill gaps and strategies to resolve them (Harvard Business School 2004, 22).

Assessing a team member's performance or behaviors *against behavior-based expectations* can provide a meaningful evaluation of an individual's competence in and commitment to safe care practices. The Safety Practices Self-Assessment is a tool that helps coaches identify (1) an individual's performance against stated goals, (2) the goals that have been achieved, (3) the goals that an individual is struggling with, (4) the obstacles that are inhibiting an individual's progress, and (5) the likelihood an individual will change his or her risky behaviors (Harvard Business School 2004, 17–18). In his book *Leading Teams*, J. Richard Hackman (2002, 205), an expert on organizational behavior, describes the benefits of good coaching for team performance: Good coaching helps teams (1) enhance the effort of individual team members, (2) ensure that each team member's work is done appropriately, and (3) make the most of team members' individual talents.

Three levels of competence can be defined in terms of team members' KSAs (Harvard Business School 2014, 117–20):

1. *Stars*—Hold up these star performers as exemplars whose behaviors should be emulated, praise them, and thank them.
2. *Steadies*—Provide these performers, who make up the vast majority of the workforce, with opportunities to grow and expand their comfort zone, and recognize and reward them.
3. *Strugglers*—Give these low performers a chance at redemption, set firm performance and behavioral expectations, and create a clear path for improvement with assistance.

THE BENEFITS OF COACHING

At the Hospital for Sick Children, known as "SickKids," in Toronto, Canada, patient safety coaches serve as patient safety experts who review error-prevention tools and techniques with their peers, observe their use by staff, provide positive reinforcement, and offer constructive criticism when they observe missed opportunities to apply safe care practices (SickKids 2017). The patient safety coach program at SickKids helps "ensure everyone is speaking the same language of safety . . . [and] working together towards the same goal, which is keeping our patients safe and reducing preventable harm." With a focus on sustainability, safety coaches meet monthly to share their experiences, debrief, and discuss challenges they are facing. The aim of the monthly patient safety coach meetings is to "build a community of practice around peer-to-peer coaching."

> You're in it to coach workers to peak performance, including acquisition of new skills and techniques.
> —Marshall Cook and Laura Poole (2011)

Patient safety coaching is an important enabler of *behavior-based safety*. Patient safety coaches (1) clearly define a set of safe behaviors and work practices, (2) identify and reinforce safe work practices, (3) reduce at-risk behaviors to a near-zero level, (4) recognize favorable behaviors, (5) correct unfavorable behaviors, and (6) problem-solve to improve work practices (Muhlenberg College 2019).

At Rady Children's Hospital in San Diego, California, patient safety coaches are unit-based frontline staff who are trained to observe the behavior of patient care team members and provide peer-to-peer support to reinforce safety practices and behavior expectations (Billman 2017). Rady has identified seven reasons why patient safety coaches are so important to their efforts to optimize patient outcomes and to achieve high-reliability healthcare for the children they serve:

1. *People make mistakes.* Coaches can help minimize the frequency of errors and mistakes.
2. *People drift.* Coaches can help keep staff focused on consistently following safe care practices.
3. *People resist change.* Coaches can foster the adoption of and adherence to new safety habits.
4. *People can't be everywhere all the time.* Peer coaches embedded in patient care teams *are* everywhere all the time to ensure the consistent use of safe care practices.

5. *People need time to form new habits.* Coaches provide safety behavior education, awareness building, and continuous reinforcement of new safety behaviors until they become habits.

6. *Lasting change occurs at the local level.* Coaches are involved with all patient care teams and provide ongoing and consistent feedback to help teams create change that results in new and improved safety habits and the provision of safe care.

7. *Coaches are volunteers for patient safety.* Volunteer patient safety coaches are committed to helping their peers develop new safety behaviors and habits to eliminate all preventable patient harm.

Volunteer safety coaches at Cincinnati Children's Hospital reinforce the use of expected safety behaviors among the caregiving staff and encourage open communication about patient safety concerns and opportunities for improvement. Safety coaches conduct behavioral observations of patient safety practices and coach staff on the performance of safety behaviors. Each safety coach completes several behavioral observations a month, providing immediate positive and negative feedback to individuals and teams. Safety coaches often lead patient safety rounds to encourage open discussion of patient safety successes and failures. Coaches help build personal accountability for patient safety throughout the organization (Muething et al. 2012).

Novant Health, an integrated healthcare system serving communities in North Carolina, Virginia, South Carolina, and Georgia, has been on a mission since 2009 to significantly reduce the number of serious safety events. By March 2015, Novant Health had achieved an 80 percent reduction in serious safety events through its "First Do No Harm" safety program. According to Dr. Herbert Clegg (2015), senior vice president for clinical excellence, Novant Health "believes that patient safety coaches will serve an important role in achieving high reliability and further reducing patient harm incidents through enhanced teamwork and peer support, feedback, and accountability." Lessons learned from Novant Health's experience with implementing patient safety coaches include the following:

- Patient safety coaches can contribute to an improved patient safety culture by their presence and actions.
- Patient safety coaches can have a positive impact on teamwork and the openness of communication.
- Patient safety coaches can be an important part of a larger improvement plan for shifting attitudes about patient safety culture and achieving high reliability.
- Patient safety coaches can have a positive impact on safety event reporting and nonpunitive response to error.

As part of its Coaching Clinical Teams educational module, the Agency for Healthcare Research and Quality has identified fives benefits of coaching teams: (1) better patient care, (2) better morale, (3) better-functioning teams, (4) improved motivation of individuals and teams to make needed changes in safety behaviors, and (5) improved identification of safe practices and areas of focus for quality and safety improvement efforts (AHRQ 2017).

COACHING KNOWLEDGE, SKILLS, AND ABILITIES

Knowledge, skills, and abilities are defined as the competencies necessary for individuals to effectively perform their assigned job responsibilities. KSAs are usually acquired through education, training, and work experience.

- *Knowledge* is a body of retained information that enables the performance of a function.
- *Skill* is an observable competence to perform an assigned task.
- *Ability* is the demonstrated competence to perform a specific task.

Patient safety coaches must first build trust among people they will be coaching. This trust is based on the coach's track record of patient safety expertise; *knowledge* of both clinical processes of care and safe care practices; observable competence in coaching *skills* such as active listening, positive reinforcement, and providing meaningful feedback; and the *ability* to work through staff resistance to achieve and sustain behavioral change. The World Health Organization (WHO) has defined the *principles of effective coaching* and the skills that are necessary for coaches to be effective change agents. "An effective coach will take the time to build a rapport with others and understand their perspective, in order to gain trust and a commitment to improve" (WHO 2015).

Coaches should demonstrate a sincere interest in helping individuals and teams develop safety behaviors; observing performance and asking open-ended questions in a nonjudgmental way will engender greater trust and team success. "Coaches who understand root causes can better facilitate solutions that are appropriate and achievable" (WHO 2015). Root causes might include environmental or contextual factors; a lack of motivation among the individuals on the team; or deficiencies in KSAs.

Patient safety coaches discuss team performance and safety practices with individual team members, provide feedback about observed safety-related performance, and identify problems and solutions to resolve risky behaviors. Coaches use strong communication skills—listening well, showing respect, and speaking clearly and concisely—to gain the trust of the patient care team and achieve sustainable improvement in safety behaviors.

According to the WHO, good coaches are (1) coachable themselves, (2) trusted and respected by their peers, (3) humble and honest, and (4) patient and flexible. Coaches who are self-motivated to improve their own practice and behaviors commonly demonstrate the insight, sensitivity, and understanding needed to coach others. Good coaches build trust over time by demonstrating their coaching skills and admitting when they don't know something. Good coaches recognize positive actions by team members and provide feedback about their observations of performance without judging what or how the team performed. Coaches give team members enough time to learn by reaching their own conclusions, identifying challenges, and forming solutions. A sample job description for a patient safety coach, based on a review of current best practices in hospital patient safety coaching, is provided as exhibit 13.1.

Exhibit 13.1: Patient Safety Coach Job Description

Patient Safety Coach

Summary of Job Functions

Patient safety coaches observe the safety performance of their peers in patient care teams, engage in coaching conversations about patient safety issues and concerns by asking open-ended questions, praise good safety behaviors, provide feedback to correct poor safety behaviors, and follow up to ensure the consistent and competent use of safe care practices and error-prevention techniques. Patient safety coaches constantly increase staff awareness of potential risks and hazards to avoid complacency. They provide regular reports of their safety observations and interventions, attend monthly patient safety coach meetings, and encourage others to report close calls and safety events.

Primary Responsibilities

1. Participate in training to enhance coaching knowledge, skills, and abilities and expertise in error-prevention tools and techniques, effective communication, and safe care practices.
2. Observe, reinforce, and provide real-time feedback regarding the safety behaviors of staff and safe care practices.

(continued)

Exhibit 13.1: Patient Safety Coach Job Description *(continued)*

3. Serve as a role model and champion for patient safety, error-prevention tools, and safety behaviors and provide coaching to team members on how to improve their safety behaviors.
4. Encourage staff to report close calls and serious safety events to the organization's event reporting system.
5. Disseminate information to staff to aid their adoption of safe care practices and error reduction tools and techniques.
6. Conduct regular evaluations of safety competence of the patient care unit.
7. Attend monthly patient safety coach meetings to discuss safety observations, share information about successful coaching interventions and failures, and discuss how to resolve existing barriers to coaching teams to improve safety behaviors.
8. Encourage team members to adopt and consistently apply error-prevention tools and safety behaviors.
9. Prepare and submit "Good Catch" and "Safety Success Stories" on a regular basis.

Competencies, Knowledge, Skills, and Abilities

1. Exhibit a passion for patient safety and service excellence and a commitment to the goal of zero preventable patient harm.
2. Exhibit a caring, empathetic, respectful, and patient-centered attitude.
3. Demonstrate the ability to communicate clearly, including active listening and appropriate assertive communications.
4. Complete required training and demonstrate superior competence in safe care practices and error reduction techniques.
5. Demonstrate the ability to identify crucial conversations and how to engage in a crucial conversation when needed.
6. Possess an understanding of medical errors, their causes, human factors, latent system weaknesses, and the importance of barriers, safeguards, defenses, and controls.
7. Demonstrate the ability to recognize safety and service concerns and emerging threats to patient safety and take appropriate action to reduce or eliminate the risk of harm to patients.
8. Demonstrate the ability to use critical thinking to proactively solve safety-related problems.

(continued)

9. Possess knowledge of the clinical environment and experience as a doctor, nurse, or other clinical provider to provide credible peer coaching to patient care teams.

Education and Experience

1. Demonstrated expertise and knowledge of patient safety principles, error-prevention tools and techniques, and safe care practices.
2. Superior coaching skills, such as effective communication, the ability to build trusting relationships, appropriate assertion, providing meaningful feedback, mentoring team members to improve their safety behaviors, modeling safe behaviors, and effectively resolving conflict and minimizing resistance.
3. Degreed and licensed as a doctor, nurse, or other clinical provider.

CORE COMPETENCIES

The International Coach Federation (ICF) is a global organization dedicated to advancing the coaching profession. The ICF sets high standards for the coaching profession and offers independent certification based on an individual's demonstration of a thorough understanding of the core coaching competencies. The ICF's Coach Knowledge Assessment comprises 11 core competencies and 60 standards that reflect the skills and approaches within the coaching profession that are "critical for any competent coach to demonstrate" (ICF 2019). The following is a summary of the ICF's 11 core coaching competencies:

1. *Meeting ethical guidelines.* Apply coaching ethics and professionalism in all coaching situations.
2. *Establishing the coaching agreement.* Come to agreement with the individual or team about the coaching process and relationship.
3. *Establishing trust.* Create a safe and supportive environment that produces ongoing mutual respect and trust.
4. *Coaching presence.* Create a spontaneous relationship with the individual or team using a style that is open, flexible, and confident.

5. *Active listening.* Focus completely on what the individual is saying, understand the meaning, and encourage and support the expression of feelings, perceptions, and concerns.

6. *Powerful questioning.* Ask questions that evoke discovery, insight, and commitment to action.

7. *Communicating directly.* Be clear, articulate, respectful, and direct in providing feedback.

8. *Creating awareness.* Make interpretations that will help the individual or team gain awareness and achieve agreed-upon results and objectives.

9. *Designing actions.* Define actions that will enable the individual or team to demonstrate, practice, and deepen new learning and take actions that will lead to agreed-upon goals.

10. *Planning and goal setting.* Create a plan with results that are SMART—Specific, Measurable, Attainable, Relevant, and Time-sensitive.

11. *Managing progress and accountability.* Acknowledge the individual's or team's progress, promote self-discipline, and hold team members accountable for what they say they are going to do, for the results of an intended action, or for a specific plan with related time frames.

The Virginia Commonwealth University Health System in Richmond launched a patient safety coaching program in 2011 in which safety coaches serve as "role model[s] for our safety behaviors and error prevention tools" (Strategies for Nurse Managers 2019). Virginia Commonwealth has identified the following KSAs and core competencies for the recruitment of patient safety coaches throughout the healthcare system:

- Be trained on the use of error-prevention tools and techniques.
- Demonstrate an exemplary ability to use error-prevention tools and safety practices and to help others use those tools and safety processes.
- Be able to use active listening skills, identify crucial conversations, and understand how to engage in a crucial conversation when needed.
- Gain an understanding of errors and their causes.
- Be a frontline staff member.
- Take advantage of coaching opportunities when they present themselves.
- Report four observations or interviews with team members regarding a discussion about error-prevention tools or safety behaviors each month.
- Report one safety success story each month describing a safety behavior in the coach's area.

- Demonstrate a passion for safety and service through commitment to the organization's goal of zero preventable harm to patients.
- Demonstrate the ability to recognize safety and service concerns and situations, take appropriate action to reduce or eliminate risks, and promote service excellence.
- Be a role model and champion for the organization's error-prevention and patient safety tools.
- Provide coaching to team members on how to adopt and apply error-prevention tools, standards, and behaviors.
- Demonstrate the ability to use critical thinking to proactively solve problems.
- Demonstrate the ability to communicate clearly.
- Be a team member in good standing.
- Complete the required training and education in the areas of patient safety and error prevention.

CONCLUSION

Chapter 13 discusses the safe care practices that define the roles and responsibilities of the patient safety coach. As demonstrated by several leading healthcare systems and the Agency for Healthcare Research and Quality, the training and deployment of peer patient safety coaches can have a significant positive impact on a hospital's ability to provide better, safer patient care and eliminate preventable patient harm. Embedded in patient care teams throughout the hospital, patient safety coaches work to address the threats of complacency, inconsistent adherence to safe care practices, and staff incompetence resulting from poor safety training and behaviors.

Patient safety coaches observe the safety performance of their coworkers, engage in discussion by asking open-ended questions, praise good safety behaviors, provide feedback to correct poor safety behaviors, and follow up to ensure the consistent adoption of safe care practices. Patient safety coaches, with their passion for service and safety excellence, are the key ingredient in a hospital's quest to achieve high-reliability healthcare. In a high-reliability care environment, every patient care provider and patient care team member consistently and competently applies safe care practices and error-prevention techniques in every patient encounter.

CHAPTER 13 SAFE CARE PRACTICES

1. Adopt the 11 core competencies and 60 standards that make up the International Coach Federation's Coach Knowledge Assessment. These core competencies and standards reflect the skills and approaches within the coaching profession that any competent coach must demonstrate.

2. Train and deploy patient safety coaches to help individuals and teams strengthen their awareness through daily practice and the acquisition of new skills.

3. Assess each patient care team member's performance and behaviors against behavior-based expectations. This kind of assessment can provide a meaningful evaluation of an individual's competence in and commitment to safe care practices.

REFERENCES

Agency for Healthcare Research and Quality (AHRQ). 2017. "Coaching Clinical Teams Module: Facilitator Notes." Accessed April 5, 2019. www.ahrq.gov/professionals/quality -patient-safety/hais/tools/ambulatory-surgery/sections/implementation/training-tools /coaching-facnotes.html.

Billman, G. 2017. "Why a Safety Coach Program May Be Our Most Important Legacy." Presentation to the Hospital Quality Institute Conference, Rady Children's Hospital San Diego. Accessed April 5, 2019. www.hqinstitute.org/sites/main/files/file-attachments /why_a_safety_coach_program_may_be_our_most_important_legacy_10.27.2017 _revised_full.pdf.

Burke, G. H., G. B. LeFever, and S. M. Sayles. 2009. "Zero Events of Harm to Patients." *Managing Infection Control.* Published February. https://insidekentuckyonehealth.org/ Portals/0/Learning/Documents/4-15%20Culture%20of%20Safety.pdf.

Canfield, J., and P. Chee. 2013. *Coaching for Breakthrough Success: Proven Techniques for Making Impossible Dreams Possible.* New York: McGraw-Hill.

Cincinnati Children's Hospital. 2019. "Safety Coaching." Accessed April 5. www.cincinnati childrens.org/service/j/anderson-center/safety/methodology/safety-coaching.

Clegg, H. 2015. "Improving Patient Safety Culture in Novant Health's Ambulatory Physi-cian Clinics." North Carolina Quality Center. *NC Quality Highlights*, March.

Cook, M. J., and L. Poole. 2011. *Effective Coaching*, 2nd ed. Madison, WI: McGraw-Hill.

Flaherty, J. 2010. *Coaching—Evoking Excellence in Others*, 3rd ed. New York: Routledge.

Hackman, J. R. 2002. *Leading Teams: Setting the Stage for Great Performances*. Boston: Harvard Business School Press.

Harton, B., and S. Ingram. 2013. "Ready for Lift Off: Implementing a Safety Coach Initiative." *Nursing Management* 44 (5): 40–45.

Harvard Business School. 2014. *HBR Guide to Coaching Employees*. Boston: Harvard Business Review Press.

———. 2004. *Coaching and Mentoring*. Boston: Harvard Business Review Press.

Hospital for Sick Children (SickKids). 2017. "About SickKids: Safety Coaches Are Helping Us to Care Safely Everywhere, Every Day." Published November 1. www.sickkids .ca/AboutSickKids/Newsroom/Past-News/2017/safety-coaches-helping-us-care-safely -everywhere-everyday.html.

Institute for Safe Medication Practices (ISMP). 2011. "Medication Safety Self-Assessment, Coach." Published April 1. www.ismp.org/assessments/hospitals.

International Coach Federation (ICF). 2019. "Core Competencies." Accessed April 5. https://coachfederation.org/core-competencies.

Jackson, P. 2013. *Eleven Rings: The Soul of Success*. New York: Penguin.

Joint Commission. 2019. "Most Commonly Reviewed Sentinel Event Types." Updated February 5. www.jointcommission.org/assets/1/6/Event_type_4Q_2018.pdf.

Muething, S. E., A. Goudie, P. J. Schoettker, L. F. Donnelly, M. A. Goodfriend, T. M. Bracke, P. W. Brady, D. S. Wheeler, J. M. Anderson, and U. R. Kotagal. 2012. "Quality Improvement Initiative to Reduce Serious Safety Events and Improve Patient Safety Culture." *Pediatrics* 130 (2): e423–31.

Muhlenberg College. 2019. "Be a Safety Coach (Part 3)—Coaching." Accessed April 5. www.muhlenberg.edu/media/contentassets/pdf/about/hr/Safety_coach_part3.pdf.

Simpson, M. 2014. *Unlocking Potential: 7 Coaching Skills That Transform Individuals, Teams and Organizations*. Grand Haven, MI: Grand Harbor Press.

Strategies for Nurse Managers. 2019. "Safety Coach Role Description." Accessed April 5. www.strategiesfornursemanagers.com/ce_detail/312906.cfm.

Weick, K. E., and K. M. Sutcliffe. 2007. *Managing the Unexpected: Resilient Performance in an Age of Uncertainty*. San Francisco: Jossey-Bass.

Whitmore, J. 2009. *Coaching for Performance: Growing Human Potential and Performance—The Principles and Practice of Coaching and Leadership*, 4th ed. London: Nicholas Brealey Publishing.

World Health Organization (WHO). 2015. "Principles of Effective Coaching." Accessed April 5, 2019. www.who.int/patientsafety/implementation/checklists/scc_effective -coaching.pdf.

Coaching Teams to Consistently Demonstrate Safe Behaviors

WHY DO TEAMS NEED PATIENT SAFETY COACHES TO IMPROVE THEIR SAFETY-RELATED BEHAVIORS AND PERFORMANCE?

Coaches provide feedback that increases the competence of individual patient care team members. The coach provides the structure for team members to work collaboratively to learn new patient safety skills and behaviors. Coaches facilitate the team's performance of safe care practices and help ensure that each team member takes personal responsibility for their behaviors and performance of safe practices. Moreover, patient safety coaches assess, through observation, the skill, will, knowledge, and abilities of team members and support their development and improvement in the use of error-prevention tools and safe care practices. Effective coaching helps others engage in self-reflection and evaluation, which leads to improved performance, fosters collaboration among team members, and ensures that all team members are invested in the team's work, goals, and outcomes (Aguilar 2016, 42, 195).

> Leading a team requires a skill set in which very few of us have ever been trained.
>
> —Elena Aguilar (2016)

Coaching teams is a process that helps team members use their collective resources to achieve peak performance and to improve team functioning and collaboration (Harvard Business School 2014, 150). According to the Harvard Business School's *Guide to Coaching*, coaches help teams avoid *process losses* and achieve *process gains*. Process losses occur when the patient care team (1) underutilizes individual team members' talents, (2) interacts with each other in a way that hampers the team's efforts, and (3) develops inefficiencies or internal breakdowns as a result of waste of time, energy, and expertise (Harvard Business School 2014, 150). Process gains are achieved when team members interact in a way that enhances the team's collective effort and results in the active development of team members' knowledge, skills, and abilities. "A coaching intervention is any action that seeks to minimize process losses and to foster process gains for any of the three performance processes"—that is, effort, performance strategy, and knowledge and skills (Harvard Business School 2014, 151).

Patient safety coaches serve to raise the safety conscientiousness of patient care team members, help the team avoid error traps and potential hazards, ensure the safe behaviors of team members, and enhance team members' knowledge, skills, and abilities related to safe care practices.

Patient safety coaches perform three interventional roles as members of patient care teams:

1. *Before active patient care.* Coaches prepare and train team members on the proper use of error-prevention tools and techniques, constructive communication skills, situational awareness, personal accountability for safe behaviors, and how to identify emerging safety threats. Coaches strive to earn the trust and respect of their teammates.

2. *During active patient care.* As peer members of patient care teams, coaches observe and modify the safety behaviors of teammates by providing constructive feedback, fostering adherence to safe care practices, ensuring the use of safety communication techniques, enhancing the awareness of all team members to counter complacency, helping to catch and correct errors and system weaknesses, and assessing the effectiveness and staff adherence to established safety barriers, defenses, and controls.

3. *After active patient care.* Coaches conduct after-action reviews to assess whether the goals of the patient care process or procedure were met, whether any unexpected events created safety concerns, and whether team members could do anything differently the next time. Coaches provide specific feedback and time for team members to reflect on their performance. Coaches participate in barrier effectiveness analysis, proactive risk assessment, and unit-based safety huddles.

COACHING: BEFORE ACTIVE PATIENT CARE

Both coaches and patient team members should receive formal training on the use of error-prevention tools and techniques, safety communication methods, behavior-based expectations, and safe care practices in simulation and classroom sessions *before* these skills are applied in actual patient care settings. After acquiring expertise in safe care practices, coaches can be part of the educational faculty and lead team skill development sessions.

> A good sports coach gives the team the tools to succeed, guides them, helps them do their best, and cheers them on as they perform.
> —Marshall Cook and Laura Poole (2011)

Before beginning active coaching—that is, coaching teams that are actively providing patient care—coaches must plan their strategy, focus, and approach to engaging the team in a coaching conversation. Coaches should first develop a *coaching session plan* that identifies the skill or behavior to be demonstrated, the team to be engaged, and the best method of teaching the skill or behavior. In other words, does the individual or team learn best using auditory learning, visual learning, or kinesthetic (hands-on) learning, or a combination of all of these methods (Cook and Poole 2011, 114)?

Coaching is best received by team members when they are not under stress and when they have enough time to talk about their performance after simulated practice. The coaching session should include the entire team if it is practical to do so (AHRQ 2017). "You'll do some of your best coaching (especially with teams) when you run with them, working out solutions and anticipating problems together" (Cook and Poole 2011, 94).

The coach and the team should work collaboratively to develop SMART goals—Specific, Measurable, Achievable, Realistic, and Time-sensitive—to guide the acquisition of new safety behaviors and knowledge about safe care practices. Solution-focused coaching should establish a clear performance objective for the patient care team based on the desired outcome of eliminating preventable patient harm (Cook and Poole 2011, 101). Solution-focused coaching is organized around four questions:

1. What do we want to achieve?
2. Why is it important?
3. How will we achieve it?
4. How will we be accountable for the results?

When conducting a training session on patient safety tools, techniques, and safe behaviors, the coach should begin by explaining what the team members are going to learn, practice, and do and why they are learning it. The coach should describe the goals and desired outcomes of the training and make the process of learning interactive with questions and feedback. During the training, the coach should (1) break the material into clear and easily digestible steps; (2) explain the task, process, or technique to be learned; (3) provide team members with enough training or practice to be able to adopt the new process or task; and (4) answer technical questions, especially about the efficacy of the new process.

For example, during a training session to review a safe care practice or error-prevention technique, the coach should (1) explain and demonstrate the process, (2) describe the desired outcome of the training, (3) observe team members practicing the new technique, (4) answer questions and provide feedback, and (5) allow time for team members to reflect and assess their own performance. The coach should provide positive reinforcement and a candid assessment of the team's performance of the new knowledge or skill (Cook and Poole 2011, 114–26). In their book *Effective Coaching*, Marshall Cook and Laura Poole (2011, 144) advise aspiring coaches to "coach toward positive behaviors."

COACHING: DURING ACTIVE PATIENT CARE

Coaching patient care teams during the active delivery of patient care requires striking a balance between not interfering with the patient care process and speaking up if something that may be harmful to the patient is observed (AHRQ 2017). The patient safety coach must use good judgment and call on his or her past clinical experiences to determine whether and when to assert active coaching. The coach should determine whether it is the best time to (1) raise a safety concern; (2) recommend or insert an error-prevention tool or safe practice; (3) question a risky behavior; (4) catch and correct an error before harm occurs; (5) assess whether safety defenses and barriers are working as intended; (6) observe and assess individual team member knowledge, skills, and abilities; (7) observe and assess team knowledge, skills, and abilities; (8) refocus the team's mindfulness to avoid complacency; or (9) recognize and praise good safety behaviors and safe practices.

Executive coach Michael Simpson identifies seven coaching skills that can transform individuals, teams, and organizations. "Perhaps the best definition of coaching is unleashing or unlocking the potential of another human being," he says (Simpson 2014, 3). According to Simpson (2014, 17), "everyone has the potential to become something better, regardless of the point of departure." Coaching patient care teams in the moment requires an acute situational awareness and quick observation and assessment of the competencies and safety behaviors of the patient care team members. Using these seven coaching skills, patient safety coaches can transform the behaviors and performance of individual caregivers so that they consistently exceed the behavior-based expectations of a high-performing, high-reliability organization (Simpson 2014, 39–99).

1. *Build trust in the coach.* The team must believe in the competence and capabilities of the coach to place trust in the coach's guidance, interventions, and feedback.

2. *Challenge paradigms.* Paradigms are the way we think about things. The coach needs to understand individuals' assumptions and rationales for their behavior and how they think to help them challenge their old paradigms and take fear out of the change process.

3. *Seek strategic clarity.* The coach should create a clear and compelling narrative (story) to clarify the strategic direction of the team. "Nothing reinvigorates team members like a timely reminder of a powerful and compelling goal" (Simpson 2014, 66). People need clarity about what is expected of them, how to accomplish the goal, and when they need to achieve it.

4. *Execute flawlessly.* Hold individuals accountable for setting, prioritizing, and achieving the goal. "Without execution, the vision is just a hope" (Simpson 2014, 72).

5. *Give effective feedback.* No team or individual can improve without feedback. Feedback helps create awareness and focus on the intended actions and the outcomes of the team's performance. A coach can help individuals identify opportunities for lasting change and performance improvement. Focused feedback should target specific behaviors and the benefits of acting in new ways.

6. *Tap into talent.* The coach can help individuals tap into the reserve of talent they already have. "Great coaches help to create a culture that unleashes the highest talents and diverse skills and contributions of people" (Simpson 2014, 99).

7. *Move the middle.* The biggest opportunity in any organization is to move the middle—those performers that are good but not yet great.

Patient safety coaches can have a significant positive impact on the patient care team's performance by resolving conflict and improving communications. When conflict among the team members occurs, the coach acts as an objective mediator, interpreting the cause of the conflict, assessing the conflicting perspectives, acknowledging their different views, and then redirecting the team's energy toward its shared goals (Aguilar 2016, 294–304).

Coaches can foster behaviors that improve communications among team members by (1) making sure that everyone's voice is heard, (2) actively listening and asking clarifying questions, (3) appreciating what others say and do, (4) respecting and valuing the input of others, (5) problem-solving, (6) being aware of their own emotions, (7) encouraging empathy for one another, (8) being flexible, and (9) offering solutions and next steps (Aguilar 2016, 149). "Great coaches know when to seize a teachable moment to give feedback in the form of a statement followed by a question. This approach gets people to realize how they can do better and gets them to feel motivated to improve" (Canfield and Chee 2013, 103).

The coach's role is to provide continuous encouragement and affirmation to patient care team members and help them establish support structures that will maximize their chances of success. Coaching enables individuals to sustain change and achieve more by staying motivated and on track (Canfield and Chee 2013, 138).

COACHING: AFTER ACTIVE PATIENT CARE

Immediately after a process or procedure is performed, the patient safety coach should gather the team members and conduct a brief after-action review and team debriefing. The coach can provide observation-based feedback and facilitate a positive and constructive discussion about the team's performance of the process or procedure. The team leader should recognize the exemplary efforts of team members and lead a discussion focused on five questions:

1.   What did we do well?
2.   What did we learn?
3.   What would we do differently the next time?
4.   Were there any systems issues or equipment problems?
5.   Who will take responsibility for making sure the identified systems or equipment issues are corrected?

The coach can focus assessment and feedback on several areas of performance, such as adherence to behavior-based expectations, team resilience in response to an unexpected safety threat, the skill and will of team members participating in the care process, the active use of safety communication techniques, or the effectiveness of controls, safeguards, barriers, or defenses.

A coach's conversation with individual team members regarding an improvement opportunity may focus on an observation of the *skill* and *will* demonstrated by team members during active patient care. Skill is developed through experience, training, understanding, and role perception. An individual's will reflects the desire to achieve and succeed, the aspiration to meet high standards, and self-motivation and confidence in the individual's abilities (Landsberg 2015, 55–67). Individuals who demonstrate both high skill and high will are the organization's "positive deviants" (Seidman and Grbavac 2013). These are team members who model positive attitudes, safe behaviors, and a commitment to operational excellence. They are the safety leaders on the front line, and patient safety coaches should both praise them and recruit their leadership in modeling the desired safe care behaviors.

DEALING WITH RESISTANCE AND RELUCTANCE TO COACHING

One of the biggest coaching challenge is dealing with resistance and reluctance (Aguilar 2016, 197). Resistance often masks an individual's fear, and it is an indirect expression of concern, anxiety, or anger. Resistance may be camouflaging an individual's underlying feeling of emotional distress and dissatisfaction with work or life generally. Resistance can take many forms, including questioning the rationale for a process or procedure, questioning the competence of the coach, attacking the messenger, changing the subject, blaming others, and exhibiting perpetual confusion (Aguilar 2016, 199).

Some team members may not have developed trust in the patient safety coach, or they may have had a negative relationship with a coach in the past that prevents them from receiving the coach's assistance, feedback, and advice. A reluctant team member may be hesitant to be coached, unwilling to admit the need or scope for improvement, overloaded with work, or mistrustful of the organization and its motives for coaching staff (Landsberg 2015, 61).

Coaches must always have the learner's approval before beginning a coaching session or a coaching conversation. One approach that coaches can use to gain an individual's agreement to be coached is called "Ask Before Coaching." "Coaching is about creating a positive path forward," so the coach must be patient with resistant or reluctant team members and work to build their trust in the coaching process and in the coach's competence (Cook and Poole 2011, 16, 152, 162). Coaches should work with team members who resist the coaching process to recognize and identify the source of their resistance and work through a process of discovery to overcome it. It may take some time for patient care team members to experience and realize the benefits of patient safety coaching as an integral component of a hospital's safety culture.

Coaches encounter many forms of resistance (Whitmore 2009, 151–54):

- Team members perceive that the organization's culture does not support their safety efforts.
- Staff are cynical about the benefits of coaching.
- Staff do not trust the coach or his or her intentions.
- Team members believe that coaching takes too much time.
- Staff perceive coaching as just another gimmick.

- Some staff prefer to be told what to do and don't want to take personal responsibility for patient safety.
- Some staff believe that what they are doing now is working just fine.
- Some staff fear that coaching is about performance evaluation, not helpful improvement.
- Some staff fear they will fail at being coached and learning new techniques and approaches.

When confronted with resistance or reluctance to coaching, coaches should express compassion and empathy for the individual and seek to understand his or her concerns and reservations. Coaches should avoid arguing, getting angry, using condescending language, or demanding that the team member participate. Those approaches will only deepen the team member's resistance.

Staff are more likely to be receptive to coaching when they are doing work that they like, that they are good at, and that is good for the organization; when they feel safe at work and can be candid, open, and connected; and when they are imaginatively engaged with their work (Harvard Business School 2004, 22). In her book *The Art of Coaching Teams*, Elena Aguilar (2016, 202), an expert on transformational coaching and team development, speaks to the roadblocks of resistance: "When resistance prevents us from learning together, it blocks our efforts at transformation."

"YOU'RE A COACH, NOT A COP"

In *Effective Coaching*, Cook and Poole (2011) emphasize that coaches seek performance change and improvement, not punishment or blame. When an organization introduces the idea of patient safety coaches, it must make clear from the outset that the coach's role is to encourage and influence staff to adopt safe behaviors that will lead to better outcomes for patients. Patient safety coaches are instrumental in bringing about organizational transformation and a culture of safety focused on eliminating all preventable patient harm. If staff believe that the coach's role is to evaluate their performance, they will be resistant to participate in coaching sessions. It is important that the patient safety coach's job description clearly describe the coach's performance and safety improvement responsibilities and clarify that the coach's activities will not be used for performance evaluations or reward and punishment decisions.

Although individuals who excel at patient safety, error prevention, and behavior-based expectations should be recognized and rewarded for their exemplary efforts, observational data and analysis from the patient safety coaching process must not be used for this purpose. The essence of coaching is "to allow people to change, to become more competent, and to become excellent at performance" (Flaherty 2010, 16).

EIGHT STEPS TO EFFECTIVE COACHING

A good coaching session, according to Cook and Poole (2011, 52, 121), depends on creating a learning environment that minimizes distractions, respects the intelligence of the participants, and respects their time. Effective coaches establish a clear purpose and vision for the coaching session, stay focused, speak clearly, initiate coaching conversations, avoid lecturing the group, and stay open to new ideas. Most importantly, coaches should encourage and verbally recognize team members who embrace new learning and take steps to adopt new safety behaviors. These individuals are taking Positive Specific Action to change their behaviors into safe behaviors by identifying the goal, practicing the new behaviors, and receiving constructive feedback and guidance from their coach.

Seeking Positive Specific Action from patient care team members, the coach should engage the team using an eight-step effective coaching process (Cook and Poole 2011, 144–84):

1. *Build rapport.* Build a connection with the team that allows them to work together, instead of at cross-purposes.
2. *Identify the goal.* State the goal and ask the team, "Do I have that right?"
3. *Create a vision.* Create a positive vision for the coaching intervention.
4. *Brainstorm approaches.* Inspire creativity among the team by brainstorming action steps that will actualize the vision.
5. *Establish an action plan.* Assign responsibilities for completing elements of the task, process, or procedure, making clear who is doing what and when it must be done.
6. *Gain commitment.* Secure the team members' commitment to the action plan and hold them accountable for their commitments and performance.
7. *Acknowledge the team's success.* After the coaching session or intervention, acknowledge both individual and team successes, creativity, engagement, and skills. The best feedback refers to specific behaviors.
8. *Follow up.* Track the team's progress in implementing the new technique, tool, or practice and provide feedback and recognition.

> Encourage your employees to be who they are. We're all a little strange.
> —Harvard Business School (2014)

Even if we're not all strange, we are all certainly different in how we learn, respond to the stimulus of change, and receive and react to coaching interventions. Patient care team members have widely different educational backgrounds, different personality types, and different learning styles. The task of engaging the team in a coaching conversation is informed by the evolutionary position of the team, the idiosyncrasies of the team members, and the learning styles that work best. Teams progress through three stages: *inclusion, assertion*, and *cooperation* (Whitmore 2009, 137–39). During the inclusion stage, individuals attempt to determine whether they are included as a member of the team, and therefore they experience anxiety, need for acceptance, and fear of rejection. During the assertion stage, team members may express their power and extend their boundaries, mark their territory, and resist cooperation. At this stage, competition among the team members is high. The team will lack cohesiveness, but it may still be productive as a result of the excellent performance of individual team members. As the team evolves, it reaches the cooperation stage, where teams perform at their best. During the cooperation stage, teams are highly cooperative, but they retain a dynamic tension that enhances productivity. Team members support one another, particularly when one member has a bad day, and celebrate together when a team member is successful.

Effective coaching also requires an understanding of the learning styles that individuals prefer. When the coach's language and approach are aligned with team members' preferred learning styles, the result is a more successful coaching engagement and greater and faster progress (Harvard Business School 2014, 103). People generally learn from their experiences and then reflect on the lessons learned from those experiences. Individuals' preferred learning styles are influenced by their personality type, past experiences, education, and cultural background. Nine types of learning styles, and the type of language that speaks best to them, can be defined as follows:

1. *Initiating.* These learners like to experiment with new courses of action and seek new opportunities. Coaches should use inspiring, energetic language.
2. *Experiencing.* These learners find meaning in deep involvement in experiences and relationships. Coaches should use sensitive and accepting language.
3. *Imagining.* These learners have many creative ideas, consider a range of solutions, and seek diverse input from many people. Coaches need to be open-minded and show empathy.
4. *Reflecting.* These learners observe others, take multiple perspectives into account, and wait to act until they are confident of the outcome. Coaches should convey a slow and thoughtful process to connect ideas and experiences through sustained reflection.

5. *Analyzing.* These learners integrate and systematize ideas and like to make plans, attend to details, and test assumptions. Coaches should use concise, logical language.

6. *Thinking.* These learners engage in disciplined logic, prefer quantitative analysis, and tend to focus on one objective at a time. Coaches should use logical and reason-based language.

7. *Deciding.* These learners like to choose a single course of action early on to achieve practical results. Coaches should use pragmatic and direct language.

8. *Acting.* These learners take assertive, goal-directed steps toward a change they care about and take risks to get things done faster. Coaches should convey dynamism and speed.

9. *Balancing.* These learners like to weigh the pros and cons of acting versus reflecting and experiencing versus thinking, adopting a variety of learning styles. Coaches should respect their flexibility.

PROVIDING FEEDBACK

Giving and receiving feedback is an essential part of the coaching relationship. Coaches should provide useful feedback to team members and, in turn, solicit feedback about their coaching style and approach. Questions such as "Is what I said clear?" or "Is that helpful?" can provide guidance on the design of future coaching conversations. The Harvard Business School's guide *Coaching and Mentoring* suggests that coaching fosters skill development, imparts knowledge, and influences behaviors to achieve the organization's goals (Harvard Business School 2004, xi).

Feedback sessions should encompass the following: (1) specifically name the behavior that is to be corrected, (2) describe the organizational significance of the behavior, (3) describe the purpose of the feedback, (4) describe the desired behavior in detail, (5) identify the expected results, (6) tailor the communication style to the learner, (7) identify and make a plan to overcome any barriers to providing the feedback, (8) identify the constructive behavior that is expected, and (9) ask for an affirmation of understanding from the learner (Harvard Business School 2004, 141).

Coaching is accomplished through a four-step process of observation, discussion, active coaching, and follow-up. During the active coaching phase, "An effective coach offers ideas and advice in such a way that the [individual] can hear them, respond to them, and appreciate their value" (Harvard Business School 2004, 8). Giving and receiving feedback during the active coaching phase is critical to achieving a coaching conversation that changes behaviors and saves lives in healthcare.

Business coach James Flaherty (2010, 25) summarizes the mission of coaching: "If the purpose of coaching is to change behavior, then the coach's mission is to find what affects behavior in a way that will bring about the desired change."

THE FLOW OF COACHING

In his book *Evoking Excellence in Others*, Flaherty describes a seven-step Flow of Coaching model. It begins with establishing a relationship between the coach and the individuals on the team and continues through observation, assessment, feedback, and agreement on future steps. The following is a summary and elaboration of the Flow of Coaching model:

1. *Establish the relationship.* The coaching relationship must be based on mutual trust, mutual respect, and mutual freedom of expression. The coach should facilitate open communications in which information is exchanged without defensiveness or argumentation. Freedom of expression is grounded in openness, listening, and confidentiality.

2. *Recognize the opening.* An opening is an event or occasion that makes the individual or team more amenable to coaching—for example, the breakdown of a process, the need for enhanced competency, or the introduction of a new process or technique.

3. *Observe and assess performance.* In addition to observing immediate concerns, the coach should observe and assess how the team is meeting its commitments, working toward future outcomes, and maintaining a constructive mood while also assessing the level of competence in group and individual behaviors.

4. *Enroll the team for a coaching session.* The coach and team should make explicit what they aim to accomplish together, discuss potential barriers, identify desired outcomes, reach mutual commitments, and identify obstacles to success.

5. *Conduct the coaching conversation.* During the initial session, the coach should clarify the desired outcome, observe the team's performance, set communication expectations, and plan a follow-up session. During the second session, the coach should report on observations, address breakdowns, discuss new behaviors, and assign practice. During the third session, the coach should report on observations of the new practice, the results of the new behavior, and the effects of the newly acquired competence and make recommendations for the future. The coach should acknowledge positive results and progress and ask the team members to

reflect on what they have learned from their own observations of their performance.

6. *Provide feedback.* Feedback should provide time for the team members to reflect on the coach's observations of their performance and on their own observations. By conducting a self-assessment, the team will better understand the behavior changes needed for sustained improvement.

7. *Agree on future steps.* The coach and the team members should agree on the focus of future coaching conversations, practice sessions, and new behaviors to master.

ANALOGOUS COACHING MODEL: PRECEPTOR SUPPORT FOR NURSE TRANSITION TO PRACTICE

Preceptor or coach, coach or preceptor? These roles are very similar. After graduating from a nursing program and receiving their license, it is important for new nurses beginning their practice in a hospital to "have an effective orientation program that will enable them to make a smooth transition from student to professional. As a result, dedicated nurse preceptors are vital to the success of healthcare organizations and to the retention of nurses in the profession" (Lippincott Solutions 2016).

Nurse preceptors serve as role models and mentors for staff nurses who are new to the hospital or unit, student nurses, and new graduate nurses who are new to the hospital and need to become familiar with the hospital's culture, clinical practices, job responsibilities, and behavior-based expectations. Nurse preceptors "combine the knowledge, skills, abilities, and roles of both coaches and mentors to help preceptees develop and mature into strong practicing professionals" (Lippincott Solutions 2016). Preceptors acclimate and support new nurses by helping them socialize with coworkers, practice care processes and procedures, and evaluate their competence. Preceptors also give advice to new nurses on managing the stress of working in a complex and often overwhelming acute care environment.

Effective nurse preceptors need to be competent in nine qualities (Lippincott Solutions 2016):

1. Assessing learning needs and setting goals
2. Developing and implementing learning plans
3. Teaching time management and prioritization of patient care
4. Evaluating clinical competence and documenting learning and clinical progress
5. Teaching and promoting clinical reasoning, critical thinking, and problem-solving

6. Providing constructive feedback and coaching
7. Modeling evidence-based professional nursing practice
8. Applying effective communication, interpersonal, and conflict management skills to foster collaboration and patient satisfaction
9. Facilitating social interaction and acclimatization to the organization's and unit's culture

"The goal of the preceptor is to provide valuable teaching and learning experiences and to role model safe patient care using evidence-based practice" (Dusaj 2014). Preceptors help acclimate new nurses to the hospital's protocols and checklists, as well as the unit and staff they will be working with. "A preceptor is much more than a teacher or mentor. A preceptor provides new nurses with a toolbox of resources and personnel to ready them to take on any situation or challenge set forth in the job. They also guide new nurses in adapting to the unit culture" (Dusaj 2014).

Preceptors establish goals and responsibilities for new nurses by setting clear expectations, giving them deadlines or time frames for each goal, and outlining a plan for advancing their knowledge and skills. Preceptors assess the clinical competence of new nurses and train them to develop their own clinical judgment. Competency checklists are used to guide the acquisition of new skills in procedures such as the care of chest tubes, administering tube feedings, using bar-code medication administration, or using electronic health records. Preceptors help new nurses learn the norms of the unit and unit culture; how best to communicate with their fellow nurses, physicians, technicians, and other staff; and the attributes of professional conduct, such as being respectful and courteous with other staff.

By providing encouraging, positive, and constructive feedback, preceptors reinforce new nurses' good work and progress. Negative feedback should always be clear, empathetic, and respectful and include specific instructions on how to improve or correct the undesirable behavior. Effective preceptors help new nurses become competent in the clinical environment by offering "them challenging situations that will prepare them to practice independently" (Dusaj 2014).

COACHING SKILLS SELF-ASSESSMENT

Flaherty (2010, 171–72) identifies five skills that are required for effective coaching: (1) speaking in a way that inspires the learner to see new possibilities, (2) listening to understand the learner's situation and observing his or her performance, (3) resolving breakdowns and creating new possibilities for revised action, (4) assessing and observing by maintaining objectivity and avoiding personal prejudices, and

(5) designing a path for the learner to achieve the desired outcome and describing the competence that the learner will master by the end of the coaching program. Flaherty poses the following nine questions as a coaching skills self-assessment:

1.   What makes my coaching most effective?
2.   What aspect of coaching makes me most uncomfortable?
3.   What part of my approach to coaching is praised?
4.   What part of my approach to coaching is being challenged?
5.   What emotional mood seems to work best?
6.   What have I learned about coaching?
7.   What have I learned about my competence as a coach?
8.   What are my strengths?
9.   What can I improve?

The Harvard Business School (2004) Coach's Self-Evaluation Checklist includes 21 questions related to the skills and qualities of an effective coach. It is intended for use by coaches to assess their own effectiveness. A sample of the questions follows:

1.   Do you serve as a role model?
2.   Do you work with the individual you are coaching to generate alternative approaches or solutions which you can consider together?
3.   Before giving feedback, do you observe carefully, and without bias, the individual you are coaching?
4.   Do you separate observations from judgments or assumptions?
5.   Do you use open-ended questions to promote sharing of ideas and information?
6.   Do you give specific and timely feedback?
7.   Are you careful to avoid using your own performance as a yardstick to measure others?
8.   Do you give positive as well as negative feedback?
9.   Do you give feedback that focuses on behavior and its consequences (rather than on vague judgments)?
10. Do you try to reach agreement on desired goals and outcomes rather than simply dictate them?
11. Do you try to prepare for coaching discussions in advance?
12. Do you always follow up on a coaching discussion to make sure progress is proceeding as planned?

Reframing the mission and vision framework offered by Aguilar in *The Art of Coaching Teams*, the following reflects the desired future state of patient safety coaching in hospital settings and the extraordinary contribution that patient safety coaches are making in pursuit of the high-reliability goal for healthcare—zero patient harm. The patient safety coach program mission and vision statements are as follows:

Mission:
Develop patient care team members and leaders who can consistently apply safe care practices that will result in safe and effective patient care for every patient, in every setting, every time they require care.

Vision:
Patient care teams will report that patient safety coaches are an essential part of patient care teams and that patient safety coaches are critical to improving the adoption of safe care practices, improving teamwork, enhancing organizational resilience, and improving patient outcomes.

CONCLUSION

Chapter 14 describes the safe care practices that will help patient safety coaches work with patient care teams so that they consistently demonstrate safe behaviors. Patient safety coaches perform three interventional roles as members of patient care teams: before active patient care, during active patient care, and after active patient care. Mastering coaching skills at each phase is critical to achieving a positive coaching result.

CHAPTER 14 SAFE CARE PRACTICES

1. Use Michael Simpson's seven coaching skills to transform the behaviors and performance of individual caregivers so that they consistently exceed the behavior-based expectations of a high-performing, high-reliability organization.

2. Engage the patient care team by following Marshall Cook and Laura Poole's eight-step effective coaching process. Effective coaches establish a clear purpose and vision for the coaching session, stay focused, speak clearly, initiate coaching conversations, avoid lecturing the group, and stay open to new ideas.

$\rightarrow$

---

3. Model patient safety coaching on James Flaherty's seven-step Flow of Coaching process. This process begins with establishing a relationship between the coach and the individuals on the team and continues through observation, assessment, feedback, and agreement on future steps.

4. Use the Harvard Business School's Coach's Self-Evaluation Checklist to assess coaching effectiveness. This checklist includes 21 questions related to the skills and qualities of an effective coach.

5. Make clear from the outset that the role of the patient safety coach is to encourage and influence staff to adopt safe behaviors that will lead to better outcomes for patients.

REFERENCES

Agency for Healthcare Research and Quality (AHRQ). 2017. "Coaching Clinical Teams Module: Facilitator Notes." Accessed April 5, 2019. www.ahrq.gov/professionals/quality-patient-safety/hais/tools/ambulatory-surgery/sections/implementation/training-tools/coaching-facnotes.html.

Aguilar, E. 2016. *The Art of Coaching Teams: Building Resilient Communities That Transform Schools.* San Francisco: Jossey-Bass.

Canfield, J., and P. Chee. 2013. *Coaching for Breakthrough Success: Proven Techniques for Making Impossible Dreams Possible.* New York: McGraw-Hill.

Cook, M. J., and L. Poole. 2011. *Effective Coaching,* 2nd ed. Madison, WI: McGraw-Hill.

Dusaj, T. 2014. "Become a Successful Preceptor." *American Nurse Today.* Published August. www.americannursetoday.com/become-successful-preceptor/.

Flaherty, J. 2010. *Coaching—Evoking Excellence in Others,* 3rd ed. New York: Routledge.

Harvard Business School. 2014. *HBR Guide to Coaching Employees.* Boston: Harvard Business Review Press.

———. 2004. *Coaching and Mentoring.* Boston: Harvard Business Review Press.

Landsberg, M. 2015. *The Tao of Coaching: Boost Your Effectiveness at Work by Inspiring and Developing Those Around You.* London: Profile Books.

Lippincott Solutions. 2016. "9 Qualities of Effective Nursing Preceptor Programs." Published January 14. http://lippincottsolutions.lww.com/blog.entry.html/2016/01/14/9_qualities_of_effec-5PTJ.html.

Seidman, W., and R. Grbavac. 2013. "Creating a Culture of Patient Satisfaction: The Four Positives Change Method Can Lead to Better Focus on Patients." *Hospitals & Health Networks Daily.* Published March 7. www.hhnmag.com/articles/5794-creating -a-culture-of-patient-satisfaction.

Simpson, M. 2014. *Unlocking Potential: 7 Coaching Skills That Transform Individuals, Teams and Organizations.* Grand Haven, MI: Grand Harbor Press.

Whitmore, J. 2009. *Coaching for Performance: Growing Human Potential and Performance— the Principles and Practice of Coaching and Leadership,* 4th ed. London: Nicholas Brealey Publishing.

PART VII

Creating a Safety Culture and Climate

Leading the Cultural Transformation to Harm-Free Healthcare

WHY CREATE A SAFETY CULTURE AND CLIMATE?

In the Agency for Healthcare Research and Quality (AHRQ) report *Making Health Care Safer II*, Sallie Weaver and colleagues suggest that a culture of safety is "a core mechanism underlying safe, effective, and timely patient care" (Weaver, Dy, et al. 2013, 362). Moreover, AHRQ found that creating a culture of safety is critical for continuous learning and effective teamwork in hospitals and healthcare systems. As healthcare leaders have worked to foster a culture of safety, safety behaviors have improved, such as error reporting and speaking up about safety concerns. The adoption of a safety culture has also been shown to improve safety outcomes, reducing, for example, the number of adverse or serious safety events.

In its 2017 "Call to Action," the National Patient Safety Foundation (NPSF) appealed to all stakeholders to pursue "coordinated, system-wide efforts necessary to accelerate progress against preventable harm" (Gandhi 2017, 27). The NPSF's six priorities for reducing preventable harm include ensuring that "leaders establish and sustain a culture of safety," providing sustainable funding for research on patient safety, and optimizing technology to improve patient safety (Gandhi 2017, 27). Investing in and enhancing the culture of safety in healthcare organizations has been shown to improve working conditions, foster an environment of teamwork and respect, and facilitate organizational resilience in response to serious safety events. In addition, safety culture improvements can lead to better management of worker fatigue—thereby reducing its negative consequences—and contribute to improved communication among patient care team members. "A commitment to these six priorities . . . will set the nation on a better course for preventing patient harm" (Gandhi 2017, 27).

Healthcare staff working in an organization with a mature safety culture will have a sense of physical and psychological safety. A culture of safety promotes best practices and reduces the physical and psychological hazards that are inherent in the healthcare environment. In a culture of safety, caregivers feel safe when they speak up about a potential safety risk, close call, or unwanted variation in care practice and feel empowered to "stop the line" if they feel the patient's safety may be at risk (Hickson et al. 2012, 7). An effective culture of safety also sets high standards for professional conduct, so that team members can be confident that what The Joint Commission (2008) has termed "behaviors that undermine a culture of safety" will be dealt with proactively and consistently.

Dr. Gerald Hickson, senior vice president for quality, safety, and risk prevention at Vanderbilt University Medical Center in Nashville, Tennessee, asserts that a supportive safety culture, effective leadership, and clearly articulated organizational values are the underpinnings of reliability and patient safety. Hickson identifies the following critical elements of a strong and effective culture of safety: (1) a state of organizational readiness to address unsafe systems or unreliable individuals, (2) multifaceted learning systems, (3) key individuals in the organization tasked with addressing systems issues and holding staff accountable for their actions, and (4) methods and procedures to analyze serious safety events and close calls, identify patterns of underlying event causes, and execute improvement plans (Hickson et al. 2012, 8).

The patient safety goal has been stated many different ways: first, do no harm; keep the patient safe; eliminate all preventable patient harm; zero harm; and harm-free healthcare. Safety culture plays a critical role in achieving patent safety goals. Safety culture reflects the beliefs, attitudes, and values of an organization's staff (Reason and Hobbs 2003, 145–46). James Reason identifies eight important attributes of a safe culture:

1. A safe culture drives the organization toward the goal of maximum attainable safety regardless of commercial pressures or top management.
2. A safe culture reminds all employees to respect operational safety risks and hazards and to expect that people and equipment will fail.
3. A safe culture accepts that failures in system and individual performance are the norm and develops defenses to counter them.
4. A safe culture is a wary culture that avoids complacency and develops a collective mindfulness of the things that can go wrong.
5. A safe culture is an informed culture characterized by an atmosphere of trust in which individuals feel safe in confessing their errors and near misses (and those of others) to help the organization identify error-provoking situations.

6. A safe culture is a reporting culture that involves the collection, analysis, and dissemination of information about serious safety events and close calls to drive improvement.

7. A safe culture is a just culture that clarifies the distinction between blame-free and culpable acts determined to be unsafe.

8. A safe culture is a learning culture that analyzes and understands the difference between what the organization intended to happen in a process and what actually happens—the tools of both reactive and proactive risk assessment are used.

The ideal model for applying Reason's eight attributes of a safety culture in a hospital or healthcare system would look something like this:

1. The hospital or healthcare system's board and senior management adopt a clear and passionate vision statement that focuses on the goal of zero patient harm—that is, eliminating all preventable patient harm—and this vision drives hospital policy, process improvement, and behavior change.

2. All staff receive safety, human factors, and error-prevention training to gain a better understanding of how and why people and processes fail and, more importantly, how to catch and correct people or process failures *before* they negatively affect a patient.

3. Hospital safety and improvement teams constantly analyze the effectiveness of the safeguards, controls, barriers, and defenses that are required to keep patients safe from the inevitable occurrence of human, equipment, process, or system failures that could harm the patient.

4. Safety huddles, CEO and chief medical officer safety walk rounds, continuous team safety training, simulation, safety communication tools, and safety coaches are all used to reinforce the need for situational awareness to avoid hazards and error traps and to avoid an attitude of complacency.

5. Senior leaders reward staff for speaking up about safety concerns, for taking personal accountability for patient safety, and for having a questioning attitude; leaders build trust by taking improvement action that demonstrates that they take staff concerns about patient safety seriously.

6. All staff can easily submit an electronic SBAR (Situation, Background, Assessment, Recommendation) to report a close call, near miss, or serious safety event to the safety or performance excellence department, where it

is analyzed to determine causal factors and systemic issues that become lessons learned for staff behavior change, process improvement, or barrier/defense enhancement.

7. The hospital consistently and actively applies the human performance culpability matrix in situations in which individual performance requires potential disciplinary action—fewer errors are committed when just actions are taken in response to human error.

8. Hospital safety and performance improvement staff conduct proactive risk assessment of care processes using failure mode and effects analysis. Root cause analyses are conducted in response to events. These processes drive process and defense improvements.

These eight safe care practices are the building blocks of a safety culture. They are interrelated and interdependent. They begin with setting a clear organizational goal and commitment to eliminating all preventable patient harm and creating and maintaining a work climate that is based on trust. Staff trust each other to be accountable for their own safe care performance and for the safe performance of their teammates, often referred to as "200 percent accountability." When everyone in the organization respects that errors occur and that processes fail, then everyone is committed to strengthening the safeguards and defenses necessary to protect patients from harm. Staff remain wary and vigilant, always looking for hazards and error-provoking situations. Staff remind each other not to become complacent when it comes to patient safety. When staff trust the leadership to respond effectively to reported safety concerns, then more reporting occurs and more learning takes place as the organization becomes better informed about the type, nature, and frequency of precursor, near-miss, and serious safety events.

Hickson recommends "promoting an increasingly reliable safety culture" by taking a balanced approach to addressing system issues and improving individual accountability. Vanderbilt has benefited from an enhanced safety culture in which team members speak up when they see undesirable variation in care processes and there is active reporting and review of safety event and close calls. Vanderbilt has also experienced greater leadership involvement in addressing system vulnerabilities and individual accountability issues (Hickson et al. 2012, 26–29).

IMPLEMENTING A HARM-FREE HEALTHCARE CULTURE

Dr. Robert Wachter (2012, 261), chief of medical services at the University of California, San Francisco Medical Center, advises that "fighting the culture of low expectations is a crucial step in creating a safety culture." In his book *Understanding*

Patient Safety, Wachter (2012, xiii) concludes that "we now understand that the problem of medical errors is not fundamentally one of 'bad apples' (though there are some), but rather one of competent providers working in a chaotic system that has not prioritized safety."

When a hospital or healthcare system is not committed to creating and maintaining a culture of safety, leadership and staff can "become accustomed to working in cultures where low expectations and mediocrity are the norm. They learn to tolerate bad things happening because 'it's always been that way'" (Kerfoot 2009, 25).

Nurse leader Karlene Kerfoot cites cases of poor safety behaviors in a culture of low expectations in which, for example, staff expect and tolerate a norm of faulty and incomplete information handoffs and exchanges or ignore soft signs that the wrong patient might be getting a treatment or procedure. Kerfoot offers five strategies for breaking the culture of low expectations. First, leaders must break through the staff's mental models that normalize deviance and low expectations. Second, leaders should use the power of patient stories to create empathy and passion for creating a culture of safety. Third, leaders can create a culture of transparency by reporting performance measures from internal and external sources that call attention to the fact that patients are being harmed in a culture of low expectations. Fourth, staff who serve as peer champions of change should reinforce, encourage, and reward desired behaviors, thereby motivating and energizing their peers. Lastly, unit-based safety champions, quality champions, or patient safety coaches are a proven and effective method of creating a culture of safety on the front line of patient care (Kerfoot 2009, 26).

Hospitals and healthcare systems that have succeeded at changing their organization's culture from one of low expectations to a culture of safety exhibit a strong and clear vision from the board and senior leadership. The WellStar Health System in Georgia, for example, brought in performance improvement and high-reliability specialists to conduct human error-prevention training and to set in motion the safe care practices that support a culture of safety. More than 11,000 team members received safety training, as well as 1,800 members of the medical staff and allied health professionals. WellStar's safety imperative—"Making Every Day a Safe Day at WellStar"—reflects its belief that patient safety "doesn't just happen—it's the result of understanding behavior and applying knowledge to further prevent and detect errors" (WellStar Health System 2017). WellStar's Safety First program applies advanced technology solutions and innovation to improve patient care quality and safety and reduce the risk of errors. It has invested in technology advances such as electronic medical records, computerized order entry, medication bar coding, and smart pumps.

Implementation of WellStar's safety culture enhancements and facilitators included the following:

- Adoption of safety behaviors and techniques that are proven to prevent errors and promote efficient and effective processes
- Training and deployment of patient safety coaches who mentor healthcare team members on the consistent use of safety behaviors and techniques
- Completion of Safety First Team Training for all healthcare team members based on an evidence-based teamwork development program to improve communication and teamwork skills
- Promotion of a safety culture that encourages communication of safety concerns and unsafe conditions
- Application of high-reliability concepts and best practices to decrease errors and streamline processes

Organizational theorist Karl Weick notes that "as people make these kind of changes, a new culture begins to emerge. The culture takes the form of a new set of expectations and standards (norms) and a new urgency that people live up to them" (Weick and Sutcliffe 2007, 111). Achieving significant culture change in a complex organization such as a hospital or healthcare system may take several years; some high-reliability organizations have reported that it took 8 to 10 years to bring about the culture change necessary to become reliably safe. The integral components of a strong safety culture are as follows:

- Articulating a clear and consistent vision of the safety culture goal from the top of the organization and providing continued support for the pursuit of that goal
- Creating an environment of trust in which staff feel safe speaking up about safety concerns and confident that leaders will take action in response to those concerns
- Training all staff on error prevention and safe care practices
- Differentiating between blame-free and culpable acts, where some unsafe acts may require disciplinary action
- Maintaining a state of mindfulness about the presence of latent and active hazards or risks in the complex system of healthcare and avoiding complacency
- Setting behavior-based expectations and holding staff accountable for modeling desired behaviors
- Routinely assessing staff opinions about the attributes of the culture of safety in their organization and focusing improvement efforts on areas of weak performance

Building a culture of safety in a hospital or healthcare system requires a clear, consistent, and continuous commitment from the board, CEO, and other senior leaders to provide the ongoing training, support, and encouragement that is required to achieve the goal of eliminating all preventable harm. Novant Health, a North Carolina–based integrated healthcare system, has been working to achieve the high-reliability goal of zero patient harm since 2009. All Novant Health team members, including physicians and nonclinical staff, received safety training in a program called "First, Do No Harm." Training at Novant Health focuses on key human behaviors that have been shown to save lives, such as complying with "red rules" (100 percent compliance on high-risk processes) and adopting a questioning attitude. Novant Health CEO Carl Armato has been a champion of the quest to achieve zero patient harm and has challenged the Novant Health team to strive to make zero patient harm an attainable goal (Mahoney 2016).

WHAT IS CULTURE?

Edgar Schein, a former professor at the Massachusetts Institute of Technology and the author of *Organizational Culture and Leadership*, defines *culture* as a set of behavioral regularities, working group norms, and dominant values established by the organization. Further, Schein describes culture as the philosophy that guides employee policy, the rules for how employees are expected to work together, and the climate in which employees interact with each other and with customers (Schein 1985, 6). Individually, we function within multiple cultures simultaneously: family cultures, religious and ethnic cultures, state and local cultures, and, in the work environment, several interactive cultures.

According to Schein, a culture involves (1) a common language, (2) inclusion and exclusion criteria, (3) rules for peer relationships and friendships, (4) parameters that define what actions are rewarded and what actions are punished, and (5) the overall ideology and purpose (Schein 1985, 65). In *Managing the Unexpected*, Weick and Sutcliffe (2007, 109) describe culture as "what holds your group together [and] sets its prevailing tone." The organization's prevailing culture shapes an individual's actions and how those actions are interpreted by others. Weick and Sutcliffe (2007, 111) suggest the following:

> An organizational culture emerges from a set of expectations that matter to people. Powerful social forces such as inclusion, exclusion, praise, positive feelings, social support, isolation, care, indifference, excitement, and anger are the means by which people make things matter for one another. All of us are products of our relationships, our mutual accommodations with

other people, and the respectful interactions that define us. This means that we shape the cultures that in turn shape us.

The leader's role in bringing about culture change is paramount. According to Schein, the most powerful change agent is the leader of the organization. The leader sets the example and reinforces the behaviors that are expected in the desired culture. Schein (1985, 224–25) identifies six leadership influences that can facilitate culture change:

1. What leaders pay attention to
2. What leaders measure and control
3. How leaders react to critical incidents
4. How leaders act as role models and coaches
5. How leaders set criteria for rewards and status within the organization
6. How leaders set criteria for recruitment and promotion

As Schein points out, there are many mechanisms or causal influences that may stimulate a change in an organization's culture. These range from natural evolution and managed evolution, on one end of the spectrum, to scandal, explosion, or coercive persuasion, on the other. Culture change can be planned, evolutionary, incremental, or revolutionary. Getting the senior leadership team and staff on the same page regarding the need for culture change is critical. "If one person views culture change as evolution, while a second views it as adaptation, while a third views it as managed, they are likely to end up in confusion and disagreement," says Schein (1985, 309).

Exhibit 15.1 depicts the relationship between the shared values, attitudes, and beliefs; individual behaviors; and performance and outcomes. This depiction reflects

Exhibit 15.1: From Setting Expectations to Effecting Culture Change

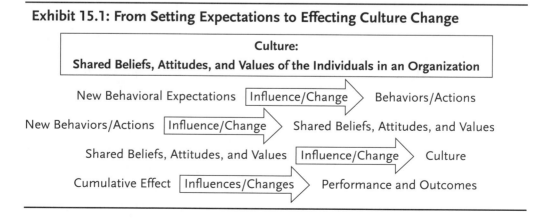

the culture change approach used by Novant Health (Mahoney 2016). To change the culture, the organization must do the following:

- *Set expectations.* When the board and CEO establish the high-reliability goal of zero patient harm and clearly define the safety behaviors expected of staff, the organization begins the transformation to a culture of safety.
- *Provide education.* Educate staff about safety behaviors and error-prevention tools. Novant's "Know Five. Save Lives" safety behaviors (e.g., having a questioning attitude and complying with red rules) are considered critical to achieving a culture of safety.
- *Reinforce and build accountability.* Patient safety coaches help staff keep safety front and center in their minds and facilitate the practice of safety behaviors and error-prevention tools.

WHAT IS A CULTURE OF SAFETY?

The term *safety culture* was coined following the nuclear power accident and ensuing disaster that occurred at Chernobyl in 1986. In its accident investigation report, the International Atomic Energy Agency noted that the root causes of the accident were grounded in the safety culture of the organization running the power plant (Itoh, Andersen, and Madsen 2012, 134). In the report, the term *safety culture* was used to refer to an organizational culture that tolerated gross violations and individual risk-taking behaviors. The report defined safety culture as "that assembly of characteristics and attitudes in organizations and individuals which establishes that, as an overriding priority, nuclear plant safety issues receive the attention warranted by their significance" (Itoh, Andersen, and Madsen 2012, 134). (Note: reactor design flaws and operator error at Chernobyl were found to be root causes that led to a reactor core explosion and the release of radioactive isotopes into the atmosphere; 31 deaths have been attributed to the Chernobyl accident, and 49,000 people were evacuated from the town of Pripyat, which is now a ghost town.)

The most widely recognized and accepted definition of a safety culture is that adopted by the Advisory Committee on the Safety of Nuclear Installations (Itoh, Andersen, and Madsen 2012, 135):

> The safety culture of an organization is the product of individual and group values, attitudes, perceptions, competencies, and patterns of behavior that determine the commitment to, and the style and proficiency of, an organization's health and safety management. Organizations with a

positive safety culture are characterized by communications founded on mutual trust, by shared perceptions of the importance of safety and by confidence in the efficacy of preventive measures.

Safety culture, then, consists of the underlying normative beliefs, attitudes, and values shared by members of the organization. Safety culture reflects the degree of leadership involvement in promoting safety, perceptions of organizational commitment to safety, and the organization's willingness to learn from serious safety events (Itoh, Andersen, and Madsen 2012, 136).

In their study "Promoting a Culture of Safety as a Patient Safety Strategy," Weaver and colleagues conducted a systematic review of the literature to assess interventions used to promote safety culture in hospital settings. Developing a safety culture is a significant component of hospital efforts to improve patient safety. The authors define safety culture as the shared values, beliefs, norms, and procedures related to patient safety among the members of an organization, unit, or team. Moreover, a culture of safety shapes clinicians' and staff's perceptions of normal behavior related to patient safety and which acts are considered praiseworthy and which are punishable. Culture influences an individual's motivation to engage in safe behaviors, if that motivation translates into daily practice (Weaver, Lubomski, et al. 2013, 369). The study identified several interventions that have a positive impact on promoting safety culture, including the multiple components of team training, tools to improve team communications, and executive involvement in frontline safety walk rounds (Weaver, Lubomski, et al. 2013, 373).

Hospital leaders play a critical role in driving the adoption of a safety culture. Leaders lead by making safety rounds; participating in daily safety huddles; attending quality and safety improvement meetings; speaking with patients, families, and staff to assess the safety culture; and recognizing staff for exemplary performance in practicing safety behaviors (Birk 2015, 20).

SAFETY CULTURE VERSUS SAFETY CLIMATE

An organization's safety culture reflects its underlying values, traditions, and beliefs and is an antecedent for individual safety behaviors. Safety culture represents the organization's expectation for safety behaviors, which are routinely measured through an assessment of the *safety climate*. The safety climate reflects the current condition of safe care practices and safe behaviors in the organization; the climate fluctuates in response to safety events.

An organization's safety climate is evaluated by conducting perception surveys of staff. The gap between the organization's perceived safety culture and the current assessment of its safety climate is the *safety performance gap*. The organization's safety management system should include metrics used to measure the safety climate and the safety behaviors of the organization, care teams, and individuals. For example, an element of an organization's safety culture might state, "Every member of the hospital team strives to make patient safety and the achievement of harm-free healthcare our number one priority and accepts personal accountability for their performance and the performance of their fellow team members." The safety mission or goal of the organization might be zero patient harm. However, a safety climate survey of staff might indicate that only 60 percent of staff believe that established safe care practices are actually being followed and that only 70 percent feel that staff are personally accountable for safe team or individual performance.

LESSONS FROM HIGH-RELIABILITY ORGANIZATIONS

US Nuclear Regulatory Commission

The Nuclear Regulatory Commission (NRC) sets policies and regulations that govern nuclear reactor and nuclear materials safety in the United States. The NRC employs more than 4,000 people and has an annual budget of about $1 billion to ensure the safe commercial use of nuclear materials in the United States. The NRC safety policies apply to all 102 nuclear power plants in the United States, as well as to the handling and storage of nuclear materials, nuclear security, and the storage of radioactive waste (NRC 2011a).

In 2011, the NRC adopted a revised Safety Culture Policy Statement that establishes expectations for all individuals and organizations subject to NRC regulatory oversight. The policy requires "a positive safety culture commensurate with the safety and security significance of their activities and the nature and complexity of their organizations and functions" (NRC 2011a).

Over the years, the NRC has modified its Safety Culture Policy to include important safety practices, such as ensuring the freedom of employees to raise safety concerns without fear of retaliation and making improvements to the reactor oversight process to strengthen the agency's ability to detect safety culture weaknesses during inspections and performance assessments. The NRC defines nuclear safety culture "as the core values and behaviors resulting from a collective commitment by leaders and individuals to emphasize safety over competing goals to ensure protection of people and the environment" (NRC 2011a).

→

According to the NRC's Safety Culture Policy Statement, a positive safety culture is defined by nine traits that describe patterns of thinking, feeling, and behaving that emphasize safety, particularly in situations in which goals conflict—for example, when safety goals conflict with production, scheduling, or financial goals (NRC 2011b).

Exhibit 15.2 shows the personal and organizational traits that are present in a positive safety culture. These attributes begin with leadership, with leaders demonstrating a strong commitment to safety in their decisions and in their behaviors. All staff are expected to be personally accountable for their behaviors and actions. A safe culture is a respectful work environment in which trust and respect are the norm and staff feel free to raise safety concerns without fear of retaliation, intimidation, harassment, or discrimination.

The key to becoming a high-reliability organization is instilling all staff with a *questioning attitude*, whereby individuals are constantly mindful of the latent and active hazards that are present in complex systems and processes and seek to identify process anomalies *before* they cause harm. The NRC's nine traits of a positive safety culture, if applied in hospitals and healthcare systems, would have an immediate positive impact on the adoption of a safety culture and reducing the occurrence of serious safety events.

JOINT COMMISSION: *SENTINEL EVENT ALERTS* ON SAFETY CULTURE

In 2008, The Joint Commission issued a *Sentinel Event Alert* on "Behaviors That Undermine a Culture of Safety." Intimidating and disruptive behaviors can compromise the safety of patients and foster medical errors (Joint Commission 2008). The uniqueness of the healthcare environment has contributed to a tolerance of or indifference toward intimidating or disruptive behaviors. The dynamic and often stressful care environment in hospitals is marked by productivity pressures, cost containment pressures, embedded hierarchies, fear of litigation, and differences in the positions of team members, including roles, authority, autonomy, and expertise. These systemic factors are exacerbated by the daily changes in shifts, rotations, patients, patient conditions, and interdepartmental support staff.

Exhibit 15.2: Nine Traits of a Positive Safety Culture

Leadership Safety Values and Actions	Problem Identification and Resolution	Personal Accountability
Leaders demonstrate a commitment to safety in their decisions and behaviors.	Issues potentially impacting safety are promptly identified, fully evaluated, and promptly addressed and corrected commensurate with their significance.	All individuals take personal responsibility for safety.
Work Processes	**Continuous Learning**	**Environment for Raising Concerns**
The process of planning and controlling work activities is implemented so that safety is maintained.	Opportunities to learn about ways to ensure safety are sought out and implemented.	A safety conscious work environment is maintained where personnel feel free to raise safety concerns without fear of retaliation, intimidation, harassment or discrimination.
Effective Safety Communications	**Respectful Work Environment**	**Questioning Attitude**
Communications maintain a focus on safety.	Trust and respect permeate the organization.	Individuals avoid complacency and continually challenge existing conditions and activities in order to identify discrepancies that might result in error or inappropriate action.

Source: Reprinted from US Nuclear Regulatory Commission (2011b).

The Joint Commission's *Sentinel Event Alert* on disruptive and intimidating behaviors recommends that hospitals take the following actions to address these unacceptable and unsafe behaviors:

- Educate all team members on appropriate professional behavior, with an emphasis on respectful interactions among team members.

- Adopt a code of conduct that defines acceptable behavior as well as inappropriate behaviors, including a zero-tolerance policy for intimidating and disruptive acts.
- Implement a process to address inappropriate behaviors.
- Hold team members accountable for modeling desired behaviors.
- Reduce fear of retribution by protecting those who report unprofessional behavior.
- Provide skills-based training and coaching for relationship building and collaborative practice.

These recommendations are a subset of The Joint Commission's "suggested actions" contained in the full version of the *Sentinel Event Alert* (Joint Commission 2008).

In its *Sentinel Event Alert 57*, The Joint Commission (2017) describes the essential role of leadership in developing a safety culture: "leadership's first priority is to be accountable for effective care while protecting the safety of patients." The alert states that leaders who have personally committed to prioritizing patient safety through their everyday actions play a critical role in creating a culture of safety.

An analysis of causal factors of events reported to The Joint Commission's Sentinel Event Database reveals that the failure of leadership to create and sustain an effective safety culture has been a contributing factor to many types of serious safety events, including wrong-site surgery and delays in treatment. The Joint Commission identifies 11 Tenets of a Safety Culture, which emphasize the important role of leadership in creating and continuously improving the hospital's culture of safety:

1. Apply a transparent, nonpunitive, approach to reporting and learning from adverse events, close calls, and unsafe conditions.
2. Use clear, just, and transparent risk-based processes for recognizing and distinguishing human errors and system errors from unsafe, blameworthy actions.
3. Encourage CEOs and all leaders to adopt and model appropriate behaviors and champion efforts to eradicate intimidating behaviors.
4. Implement, communicate, and enforce policies to support safety culture and the reporting of adverse events, close calls, and unsafe conditions.
5. Recognize patient care team members who report adverse events and close calls, identify unsafe conditions, or have good suggestions for safety improvements and share these lessons with all team members.
6. Determine an organizational baseline measure for safety culture performance using a validated tool.

7. Analyze safety culture survey results from across the organization to find opportunities for quality and safety improvement.

8. Use information from safety assessments or surveys to develop and implement unit-based quality and safety improvement initiatives designed to improve the culture of safety.

9. Embed safety culture team training into quality improvement projects and organizational processes to strengthen safety systems.

10. Proactively assess system strengths and vulnerabilities and prioritize them for enhancement or improvement.

11. Repeat organizational assessment of safety culture every 18 to 24 months to review progress and sustain improvement.

THE HIGH-RELIABILITY COMMITMENT INDEX

Hospital and healthcare system leaders should ask seven critical questions to determine the veracity of their organization's safety culture and their commitment to achieving a highly reliable level of performance. When a hospital's board and senior leaders can answer these questions in the affirmative, the organization is on its way to achieving high reliability and harm-free healthcare for the patients it serves:

1. Has the board established an organizational commitment to achieving zero preventable patient harm?

2. Does the organization provide staff with opportunities for deliberate practice and simulation to improve motor and cognitive skills, especially for the preparation of performance of safety-critical tasks and procedures?

3. Do senior leaders know the type and frequency of preventable harm that is occurring in the hospital each day and the specific human and systems-related causes of the harm?

4. Are all staff routinely trained on the use of safe care practices, safety communication techniques, and error-prevention tools?

5. Does the organization conduct functional hazards analysis to identify and control hazards and barrier effectiveness analysis to improve the strength of its defenses and controls?

6. Are patient safety coaches embedded in all patient care teams, with the primary responsibility of ensuring that staff consistently exhibit safe behaviors?

7. Are senior leaders continuously involved in safety rounds, safety huddles, safety committee meetings, and safety improvement team report-outs and committed to building trust by responding effectively to safety concerns?

HARM-FREE HEALTHCARE: EXEMPLARY PRACTICE

Nationwide Children's Hospital

Nationwide Children's Hospital in Columbus, Ohio, has been on a mission of cultural transformation since 2008, when its board of directors issued a call to action to reduce the incidence of preventable patient harm to zero and directed the organization to "aspire to eliminate preventable harm" (Brilli et al. 2013, 1639). Nationwide Children's Hospital is the largest children's hospital in the United States, with about 25,000 hospital admissions a year and approximately 10,000 staff and 1,000 medical staff. Concerned that progress to reduce patient harm in US hospitals had been slow, Nationwide Children's Hospital adopted the goal of eliminating all preventable patient harm by the end of 2013.

A key component of this initiative was a cultural transformation to become a high-reliability organization. The hospital focused on eliminating harm in the eight domains measured by the Preventable Harm Index. These include hospital-acquired infections, surgical site infections, central line–associated bloodstream infections, adverse drug events, and all serious safety events. Error-prevention tools were selected based on common causes of past events, and a training course on error prevention was provided to staff. With the goal of moving the hospital to high reliability, the hospital made a concentrated effort to improve consistent performance by everyone.

Nationwide Children's Hospital created the "Zero Hero" patient safety program to rally staff behind the zero-harm goal and provided basic error-prevention training to more than 8,000 clinical and nonclinical staff members. In addition, more than 600 leaders received training in leadership methods and techniques they could use to reinforce the high-reliability concepts taught to all staff. Finally, a patient safety coach program was launched to train frontline staff to coach their peers to apply the error-prevention methods and patient safety tools they had been taught (Brilli et al. 2013, 1638–39). Nationwide Children's Hospital has experienced significant improvement in its safety climate as well as significant reductions in serious safety events, preventable harm, and hospital mortality (Brilli et al. 2013, 1642).

→

Nationwide Children's Hospital strives to continuously enhance its culture of safety through actions related to the five pillars of quality and safety, which reflect patients' expectations of the hospital: do not harm me, cure me, treat me with respect, navigate my care, and keep us well (Nationwide Children's Hospital 2019a). The hospital is committed to transparency and demonstrates its commitment by sharing safety performance information internally and externally. For several years, Nationwide has published its serious safety event rate on its website (Nationwide Children's Hospital 2019b). Nationwide Children's Hospital's commitment to patient safety is exemplified by its nationally recognized Zero Hero program, in which "zero is the only acceptable goal, and one that we all strive for" (Nationwide Children's Hospital 2019a). From 2010 to 2019, Nationwide Children's Hospital reported an 82 percent decrease in the serious safety event rate, and the number of days between events improved from once every 11 days to once every 122 days (see exhibit 15.3).

Exhibit 15.3: Serious Safety Event Rate—Nationwide Children's Hospital

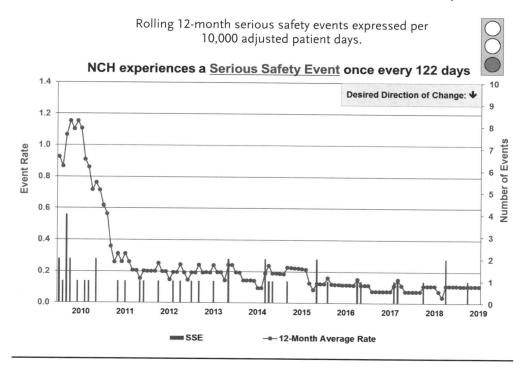

Rolling 12-month serious safety events expressed per 10,000 adjusted patient days.

NCH experiences a <u>Serious Safety Event</u> once every 122 days

Source: Nationwide Children's Hospital (2019b). Used with permission.

Hospital leaders who can confidently answer yes to these seven questions understand the importance of leadership's active presence and participation in safety-critical activities. Paying attention to the details can result in a level of consistent excellence in patient care—care that is considered highly reliable for its high quality and absence of harm.

CONCLUSION

Chapter 15 presents the safe care practices that will strengthen leadership's role in achieving the high-reliability goal of zero patient harm. This patient safety goal has been stated in many different ways: first, do no harm; keeping patients safe; eliminating all preventable patient harm; zero harm; and harm-free healthcare. Safety culture plays a critical role in achieving these patient safety goals. According to Edgar Schein, the most powerful change agent is the leader of the organization. The leader sets the example and reinforces the behaviors expected in the new, desired culture.

CHAPTER 15 SAFE CARE PRACTICES

1. Build a culture of safety by making a clear, consistent, and continuous commitment to provide the ongoing training, support, and encouragement required to achieve the goal of eliminating all preventable harm.

2. Take the lead by making safety rounds; participating in daily safety huddles; attending quality and safety improvement meetings; speaking with patients, families, and staff to assess the safety culture; and recognizing staff for exemplary performance in practicing safety behaviors. Hospital leaders play a critical role in driving the adoption of a safety culture.

3. Evaluate the hospital or healthcare system's commitment to achieving high reliability and a culture of safety by completing the High Reliability Commitment Index. Leaders who can answer yes to these seven questions understand the importance of leaders' active presence and participation in safety-critical activities. Paying attention to the details can result in patient care that is considered highly reliable for its high quality and absence of harm.

REFERENCES

Birk, S. 2015. "Accelerating the Adoption of a Safety Culture." *Healthcare Executive*, March/April, 19–26.

Brilli, R. J., R. E. McClead Jr., W. V. Crandall, L. Stoverock, J. C. Berry, T. A. Wheeler, and J. T. Davis. 2013. "A Comprehensive Patient Safety Program Can Significantly Reduce Preventable Harm, Associated Costs, and Hospital Mortality." *Journal of Pediatrics* 163 (6): 1638–45.

Gandhi, T. 2017. "Coordinated, Systemwide Efforts Necessary to Accelerate Progress Against Preventable Harm." *Modern Healthcare* 47 (11): 27.

Hickson, G., I. Moore, J. Pichert, and M. Benegas. 2012. "Balancing Systems and Individual Accountability in a Safety Culture." In *From Front Office to Front Line: Essential Issues for Health Care Leaders*, 2nd ed., edited by S. Berman, 1–36. Oakbrook Terrace, IL: Joint Commission Resources.

Itoh, K., H. B. Andersen, and M. D. Madsen. 2012. "Safety Culture in Health Care." In *Handbook of Human Factors and Ergonomics in Health Care and Patient Safety*, 2nd ed., edited by P. Carayon, 133–62. Boca Raton, FL: CRC Press.

Joint Commission. 2017. "The Essential Role of Leadership in Developing a Safety Culture." *Sentinel Event Alert* 57. Published March 1. www.jointcommission.org/sea_issue_57/.

———. 2008. "Behaviors That Undermine a Culture of Safety." *Sentinel Event Alert* 40. Published July 9. www.jointcommission.org/assets/1/18/SEA_40.PDF.

Kerfoot, K. M. 2009. "Good Is Not Good Enough: The Culture of Low Expectations and the Leader's Challenge." *ANNA Update*. Published September/October. https://pdfs.semanticscholar.org/b380/1509ff74a091e686da40e090c1883ff1aa9a.pdf.

Mahoney, D. 2016. "At Novant Health, Safety Is Woven into the Fabric of Its Culture." *Industry Edge*. Published May. www.pressganey.com/resources/articles/at-novant-health-safety-is-woven-into-the-fabric-of-its-culture.

Nationwide Children's Hospital. 2019a. "Impact and Quality." Accessed April 8. www.nationwidechildrens.org/impact-quality.

———. 2019b. "Serious Safety Event Rate (SSER)." Accessed April 17. www.nationwidechildrens.org/impact-quality/patient-safety/serious-safety-event-rate-sser.

Reason, J., and A. Hobbs. 2003. *Managing Maintenance Error: A Practical Guide*. Burlington, VT: Ashgate Publishing.

Schein, E. H. 1985. *Organizational Culture and Leadership*. San Francisco: Jossey-Bass.

US Nuclear Regulatory Commission (NRC). 2011a. "Safety Culture Policy Statement." Accessed April 7, 2019. www.nrc.gov/about-nrc/safety-culture/sc-policy-statement.html.

————. 2011b. "Traits of a Positive Safety Culture." Accessed April 7, 2019. www.nrc.gov /about-nrc/safety-culture/sc-policy-statement.html#traits.

Wachter, R. 2012. *Understanding Patient Safety*, 2nd ed. New York: McGraw-Hill Medical.

Weaver, S. J., S. Dy, L. H. Lubomski, and R. Wilson. 2013. "Promoting a Culture of Safety." In *Making Health Care Safer II: An Updated Critical Analysis of the Evidence for Patient Safety Practices*, 362–71. Rockville, MD: Agency for Healthcare Research and Quality.

Weaver, S. J., L. H. Lubomski, R. F. Wilson, E. R. Pfoh, K. A. Martinez, and S. M. Dy. 2013. "Promoting a Culture of Safety as a Patient Safety Strategy." *Annals of Internal Medicine* 158 (5, Part 2): 369–74.

Weick, K. E., and K. M. Sutcliffe. 2007. *Managing the Unexpected: Resilient Performance in an Age of Uncertainty*. San Francisco: John Wiley & Sons.

WellStar Health System. 2017. "Making Every Day a Safe Day at WellStar." Accessed April 8, 2019. www.wellstar.org/about-us/safety-and-quality/pages/safety-first.aspx.

Index

Agency for Healthcare Research and Quality (*continued*)

> *Evidence-Based Handbook for Nurses,* 144, 149; *Fall Prevention Toolkit,* 97, 98; "Guide to Patient and Family Engagement in Hospital Quality and Patient Safety," 59, 221; *Making Health Care Safer II* report, xxvii, 93, 112, 191, 283; *National Healthcare Quality and Disparities Report,* xix; "Patient Care Technology and Safety," 135; patient safety practice defined by, 94; Patient Safety Primer on simulation training, 72; Pressure Ulcer Bundle, 110, 111; *Preventing Pressure Ulcers in Hospitals,* 111; safe practices for preventing central line–associated bloodstream infections, 105; study of simulation exercises, 71–72; TeamSTEPPS program, 54; team training in healthcare report, 49; Universal Fall Precautions, 92, 210

Agrawal, A., 60

Aguilar, Elena, 263, 270, 277

AHRQ. *See* Agency for Healthcare Research and Quality

Air-filled mattresses, 143

Airline pilots: simulation-based training for, 77

Airline safety: improving, human factors analysis used in, 197–98

Air traffic control: safety management in, 219–20

Air Traffic Control collective: T²EAM assessment tool, 126–27, 129

Air Traffic Organization (ATO): Risk Analysis Process, 219, 220; Runway Safety Program, 220; Safety Management System maintained by, 219

Allianz, 78

Ambiguity, 192

American Association of Critical-Care Nurses (AACN), 29

American Board of Medical Specialties, 182

American College of Healthcare Executives (ACHE), xiii

American Hospital Association, xix, 112

American National Standard: on benefits of resilience, 121

American Nurse Today, 195

American Society of Health-System Pharmacists (ASHP): "Guidelines on Preventing

Medication Errors in Hospitals," 106–7; Self-Assessment Checklist, 110

American Society of Health-System Pharmacists 11-step medication-use system, summary of, 107–10; administration, *107,* 109; dispensing, *107,* 109; evaluation, *107,* 110; monitoring, *107,* 109; ordering, transcribing, and reviewing, *107,* 108–9; patient admission, *107,* 108; patient discharge, *107,* 109–10; planning, *107,* 108; preparation, *107,* 109; selection and procurement, *107,* 108; storage, *107,* 108

Analysis of variance, 235

Analyzing learning style: coach's language and approach with, 273

Anesthesia Crisis Resource Management program (Stanford University School of Medicine), 54, 79

Anesthesiologists: simulation training for, 79–80

Anesthetists' Non-Technical Skills (ANTS) training program, 32

Anticoagulants: oral, adverse drug events in emergency room patients and, 106

Antiplatelet agents: adverse drug events in emergency room patients and, 106

Antisepsis: introduction of, 135

ANTS training program. *See* Anesthetists' Non-Technical Skills training program

Appropriate assertion: teamwork and, 57–58, 64

Armato, Carl, 289

ARMI analysis, *17–18*

Arthur Andersen, 204

Art of Coaching Teams (Aguilar), 270, 277

Ascension Health, 143, 227

ASHP. *See* American Society of Health-System Pharmacists

"Ask Before Coaching" approach, 269

Aspirations: definition of, 8

Aspirin: adverse drug events in emergency room patients and, 106

Assertion/assertiveness: appropriate, 38, 57–58; characteristics of, in communication, 34

Assertion stage: teams and, 272

Assessment: defenses and barriers and, 168

Association for Professionals in Infection Control and Epidemiology, 112–13

Association of periOperative Registered Nurses, 29

ATO. *See* Air Traffic Organization

Attention and alertness: as human defensive actions, 213

Attitude: behavior and, shaping, 39

Atun, Rifat, 177

Availability: defenses and barriers and, 168

Aviation industry: crew resource management in, 175; crew resource management training modules in, 32; nontechnical skills and, 31; simulation-based training in, 72; simulation training as effective form of deliberate practice in, 76–78

Awareness: complacency counteracted with, 248; creating, in International Coach Federation's core coaching competencies, 259; resilience training, competence, and, 126–27; training, 44. *See also* Situational awareness

Backup behavior, 58; definition of, 56; team members and, 51

Bad organizational design, 180

Bad system design, 180

Bainbridge, Lissane, 143

Baker, D. P., 62

Balancing learning style: coach's language and approach with, 273

Bar-code medication administration (BCMA), 136, 138, 139, 207, 209

Bar-code technology, 138, 139–40, 175

Barrier effectiveness analysis, 168, 169, 173, 192, 229; analyzing strength of defenses through, 215–16, 218; five elements considered in, 216; of patient falls, sample, *217*; safety cases and, 218; thorough, defensive states revealed in, 216

Barriers: for Air Traffic Organization, categories of, 220; designing, 205; ineffective or missing, 212; intended use of, 203; mitigation, 206; at nuclear power plants, 208; "pragmatic criteria" defined for, 218; retrospective analysis of, 216

BARS. *See* Behavior-anchored rating scales

Basketball: "efficiency" rating in, 222; situational awareness in, 249

Bates, David, 133

Battles, James B., 55, 62

BCMA. *See* Bar-code medication administration

Beer's Eight Steps to Create Real Change, 10

Behavioral approach: to facilitating change, 14

Behavioral influence: six sources of, 38–39

Behavior-anchored rating scales (BARS), 59

Behavior-based expectations: assessing patient care team member's performance or behaviors against, 252, 261; coaching before active patient care and, 265; at Sentara Healthcare, 40–41; setting, 36, 38–39, 46

Behavior-based safety: patient safety coaching as enabler of, 253

Behavior(s), 45, 50; attitude and, shaping, 39; interrelationships between competence, performance, and, *28, 46*; in patient engagement, 221; positive deviants and, 36; reasons for focus on, 27–29. *See also* Action(s); Behavior-based expectations; Unsafe behaviors

Beliefs: harm-free performance and, 39

Best practices: facilitating adoption of, 10

Big Y formula, xxii–xxiv

Bladder bundle: definition of, 99

Bladder Bundle Initiative, 92

Bloodstream infections: financial impact of, 104–5; prevalence of, 104

Blue Box, 77

"Blunt" end of patient care experience. *See* Macrosystem(s) (or "blunt" end of patient care experience)

Board: building a safety culture and commitment from, 289; culture of safety and vision of, 287; High-Reliability Commitment Index and, 297; safety as job number one for, 155

Boeing: human factors analysts at, 198

Bounce (Syed), 74

Boundaries: system tendencies and, 178

Bounding, *16–17*

Bowel perforation: Unintended retained foreign objects and, 102

Bowen, Ronda, 240

Brady, P. Jeffrey, 55

Brady, Tom, 61

Briefing, 65

Change, assimilating, 13–16, 23; motivations and, 14–15; resistance and complacency and, 15–16

Change Acceleration Process model: pillars of, 8

Change agents: defining, 22; five stages of consulting process used by, 21–22; responsibilities and roles of, 16, 21–22, 23

Change facilitation tools (CFTs): ARMI analysis, *17–18*; bounding, *16–17*; changing systems and structures, *20*; elevator speech, *19*; force field analysis, *19–20*; GRPI team effectiveness assessment, *18*; more/less of project shaping, *18–19*; plus/delta assessment, *20*; SIPOC diagram, *17*; team charter, *17*; TPC analysis, *19*; WWW action plan, *20*

Change implementation team (CIT), 16

Change initiative: determining task readiness for, 9–10

Change leader: goal of, 5

Change management: inadequate, 214; organizational transformation and, 6

Change management errors: awareness of, 12

Changing systems and structures, *20*

Chassin, Mark, xiv

Check-backs, 66

Checklist for Assessing Institutional Resilience (Reason), 123–25, 129

Checklist Manifesto (Gawande), 211

Checklists, 175; as administrative defense, 211; as defense against active errors, 211; hospital health information technology purchasing decisions, 144, 149; I'M SAFE, 66; for nurse preceptors, 276; routine use of, 194; safety, 59

Chernobyl nuclear power plant accident (1986): investigating root causes of, 291

CHFG. *See* Clinical Human Factors Group

Chief executive officers (CEOs): building a safety culture and commitment from, 289; as champions for change initiative, 8

Cincinnati Children's Hospital: Safety Coaching Program at, 248; volunteer safety coaches at, 254

Cipriano, Pamela, 195

"Circle-slash" method, 67

CIT. *See* Change implementation team

Civility: patient safety and, 53

CLABSI bundles: applying, in intensive care unit settings in Michigan hospitals, 105

CLABSIs. *See* Central line–associated bloodstream infections

Clarity: team alignment and, 63

Clegg, Herbert, 254

Clinical care staff: concerns about caregiver incompetence, 29

Clinical decision support (CDS), 136; coupling systems of, with computerized provider order entry, 140; electronic health records integrated with, 142

Clinical departments: as microsystems, 227

Clinical Human Factors Group (CHFG): *Implementing Human Factors in Healthcare—Taking Further Steps,* 196

Clinical Practice Guideline for Preventing and Treatment of Pressure Ulcers (Institute for Healthcare Improvement), 110

Clinical references: note about, xxvii

Clinical skills: deliberate practice and improvement in, 82

Closed-loop communication, 51, 58, 66

Clostridium difficile infections: reducing, Centers for Disease Control and Prevention reports on hospitals' progress in, 103

CMS. *See* Centers for Medicare & Medicaid Services

Coaching: benefits of, 253–55; dealing with resistance and reluctance to, 269–70; deliberate practice sessions, 82; effective, eight steps to, 271, 278; effective, five skills for, 276–77; effective, World Health Organization principles of, 255; essence of, 270; flow of, 274–75, 279; International Coach Federation's core coaching competencies, 258–59; learning styles and types of language used by, 272–73; mission of, 274; purpose of, 251; seven transformative skills in, 266–67, 278; solution-focused, 265. *See also* Patient safety coaches

Coaching agreement: establishing, International Coach Federation's core coaching competencies and, 258–59

Coaching and Mentoring guide (Harvard Business School), 273

Coaching—Evoking Excellence in Others (Flaherty), 251

Coaching excellence: benefits of, 248

CPOE. *See* Computerized provider order entry

Creasey, Timothy, 6, 10, 13

CREW (Civility, Respect, and Engagement at Work), 53

Crew resource management (CRM): patient care teams and, 175; training modules, 32

Crichton, Margaret, 32, 33, 35

Cross-checks, 175

Crossing the Quality Chasm: A New Health System for the 21st Century (Institute of Medicine), xix, xxi

Cross-monitoring, 65

Crucial conversations: about patient safety, 30

Cultural transformation: foundational changes in, 22

Culture: definition of, 289; elements of, 289; just, 108; of low expectations, five strategies for breaking, 287; prevailing, actions shaped by, 289–90

Culture change: effecting, from setting expectations to, 290, *290*; facilitating, six leadership influences on, 290; performance improvement and, 7, 22

Culture of safety: achieving, by changing practices and behaviors, 4–6; building, commitment required in, 289, 300; coining of term for, 291; creating informed culture and, 157; fostering, 283; integral components of, 288; at Nationwide Children's Hospital, 298–99, *299*; strong and effective, critical elements of, 284. *See also* Safety culture

Cummings, Joseph, 139

CUSP. *See* Comprehensive Unit-based Safety Program

CUSS technique: protecting patients from harm with, 34, 58, 65

CVCs. *See* Central venous catheters

Debriefings, 57, 64, 65

Deciding learning style: coach's language and approach with, 273

Decision-making, 32, 33; cognitive ergonomic issues and, 190; in Kaizen projects, 3G approach to, 240; shared, 221

Defects in healthcare: Lean targeting of, 235

Defects per million opportunities (DPMO), xix

Defense and controls performance, 171–72, 185

Defense-oriented safe care technologies, 138

Defenses: administrative, 205, 209–11, 223; barrier effectiveness analysis of strength of, 215–16, 218; defeating, factors related to, 214–15, 224; definition of, 206; developing and implementing, 205; human, 205, 213–14, 223; mitigation, 206; multiple, layers of protection and, 207; physical and technical, 205, 211–13, 223; prevention, 206; purposes of, 205–7; retrospective analysis of, 216; understanding effectiveness of, in keeping patients safe, 203–5

Defenses-in-depth, 207–9, 224; in football, 207–8; nuclear power plants, 208–9

"Defensive" competencies: "offensive" competencies, saving lives, and, 203–5

Defensive controls: computerized provider order entry, 207

Defibrillators: invention of, 135

Deficit Reduction Act (2005), xix, 93

Deliberate practice, 86; competency enrichment and, 83; in competitive sports, 73–74; elite performers and, 81; examples of, 73–75; importance of, 71; mastery learning and, 81; naive practice *vs.,* 75; preparing to deliver safe care through, 82–86; reasons for patient care teams' involvement with, 71–73; simulation-based, 72, 82–83; simulation training in aviation industry as form of, 76–78; through simulation in healthcare: exemplary practice, 79–80; twelve attributes of, 76, 86

Delta: as symbol of change, 23n

Deming, W. Edwards, 234, 239

Design controls, 166–67

Design for Six Sigma, 238–39

Diagnosis stage: of consulting process used by change agents, 21

Diagnostics: running on each system, 228–29, 241

Diffusion of Innovations (Rogers), 22

Digital Doctor (Wachter), 133

Disruptive behaviors: addressing, 39, 41–42, 46, 295–96; medical errors, compromised patient safety, and, 294

Distractions: minimizing, 56, 175

Disturbance management, 119

Diversity: defenses-in-depth and, 209

FAA. *See* Federal Aviation Administration

Failure mode and effects analysis, 168, 173, 192, 195, 229

Fairbanks, Rollin J., 119, 129

Fall alarms, 135

Fall Prevention Toolkit (Agency for Healthcare Research and Quality), 92, 97–98; twelve Universal Fall Precautions in, 97, 98

Falls. *See* Patient falls

Fatigue, 192; decision-making compromised by, 33; decreasing, through work hour limitations, 175; definition of, 36; minimization of, 32, 36; nontechnical skills and levels of, 31; situational awareness compromised by, 33; solution for, 45

Federal Aviation Administration (FAA), 77, 219; Fitness-for-Duty program, 31; Human Factors Policy Order 9550.8, 197; "sterile cockpit" rule, 33, 41, 56–57; on system design and safety, 241

Feedback: on adequacy of defenses, 205; debriefing and, 65; effective, coaching during active patient care and, 267; by nurse preceptors, 276; observation-based, coaching after active patient care and, 268; positive, patient safety coaches and, 252; providing, in coaching relationship, 273–74, 275; in simulation environment, 85; structured deliberate practice and, 83; team knowledge, skills, and abilities and, 58; team training programs and, 54

Feedback loops: system tendencies and, 178

Feeley, Derek, xii

FFD. *See* Fitness for duty

First Do Less Harm (Koppel), 136

Fitness for duty (FFD): assessing, concerns about, 30; at nuclear power plants, addressing, 31

Fitness-for-work expectations: establishing, 56

5P safety check, 68

Five Cs of Effective Teamwork, 60, 64

Five Disciplines of Performance Excellence, xv–xvii, *xvi,* xxiv, xxviii, 158; actualizing aspiration of zero patient harm and, 5; applying proven safe care or offensive strategies, *xvi,* xxiv, 5; Big Y formula and, xxii; coaching individuals and teams, *xvi,* xxiv, 5; facilitating adoption of, 10; maximizing controls or defenses, *xvi,* xxiv, 5; minimizing errors and mistakes, *xvi,* xxiv, 5; preparing to deliver safe care, *xvi,* xxiv, 5, 174. *See also* Zero patient harm

Flaherty, James, 251, 274, 276, 279

Flattened hierarchy: effective teamwork and, 56, 64

Flight simulators, 78

Flin, Rhona, 32, 33, 35

Florence Nightingale Pledge: for nursing graduates, xv

Flow: in Lean methodology, 236, 237

Flow of Coaching model: steps in, 274–75, 279

Foley catheter, 98

Follow-on actions: identifying, 320

Football: offensive and defensive teams, championship seasons, and, 204; teams with excellent defenses-in-depth in, 207–8

Force field analysis, *19–20*

Forcing functions: human factors and, 186

Forest thinking: tree-by-tree thinking *vs.,* 181

Foundational Tenets for Change Management (Hiatt & Creasey), 10

Four Cornerstones of Resilience, 125, 129

Free from Harm (National Patient Safety Foundation), xii

Frontline caregivers: concept of control and, 126

Functional hazard analysis, 229–30; documenting, 320; seven steps in, 229–30

Gaba, David, 79

Gandhi, Tejal, xx

Gawande, Atul, 81, 133

Gel pads, 142

Gemba (place or location): in Kaizen projects, 240

Genbutsu (the product): in Kaizen projects, 240

Genjitsu (the problem specifically being looked at): in Kaizen projects, 240

Germ theory, 135

Global Aviation Study: on airline safety performance, 77–78

Global Trigger Tool, xx

Goal execution: flawless, coaching during active patient care and, 267

Goal setting: facilitating change and, 14; in International Coach Federation's core coaching competencies, 259

Organization's six "building blocks" for system analysis and improvement of, 181, 184

Healthcare workforce: World Health Organization framework for system analysis and improvement and, 181. *See also* Employees; Staff

Health financing: World Health Organization framework for system analysis and improvement and, 181

Health information: World Health Organization framework for system analysis and improvement and, 181

Health Information Technology for Economic and Clinical Health Act: passage of, 136

Health technology: World Health Organization definition of, 135

Henriksen, Kerm, 188, 189, 190

Heparin, 106, 138

Heterogeneous evidence: on simulated deliberate practice and safer patient care, 82

HFE. *See* Human factors and ergonomics

Hiatt, Jeffrey, 6, 10, 13

Hickson, Gerald, 284, 286

Hierarchy: flattened, teamwork and, 56, 64

High-alert medications: adverse drug events and, 106

High-fidelity full-body mannequins, 78, 80, 83

High-hazard industries: precursors and, 166

High-performing teams: characteristics of, 34–35

High-Reliability Commitment Index, 155, 297, 300

High Reliability Operations: A Practical Guide to Avoid the System Accident, 212

High-reliability organizations (HROs), 228; achieving significant culture change in, 288; achieving zero patient harm in, 155; adopting safe practices of, 4; defenses-in-depth at nuclear power plants, 208–9; diagnostic tools used by, 229; Hoar Construction, 165; human factors analysis used to improve airline safety, 197–98; learning directive in, 186; resilient operation of, abilities related to, 121; safety cases developed by, 232; safety management in air traffic control, 219–20; simulation training in aviation, 76–78; US Department of

Energy, xxiii; US Nuclear Regulatory Commission, 293–94

Hippocrates, xv, 180

Hippocratic Oath, xv

HIT. *See* Healthcare information technology

Hoar Construction: "Safety Moment" smartphone app, 165

Hobbs, Alan, 157, 215

Hockey: "plus/minus" rating for performance in, 222

Hogan, Ben, 74

Hollnagel, Erick, 125, 129, 218

Homeostasis: definition of, 8; system tendencies and, 178

Hospital-acquired conditions (HACs): fourteen categories of, according to Centers for Medicare & Medicaid Services, 94; leading types of, xix

Hospital-Acquired Conditions (HAC) Initiative (Centers for Medicare & Medicaid Services), xix, 93

Hospital Corporation of America, 227

Hospital for Sick Children, or "SickKids" (Toronto): patient safety coaches at, 253

Hospital health information technology purchasing decisions: checklist for, 144, 149

Hospitals: assessment tools for, 163–64; counteracting tendency toward oversimplification in, 227; defenses-in-depth approach for, 209; developing safety culture in, 292; diagnostics run by, 228–29; dynamic complexity of, 177–78; enhancing capacity for resilience in, 123–26, 129; health information technology purchasing checklist for, 144, 149; human factors analysis used by, 185; improving teamwork in, interventions for, 59; patient care teams in, composition of, 53; patient falls in, 96, 97; pressure ulcer rates in, 110; right improvement tools for, to build safer "home" for patients, 234; safety-related aspiration for, 8; stressful care environments in, 294; Systems Improvement Plan for, 179–80

Hospital Value-Based Purchasing, xxi

HROs. *See* High-reliability organizations

Human defenses, 205, 213–14, 223; for Air Traffic Organization, examples of, 220; cultural norms and, 213; safe defensive attitudes and, 167

Institute of Medicine (IOM): Committee on Quality of Health Care in America, xxi; creation of, xxi; quality chasm described by, xix; six aims of, xxi–xxii

Institute of Nuclear Power Operations: on warning signs indicating degradation of defenses/controls, 214–15

Instrument counts: World Health Organization guidelines for, 103

Insulin, 106, 138

Intensive care units (ICUs): mix of monitoring systems in, 189; organizational characteristics of, in human factors assessment, 191; safety assessment reports performed for, 230; as systems, 227

International Atomic Energy Agency, 291

International Coach Federation (ICF): Coach Knowledge Assessment, 258, 261; core coaching competencies, 258–59, 261

Interpretation: defenses and barriers and, 168

Intervening stage: of consulting process used by change agents, 21

Intimidating behaviors: addressing, 295–96; medical errors, compromised patient safety, and, 294

Intravenous (IV) infusion pumps, 135; early programmable, 212–13; first-, second-, and third-generation designs for, 138; safety case for, 218; smart, medication safety and, 212, 213

Inventory waste: Lean targeting of, 236

IOM. *See* Institute of Medicine

"Ironies of automation" precept (Bainbridge), 143

Isolationism, 214

IT. *See* Information technology

IV infusion pumps. *See* Intravenous infusion pumps

Jackson, Phil, 249

James, John, xx

Johns Hopkins Medicine: benefits of human factors analysis described by, 195–96; central line checklist developed at, 211

Joint Commission: on behaviors undermining culture of safety, 284; Center for Transforming Healthcare, 113, 215; on 11 Tenets of a Safety Culture, 296–97; fall prevention recommendations, 98;

"Human Factors Analysis in Patient Safety Systems," 194; Lean Six Sigma use by, 234, 235; on main causes of wrong-site, wrong-patient, and wrong-procedure surgeries, 215; medication management system, 106; National Patient Safety Goals established by, 93; patient suicides reported to, 100; safety event standards of, 155; *Sentinel Event Alert* on "Behaviors That Undermine a Culture of Safety," 41, 294, 295–96; Sentinel Event Database, ix–x, 96, 102, 113, 296; suicide ideation recommendations, 101

Jones, Daniel, 235

Just culture, 108

Kaiser Permanente, 227; Critical Incident Response program, 128

Kaizen: "change for the better" with, 239–40; definition of, 239; process improvement and principles of, 240

Kaizen activity: seven phases in continuous cycle of, 240

Kaizen event (or "blitz"): definition and focus of, 240

Kerfoot, Karlene, 287

Kianfar, Sarah, 191

King, H. B., 62

King, Rosemary, 238

Klein, Cameron, 49

Knowledge, skills, and abilities (KSAs), 4, 5, 14, 21, 28, 29, 42, 50; coaching, 255–56, *257–58*; complementary, team members and, 53; diminished, incompetence and, 248; interdependent teamwork and, 53; nurse, effective, 52; for patient safety coaches at Virginia Commonwealth University Health System, 259–60; simulation-based deliberate practice and, 84; team-based, descriptions of, 58; team-based, development of, 51, 52; of team members, competence levels defined in terms of, 252; team training in healthcare and, 61; team training program evaluation and, 63; trigger events in simulation training and, 85. *See also* Competency(ies)

Knowledge-based performance, 44, 159–60, 176–77

Kohanna, Fred, 30

National Academy of Sciences, xxi; on accident or safety event precursors, 164; on medication-related errors, 105

National Action Alliance for Suicide Prevention, 100–101

National and State Healthcare-Associated Infections Progress Report (Centers for Disease Control and Prevention), xix

National Center for Human Factors in Healthcare (MedStar Health), 195

National Football League, 204

National Healthcare Quality and Disparities Report (Agency for Healthcare Research and Quality), xix

National Health IT Plan: on benefits of health information technology, 136–37

National Institute for Clinical Excellence (NICE): ultrasonography guidelines, 141

National Patient Safety Foundation (NPSF), xii–xiii; "Call to Action," 283

National Patient Safety Goals (Joint Commission), 93

National Pressure Ulcer Advisory Panel (NPUAP), 110; *Prevention and Treatment of Pressure Ulcers: Clinical Practice Guidelines,* 111; Support Surfaces Standards Initiative, 142

National Quality Forum (NQF): Health IT Safety Committee, goals of, 143; *Identification and Prioritization of Health IT Patient Safety Measures,* 143; never events identified by, 93, 95

National Quality Strategy, xxi; establishment of, xii; six priorities of, xx

National Scorecard on Rates of Hospital-Acquired Conditions, 95

National Strategy for Suicide Prevention, 100

National Transportation Safety Board, 204

Nationwide Children's Hospital (Columbus, Ohio): serious safety event rate at, 299, *299*; "Zero-Hero" patient safety program at, xiii, 298–99

Natural disaster casualties: resilience and adaptability in face of, 119, 120

Natural human tendencies: TWIN analysis of, 161, 169, 174

Nemeth, Christopher, 119

Never events, xix; identified by National Quality Forum, 93, 95; other examples of,

96; surgery-related, prevalence of, 113; in surgical care, 95

New England Journal of Medicine, 133

New England Patriots, 204

NICE. *See* National Institute for Clinical Excellence

Nicklaus, Jack, 74

Nightingale, Florence, 180

Nonretaliation clauses, 42

Nontechnical skills, 45–46; communication, 32, 34; decision-making, 32, 33; definition of, 31; essential, 32–36; fatigue minimization, 32, 36; mastering, 31–32, 46; situational awareness, 32–33; stress minimization, 32, 35–36; team safety leadership, 32, 35; teamwork, 32, 34–35

NOTECHS, 33

Novant Health (North Carolina): building culture of safety at, 289; culture change approach used by, 291; "First Do No Harm" safety program at, 254; "Know Five. Save Lives" safety behaviors, 291

NPSF. *See* National Patient Safety Foundation

NPUAP. *See* National Pressure Ulcer Advisory Panel

NQF. *See* National Quality Forum

NRC. *See* US Nuclear Regulatory Commission

Nuclear power plants: addressing fitness for duty at, 31; defenses-in-depth approach and, 208–9

Nurse preceptors: effective, competencies for, 275–76; role of, 275

Nurses: concerns about caregiver incompetence, 29; medical technology use by, 135; simulation training for, 82; systems thinking focus and, 182; tips for influencing technology at bedside, 144–45; workplace layout and, 189–90

Nursing: human factors considerations for, 190; teamwork in, benefits of, 52

Nursing homes: pressure ulcer rates in, 110

Observability: rate of change adoption and, 8

Occupational Safety and Health Administration, 231

O'Connor, Paul, 32, 33, 35

"Offensive" competencies: "defensive" competencies, saving lives, and, 203–5

Physicians: concerns about caregiver incompetence, 29; defining and enforcing behavioral expectations for, 41; involved in serious safety events, support for, 127; simulation training for, 82; systems thinking focus and, 182–83

Pictorial reminders, 194

Place-keeping technique, 44, 67

Plan-Do-Check-Act process improvement cycle: development of, 234

Plus/delta assessment, 20

Pneumothorax: mechanical ventilation and, 111

"Point-and-shoot" ultrasound with mobile devices, 135

Poole, Laura, 253, 265, 266, 270, 271, 278

Poon, Eric, 207

Positive controls, 211–12

Positive deviance, 38

Positive deviant behaviors: identifying, 42; widespread adoption of, 38

"Positive deviants": high skill and high will in, 268; identifying, 36

Positive images, 38

Positive practice, 38

Positive reflection, 38

Positive Specific Action: seeking, effective coaching and, 271

Potassium chloride, 106

Pounds, Jerry, 42

Practices and behaviors: changing, to achieve a culture of safety, 4–6

Precursor reporting systems, 164

Precursors: in high-hazard industries, 166

Pre-job briefings, 45, 56, 161, 213

Presence: in International Coach Federation's core coaching competencies, 258

Presenteeism: reducing effects of, 30–31, 46

Pre-simulation conditions: establishing, 84

Pressure Ulcer Bundle (Agency for Healthcare Research and Quality), 110, 111

Pressure ulcers, xix; preventing, 110–11, 138; problem of, 110; reducing, specialized support surfaces (mattresses) and, 142–43

Preventable Harm Index: eight domains measured by, 298

Preventable patient harm: excuses for tolerance of, xvii–xviii; National Patient Safety Foundation's six priorities for reducing, 283

Preventing Pressure Ulcers in Hospitals (Agency for Healthcare Research and Quality), 111

Prevention and Treatment of Pressure Ulcers: Clinical Practice Guidelines (National Pressure Ulcer Advisory Panel), 111

Prevention barriers or defenses, 166, 206, 207

Proactive resilience strategies, 123

Proactive safe care technologies, 138

Procedural Event Analysis Tool (PEAT): Boeing's use of, 198

Procedural lapses/slips, 158, 169, 175, 192

Procedural skills: deliberate practice and improvement in, 82

Process: changes in, performance improvement and, 7; great teams and, 53

Processes and procedures: reviewing and simplifying, 194; standardizing, 194

Process gains: achieving, coaching teams and, 263, 264

Process improvement tools: building safe hospital "home" and, 234

Process losses: avoiding, coaching teams and, 263–64

Product: great teams and, 53

Production over protection prioritization: Reason's assessment of, 222–23

Production priorities, 214

Professional conduct: effective culture of safety and, 284

Progress: managing, in International Coach Federation's core coaching competencies, 259

"Promoting a Culture of Safety as a Patient Safety Strategy" (Weaver et al.), 292

Pronovost, Peter J., 188

Propofol, 138

Prosci ADKAR Model of Individual Change, 10

Prospective analysis, 173, 183

Prospective risk assessments, 194

Protocols: importance of, in healthcare, 194

Psychodynamic approach: to facilitating change, 14

Psychological safety: mature safety culture and, 284

Puerperal fever: monthly mortality rates, Vienna General Hospital, 1841–1849, 134, *134*

Pull: in Lean methodology, 236, 237

Safety huddles, 161, 285, 300
Safety management: in air traffic control, 219–20
Safety management system: organizational metrics for, 293
Safety performance gap, 293
Safety Practices Self-Assessment, 252
Safety-related behavioral expectations: types of, 43
Safety-significant functions: decomposing, into components, 220
Safety-significant subsystems: identifying, 229
Safeware, 147–48
Safeware Guiding Principles, 147–48, 149
Salas, Eduardo, 49, 53, 60, 64, 84, 86
SAR. *See* Safety assessment report
Save Our Skin program: reduction in pressure ulcers and, 92
SBAR (Situation, Background, Assessment, Recommendation): safety culture and staff submission of, 285–86
SBARQ technique, 65
SBP. *See* Systems-based practice
Schein, Edgar, 289, 290, 300; Model of Transformative Change, 10, 12–13, 23
Schlitterbahn Waterpark (Kansas): lack of safety defenses and child fatality at, 204
Schmidt, E., 81
Schyve, Paul M., 180
Scrub Practitioners' List of Intraoperative Non-Technical Skills (SPLINTS), 32
Seattle Seahawks, 75
Second-person verifications, 213
Second victims: definition of, 127; recovery stages for, 128
Sehgal, Niraj, 60
Self-Assessment Guides for High Priority Practices (Office of the National Coordinator for Health Information Technology), 146–47, 149
Self-checking: human defenses and, 213; STAR method for maintaining attention on performance, 45
Self-criticism: lack of, 215
Self-reflection: effective coaching and, 263
Semmelweis, Ignaz, 134
Senior leaders: applying Reason's eight attributes of a safety culture and, 285; assessment of error-prone environments

by, 163, 169; building a safety culture and commitment from, 289; as champions for change initiative, 8; culture change and, 290; culture of safety and vision of, 287; High-Reliability Commitment Index and, 297, 300; safety as job number one for, 155
Senior management: training in behavior-based safety processes and, 42
Sensing data, 21
Sentara Healthcare (Virginia): behavior-based expectations, 40–41; patient safety coaches at, 250–51
Sentinel Event Alerts (Joint Commission): on "Behaviors That Undermine a Culture of Safety," 294, 295–96; patient safety priorities and, 93
Sepsis: unintended retained foreign objects and, 102
Serious safety events: active errors and analysis of, 177; estimating probability of, 229; failed defenses, barriers, or controls and, 167; five-step dynamic in, 206; Novant Health and steep reduction in, 254; rate of, at Nationwide Children's Hospital, 299, *299*; support for staff involved in, 127–29, 130
Service delivery: World Health Organization framework for system analysis and improvement and, 181
Seven Stages of Change (Cameron & Green), 10
Shared decision making, 221
Shared mental models, 65
"Sharp" end of patient care experience. *See* Microsystem(s) (or "sharp" end of patient care experience)
Sharp-end workers: resilient systems and, 129
Sharp HealthCare (San Diego): "Attitude Is Everything" at, 37
Sharps count: World Health Organization guidelines for, 103
SHEA. *See* Society for Healthcare Epidemiology of America (SHEA)
Shewhart, Walter, 234
Shift work and rotations: changing team membership and, 60
Significance: team alignment and, 63
SimMan, 79
Simon, Mark, 41

Simpson, Michael, 266, 278

Sims, Dana, 49

Simulation-based deliberate practice, 82–83; ultimate goal of, 83–84

Simulation-based training, 59, 175; advantages of, in healthcare, 78, 80–82; Agency for Healthcare Research and Quality's Patient Safety Primer on, 72; for anesthesiologists, 79–80; applying sound instructional principles in, 85; approaches to, in healthcare, 80–81; in aviation industry, 76–78; designing, principles for, 83–86; determining effectiveness of, 85–86; developing performance measures for, 85; ensuring trainee motivation, 84–85; goal of, 72–73; knowledge-based performance and, 160, 176; for physicians and nurses, 82; preparing for transfer environment in, 85; preparing healthcare organizations for, 84; procedural safety improvements from, 73; teamwork and, 86

Simulation environment: establishing, 85

Simulation exercises: Agency for Healthcare Research and Quality study of, 71–72

Sinek, Simon, xxvi

SIPOC: diagram, 17; Joint Commission's use of Lean Six Sigma and, 235; safer system design and, 228

Situational awareness, 32–33; of changing patient care environment dynamics, 249; in coaching patient care teams, 266; definition of, 56; effective teamwork and, 56–57, 64; enhancing, 33; human defenses and, 213; strategies contributing to, 56; team huddles and, 65

Situation monitoring, 51, 64, 65

Six Sigma, xix; Big Y formula and, xxii; building safe hospital "home" and, 234; Design for Six Sigma methodology, 238–39; development of, xxii; process redesign, violations of flawed rules/procedures and, 160

Six Sigma improvement tools. See Lean Six Sigma improvement tools

Skill-based performance, 43, 158–59, 176

Skills: coaching self-assessment of, 276–78; improving, coaching after active patient care and, 268. See also Knowledge, skills, and abilities

Sleep, 36, 45

SMART goals: patient safety coaches in patient care teams and, 265

SMART method: performance objectives and, 43

SMART planning: in International Coach Federation's core coaching competencies, 259

Smart pumps, 136, 138–39; active engineered defense for, 167; dose error controls on, 166; medication safety and, 212, 213; reengineered, 138

Smith, Douglas, 4, 7, 10, 13, 15, 23

Smith, Rick, 74

Social ability: positive deviant behaviors and, 38

Socially toxic workplaces, 52

Social motivation: positive deviant behaviors and, 38

Society for Healthcare Epidemiology of America (SHEA): "Strategies to Prevent Ventilator-Associated Pneumonia in Acute Care Hospitals," 112–13

Society for Simulation in Healthcare, 80

Sociotechnical systems: definition of, 143; workplace interaction of people and technology and, 145

Software: physical and technical defenses and, 211; reliable, 147

Software criticality indices: identifying, 320

Solution-focused coaching: four questions for organizing, 265

Solutions for Patient Safety, xiv

Sound control, 189

South Canyon Fire, 204

SPLINTS. See Scrub Practitioners' List of Intraoperative Non-Technical Skills

Sponge counts: World Health Organization guidelines for, 102–3

Sports: great performers in, deliberate practice and, 73–75

SSIs. See Surgical site infections

Staff: emergency department, adaptive strategies used by, 119–20; involved in errors and adverse events, support for, 127–29, 130; resilience training for, 126; safety as job number one for, 155

Stakeholder analysis, 235

Standardization: human factors and, 186

About the Author

Charles A. Mowll, LFACHE, served as executive vice president of The Joint Commission for more than 20 years, acquiring expertise in patient safety, high reliability, and Lean Six Sigma. In this role, Mr. Mowll had the opportunity to interact with and learn from some of the world's leading experts in these fields. Mr. Mowll also understands the financial constraints that healthcare organizations face, having spent the first half of his career as a healthcare financial management executive.

Following his retirement from The Joint Commission in 2015, Mr. Mowll formed the Patient Safety Coaches Academy. The Academy recognizes that even great players and great teams need a great coach to master their skills and achieve a level of consistent excellence. The Patient Safety Coaches Academy is focused on helping hospitals develop patient safety coaching programs, enhance the competence of their patient safety coaches, and spread the consistent use of safe care practices.

Mr. Mowll earned his master's degree in public health from the Robert Wood Johnson Medical School at Rutgers University. He is a Life Fellow of the American College of Healthcare Executives and previously was a fellow of the Healthcare Financial Management Association and an American Society for Quality–Certified Six Sigma Black Belt.